羅常培文集

The Collected Linguistic Works of Luo Changpei

山东教育出版社
Shandong Education Press

罗常培在美国。

罗常培（中）与老舍（右）、李抱忱在美国。

1946 年在美国芝加哥。

1945 年在美国加州。

國立西南聯合大學用箋

濟之吾兄：

返滇已上兩函，想來得覆，不知已收到否。聯大運輸處胡君送來圖紙一捲、牛津小字典兩大本，現存弟處，應如何處理，祈即示知。老伯大人近況如何？前附致兄信中亦有一稟，不悉登覽否。當代評論所刊蜀道難想已見及，望指教。一切匆匆，即頌

近安

弟常培 三一、一、十四。

罗常培手迹。

编印说明

本卷包括五个部分:一是外文论著,包括英法文稿 10 篇,按发表的时间先后编次。文中的罗马拼音按原样,有些文章曾用中文发表,有的是未曾发表过的英文演讲稿,由罗慎仪编校。二是游记。虽为旅行散文纪实,但颇具资料性。《蜀道难》,1944 年由重庆独立出版社出版,1946 年上海再版。《苍洱之间》,南京独立出版社 1947 年出版。此次由高更生根据辽宁教育出版社 1996 年版《书趣文丛》第三辑之《苍洱之间》编校。三是零星文章,如自传及有关散文,便于读者更全面地了解著者,由罗圣仪编校。四是罗常培年表,由杨力立编。五是《罗常培文集》总目,由罗圣仪编。本卷涉及近百人名,当时或出于尊敬,或由于亲近,作者对有些人用“号”称呼。为了方便读者,我们加注了“名”,用“[　]”标明,以区别于“(　)”中作者所加的注。

目 录

外文论著

蜀道难

苍洱之间

零星文章

外 文 论 著

Indian Influence on the Study of Chinese Phonology[①]

Ⅰ. INTRODUCTION

The Chinese scholar Cheng Ts'iao(郑樵 1104 – 1162 A.D.) of the Song dynasty, while discussing the various characteristics of the Chinese and Sanskrit languages in his "Outline of Six Orders"(《六书略》) in *T'ung-che* (《通志》) says: "What counts with the Indians is the sound of a word; it is the discrimination of sound that is emphasised. With the Chinese it is the characters that count and the student is concerned with the discrimination of characters. So the Indian writing is simple in form, consisting only of the turns and the twists of a single line. There is little variety and no intricate arabesques and yet a great range of sounds is rendered thereby. The Chinese writing is much cramped for want of discrimination in sounds. Before the Han dynasty few knew any sort of spelling. The knowledge of spelling came to China later from the Western countries. So rimetables can usually be read by most Buddhist monks while the Chinese scholars can hardly make head and tail of them as they are derived from India. . . . So the Indians have a vast

① This paper was read in Viśva-Bhāratī Cheena-Bhavana, Santiniketan, Bengal, on the 23rd November, 1944.

number of sounds but the Chinese have as many characters. The Indians excel in hearing and they acquire their knowledge mainly through the ear; the Chinese excel in sight and they rely more upon the eye."

Cheng Ts'iao has thus fairly succeeded in representing the difference between the two languages. For though the Chinese characters may be divided into six orders according to the old usages, the so-called *liu-shu*（六书）such as: (1) Siang-hing（象形）or hieroglyphs, (2) Hui-yi（会意）or ideograms, (3) Che-she（指事）or emblematic characters, (4) Sie-sheng（谐声）or phonetic compounds, (5) Chuan-chu（转注）or homonymic synonyms and (6) Kia-tsie（假借）or derivatives, to judge by their general traits, hinge upon the structure of the characters and their sense and not upon their sounds. In the square pattern of a Chinese character, the image and sense it represents can often be perceived, but there is no indication in it as to how it is to be pronounced. In the phonetic compounds, the part of sound symbol is indeed purported to be phonogram, but the phonogram itself does not show the sound for it is still character and not a letter and does not represent any phonetic element. Every character, as it has its own structure, has also its own sound. Yet every character having its own sound and the sound not being indicated by its structure, there is of course a chaos which it is hard to reduce to order. Even if some phonetic system could be educed, the symbols that represent the phonetic elements have yet to be found. This is the main obstacle with which the student of Chinese phonology is faced. For illustrations let us consider four sets of Chinese characters:

a. 牛: [illegible] [illegible] "cow" Ancient Chinese [$_{c}$ngəu], Mandarin [niu$_2$]

b. 羊: [illegible] [illegible] "goat" Ancient Chinese [$_{c}$ĭang], Mandarin [iang$_2$]

c. 犬: [illegible] [illegible] "dog" Ancient Chinese [^{c}k'ĭwen], Madarin [k'üen$_3$]

d. 马: "horse" Ancient Chinese[^{c}ma], Madarin[ma$_3$]

Even if we had known little Chinese, we could guess what these characters represent. We shall consider another set of characters:

e. "拱手" a sort of salute by holding up the two loosely clenched fists as high as the nose. Ancient Chinese [^{c}kǐwang], Mandarin [kung$_3$]

f. "攀"或"扳" pull down with two hands. Ancient[$_c$pwan], Mandarin[pan$_1$]

g. "多手抬物" to lift or raise with many hands. Ancient[$_c$ǐwo], Mandarin[ü$_2$]

h. "两手对举" to hold in both hands. Ancient[kīuk$_ɔ$], Mandarin [tśü$_2$]

We can infer the idea which these characters convey from their structure, but can either foreigners or the Chinese find any shadow of a hint as to their phonetic value? The Chinese characters are thus peculiarly unsuited to indicate sound. So the study of Chinese phonology cannot successfully progress without the help of phonetic languages.

With the languages of India however the case is altogether different. Since they, along with other languages of the Indo-European family, belong to the order of phonetic languages. They have besides a well-developed phonology. The study of phonology was pursued in ancient India with an interest that has few parallels in antiquity. The origin of this interest may be traced in the Rgveda which dedicates two entire hymns to speech. Besides the first of the six Vedāṅgas called Śikṣā and the applied phonetics viz. the

Prātiśākhya contain many valuable phonetic theories.[①] Hiuan-tsang (玄奘) in his *Records of the Western World* (《西域记》) says: "In beginning the education of their children and winning them on to progress they follow the 'Twelve Chapters' (Siddhirastu). When the children are seven years of age the great treatise of the Five Sciences (Pañcavidyās) are gradually communicated to them. The first Science is Grammar (Sabda-vidyā) which teaches and explains words, and classifies their distinctions".[②] In Yi-tsing's (义净) *A Record of the Buddhist Religion as practised in India and the Malay Archipelago* (《南海寄归内法传》), it is said: "The *Si-t'ang-chang* (Siddha composition) for beginners.-This is also called Siddhirastu, signifying 'Be there success' (Ch. lit. 'complete be good luck') for so named is the first section of this small (book of) learning".[③] Now as the discrimination of sounds was regarded as rudiments to be learned by children before they were seven and the language itself is suited to the analysis into its phonetic elements, it is small wonder that phonology should have been much more developed in India than in China.

From the time when the Indian culture began to spread into China i.e. towards the end of the Han dynasty, it has exercised a great influence on Chinese philosophy and religion. But it also has had a signal effect on Chinese philology and specially on phonology. In the "Chapter of Bibliography" in the *History of the Sui dynasty* (《隋书·经籍志》) it is

---

① Cf. Siddheswar Varma's *Critical Studies in the Phonetic Observations of Indian Grammarians*, pp. 4 – 16.

② Watters-*On Yuan Chwang's Travels in India*, I, pp. 154 – 155.

③ Translated by Takakusu, Oxford, 1896, section on the *Method of Learning in the West*, pp. 170 – 171.

said: "Since Buddhism prevailed in China from the later Han dynasty, there came the foreign letters of the Western Countries which can represent all vocal sounds with fourteen characters. It is concise and compendious and is called Brahman letters; it differs altogether from our characters which are divided into the eight styles or six orders". This just shows the sense of difference between the Indian and the Chinese languages. But in the *Biographies of Eminent Monks*(《高僧传》) it is recorded that Sie Ling-yun (谢灵运) invented the fourteen phonetic symbols under this influence. To my mind the greatest effect of Indian influence on Chinese phonology are exhibited in the invention of three things:

1. Shou-wen's (守温) Chinese initial system
2. The four divisions of Rime
3. Transliterated Sanskrit texts and the ancient pronunciation of Chinese

Let us consider them in detail.

Ⅱ. SHOU-WEN'S CHINESE INITIAL SYSTEM

The thirty-six tseu-mu(字母) or phonetic radicals used by the Chinese phonologists have been attributed by tradition to Shou-wen, a monk of the end of the T'ang dynasty. Little is now known of him. What is left is only the record that he had a book on the thirty-six tseu-mu, found in the "Outline of Bibliography"(《艺文略》) in Cheng Ts'iao's *T'ung-che* (《通志》) and Wang Ying-lin's (王应麟) *Yü-hai*(《玉海》) or *Jade Sea*. In the "Chapter of Bibliography" in the History of the Song dynasty(《宋史·艺文志》), it is also recorded that there was a book named Shou-wen's *Key to Surds and Sonants* (守温《清浊韵钤》). These two books are now lost and we can hardly guess at their contents. In the collection of the Bibliothèque Nationale of Paris there is a manuscript in three fragments. No. 2012 which was discovered by Paul Pelliot in the *Caves of Thousand Buddhas at Tun-huang*. At the commencement of one fragment we have the words "Written by the Chinese Bhikṣu Shou-wen of Southern Leang"(南梁汉比丘守温撰). It also contains the thirty-six tseu-mu arranged in the following order:

唇音	不芳并明	Labials: p, p‘, b‘, m
舌音	端透定泥是舌头音	Linguals: t, ṭ‘, d‘, n are the sounds on the tip of tongue.
	知彻澄日是舌上音	ṭ, ṭ‘, ḍ‘, ṇ are the sounds above the tongue.
牙音	见[君]溪群来疑等字是也	Gutturals: such as the characters which have the initials k, k‘, g‘, l(?), ng
齿音	精清从是齿头音	Dentals: ts, ts‘, dz‘ are the sounds on the tip of teeth.
	审穿禅照是正齿音	ś, tś‘, dź‘, tś are the sounds just on the teeth.
喉音	心邪晓是喉中音清	Glottals: s(?), z(?), χ are the sounds of glottal.
	匣喻影是喉中音浊	γ, j, ? are the sonants of glottal.

The number of tseu-mu and the headings under which they are arranged are much the same as those of the "An Example of the Thirty tseu-mu", a manuscript kept in the British Museum. Only there is some slight difference in the order of arrangement. My studies of these two manuscripts which were published in *CYYP* vol. Ⅲ, Part 2, have led me to think that Shou-wen could not have lived earlier than the reign of Tai-tsong (代宗) and Tö-tsong (德宗) of the T'ang dynasty. The tseu-mu originally fixed by him were thirty in number. The monks of the Song dynasty added the six tseu-mu 帮 p, 滂 p', 奉 bv', 微 mj, 床 dz, 娘 ń for the sake of symmetry and changed 不芳 into (非) pf, 敷 pf' with other alterations in classifying the sounds. In this way there came to be thirty-six tseu-mu of the "Rime-tables of the four divisions" of the Song and Yuan dynasties.

This set of tseu-mu, invented by a Buddhist monk, of course owed much to the influence of Indian culture. Some say that it was based on the forty-two letters of the *Avataṃśaka Sūtra*. Some refer it to the forty-seven letters of the Mahāparinirvāṇa Sūtra. But if we compare the thirty-six tseu-mu with those in the two Sūtras, we can see at once that the first opinion is untenable and that the second is quite correct. For the letters in the Avataṃśaka Sūtra ष्ट *ṣṭa* श्व *śva*, क्ष *kṣa*, स्त *sta*, स्थ *stha*, स्म *sma*, ह्व *hva*, स्क *ska*, स्य *sya and* श्च *śca* and the like do not bear on Shou-wen's tseu-mu at all which were really derived from the forty-seven letters in the Mahāparinirvāṇa Sūtra adapted to the Chinese phonetic elements. Such sounds as are not found in Sanskrit were supplied from Tibetan. The following table will prove our contention clearly:

1	2	3	4	5
Sanskrit	Tibetan	Shou-wen	Song, Yuan Rime-tables	Mahāparinirvāṇa Sūtra
ka	ka	见	见	迦
kha	kha	溪	溪	法
ga	ga			伽
gha	(gha)	群	群	伽(重)

1 Sanskrit	2 Tibetan	3 Shou-wen	4 Song, Yuan Rime-tables	5 Mahāparinirvāṇa Sūtra
ṅa	ṅa	疑	疑	俄
ca	ca	照	照	遮
cha	cha	穿	穿	车
ja	ja			阇
jha	(jha)	禅	床	阇(重)
ña	ña	日	日	若
ṭa	(ṭa)	知	知	○
ṭha	(ṭha)	彻	彻	侘
ḍa	(ḍa)			茶
ḍha	(ḍha)	澄	澄	茶(重)
ṇa	(ṇa)		娘	拏
ta	ta	端	端	多
tha	tha	透	透	他
da	da			陀
dha	(dha)	定	定	陀(重)
na	na	泥	泥	那
pa	pa	不	帮	波
pha	pha	芳	滂	颇
ba	ba			婆
bha	(bha)	並	並	婆(重)
ma	ma	明	明	摩
	tsa	精	精	
	ts‘a	清	清	
	dza	从	从	
	wa			

1 Sanskrit	2 Tibetan	3 Shou-wen	4 Song, Yuan Rime-tables	5 Mahāparinirvāṇa Sūtra
ya	ya	喻	喻	邪
	ža	禅	禅	
	źa	邪	邪	
	ḥa	匣	匣	
ra	ra			啰(轻)
la	la	来	来	罗
va	va			和
śa	śa	审	审	赊
ṣa				沙
sa	sa	心	心	娑
ha	ha	晓	晓	呵
a	ʻa	影	影	阿
			非	
			敷	
			奉	
			微	

On the evidence of the above table we can say that when Shou-wen invented his tseu-mu, he must have classified the characters used in Chinese spelling with reference to the Vyāñjanam in Sanskrit. Such sounds as could be found in Sanskrit and Tibetan but were absent in Chinese, were of course left out while the sounds that Chinese possess but are wanting in Sanskrit and Tibetan were not supplied. So the Sanskrit *ra*, *va* (Tibetan *wa*) having no equivalents in Chinese were omitted and at the same time the four sets of sounds in the Chinese spelling: 庄t̤s̤, 初t̤s̤ʻ, 崇d̤z̤ʻ, 以(characters without initial consonant) were subsumed under 照ṫś, 穿ṫś', 禅ḋż, 喻 j because there were no equivalents in Sanskrit and Tibetan. However, generally speaking, it is now beyond dispute that Shou-wen's Tseu-mu was modelled on the system of Vyāñjanam.

Ⅲ. RIME-TABLES OF THE FOUR DIVISIONS

The so-called Rime-table of the four divisions is the Chinese syllabary modelled on the Indian Siddhirastu. It arranged initials in a perpendicular line and the finals in a horizontal one. As Chinese characters are written from the top to bottom and not from the left to right like Sanskrit, so the table also is arranged in a converse way. They are further divided into four tones according to their difference in pitch accent and into four divisions according to the difference between the open and the close in vowel quality. All these are absent in Sanskrit. Therefore the Chinese rime-table is much more complex than the Siddhirastu.

As to the time when the rime-table was invented, we know nothing definitely. But it could not have been much later than the publication of the Ts'ie-yün (601 A.D.). In the fragments of a T'ang manuscript of Shou-wen's book on phonology found at Tun-huang there is a passage on the four divisions. The examples adduced there agree with those of the Rime-tables of the Song and Yuan dynasties in regard to their method of division.[1] So it is clear that the classifications of rimes into divisions prevailed even before the

---

① Cf. *CYYP*, (Bulletin of the National Research Institute of History and Philology, Academia Sinica) vol. Ⅱ, part 2.

time of Shou-wen. Rime-tables have come down to us. They often occur in the bibliography of ancient books. The Buddhist monks had a hand in most of them. For example the *Sseu-sheng-teng-tseu*(《四声等子》) or the *Division of the Four Tones of the Song dynasty*, though not very likely the same book as the *Sseu-sheng-teng-ti-t'u*(《四声等第图》) or the *Division of the Four Tones* with the tables by the monk Tsong-yen(宗彦) as was supposed by Ch'en Li(陈澧), it was in any case written by a monk. Apart from this, books like *Yun-king*(《韵镜》) or the *Mirror of Rime*, *Ts'i-yin-leo*(《七音略》) or an *Outline of Seven Vocal Sounds*, *Ts'ie-yün-che-chang-t'u*(《切韵指掌图》) or the *Tables of Spelling* and *Ts'ie-yün-che-nan* (《切韵指南》) or *Guide to Spellings* have all more or less to do with monks. The *Yun-king* current in Japan are almost all annotated by monks. And it was by monks too that the older editions of the *Ts'ie-yün-che-nan* were published. Even the chapter in spelling placed in the beginning of the popular *K'ang-hi Dictionary*(《康熙字典》) was originally current in book form and called *The Key to Spelling the tseu-mu in the Tripiṭaka*(《大藏字母切韵要法》). The frontispiece is the portrait of Buddha and the next page is a Buddhistic hymn. On the third page there is the title: *Ta tsang tseu mu ts'ie yun yao fa* translated by the Indian monk Amaladhi(《大藏字母切韵要法》,天竺沙门阿摩利谛译). It was after all in such books that the key to spelling is found. So the relation between these books and the monks is still closer. Probably the monks had to drill their tongue in order to read their dhāraṇīs. So they made tables of phonetic elements to facilitate their practice. It was in this way that the tables came to be transmitted. And the people went even so far as "to regard meditation as the major way of self-realisation and the spelling the minor way". The religious flavour was thus enhanced.

Ⅳ. TRANSLITERATED SANSKRIT TEXTS AND THE ANCIENT PRONUNCIATION OF CHINESE CHARACTERS

Following Abel Rémusat, ①Eugéne Burnouf, ②Stanislas Julien, ③Ernest J. Eitel④ and Bernhard Karlgren, ⑤ Baron Alexander von Staël-Holstein the Russian Sinologist, wrote in 1922 *Transliterated Sanskrit Texts and the Ancient Pronunciation of Chinese Characters*⑥. An Indian monk called Fa-t'ien(法天)or Dharmadeva who lived and worked at the beginning of the Song dynasty transcribed some short dhāraṇīs as well as longer religious hymns with Chinese characters. The Sanskrit originals of some of his texts have been found. A few texts of which the originals have not yet been discovered had been restored into Sanskrit by Staël-Holstein, with the additional help available from Tibetan versions. This restoration enabled Staël-Holstein to compare the Sanskrit and the Chinese of a work called *Kien-chuei-fan-tsan* or *Gaṇḍīstotra-gāthā*(犍稚梵赞) and with the help of the results arrived at by Bernhard Karlgren he came to the conclusion that

---

① L'étude des Langues étrangères chez les Chinois-*Le Magazine Encyclopédique*, Octobre, 1811.

② Le Lotus de la Bonne Loi, 1852.

③ Méthode pour déchiffrer et transcrire les Noms sanscrits qui se rencontrent dans les Livres chinois, 1861.

④ *Handbook of Chinese Buddhism*, 1904.

⑤ Prononciation ancienne des caractères Chinois figurants dans les Transcriptions bouddhiques, *T'oung Pao*, XIX, 1920.

⑥ *KHCK*, (Sinological Quarterly, National University of Peking) vol. I, part 1, translated into Chinese by Dr. Hu-shih.

the Chinese which Dharmadeva used was the dialect of North-West China at the beginning of the Song dynasty. He expressed the wish that the Chinese scholars should take up the study of other similar transcriptions of Sanskrit texts which may yield more important results than those of Dharmadeva's versions as there are versions made in the kingdom of Wu in the time of the three kingdoms and others which even go back to the time of the Later Han dynasty. Such studies, if taken up in right earnest, will not only benefit the history of Chinese phonology but also the study of the antiquities of India and Eastern Turkestan.

Staël-Holstein's suggestion was not in vain as may be seen from the researches of Wang Jong-pao(汪荣宝). Not long after the publication of Staël-Holstein's paper Wang published his article *On the ancient pronunciation of the characters of the Group* 歌戈(o)鱼虞(ü)and 模(u)(歌戈鱼虞模古读考)①. He says in that article: "The Chinese language relies upon the structure of the character and has no phonetic symbols. So it is the more liable to change in regard to its pronunciation. Modern scholars have tried to reconstruct the ancient pronunciation with the help of phonetic compounds and rimes of the classics and have accomplished signal results. But the phonetic compounds and the rimes can carry one no further than marking the differences in the classification of the rimes of the ancient and modern systems. As to how the orders of characters were pronounced in ancient times and wherein they differ from their modern pronunciations the ancient literature can never lead to any certainty. The ancient utterence is beyond recovery and written words are not adequate to render it. So it is only

① *KHCK*, vol. I, part 2.

with the aid of external evidences afforded by the phonetic languages that had intercourse with ancient Chinese that the problem can ever be solved. There are two methods to deal with such evidences:

1. To note the pronunciation of phonetic transcriptions of Chinese words in foreign languages.

2. To note the phonetic transcriptions of foreign words in Chinese and find out how the originals were pronounced."

By these methods Mr. Wang proved that before the T'ang and Song dynasties all words that rime with 歌 and 戈 were pronounced not with [o] sound but with [a] sound and that as late as the Wei and Tsin dynasties all characters of 鱼虞模 rime were pronounced with [a] sound and not with [u] or [ü] sound. In order to prove his first contention he has adduced the following Sanskrit instances collected from the old texts.

Agada—阿伽陀	Dhuta—头陀
Anuttara—阿耨多罗	Nīlapīṭa(?)—尼罗蔽茶
Amita—阿弥陀	Panasa—婆那娑
Aśoka—阿输迦	Paramārtha—婆罗末陀
Asura—阿修罗	Pāramitā—婆罗密多
Kapiñjala—迦频阇罗	Buddha—佛陀
Karpūra—羯布罗	Bodhisattva—菩提萨埵
Karmadāna—羯磨陀那	Brāhmaṇa—婆罗门
Gada—伽陀	Muhūrta—牟呼栗多
Candra—战达罗	Yama—阎魔,餤摩
Cintā—振多	Vihāra—毗诃罗
Deva—提婆,提桀	Rāhula—罗睺罗

In order to prove that during the Han and Wei dynasties even characters with 鱼虞模 rimes were also pronounced with the [a] sound he has collected the following examples from the old texts:

Buddha——佛陀 or 浮屠,浮图

Upāsaka——优婆塞 or 伊蒲塞

Māyā-devī——摩耶 or 莫邪

Pāṇḍurā——宾度罗 or 宾头卢

Sinra(?)——新罗 or 新卢

In the current opinion of the scholars, the latter half of Wang's conclusions may yet be disputed, the former half is no more refutable. It is to this skilled use of Sanskrit and Chinese transcriptions of sounds that he owes his achievement. By the same method I have also attained results that have been embodied in the treatise *On the Ancient Pronunciation of the Initials* 知彻澄娘"(《知彻澄娘古读考》).①

The last but not the least, Dr. Hu Shih in his "Preface to the *Ts'e-t'ung*(《辞通》)" has said: "As one goes through this gigantic work one cannot help regretting one group of important omissions, namely the variations of the Buddhist words and phrases which very frequently trouble readers of Chinese literature and history. The inclusions of various transcriptions of Sanskrit terms in such dictionary would not only greatly enhance its usefulness but also help to familiarise the untrained reader in the phonological principles involved in the vast majority of the troublesome variants of pure Chinese words"② This opinion is as important as the pure phonological researches.

---

① *CYYP*, vol. Ⅲ, part 1.

② *Quarterly Bulletin of the Chinese Bibliography* (English edition), vol. I, no. 2.

In the communion between Indian and Chinese cultures philology or phonology does not play an important role. But even in this sphere alone, we have successively received much aid from India in course of thousand years from the end of the Han dynasty to the present times, let alone what Indian religion, philosophy and other branches of culture have given us. I am glad to be able to convey this sentiment of gratefulness so far as my special field of studies is concerned just on my arrival in India. I hope that the two nations will not only maintain the relations that have existed so well through long ages but make them still deeper and more intimate, so that even the philological studies in the both countries will also rise to new heights and fresh splendours through mutual collaboration.

(*Sino-Indian Studies* I. pt. 3. March 1945, Calcutta)

A Preliminary Study on the Trung Language of Kung-shan

In the northwestern most part of Yunnan, there is a tribe called Ch'iu-Chi by the Chinese and called Trung by its own members. They form a minority population distributed over an area between long. 97°50′ and 98°50′ E and between lat. 27° and 28°N, bounded by Kiang Sin P'o on the West and by Kau Li Kung Shan on the East.

During my visit to Tali in the early Spring of 1942 for the purpose of studying the local speech, I came to know a Trung student of National Tali Normal School who acted as my informant. We spent about fifty hours together and I was enabled to record from his lips more than seven hundred words and a few pieces of conversation. From this material I have worked out the phonetic system of the Trung language, from the point of view of analysis into initials, finals, and tones, as follows:

57 Initial Consonants and Consonant-clusters

p, *p'*, *b*, *m*; *t*, *t'*, *d*, *n*, *l*; *ts*, *ts'*, *dz*, *s*; *ch*, *ch'*, *j*, *sh*, *zh*, *r*, *hl*; *ch*(*i*), *ch'*(*i*), *j*(*i*), *sh*(*i*), *gn*; *k*, *k'*, *g*, *ng*, *h*; *pl*, *pr*, *bl*, *br*, *ml*, *mr*; *tl*, *tr*, *dr*; *kl*, *kr*, *k'l*, *k'r*, *hr*; *sl*, *sr*, *sn*, *sm*, *sd*, *sk*, *sk'*, *sg*; *shn*, *spl*, *spr*, *skl*, *sch*(*i*).

80 Finals

y, *a*, *ia*, *ua*, *o*, *io*, *uo*, *ə*, *iə*, *e*, *ie*, *i*, *u*, *iu*, *ui*, *ai*, *ei*, *əi*, *oi*; *am*, *iam*, *uam*, *om*, *əm*, *iəm*, *iem*; *an*, *uan*, *on*, *en*, *ien*, *üen*, *ən*, *in*, *un*; *ang*, *iang*, *uang*, *ong*, *iong*, *əng*, *ing*, *ung*, *iung*; *al*, *ial*, *ual*, *ol*, *iol*, *el*, *iel*, *əl*, *iəl*, *ul*; *ap*, *iap*, *uap*, *op*, *əp*, *iəp*, *uəp*, *ep*, *ip*; *at*, *iat*, *uat*, *ot*, *iot*, *uot*, *et*, *iet*, *ət*, *it*, *ut*; *ak*, *uak*, *ok*, *iok*, *ək*, *ik*.

6 Tones

(1) half-high level, (2) high rising, (3) low rising, (4) middle falling, (5) short level, (6) short falling.

For typographical convenience in dealing with a large amount of text or vocabulary, all sounds can be represented by the following letters and numerals:

p, *p*‘, *b*, *m*; *t*, *t*‘, *d*, *n*, *l*; *k*, *k*‘, *g*, *ng*, *h*; *ch*, *ch*‘, *j*, *sh*, *zh*, *gn*; *ts*, *ts*‘, *dz*, *s*; *hl*, *r*.

a, *o*, *ə*, *e*, *i*, *u*, *y*, *ü*.

1,2,3,4,5,6.

The values of the sounds in terms of phonetic symbols and those of the tones in terms of Chao's "tone-letters"[①] are given in the accompanying cut. The value of [ɑ] is a slightly fronted cardinal [ɑ]; [o] is a little lower than

① Y. R. Chao's A System of Tone-letters, *Le Maître Phonétique*, 1930, p. 24.

cardinal [o]; and [ə] is more fronted and higher than average. The romanization given at the left is much simpler than the Lisu alphabet devised by J. O. Fraser or that for Kachin by O. Hanson.

TABLE OF PHONETIC VALUES OF TRUNG ROMANIZATION

	Romanization	Values in Phonetic Symbols
Bilabials	p p‘ b m	p p‘ b m
Dentals	t t‘ d n hl l	t t‘ d n ɬ l
Gutturals	k k‘ g ng h	k k‘ g ŋ h
Retroflexes	ch ch‘ j sh zh r	tʂ tʂ‘ dʐ ʂ ʐ ɻ
Palatals	chi ch‘i ji gn shi	tɕ tɕ‘ dʑ ɲ ɕ
Dental Sibilants	ts ts‘ dz s	ts ts‘ dz s
Low Vowel	a	ɑ
Mid Vowels	o ə e	o ə
High Vowels	i u ü y	i u y ɹ̣
Tones	1 2 3 4 5 6	˦ ˥˧ ˧˥˧ ˦˧ ˥ ˥˩

While it is not yet possible, with the material at my disposal, to work out a complete grammar, certain important features of order, classifiers after nouns, and affixes are already clearly discernible. We shall illustrate each in turn.

(a) Word order

The subject comes first, the verb follows, and the object, if any, precedes the verb. Examples are: *ang*^{4} *chiəm*^{4} *ra*^{4} *ngə*^{4} "that child cry", i. e. "that child cries"; *na*^{4} *ang*^{1} *dza*^{1} *na*^{4} *kai*^{4} "you rice eat", i. e. "you eat rice".

The adjective either precedes or follows the noun modified, thus *pu*^{5} *sai*^{4} *shing*^{1} *uat*^{5} "red flower"; *məl*^{6} *shing*^{1} *lap*^{5} "green leaf"; *ik*^{5} *ra*^{4} *də*^{5} *mang*^{1} "elder brother"; *ik*^{5} *ra*^{4} *a*^{6} *dəi*^{1} "young brother".

The possessor is followed by what is possessed, thus *ik*^{5} *a*^{6} *sa*^{1} "our field"; *gnie*^{1} *gnik*^{5} *ka*^{4} *ti*^{1} "your(pl.) chicken".

(b) Classifiers

1. *Kə*^{1} is used after the names of animals together with the numerical particle *ti*^{1}, e. g. *mə*^{1} *kə*^{4} *ti*^{1} *kə*^{1} "a horse", *ka*^{4} *ti*^{1} *kə*^{1} "a chicken", *pling*^{1} *ti*^{1} *kə*^{1} "an insect", *am*^{1} *pla*^{4} *ti*^{1} *kə*^{1} "a fish", etc. (cf. Chinese 一匹马、一只鸡、一条虫、一条鱼)

2. *kəi*^{1} corresponding to Chinese 根 *kên*, *e. g. i*^{4} *jiə*^{1} *ti*^{1} *kəi*^{1} "a rope", *a*^{6} *ji*^{4} *ti*^{1} *kəi*^{1} "a straw". (cf. Chinese 一根绳子、一根茅草)

3. *plang*^{4} corresponding to Chinese 把[ᶜpa], e. g. *ul*^{6} *ti*^{1} *plang*^{4} "an axe", *shiam*^{4} *ti*^{1} *plang*^{4} "a knife". (cf. Chinese 一把斧头、一把刀)

4. *ko*^{4} corresponding to Chinese 棵 *k*ʻ*o*^{1}, e. g. *sru*^{1} *ti*^{1} *ko*^{4} "a pine", *sa*^{1} *ti*^{1} *ko*^{4} "a mulberry tree". (cf. Chinese 一棵松树、一棵桑树)

5. *lung*^{1} after the names of mountains, houses, fruits, teeth, etc., e. g. *lak*^{5} *ka*^{1} *ti*^{1} *lung*^{1} "a mountain", *chiəm*^{4} *ti*^{1} *lung*^{1} "a house", *shik*^{5} *shi*^{1} *ti*^{1} *lung*^{1} "a fruit", *sa*^{4} *ti*^{1} *lung*^{1} "a tooth".

6. *mai*^{4} after the names of the river, bench, flower, etc., e.g. *uak*^{6} *ch'ial*^{6} *ti*^{1} *mai*^{4} "a river", *sa*^{1} *ra*^{1} *ti*^{1} *mai*^{4} "a bench", *shing*^{1} *uat*^{5} *ti*^{1} *mai*^{4} "a flower".

7. The names of the parts of human body are reduplicated with the insertion of the numerical particle *ti*^{1}, e.g. *səl*^{5} *ti*^{1} *səl*^{5} "a leg", *ul*^{5} *ti*^{1} *ul*^{5} "a hand". (cf. Chinese 一条腿、一只手

8. Likewise the numerical particle alone is sometimes inserted in the name of a thing, e.g. *shing*^{1} *ti*^{1} *lap*^{6} "a leaf".

9. Some classifiers are of limited use with some particular things, e.g. *a*^{6} *tsang*^{4} *ti*^{1} *jiok*^{6} "a person", *tung*^{1} *ol*^{5} *ti*^{1} *k'lang*^{4} "a stick", *ang*^{1} *dza*^{1} *ti*^{1} *lap*^{6} "a meal", *ang*^{1} *dza*^{1} *ti*^{1} *pəl*^{5} "a bowl of rice", *shia*^{4} *ti*^{1} *jïong*^{4} "a piece of meat", *shing*^{1} *ti*^{1} *pra*^{4} "a bundle of wood (sticks)", *jï*^{4} *ge*^{1} *ti*^{1} *lang*^{4} "a sheet of paper".

(c) Affixes

1. The personal subjective prefixes and suffixes of the verbs.—An interesting grammatical feature of this language, like Nung and some Nepalese dialects, is that the reduced forms of the personal pronouns except the third are used as prefixes and suffixes of the verb to form verbal conjugations, e.g.

nga^4	*ang*^{1} *dza*^{1}	*kai*^{4}	*chia-ng*^{4}	
I	*food*	*eat*	can	I can eat
na^4	*ang*^{1} *dza*^{a}	*kai*^{4}	*nə-chia*^{4}	
You	food	eat	can	You can eat
ang^4	*ang*^{1} *dza*^{1}	kai^4	*chia*^{4}	
He	food	eat	can	He can eat

ing^{1}		*ang*^{1} *dza*^{1}	*kai*^{4}	*chia-i*^{4}		
We		food	eat	can		We can eat
gnie^{1} *gning*^{4}		*ang*^{1} *dza*^{1}	*kai*^{4}	*nə-chia-n*^{4}		
You		food	eat	can		You can eat(pl.)
ang^{4} *gning*^{4}		*ang*^{1} *dza*^{1}	*kai*^{4}	*chia*^{4}		
They		food	eat	can		They can eat

2. The personal possessive prefixes.—Besides, the reduced forms of the personal pronouns can be used as possessive prefixes of kinship terms, e.g.

na^{4} *n-a*^{6} *pai*^{4}

you you father your father

na^{4} *n-a*^{6} *mai*^{4}

you you mother your mother

3. *a*^{6} is prefixed to some numerals, nouns, pronouns, adjectives and verbs, e.g. *a*^{6} *səm*^{4} "three", *a*^{6} *sa*^{1} "field", *a*^{6} *də*^{4} "self", *a*^{6} *rom*^{1} "far distant", *a*^{6} *hra*^{4} "to tie, to fasten".

4. *də*^{5} or *tə*^{5} is prefixed to some nouns, numerals, adjectives and verbs, e.g. *də*^{5} *gəi*^{1} "dog", *tə*^{5} *k'ri*^{1} "mule", *də*^{5} *gə*^{4} "nine", *də*^{5} *grang*^{4} "pretty, beautiful", *tə*^{5} *kəng*^{4} "diligent", *tə*^{5} *kə*^{1} "to pull".

5. *pu*^{5} is prefixed to some nouns, verbs and adjectives, e.g. *pu*^{5} *shin*^{1} "heart", *pu*^{5} *sa*^{4} "to itch", *pu*^{5} *sai*^{4} "red".

6. *pə*^{5} is a verbal prefix, e.g. *pə*^{5} *kap*^{5} "to cover (up)", *pə*^{5} *tom*^{4} "to pour (water)".

7. *mə*^{5} is usually prefixed to some adjectives and verbs, e.g. *mə*^{5} *kam*^{1} "rich", *mə*^{5} *jio*^{5} "to rail at or against", sometimes with a negative sense, e.g. *guot*^{6} "clever, wise" : *mə*^{5} *guot*^{6} "muddle-headed, unwise"; *k'a*^{1} "tasting of salt" : *mə*^{5} *k'a*^{1} "unsalted".

8. *ma*^{6} or *m*-is an adjectival prefix with an opposite or contrary sense,

e.g. *a*^{6} *pra*^{1}"quick": *ma*^{6} *pra*^{1}"slow"; *tsən*^{4}"tight": *ma*^{6} *tsən*^{4}"loose".

9. *zhy*^{3} is prefixed to nouns and adjectives, e.g. *zhy*^{3} *mət*^{5}"cloud", *zhy*^{3} *na*^{4}"deep".

10. *shiə*^{4} is mostly suffixed to intransitive verbs, e.g. *tol*^{5} *shiə*^{4}"to run", *a*^{6} *kəi*^{1} *shiə*^{4}"to walk", *a*^{6} *glai*^{1} *shiə*^{4}"to jump", *ngat*^{5} *shiə*^{4}"to move".

11. *di*^{4} is a verbal suffix to express past tense or completed action, e.g. *a*^{6} *kəi*^{1} *di*^{4}"walked away", *tol*^{5} *shiə*^{4} *di*^{4}"ran away".

12. *mie*^{1} is an adjectival suffix with an opposite or contrary sense, e.g. *ak*^{5} *sal*^{5}"fresh": *ak*^{5} *sal*^{5} *mie*^{1}"stale"; *tsang*^{1} *na*^{1} *e*^{1}"clean": *tsang*^{1} *na*^{1} *mie*^{1}"dirty".

These grammatical features, as outlined above, suggest strongly that Trung is a member of the Tibeto-Burman family, though it is hard to decide to which group it belongs. The latter question has so far received only scant attention. My colleague in Academia Sinica Mr. Ling Shun-shêng assigns it to the Burman group, though he has given no reason for it. I have tried to attack this problem from two points of view. On the one hand, I have picked out some thirty Trung words which seem least likely to have been borrowed and compared them with those of the other languages of the same family taken from the Comparative Vocabulary of G. A. Grierson's *Linguistic Survey of India*, vol. 1, part 2. From this, I have found that Trung bears very many resemblances in general phonetic aspects to the languages of the Lolo-Moso group, particularly to Nung, so far as can be seen from the probable cognates. On this ground, I hope to be not entirely unjustified in classifying it tentatively along with the Lolo-Moso languages, provided that Grierson's classification of Nung to the same group is reliable. On the other hand, in the light of the personal prefixes and suffixes of the verb, the indications are that it belongs to the Si-Fan branch, as is the treatment of the Nung languages by H. R. Davies in his *Yun-Nan*. Definite conclusion on this question must therefore be withheld until more thorough study based on more extensive material has been done.

(*HJAS* Ⅷ, no. 3 & 4, March 1945, Boston)

The Genealogical Patronymic Linkage System of the Tibeto-Burman Speaking Tribes[①]

The genealogical patronymic linkage system is a dominant cultural trait of the Tibeto-Burman speaking tribes which, besides the physiological and linguistic factors, can help to determine the relations between the various tribes and throw light on some of the historical problems about the descent and inter-relationship of the Houses which have long baffled inquiry. According to this tradition of the Tibeto-Burman people, which is of great antiquity, generally the names of the father and the son overlap; that is, the last one or two syllables of the father's name are transmitted to the name of the son and become its first one or two syllables; and this is done continuously from generation to generation. It has, to be precise, the following forms:

For example:

1. A B C-C D E- D E F- F G H

En-hêng-no No- pên-p'ei Pên-p'ei-k'o K'o-kau-lie

① Read at the All India Oriental Conference, December 31, 1944.

2. A □.[①] B - B □ C - C □ D - D □ E

Kung-a-lung Lung-a-kau Kau-a-shou Shou-a-mei

3. A B C D - C D E F - E F G H - G H I J

Yi-tsun-lau-sho Lau-sho-tu-tsai Tu-tsai-a-tsung A-tsung-yi-k'u

4. □A □B □B □C □C □D □D □E

A-tsung-a-liang A-liang-a-hu A-hu-a-lie A-lie-a-kia

In each branch, there may be some slight variations but, as a rule, the forms do not go beyond the above four.

My interest in this subject was first aroused by some casual readings. In 1942 I made a trip to Chi-tsu-shan（鸡足山）, a mountain in the west of Yunnan; and there in a temple called Hsi-t'an-ssŭ（悉檀寺）I came upon the records of the house of Mu（木）, the native governor of Li-kiang（丽江）. The records are called "The Genealogy of the House of Mu（木）with Portraits". My curiosity was thus further piqued. After the trip I referred myself to the various treatments of the subject in the writings of Dr. T'ao Yun-k'uei（陶云逵）, Mr. Tung Tso-pin（董作宾）, and Dr. Ling Shun-shêng（凌纯声）; and, putting my notes in order, I wrote the "Genealogy of the House of Mu at Hsi-t'an-ssŭ on Chi-tsu-shan", which was published in issue 25, volume 3 of the *Contemporary Review*（《当代评论》）. After that, through my own researches and the aid of friends I have gathered together varied other data. With these I now write this study in the hope that those interested in the problem, whether anthropologists, ethnologists, or linguists, may supplement or revise what is put forward here so as to solve this problem adequately.

---

① The sign □ shows a constant inserted sound.

I shall discuss the subject under three headings, each with its items and sub-items.

A. The Burman Branch

1. The Burman

About this branch I have acquired as yet no first-hand data; however I have discovered the genealogical patronymic linkage practice in their histories. The Dynasty Moriya (孔雀王朝) of Burma, covering the period from the second to the fourth century A.D., did also use the system, as can be seen in the following genealogy of theirs:

Pyo-so-ti	Ti-min-yi	Yi-min-baik
Baik-then-li	Then-li-jong	Jong-du-yit①

I hope the above to be supplemented by scholars versed in Burman lore and history.

2. The A-chit 茶山.

The A-chit is a branch living in tracts of country bordering on Burma in the northwest of Yunnan. I got, last spring, two genealogies of this branch. One is of a man called K'ung K'o-lang (孔科郎) and includes forty-six generations. The other is of one named Tung Ch'ang-shao (董昌绍) and counts nine generations. We now reproduce them here:

① Phayre: *History of Burma*, p. 279, quoted by Dr. Ling Shun-shêng in his article "A study of the U-man and Pei-man of Yunnan in the T'ang dynasty", The Anthropological Journal of *CYYY*, 1938.

I. The genealogy of K'ung K'o-lang

1. Ya be bawm①	17. Te maw yaw	33. Bau myaw
2. Mashaw bawm	18. Maw yaw p'yau	34. Myaw t'uk
3. Bawm shaw chung	19. P'yau byaw yang	35. T'uk bawm
4. Chung shaw nin	20. Yang lawm lik	36. Bawm zing
5. Shaw nin k'ying	21. Lik ding chit	37. Zing yaw
6. K'ying da ê	22. Chit kang yau	38. Yaw bawm
7. Da ê saw	23. Kang yau gwi	39. Bawm K'aw
8. Shaw yaw chu	24. Gwi chung chyit	40. K'aw ying
9. Chu fu fek	25. Chung chyit yaw	41. Ying sau
10. Fu fek k'um	26. Yaw au ding	42. Sau ying
11. K'um kwe zik	27. Ding law waw	43. Ying yaw
12. Zik k'u lam	28. Waw law jang	44. Yaw ying
13. K'u lam pe	29. Jang law bawm	45. Ying K'aw
14. Shaw gyaw la ts'ang	30. Bawm law nu	46. K'aw lang
15. Ts'ang zaw byu	31. Nu kyang	
16. Byu zaw te	32. Kyang bau	

Of the forty-six names above, except the first and the second which are of the same generation, all the rest show name-linkage practice between the father and the son. There is indeed a break between the thirteenth and fourteenth generations. But according to K'ung K'o-lang, "from the thirteenth

① The notation used here follows O. Hanson's system for Kachin with a little modification. The tone-marks in this article are omitted in order to simplify the printing.

generation up, they could still talk with oxen, dogs, trees and plants as they were not yet men altogether." If so, are the names from that generation up yet legendary perhaps, and not to be accepted as the true genealogy of the house of K'ung K'o-lang?

Ⅱ. The genealogy of Tung Ch'ang-shao

1. Yawn sau
2. Sau chang
3. Chang lang
4. Lang bau; Lang gying
5. Bau zung; Bau ying; Bau taik
6. Zung ying
7. Ying sau
8. Sau chang
9. Chang sau

In this genealogy the fourth generation consists of two brothers and the fifth of three brothers. Tung's line seems to have derived from the eldest brother. According to Tung Ch'ang-shao, P'ien-ma (片马) was quite a jungle when his ancestor of the first generation in the genealogy, Yawn Sau, went there four hundred years ago, and began to reclaim the place. His grave is now at Lower P'ien-ma (下片马). There are monuments with inscriptions in Chinese and engraved portraits at the grave. The grave of his ancestor of the fourth generation is on the Gyang Gyang mountain also at Lower P'ien-ma. There are no monuments at these two graves.

Comparing these two genealogies, it is evident to us that the genealogy of Tung's house is later by far than that of the house of K'ung. If the words of Tung Ch'ang-shao are to be believed, the Tung's seem to have moved to P'ien-ma at the end of the reign of Chia-ching (嘉靖) in the Ming Dynasty, that is about 1541-1566 A.D.

B. The Moso or Na-khi(么些[①]或那喜)

Mr. Yü Ch'ing-yüan 余庆远 made the following statement on the Moso in his *Notes about Wei-hsi* 维西见闻录:"The Moso have no names and surnames. They use the last word of the name of the grandfather and that of the name of the father together with a new word to form their own name. The names of the successive generations link themselves like a chain and the removes in kinship are thus shown." As a matter of fact, if we examine with care the two genealogies of the Moso given below as well as the ways of name-linkage shown above, the words of Mr. Yü will soon be found to be but plausible and by no means accurate. The data we have come at are as follows:

(a) The religious classics of the Moso at Li-kiang (丽江) which record the six generations after the great deluge:

1. Tsung-chang-li-ên[②]	3. No-pên-p'ei	5. K'o-kau-lie
2. En-hêng-no	4. Pên-p'ei-k'o	6. Kau-lie-ts'u[③]

According to Mr. Yü the name of the third generation should be *Ên-no-p'ei*, that of the fourth should be *No-p'ei-k'o*. It is evidently at odds with the data.

(b) The genealogy of the house of Mu (木) at Li-kiang (丽江).

---

① Also written as 此 over 夕, 些.

② The Moso's genealogies (a) and (b) are read in Mandarin from the Chinese translation, and transcribed by a modified Wade spelling.

③ Quoted by Mr. Tung Tso-pin, in his article "New Evidence concerning the genealogy of Tibeto-Burman people," *Bulletin of Ethnological Studies*, no. 2, pp. 181-200, 1940, published by the Sun-Yat-sen Cultural and Educational Institute. *CYYY* 7, 121 - 135, 1938.

The head of the house of Mu was successively the native governor of Li-kiang from about the reign of Wu-tê (武德 618—626 A. D.) to the beginning of the Ch'ing Dynasty. There are four extant documents about the genealogy of the house:

(1) The introduction to the genealogy of the house of Mu by Yang Shên (杨慎) written in the twenty-fourth year of the reign of Chia-ching in the Ming Dynasty (1545 A. D.), now kept at Mu's house at Li-kiang.

(2) The genealogy of the house of Mu with portraits; bound in one volume with Yang's introduction. There are two extant copies: one was inscribed on the cover as "The Picture of Mu's Tendering Allegiance" by Ch'ên Chao-chung (陈钊钟) of Hai-nan (海南) and had an addendum and epilogue in verse by the same. It is now at Mu's house at Li-kiang. The other, inscribed as "The Genealogy of the House of Mu with Portraits", is now in Hsi-t'an-ssŭ (悉檀寺) on Chi-tsu-shan (鸡足山).

(3) The monument engraved with the genealogy of the house of Mu now in the graveyard of the house at Shê-shan (蛇山) about ten *li* southeast of Li-kiang, erected in the twenty-second year of Tao-kuang (道光) in the Ch'ing Dynasty (1842 A. D.).

(4) A draft of the genealogy of the house of Mu in the notes appended to the Moso Chao (么些诏) in the records about the natives of the south in the draft of a sequel to the provincial gazetteer of Yünnan compiled by Wang Wên-shao (王文韶) and others in the twenty-seventh year of Kuang-hsü (光绪) (1901 A. D.).

The agreements and divergences among these four kinds of data detailed in the article "On the Name, the Habitation and the Migrations of the Moso"[①] by T‘ao Yün-k‘uei and my article "The Genealogy of the House of Mu at Hsi-t‘an-ssŭ on Chi-tsu-shan". We shall not enlarge upon them here but just give the genealogy as engraved on the monument:

1. Ts‘in-yang
2. Yang-in-tu-ku
3. Tu-ku-la-kü
4. La-kü-p‘u-mêng
5. P‘u-mêng-p‘u-wang
6. P‘u-wang-la-wan
7. La-wan-si-nai
8. Si-nai-si-k‘o
9. Si-k‘o-la-t‘u
10. La-t‘u-ngo-kün
11. Ngo-kün-mou-kü
12. Mou-kü-mou-si
13. Mou-si-mou-ts‘uo
14. Mou-ts‘uo-mou-lê
15. Mou-lê-mou-pau
16. Mou-pau-a-tsung
17. A-tsung-a-liang
18. A-liang-a-hu
19. A-hu-a-lie
20. A-lie-a-kia
21. A-kia-a-têh(Mu-têh)
22. A-têh-a-ch‘u(Mu-ch‘u)
23. A-ch‘u-a-t‘u(Mu-t‘u)
24. A-t‘u-a-ti(Mu-shen)
25. A-ti-a-sŭ(Mu-k‘in)
26. A-sŭ-a-ya(Mu-t‘ai)
27. A-ya-a-ts‘in(Mu-ting)
28. A-ts‘in-a-kung(Mu-kung)
29. A-kung-a-mu(Mu-kau)
30. A-mu-a-tu(Mu-tung)
31. A-tu-a-shêng(Mu-wang)
32. A-shêng-a-chai(Mu-ts‘ing)
33. A-chai-a-sŭ(Mu-tseng)
34. A-sŭ-a-chun(Mu-yi)
35. Mu-hsi
36. Mu-sung
37. Mu-run
38. Mu-tsi
39. Mu-ren

In the thirty-nine generations above, the first and second generations are seen to use the first form of patronymic linkage system; from the third to the sixteenth they used the third form; from the seventeenth to the thirty-fourth they used the fourth form. Though the surname of Mu was conferred by the Ming Dynasty since its beginning, they could not yet give up their

① *CYYY* 7, 121-135, 1938.

habit of name-linkage and merely added the last word of their name to the surname Mu to form the required name. Thus, A-kia-a-têh（阿甲阿德）was also called *Mu-têh*. It was not till the K'ang-hsi（康熙）era（after 1662 A.D.）that such a cultural trait began to disappear in the name of Mu-hsi（木樑）.

As to those branches of Hsi-fan（西番）beside the Moso we have to pass them over for the present for want of reliable data.

C. The Lolo Branch

About this branch the data I have gathered are more ample; it may be treated under three items and six sub-items.

1. The Lolo（倮倮）.

I haves so far seen five genealogies of the branch.

(a) The thirty generations before the deluge in the so-called "Royal Genealogy"（《帝王世纪》）in *A Collection of Lolo Writings*（《爨文丛刻》）by V.K.Ting（丁文江）. They read as follows:

1. Hsi-mu-chê[①]	7. Ch'ang-kuai-tsuo	13. p'ê-nêng-tau
2. Chê-tau-kung	8. Tsuo-a-ts'ie	14. Tau-mu-yi
3. Kung-chu-shih	9. Ts'ie-a-tsung	15. Mu-yi-ch'ih
4. Shih-a-li	10. Tsung-a-yi	16. Ch'ih-a-suo
5. Li-a-ming	11. Yi-a-tsi	17. Suo-a-têh
6. Ming-ch'ang-kuai	12. Tsi-p'ê-nêng	18. Têh-si-suo

① The Lolo's genealogies（a），（b），and（c）are read in Mandarin and transcribed by modified Wade.

19. Si-suo-to
20. To-pi-yi
21. Pi-yi-tu
22. Tu-si-sien
23. Si-sien-t'o
24. T'o-a-ta
25. Ta-a-wu
26. A-wu-no
27. No-chu-tu
28. Tu-chu-wu
29. Wu-lau-ts'uo
30. Ts'uo-chu-tu

The translator Lo Wên-pi (罗文笔) said in the introduction: "During the thirty generations from the first man Hsi-mu-chê to Ts'uo-chu-tu, there was no writing of any sort; all things were transmitted orally. In the twenty-ninth generation, it pleased God to send down a priest, Mi-a-tieh (宓阿叠) by name, who instituted sacrifices, rites, and laws and invented writing. Thus culture dawned and manners began. I have not here the book called *Notes on the Deluge* and so can not describe what happened then more circumstantially." The so-called Deluge seems to have been an epoch from which we may trace back to their legendary first man Hsi-mu-chê and forward to their connection with the house of An (安) at Shui-hsi (水西) to whose first ancestor, Tu-mu-wu, Ts'uo-chu-tu the thirtieth and last of the genealogy transmitted the last syllable of his name.

(b) The genealogy of the Lolo house of An at Shui-hsi in Kweichow in the so-called "Royal Genealogy" in *A Collection of Lolo Writings*.

There are eighty-four generations in all from Tu-mu-wu to Yi-fen-ming-tsung (also called An-k'un 〈安昆〉 in Chinese):

1. Tu-mu-wu
2. Mu-ts'i-ts'i
3. Ts'i-a-hung
4. Hung-a-têh
5. Têh-ku-sha
6. Sha-ku-mu
7. Ku-mu-kung
8. Kung-a-lung
9. Lung-a-kau
10. Kau-a-shou
11. Shou-a-mei
12. Mei-a-têh
13. Têh-a-shih
14. Shih-mei-wu
15. Mei-wu-mêng
16. Mêng-tie-to
17. To-a-chih
18. Chih-wu-shuo

19. Wu-shuo-pi	41. To-a-t'a	63. A-tung-ta-wu
20. Pi-yi-mei	42. T'a-a-k'i	64. Ta-wu-lau-nai
21. Mei-a-liang	43. K'i-a-fou	65. Lau-nai-lau-tsai
22. Liang-a-tsung	44. Fou-na-chih	66. Lau-tsai-a-k'i
23. Tsung-a-pu	45. Na-chih-tu	67. A-k'i-lau-ti
24. Pu-a-shuo	46. Tu-a-kêng	68. Lau-ti-pu-chih
25. Shuo-a-t'au	47. A-kêng-a-wên	69. Pu-chih-na-k'au
26. T'au-a-ch'ang	48. A-wên-lo-nan	70. Na-k'au-pêng-tsai
27. A-ch'ang-pi	49. Lo-nan-a-k'ê	71. Pêng-tsai-lau-chih
28. Pi-yi-mêng	50. A-k'ê-yi-tien	72. Lau-chih-lau-p'u
29. Mêng-wu-shou	51. Yi-tien-tsi-k'i	73. Lau-p'u-pu-tsu
30. Shou-a-tien	52. Tsi-k'i-ren-yi	74. Pu-tsu-chih-pa
31. Tien-a-fa	53. Ren-yi-pu-yie	75. Chih-pa-an-tsuo
32. Fa-yi-yi	54. Pu-yie-yi-tsun	76. An-tsuo-chih-wu
33. Yi-yi-ch'ih	55. Yi-tsun-lau-shuo	77. Chih-wu-lau-ch'êng
34. Ch'ih-a-chu	56. Lau-shuo-tu-tsai	78. Lau-ch'êng-lo-si
35. Chu-a-tien	57. Tu-tsai-a-tsung	79. Lo-si-fei-shuo
36. Tien-a-tsi	58. A-tsung-yi-k'u	80. Fei-shuo-lau-ku
37. Tsi-a-têng	59. Yi-k'u-pu-yi	81. Lau-ku-lau-têh
38. Têng-a-tu	60. Pu-yi-a-yi	82. Lau-têh-lau-tien
39. Tu-a-ta	61. A-yi-a-lo	83. Lau-tien-yi-fen
40. A-ta-to	62. A-lo-a-tung	84. Yi-fen-ming-tsung

It was said by Lo Wên-pi, "I have found in the genealogy that there are eighty-four generations from our ancestor Mu-ts'i-ts'i to our lord An-k'un who was captured by Wu San-kuei(吴三桂)." The vicissitudes of peace and war, prosperity and decline in the course of the long ages cannot be here minutely recorded. From the ruin of the houses by Wu San-kuei to Lo Wên-pi, there are six more generations. So if we are to count from their first ancestor *Hsi-mu-chê*, there are one hundred twenty generations altogether which used uniformly the patronymic system.

(c) The ancient history of the Lolo of Wu-ting(武定).

The data on this subject were got by Mr. Ma Hsüeh-liang (马学良) from the house of the native governor Fêng 凤. One of the data is a genealogy of six consecutive generations.

1. Chu-ch'ê-k'ê	3. Shih-a-sha	5. Lu-cho-ch'u
2. Ch'ê-k'ê-shih	4. Sha-lu-cho	6. Ch'u-shu-tsu

There is another of ten generations:

1. Mu-a-ts'i	5. Suo-wu-mu	9. Lu-a-shih
2. Ts'i-a-hung	6. Wu-mu-ch'ou	10. Shih-a-mê
3. Hung-a-têh	7. Ch'ou-a-nu	
4. Têh-wo-suo	8. Nu-a-lu	

The first three generations of the second genealogy are the same as the second, third, and fourth generations of the genealogy of the An's of Shui-hsi. There are more than twenty such genealogies in the data collected by Mr. Ma. We here reproduce two of them.

(d) The patronymic linkage system of the Lolo at Mien-ning (冕宁) in Szechwan.

This is put down by Mr. Fu Mao-chi (傅懋勣) from the report of the Black Lolos of Hsiao-hsiang-kung-ling (小相公岭) at Mienning, and Mr. Fu has written an article "The Genesis in the Lolo Lore" published in *Frontier Service*, a journal of Ch'êngtu. A copy of the data he sent me is reproduced below:

V jê shih l *tsŭ*① (*tsŭ* means "from")
Shih l hê t'ê *ts'ŭ* (*ts'ŭ* means "lst generation")
Hê t'ê vo lê *gnie* (*gnie* means "2nd")
Vo lê ch'u pu *sua* (*sua* means "3rd")
Ch'u pu ju m *l* (*l* means "fourth")
Ju m *zê so go* (*zê so* means "three sons"; *go* means "measure" in the original sense, here it is used in the sense of "having")
Ju m ju t'ê *ge* (*ge* means "without issue")
Ju m ju l *ge*
Ju m v v *dzu* (*dzu* means "having descendants")
V v zê so *go*
V v ki tsih *le no su* (*le* is a particle used as a connecting word, *no su* "black man")
V v la ie ie *le he ngga* (*he ngga* is the name used by Lolo to Chinese)
V v sŭ sha le *o dzu* (*o dzu* is the name used by Lolo to Hsi-fan)

In this example we see words of specific sense added to the names; all those italicized are such words. It counts but six generations but the patronymic linkage system therein is quite evident while the relations of Lolo, Chinese, Hsi-fan in the mind of the Lolo are also betrayed.

Dr. Ling Shun-shêng said "in 1935 when I came upon at Yunnan a young Lolo of the vicinity of Ta-liang-shan (大凉山), called Ch'ü-mu-tsang-ming (曲木藏明), he told me that his father could recite with

① Mr. Fu's original transcription was in I. P. A., here I have changed it into modified Wade.

precision the genealogy of their house which comprehended scores of generations all linked with names."① Corroborated by the testimony of Mr. Fu, it is proved that this practice of linking names is equally current with the Lolo of Szechwan.

2. The Woni（窝尼）

Woni is the name given by Chinese to those speaking a language related with Lolo in the south of Yunnan. They live in places none of which is north of long. 24°N. In book 8 of *Man-ssŭ-ho-chih*（《蛮司合志》）, the Combined Records of Native Tribes, by Mao Ch'i-ling（毛奇龄）, it is said "The natives of the region, the Lolo and the Woni, are given to fighting with each other. Deaths are paid for with money. They have no family names; their names are formed with the last word of the father's name. In the reign of Hung-chih（弘治 1488-1505 A.D.）the chief magistrate Ch'ên Ch'êng（陈晟）assigned severally the first eight surnames in the book of *Pai-chia-hsing* or one hundred surnames to the eight districts to be added to their names. Each district accepted its surnames except the Na-lou（纳楼）." We see here that the Woni use the patronymic linkage system as well. Last summer Mr. Kao Hua-nien（高华年）and Professor Yüan Chia-hua（袁家骅）went to Hsin-p'ing（新平）and O-shan（峨山）, two districts in south Yunnan to inquire into the Woni language. However, they have not noted this practice of theirs. Probably the Woni in those districts are deeply imbued with Chinese influence and gradually forget their old ways. So I can not verify the words of Mao Ch'i-ling as I can do in the case of the Lolo.

① Ling Shun-shêng, *Ibid*., p.70.

3. The A-ka（阿卡）

The A-ka are very numerous in the east part of Keng Tung（景栋）and the adjoining parts of French Laos and Southern Yunnan. In 1935, Dr. T'ao Yun-k'uei made an anthropological investigation of the Shan people of Southern Yunnan; and in his journey from Mong-lem（孟连）to Mong-chieh（孟遮）he came upon an A-ka village where from the mouths of two A-ka old men he got the two following genealogies:

(a) The genealogy of Bluo-sa, fifty-six generations in all:

1. Su-mi-o①
2. O-tzuo-lö
3. Tzuo-lö-tzung
4. Tzung-mö-yieh
5. Mö-yieh-ch'ia
6. Ch'ia-di-hsi
7. Di-hsi-li
8. Li-hǒ-bä
9. Hǒ-bä-wu
10. Wu-nio-za
11. Nio-za-tzuo
12. Tzuo-mö-er
13. Mö-er-chü
14. Chü-tuǒ-p'uo
15. Tuǒ-p'uo-muo
16. Muo-kǔo-tuǒ
17. Kǔo-tuǒ-ji
18. Ji-lê-nio
19. Nio-ch'i-la
20. La-tang-buǒ
21. Buǒ-muo-buo
22. Muo-buo-ji
23. Ji-la-bi
24. Bi-mǒ-tzuo
25. Tzuo-huā
26. Huā-jiä
27. Jiä-tzä
28. Tzä-jiō
29. Jiō-blung
30. Blung-läi
31. Läi-mi
32. Mi-hsia
33. Hsia-yi
34. Yi-ch'iä
35. Ch'iä-kung
36. Kung-kang
37. Hsia-tzuo
38. Tzuo-ji
39. Ji-zá
40. zá-bang
41. Bang-läi
42. Läi-ni
43. Ni-buo
44. Buo-pö
45. Ma-buo

① According to Dr. T'ao's own transcription.

46. Buo-gong
47. P'u-da
48. Da-tzung
49. Tzung-ch'iuo
50. Ch'iuo-ji
51. Ji-z'a
52. Z'a-nio
53. Nio-chuo
54. Chuo-zä
55. Zä-bluo
56. Bluo-sä

(b) The genealogy of Ou-la, forty-seven generations:

1. Su-mi-o
2. O-tzuo-lö
3. Tzuo-lö-tzung
4. Tzung-mö-yieh
5. Mö-yieh-ch'ia
6. Ch'ia-di-hsi
7. Di-hsi-li
8. Li-ho-bä
9. Ho-bä-wu
10. Wu-nio-za
11. Nio-za-tzuo
12. Tzuo-mö-er
13. Mö-er-chü
14. Chü-tuŏ-p'uo
15. Tuŏ-p'uo-muo
16. Muo-kŭo-tuŏ
17. Kŭo-tuŏ-ji
18. Ji-lê-nio
19. Nio-ch'i-la
20. La-tang-buo
21. Tang-buo-sö
22. Buo-sö-läi
23. Läi-lang-buo
24. Buo-yi-nŏ
25. Nŏ-muo-buo
26. Muo-buo-di
27. Di-hsia-biä
28. Biä-muŏ-tzö
29. Tzö-wo-yi
30. Wo-yi-jia
31. Jia-tzä
32. Tzä-jio
33. Jio-blung
34. Blung-läi
35. Läi-hsia
36. Hsia-yi
37. Yi-chiä
38. Chiä-kung
39. Kung-kang
40. Hsia-tzuo
41. Tzuo-ji
42. Ji-za
43. Za-bang
44. O-dë
45. Dë-gong
46. Gong-tzuo
47. Ou-lä

The two genealogies are the same for the first twenty generations. The first genealogy from the twenty-seventh to the fortieth generation corresponds to the second from the thirty-first to the forty-third generation. Yet the first genealogy from the twenty-first to the twenty-sixth and the forty-first to the fifty-sixth as well as the second from the forty-fourth to the forty-seventh have their own several lines. We see, however, the two genealogies are, at all events, very near in kinship. The breaks at the twenty-seventh and thirty-seventh generations in the genealogy A, and at the fortieth and forty-fourth generations in the genealogy B, may be due to errors of the recital or some other causes about which we cannot yet be sure in the present state of our knowledge.

The above discussion is limited to the data to which we have access so far. It seems to be a matter of course that there is many another branch in the Tibeto-Burman speaking tribes as well as other peoples that have the same cultural tradition. In this account, I propose that scholars similarly interested may help to find out the spread and antiquity of the practice among the related peoples.

Now it may well be asked what is the real use of such a practice. To our mind, it is, in the first place, mnemonic. All the branches except the Lolo and Moso have no writings; or, where they have some writing, it is not for everyday use. When names are given thus overlapped in a sequence, they are much easier to remember. Everyone can then keep in mind the names of all his known ancestors down to himself and therewith identify their kinsmen and know their removes from himself. It is therefore of evident importance to them.

The other use is that it is of aid to us in solving the problems about descent of families in history.

As to the ancient history of Yunnan, though there are records of it in ancient Chinese histories such as the book of Historical Records by Ssŭ-ma Ch'ien (司马迁), the *History of the Han Dynasty* by Pan Ku (班固), the *Hua-yang-kuo-chih* (《华阳国志》) by Ch'ang Ch'ü (常璩) and *Man-shu*

(《蛮书》) by Fan Ch'o (樊绰), they are, one and all, too brief and general. It was in the Yüan and Ming Dynasties that the Chinese came to have access to the *Pa's Ancient History* (《白古记》) written in the pa-tsi (白子) language and began to know more about the ancient history of Yunnan. Then there came in the Yuan Dynasty the *Records of Ancient Yunnan* (《记古滇说》) by Chang Tao-tsung 张道宗, in the Ming Dynasty the *Legends of Nan-chao* (《南诏野史》)[①] by Juan Yuan-shêng (阮元声); and Yang Shên (杨慎) wrote the *Records of Ancient Yunnan* (《滇载记》). They all have accounts of the genealogy of the ancient Kingdom of Nan-chao. But they are often mixed up inextricably with Ai-lao's (哀牢夷) tale of Sha-i (沙壹) related in the *History of the Later Han Dynasty* on the one hand, and on the other the legends about Açoka (阿育王) brought in by Buddhism. Mr. Tung Tso-pin in his *New Evidences Concerning the Genealogy of the Tibeto-Burman People* made a comparison between the nine sons of Ti-mung-tso (低蒙苴) in the *Pa's Ancient History* and the twelve sons of Tu-chu-wu (渎侏武) (or Tu-wu-chu 〈渎武朱〉, according to Mr. Tung) in the *Royal Genealogy* of the Lolo and adduced many valuable ideas which we cannot dwell upon in detail here. We shall rather confine ourselves to the genealogy of Nan-chao.[②]

There are historians, western sinologists, and students of the Shan history, such as Hervey de Saint-Denis, Parker, Rocher, Cochrane and others who are of opinion that the Nan-chao was very akin to the Shan and should

① The word *Chao* 诏 means kingdom here.

② The genealogies of the six Chao's are determined with reference to Fan Ch'o's *Man-shu*, *Nan-man-chuan* in the *New History of the T'ang Dynasty* and *The Legends of Nan-chao* by Yang Shên. These, as well as the genealogies of the houses of Tuan and Kao, are read in Mandarin from the Chinese translation.

therefore be referred to the Tai people; and they go so far as to assert that Nan-chao was a kingdom founded by the Shan.

With regard to such opinion the evidence of the genealogy itself, let alone other objections, is enough to refute them.

In the *Legends of Nan-chao* compiled by Yang Shên, the genealogy of Nan-chao according to *Pa's Ancient History* is:

Pyo-tso-ti — Ti-mung-tso — Mung-tso-tu ———

After that there are thirty-six generations down to the following:

1. Si-nu-lo
2. Lo-ch'êng
3. Ch'êng-lo-p'i
4. P'i-lo-ko
5. Ko-lo-fêng
6. Fêng-kia-yi
7. Yi-mou-sün
8. Sün-lo-k'üan
9. K'üan-lung-ch'êng
10. Ch'êng-fêng-you
11. Shih-lung
12. Lung-shun
13. Shun-hwa-chên

If we acknowledge the name-linkage practice to be the cultural trait of the Tibeto-Burman speaking tribes, the opinion referred to above will fall to the ground of itself when confronted with the evidence of the genealogy of Nan-chao.

Besides Nan-chao there are five other Chao's which also use name-linkage system: The four generations of Mêng-chün-chao (蒙隽诏) are

1. Tsün-fu-shou
2. K'a-yang-chau (Tsün-fu-shou's brother)
3. Chau-yuan
4. Yuan-lo

The two generations of Yüeh-hsi-chao (越析诏) or Moso-chao (么些诏) are

1. Po-ch'ung
2. Yu-tsêng (Po-ch'ung's nephew)

The six generations of Lang-ch'iung-chao (浪穹诏) are

1. Fêng-shih
2. Lo-to
3. To-lo-wang
4. Wang-p'ien
5. P'ien-lo-yi
6. Yi-lo-kun

The five generations of Têng-yan-chao(澄赕诏)are

1. Fêng-mie 3. P'i-lo-têng 5. Tien-wên-to
2. Mie-lo-p'i 4. Têng-lo-tien

The four generations of Shih-lang-chao(施浪诏)are

1. Wang-mu 3. Ts'ien-pang
2. Wang-ts'ien(Wang-mu's brother) 4. Pang-lo-tien

In the house Tuan (段) at Tali (大理) which was later more deeply imbued with Chinese influence, such a cultural trait was no longer salient. Yet the son of Tuan Chih-hsiang (段智祥) was called Hsiang-hsing (祥兴); his grandson was called Hsing-chih (兴智). So traces of name-linking practice were still betrayed.

As to the house of Kao (高) which founded their so-called "Ta-chung-kuo" (大中国), they, too, preserved the custom, as is shown in the following genealogy:

1. Kao Chih-shêng(高智升) 3. Kao T'ai-ming(高泰明)
2. Kao Shêng-t'ai(高升泰) 4. Kao Ming-ch'ing(高明清)

The descendants of the house of Kao (高) were in succession the native governors of Yao-an-fu (姚安府) at the beginning of the Ch'ing Dynasty, and they also observed the name-linkage practice. On page 17, volume 135 of the provincial gazetteer of Yunnan compiled in the twentieth year of the reign of Kuang-hsü (光绪 1894), there is the following statement which is a quotation of the old records:

"At the beginning of the reign of Shun-chih (顺治 1644 A.D.) Kao Kuêng-yêng (高⊙[1]映) offered allegiance and was confirmed in his

---

① Written 天 over 明,奣.

herditary powers. At his death, his son Yêng-hou (映厚) succeeded who was again succeeded by his son Hou-têh (厚德). In the third year of Yung-chêng (雍正 1775 A.D.) he was deposed for defiance of the law and exiled to Kiang-nan (江南)."①

From this note the prevalence of the custom of name-linkage is further brought home to us.

It occurred to me that Dr. Hu Shih had also a note on "the Absence of Surnames in India" in his *Ts'ang-hui-shih Diary* (《藏晖室劄记》), volume 5, entered under July seventh, 1914. It said: "Happening to meet Mr. So and so of India, I was told that there are no family names there. They have only names. The transmission of the names is like this: If the name of the father is John Joseph Mathew, the son's name will be Joseph Mathew Richard. Richard is the new name; the former two are derived from his father's name. And the grandson's name is to be Richard Philip Charles and the great grandson's, Philip Charles William and so on." The names John, Richard and the like are of course just borrowed the west to make clear the practice to foreigners. I am much interested in this; and I regret that my knowledge of India is so meager. It is my hope, however, that the serious interest implied in dedicating this article to the 11th All-India Oriental Conference could induce some response from Indian scholars and this common point in the cultures of India and China be illuminated by their blent light.

(*HJAS* Ⅷ no. 3 & 4, March 1945, Boston)

① Quoted by Dr. Ling Shun-shêng in his article mentioned above.

The Traits of the Chinese Language

今天我要讲的题目是中国语言的特质。That means "The subject which I shall talk about today is the traits of the Chinese Language".

During thirty minutes, it is impossible to discuss this subject in detail. What I want to say I shall have to confine to a few main points.

In the first place, it seems fair to say that the Chinese characters are good for sense but hard for sound; in other words, they are more visible than audible. There have been some people who have said that Chinese Characters are a kind of picture-writing or hieroglyphs. This theory is not quite inclusive. On the ground of their structure, the Chinese characters can be divided into four kinds:

(a) Hieroglyphs as

牛 "cow" ngəu > niu$_2$

羊 "goat" ĭang > iang$_2$

犬 "dog" k'ĭwen > k'üen$_3$

马 "horse" ma > ma$_3$

(b) Emblematic

二 丄 上 above the horizon

"up, above" ẑĭang > shang$_4$

二 丅 下 beneath the horizon

"beneath, down": γa > hsia$_4$

刃 knife with the edge marked by a dot

"edge of a blade": ńzĭen > jen$_4$

寸 located one inch behind the right hand

"inch, the arteries": ts'uən > ts'un$_4$

(c) Composite ideograms as

拱手 hands folded

"joined hands": kung > kung$_3$

攀或扳 "pull down with two hands": pan > pan$_1$

舁 "to lift or raise with many hands": ĭwo > yü$_2$

臼 "to hold in both hands": kĭuk > chüe$_2$

These three types of Characters illustrated above, still hinge on the image and the sense and not upon the sound. In the "square pattern" of a Chinese character the image and sense it represents can often be perceived, but it indicates in no way how it is to be pronounced. If a person just glances over the above Chinese characters, even if he has never studied them at all, maybe he could conjecture the ideas that these words convey from their structure, but can either foreigner or Chinese find any shadow of a hint as to their phonetic value?

To supply the above shortcomings the fourth kind of Chinese characters were invented:

(d) phonetic Compounds as

江 "river" kang > chiang

河 "stream" *ga > γa > ho

松 "pine" zĭwong > sung

柏 "cypress" pek > po, pai

The method of this type no doubt had improved very much, and its quantity appropriated eight-tenths of *Shuo-wen* in Han dynasty. It uses the left side for the radical or category, and the right side for the phonetic or sound. It is more phonetic than ideographic. According to the development of world languages, some phonetic letters can be traced back to a hieroglyphic origin. All English speaking people should know that the English letters A, B and G were derived from the Greek letters Alpha, Beta and Gamma, which were borrowed from the Phoenician letters Aleph, Beth and Gimel, meaning "ox", "house" and "camel" respectively. Evidently these names were applied by the Semites because they employed the picture of an ox head to represent the first sound "A" in Aleph, the symbol of a house to represent the sound "B" in Beth, and the head and neck of camel to represent the sound "G" in Gimel. If the Chinese phonetic-compound inventors of ancient time could have accelerated their movement more radically, if they could have found the Chinese Phonological system and could have created a series of phonetic letters as simple as the thirty-nine Sound Notation announced by the Chinese Board of Education in 1917, then, no doubt, the Chinese language would long ago have changed its countenance and would now be a kind of phonographic language just like the languages of the Indo-European family. But the ancient Chinese phonetic-compourd inventors were not intelligent enough to do that. Instead they only turned a somersault inside the circle of traditional characters. The catastrophe is that one must learn 214 radicals and 1350 phonetic symbols before one can master all the Chinese sounds! Furthermore, a so-called phonetic-compound, even though the sound symbol is purported to be a phonogram, the phonogram itself does not show the sound; for it is still a character and not a letter and does not represent any phonetic element. Every character, as it has its own structure, has also its own sound. Yet, since the sound is not indicated by its shape, there is of course a chaos which is hard to reduce to order. This is the main obstacle that the students of Chinese language, both Chinese and foreigner, have to encounter.

In the second place, I want to point out the importance of tone in the Chinese language. From the musical point of view the tone means the relative pitch accent. It is the particular linguistic trait of Chinese and other Sino-Tibetan languages that they use the tone as a sense or semantic unit. So far as I know, in the Indo-European family only the Scandinavian has this characteristic. Otherwise, I have not yet found it in English, French or German. Some one may ask me "Why not?" According to Professor Daniel Jones, an authority on Phonetics, there are five different tones for "yes" and two for "no" in English:

"that is so." "of course it is so." "Yes, I understand that, please continue." This form so very frequently used when speaking on the telephone. This same intonation would be used in answering a question if a further question were expected, for instanse a shopman would use it in answering the question "Do you keep so and so."

"yes?" "that may be so."

no

rejoinder to a statement

emphatic answer to a question

Are they not the relative pitch accents of English language?① Then, I would say, "Well, of course they are, but they are only used for effectiveness of expression or the intonation of mood; the meaning of "yes" (used to express affirmation, assent, or confirmation in answering a question) and "no" (not so — the opposite of "yes") are never changed. The tone in Chinese and other Sino-Tibetan languages is quite different from this.

To save time, I shall give only the tone system of the Chinese National language—viz. Peking dialect or so-called Mandarin—for illustration. In the Chinese national language we now have four tones only: the first tone is high level, the second tone is high-rising, the third tone is low-falling and half-high rising, the fourth tone is complete falling. If we illustrate it in relative musical pitch, then they will be:

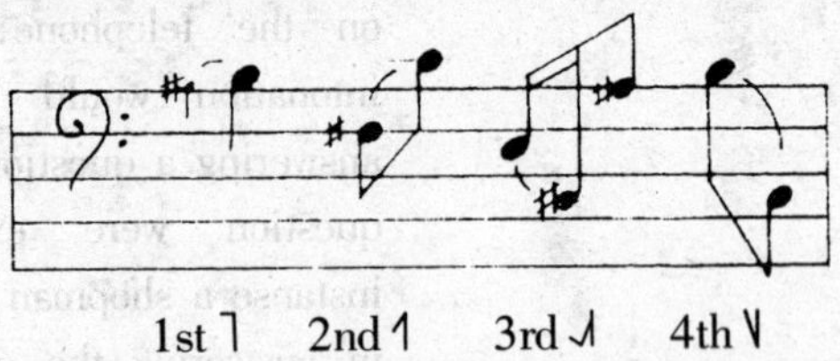

Although the key and the range are different by sex, age, and

① Cf. Daniel Jones' *An Outline of English Phonetics*, 5th ed., p. 257 – 258.

circumstance, yet the proportion of the relative pitch is never changed. We should notice that the rising or falling tone in Chinese is not like two notes on the piano where one <u>jumps</u> to another, but like two notes on the violin where one <u>slips</u> to another. The following examples are very important to the beginner who wants to learn Chinese language:

	1st	2nd	3rd	4th
	˥	˧˥	˨˩˦	˥˩
ma	"mama"	"hemp"	"horse"	"curse"
mai		"bury"	"buy"	"sell"
yi	"clothes"	"soap"	"chair"	"meaning"
ye	"choke"	"sire"	"wild"	"leaf"
	sol	what	well	then

Unless you can hear and pronounce the difference between "mai_3" and "mai_4", you won't be able to distinguish between "buy" and "sell"; unless you can separate the exact tone between "ma_1" and "ma_3" you will miscall someone's mother as a horse; unless you pronounce the 2nd and 3rd tones of "yi" very clearly, you will get a chair "yi_3tz" when you really want a cake of soap "yi_2tz". So you see, if you want to learn spoken Chinese, the system of tones is the fundamental element you must master.

In the third place, some linguists have said that Chinese is a monosyllabic language. Let me quote Lin Yutang's theory for an example. In his "My Country and My people", he says "By Comparison with the European languages it is possible to trace how much of the peculiarities of Chinese thought and literature are due simply to their possession of a so-called monosyllabic language. The fact that the Chinese spoke in syllables like Ching, Chong, Chang was appalling in consequence. This monosyllabism determined the character of Chinese writing, and the character of Chinese writing brought about the continuity of the literary heritage. Therefore it even influenced the conservation of Chinese thought. It was further responsible for the development of a literary language quite distinct from the spoken language. . . . Had the Chinese been speaking a language with words like the German Schlacht and kraft or the English scratched and scalpel, they would have, by sheer necessity, invented a phonetic script long ago."(pp. 216—217). Unfortunately, my opinion is just contrary to Dr. Lin's. I should like to venture the opinion that proto-Chinese may be not the so-called monosyllabism like Dr. Lin's hypothesis, but the monosyllablic Character had made it change its original countenance. So, it seems to me, the monosyllabism did not determine the character of Chinese writing, but the Chinese Character did determine the monosyllabism of Chinese Language. If Dr. Lin had not forgotten his own article "The Consonant-cluster in Archaic Chinese" in his Philological Essays which were published twenty years ago, then he should have remembered that he had really advocated that in Archaic Chinese we had had the words such as:

*k'lung	kung	means	"hole"
*dluan	duan	means	"round"
*glak	lak lu	means	"road"
*plum	pĭum fung	means	"wind"

Then, from the phonological point of view what is the difference between Archaic Chinese *klung, *glak, *plum, and the German Schlacht, kraft, or the English scratched, scalpel? Only because the "square-pattern"

Chinese Character was quite unfitted for transliterating sound, therefore by and by our language lost its original characteristic. The best evidence is the Sanskrit word Vedurya when this four syllable word was borrowed by the Chinese becoming the monosyllabic character 珋(lĭǝu).

Furthermore, as a matter of fact, we really have a lot of bisyllabic words in ancient as well as in modern time. We call parrot as "ying-wu_3", only the syllable "ying" or "wu" can not define the bird, just as the syllables "par" or "rot" would not define it for you. We call grape as "p'u-t'ao_4", neither the syllable "p'u" nor "t'ao" means this fruit, just like "grape" can not be divided into two syllables. As to the modern spoken Chinese, there are still a lot of examples of bisyllablic tendency. We never call stone as "$shih_2$" but "$shih_2$tou"; we never call chair as "yi_3" but "yi_3tz"; such as "yi-fu_2" for clothes, "jih_4-tou" for sun, "$yüe_4$-$liang_4$" for moon, "mei_3 li_4" for beautiful, "hsi_3-huan", for glad — these are all the bisyllabic equivalents of the monosyllabic characters: 衣, 日, 月, 美, 喜 respectively.

But, Dr. F. K. Li says: "By monosyllabism we do not mean that all words in these languages (Indo-Chinese) consist of single syllables, which is obviously false; but we mean by it that a single syllable is a phonological unit, the structure of which is rigidly determined by the phonologic rules of the language as serves as the basis for the formation of words, phrases, and sentences. The Tibeto-Burman branch of this family still possesses some of the prefixes, sometimes syllabic and sometimes asyllabical, but the Chinese and the Kam-Tai group have early lost all active use of the prefixes. It is probable that prefixes, suffixes, vocalic change, and consonantal alternations have been in use in primitive Indo-Chinese to form causatives, denominatives, and to modify the meaning in general, such as in classical

Tibetan: hgeṅs-pa (present), bkaṅ (perfect), dgaṅ (future), khoṅ (imperative) "to fill", but such derivative processes have long been dead in most languages of this family, so that we have only inflexible monosyllabic stems as are found in Chinese now (*Languages and Dialects*, China Year Book, 1937). Of course Dr. Li's insight is deeper than Lin Yutang's, and I may be convinced from this point, but not by Lin Yutang's argument.

In the fourth place, in spite of whether the ancient Chinese language was monosyllabism or not, according to its morphologic type, it is really an isolating or inflexible language at present. That is to say there are no bound forms appearing among the constituents of the modern Chinese words. The English words: man, men, woman, and women are all called "jen_2" by the Chinese. The numbers are indicated by adding numerals, and the genders are distinguished by two other words "nan_2"(男) for male and "$nü_3$"(女) for female. Instead of the words Do, did, doing, done, there is a single word "$tsuo_4$"(作); instead of the words go, went, going, gone, there is a single word "ch'$ü_4$"(去), The past tense is expressed by the adverb "kuo_4"(过) or the particle "le"(了), the progressive tense by the particle "cho_2"(着), the perfect tense by the adverb "yi_3 ching", (已经) and the future tense by using the auxiliary verb "yao_4"(要) just as in English we use "shall" and "will". The passive voice is not so often used as in English. We really use it only in cases of unintended action. When it is used, the verb keeps its original form un-changed and the verb "to be" is never added before it. As in the English sentence "I was beaten by him," the Chinese equivalent is "Wo_3 pei_4 t'a_1 ta_3 le". If we translate this literally word for word it should be "I by him beat + (the past tense particle) le". You see I have formed the passive voice by simply placing "by him" before the verb "beat". For the comparison of adjectives we do not have the bound forms-er and -est. Instead we use the adverb "keng$_4$"(更) for comparative degree, and "tsui$_4$"(最) for superlative degree. For example, "good", "better", "best" is translated "hao$_3$"(好), "keng$_4$ hao$_3$"(更好), "tsui$_4$hao$_3$"(最好), and "small", "smaller", "smallest", is translated "hsiao$_3$"(小) "keng$_4$hsiao$_3$"(更小), "tsui$_4$hsiao$_3$"(最小).

In addition to these above grammatical peculiarities there is another one, the so-called Classifier or Noun-adjoint, which is also found in other Sino-Tibetan languages. If you translate some English words into chinese, "a man" is not equal to "yi$_4$yen$_2$"(一人) but "yi$_2$ ke$_4$ yen$_2$"(一个人); "a horse" is not equal to "yi$_4$ ma$_3$"(一马) but "yi$_4$ pi$_1$ ma$_3$"(一匹马); "a table" is not "yi$_4$ cho$_1$ tzu"(一桌子) but "yi$_4$ chang$_1$ cho$_1$ tzu"(一张桌子); "a chair" is not "yi$_4$ yi$_3$ tzu"(一椅子) but "yi$_4$ pa$_3$yi$_3$tzu"(一把椅子), and so forth. The time does not allow me to describe them in detail. Here I am only pointing them out, and opening the problem for discussion. I shall discuss it in my other article "The Classifier or Noun-adjoint in the Sino-Tibetan languages".

My conclusion is that because the Chinese characters are more visible than audible and quite different from the Indo-European letters, it is therefore better for foreign students to study them after they have mastered the spoken-Chinese. In learning the spoken-Chinese, first of all, they should distinguish the system of the tones very carefully and clearly. In spite of whether the ancient Chinese was monosyllabism or not, the modern Chinese is really an isolating and inflexible language. From the morphological point of view, it is easier to learn than the agglutinative (like Turkish), the polysynthetic (like Eskimo) and the inflecting languages (like English and other Indo-European languages).

(Read before the College Club, June 19, 1945, Claremont, California)

Languages and Dialects in China

The linguistic situation in China is a very complicated one. Aside from the Chinese with its numerous dialects, there are many other languages, our knowledge of which is of an extremely uncertain quality. Some of them have not been adequately studied, some of them are scarcely known to us, and many of them have not been sufficiently recorded. The material of these languages is therefore scanty, their history unknown, and their relation with other groups very vaguely understood. However the great migration during the last Sino-Japanese War time has put many students who are interested in linguistics in close contact with speakers of different languages and dialects particularly of South-west China. A scientific recording and a systematic study of these languages and dialects has begun, and our knowledge is therefore considerably increased, but it will be many years before a precise knowledge of their distribution and classification can be obtained.

In the following description the languages in China are grouped into branches and families, and under each group are pointed out some of the characteristics which distinguish it from the other groups. We need, therefore, a few words of introduction about the classification of these languages. Languages are classified into families, with the assumption that they are historically related. Among a group of languages we find some similarities of correspondences in the word forms, in the grammatical elements such as the prefixes, the suffixes, the vacalic and consonantal alterations, etc. and in the general structure. These similarities and correspondences sometimes can be formulated into definite and exact statements. Particularly in the domain of sounds, these statements are known as sound laws. With the relations among the different languages thus formulated, it is apparent that these similarities cannot be due to chance or mere borrowing but are due to the fact that these languages are the descendents of a common parent speech. As time goes on, this parent speech splits into various dialects and through successive evolutions will develop into such different languages as English, Russian, and Bengali. Sometimes the changes that these languages have undergone are far reaching. The farther they have differentiated from each other, the more difficult it is to trace their relations, unless ancient documents which reveal the older state are available with languages, which have no records and which are known only in their modern forms, we encounter a great difficulty in establishing relationships. Many languages in China not only do not possess records of their own, but are known to us very fragmentarily. Their classification is therefore tentative.

Ⅰ. INDO-CHINESE OR SINO-TIBETAN FAMILY

One of the largest families of speech in China is known as the Indo-Chinese or Sino-Tibetan. Languages of this family are spoken throughout China Proper and Tibet, and extend into Manchuria and Chinese-Turkestan, as well as to places outside of China such as French Indo-China, Burma, Siam, etc. One of the characteristics of this family is the tendency towards monosyllabism. By monosyllabism we do not mean that all words in these languages consist of single syllables, which is obviously false; but we mean by it that a single syllable is a phonological unit, the structure of which is rigidly determined by the phonologic rules of the language and serve as the basis for the formation of words, phrases, and sentences. The Tibeto-Burman branch of this family still posses some of the prefixes, sometimes syllabic and sometimes asyllabical, but the Chinese and Kam-Tai group have early lost all active use of the prefixes. It is probable that prefixes, suffixes, vocalic change, and consonantal alternations have been in use in Primitive Indo-Chinese to form causatives, denominatives, and to modify the meaning of the steam in general such as in classical Tibetan: hgeṅs-pa (present), bkaṅ (perfect), dgaṅ (future), khoṅ (imperative) "to fill", but such derivative processes have long been dead in most languages of this family, so that we have only inflexible monosyllabic stems as are found in Chinese now.

The tendency of develop a system of tones is another characteristic of this family. We do not know whether tones existed in the primitive Indo-Chinese speech, and it is doubtful whether tones existed in classical Tibetan, but modern Chinese, modern Tibetan and Kam-Tai languages, and the Miao-Yao languages all posses tones. These tones are further influenced by the nature of the initial consonant and are divided into two main categories: those with an original voiceless consonant and those with an original voiced consonant. Such has been found to be the case with Chinese, Tibetan, Burmese, and the Kam-Tai languages, and is considered as the most powerful argument for the common origin of these languages.

Another phonetic tendency in common with this family of languages is the unvoicing of the voiced initial consonants but this has not been carried out in all dialects. It occurs in most Chinese dialects except the Wu and the Hsiang, in practically all the Kam-Tai languages, and in many Tibeto-Burman languages, so that what was originally a voiced initial is only detected in the nature of the tone.

Aside from these there are of course many points in the vocabulary which seem to be common in this family. Exact correspondences of sounds, however, have not been worked out. Four main branches are known in this family: Chinese, Kam-Tai, Miao-Yao, and Tibeto-Burman.

A. CHINESE—Chinese is the most important member of this family. The earliest records consist of numerous bone and tortoise shell inscriptions of around 1400 B.C., the excavation of which has been systematiclly carried out in Honan, but unfortunately interrupted by the Japanese invasion. The reading of these inscriptions is in progress but still presents many difficulties. Our knowledge of the archaic texts, principally the *Shi-king* and of the phonetic compounds of the written characters. It has been shown that initial consonant clusters such as *gl-*, *bl-*, *ml-*, etc., and many final consonants such as *-b*, *-d*, *-g*, *-p*, *-t*, *-k*, etc. existed in Archaic Chinese, but up to about 600 A.D., when we have the system of Ancient Chinese well represented by the rime books such as the *Ts'ie-yün*, the initial consonant clusters were already simplified and final *-b*, *-d*, *-g* dropped. From that time on the Chinese language has gone through a series of evolutions such as the unvoicing of initial sonants, the dropping of final *-p*, *-t*, *-k*, and the simplification of rime. The modern Peiping dialect which is taken as the National Language has now only some 400 possible syllables; and each syllable may have theoretically four tones. This phonetic simplification which causes the existence of many homophones, is counter-balanced by a great increase in use of compounds, so that what was formerly expressed by one syllable must now be expressed in the colloquial by two or more syllables.

We may divide the Chinese dialects into the following groups:

(1) The Northern Mandarin group occupies a large area in North China, in the provinces of Hopei, Shansi, Shensi, Honan, and Shantung, and extends into Sinkiang, Inner Mogolia in the north and into Hupei, Anhwei, Kiangsu in the south. It is characterized by the unvoicing of the ancient voiced stops, affricates, and fricatives, and by the disappearance of the "entering or abrupt tone". All the characters of the abrupt tone with unaspirated sonants or surds in Ancient Chinese become the 2nd tone in Mandarin, those which with aspirated sonant or surds in Ancient Chinese become the 4th tone in Mandarin. There are as a rule only four tones: *yin-p'ing*, *yang-p'ing*, *shang*, and *ch'ü*. Further division into sub-groups is possible.

(2) The Eastern Mandarin group is spoken along the lower Yangtze in the provinces of Anhwei and Kiangsu. It is differenciated from the Northern group by the existence of the "entering tone" as a short tone, but the original final consonants *-p*, *-t*, *-k*, which accompanied the entering tone, are substituted by the glottal stop. It presents therefore five tones.

(3) The South-Western Mandarin group is a fairly uniform type of speech spoken in Szechwan, Yünnan, Kweichow, and parts of Hupei and Kwangsi. It has as a rule no "entering tone", but in the central part of Szechwan along the Yangtze, the "entering tone" is preserved but the final consonants have completely disappeared without leaving a trace. Further

division into sub-groups is possible.

(4) The Wu group of dialects is spoken south of the Yangtze in Kiangsu, and Chekiang, and in a few districts in the eastern part of Kiangsi. It is characterized by the preservation of the ancient voiced stops, etc. as aspirated voiced consonants and by the preservation of the "entering tone" as a short tone with the loss, however, of the final *-p*, *-t*, *-k*, (or rather substituted by the glottal stop). It often presents six or seven tones.

(5) The Kan-Hakka group is spoken principally in the provinces of Kiangsi and Kwangtung. It is characterized by the change of the ancient voiced stops, etc. into aspirated surds in all four original tone classes (aspirated in *p'ing-sheng* only in the three Mandarin groups). The "entering tone" is preserved and the final *-p*, *-t*, *-k* are more or less preserved according to dialects, and there are often six or seven tones. The Northern or Kan group, particularly around the Poyang lake, has the tendency to prononce all aspirated surds as voiced in connected speech. The Hakka group preserves the final consonants such as -m, -p, -t, -k much better. Settlements of Hakka people can be found in various districts in Kwangtung, Kwangsi, and in Indo-China, Malay Penninsula, and the South Seas.

(6) The Min group can be further divided into two sub-groups. The Northern group is spoken in the northern part of Fukien and the Southern group is spoken in southern part of Fukien, in the Eastern part of Kwangtung, in Hainan Island, and in parts of the Leichow Penninsula. It is characterized by the change of the original voiced stops, etc. into unaspirated surds, even in p'ing-sheng where the aspirated pronunciation is the prevalent one, by the preservation of the Ancient Chinese prepalatal *ť-*, *ť'-*, *ď'-* (知 ťiȩ 池 ďiȩ 痴 ťi') as dental plosives which were the archaic forms from which

the ancient pre-palatals were derived, and by the preservation final -*p*, -*t*, -*k* (sometimes in modified and simplified forms). It has as a rule seven tones. The Hainan dialects present many phonetic peculiarities, possibly under the influence of an aboriginal speech, presumably a Tai language. Settlements of the Southern group (Amoy, Swatow, Hainan, etc.) may be found in large numbers in Taiwan Indo-China, Burma, Siam, Malay Penninsula, and the South Seas.

(7) The Cantonese group is spoken in the provinces of Kwangtung and Kwangsi. It is characterized by the preservation of the final consonants -*m*, -*p*, -*t*, -*k*. It presents a system of eight or more tones. The distinction of long and short vowels as in cantonese is also a special feature. Certain distinctions of tone depend on the length of the vowel. Settlements of speakers of this group are found in large numbers in Indo-China, Siam, Burma, Malay Peninnsula, and South Seas.

(8) The Hsiang group is spoken principally in Hunan. The Ancient voiced stops, etc. are as a rule kept as truly voiced consonants (Changsha dialect excepted), the final -*p*, -*t*, -*k* are usually lost, but the entering tone is preserved as distinct tone class. It often presents a system of six or seven tones.

(9) Certain isolated groups, such as the dialects spoken in the southern part of Anhwei, certain dialects in Hunan and in the north eastern part of Kwangsi may be mentioned here.

Aside from the phonological features specific to the groups mentioned above, there are also elements of vocabulary more or less peculiar to each of these groups, but these are too minute to get into here. Among these various groups some are mutually intelligible, while some are quite unintelligible.

B. KAM-TAI—The Kam-Tai branch is proposed by my colleague Dr. F. K. Li to include the Tai languages on the one hand and the Kam-Sui(侗水) languages on the other. The term Tai is used here in a strict sence and will not include languages whose kinships have not been sufficiently clarified, such as the Annamite (by Maspero) and the Miao-Yao (by Schmidt). The Kam-Sui languages on the other hand can be shown to be definitely related to the Tai, but must have separated from the primitive Tai sufficiently early to develop their particular features, while the Tai languages develop fairly uniformly among themselves. Such is illustrated by words such as Kam *q'wa:u*, *k'wa:u*, Sui *q'a:u*, *k'a:u*, *ha:u*, Hak *la:u*, T'en *la:u* against the type *lau* "wine" in all Tai languages, or Kam *pa:u*, Sui *pa:u*, *qa:u*, Mak *ka:u*, T'en *pa:u* against *k'au*, *kau*, *xau* "horn" in the Tai languages. It seems therefore proper to include the Kam-Sui and the Tai languages under one general group Kam-Tai, keeping the other closely related languages, such as Siamese, Lao, Shan, Lü, Nung, Tho, Chuang, etc. under the name Tai. It may be noted that the name Tai with its various dialectal pronunciations is only used by a portion of the Tai speakers, and are not known to Tho, Chuang, Chung-chia or Dioi.

This branch is closely related to the Chinese and possesses four tone classes analogous to the *p'ing*, *shang*, *ch'ü*, *ju* of the Chinese. These four tone classes are each further divided into two according to whether the initial consonant was originally voiced or voiceless, so that the modern Kam-Tai languages often possess eight, and sometimes nine or more tones as a further development according to vocalic length (I have counted those tones with *-p*, *-t*, or *-k* separately according to the customary method of treating Chinese tones). It has a series of preglottalized consonants, limited to ʔ*b*-,

ʔd- and *ʔj*- in the Primitive Tai but far more extensive as proved by the Kam-Tai evidence. Several Sui dialects possess *ʔb*-, *ʔd*-, *ʔm*-, *ʔn*-, *ʔng*-, *ʔv*-, etc., beside the ordinary *b*-, *d*-, *m*-, *n*-, *ng*-, *v*-, etc. Initial consonant clusters such as *kl*-, *pl*-, etc. are preserved by some dialects to this day, i.e. Siamese and the Tai language of Wuming and Lung'an in Kwangsi, but become voiceless in the modern dialects. Word order in Kam-Tai is also slightly different from the Chinese. For instance, "good man" in Chinese becomes "man good" in Kam-Tai. The earliest monument is a Siamese inscription in the 13th century. In China most of the Kam-Tai languages have no writing of their own, except some in Yunnan which employ either the Shan alphabet (derived from Burmese) or one closely related to the Southern Tai alphabet, both derived from Hindu sources.

(1) The Kam-Sui group is spoken in Southeastern Kweichow and in a few districts in Northern Kwangsi, and may be divided into four sub-groups: Kam (侗语), Sui (水语), Mak (莫语), and T'en (羊黄语). Initial consonant clusters like *kl*-, *pl*-, etc. are not allowed but must have existed; there is a series of voiceless nasals in Kam and Sui, but it disappears in Mak and T'en; there is also a distinction of velar and palatal plosives in Kam and Sui, pre-palatal and palatal in Mak, but confused in T'en; there is further a series of pre-glottalized consonants, more extensive in Sui, limited in Mak and Kam. The lengthening of the corresponding short vowels in the Tai languages is apparent in this group in many words common to them both.

(2) The Tai group may be divided into two subgroups:

a) The Chuang group consists of many dialects spoken in a great part of Kwangsi (known as Chuang 僮 or T'o 土) and in the southern part of Kweichow (known as Chung-chia 仲家, Man 蛮, Penti 本地 or Dioi), and in the southeastern part of Yunnan (known as Sha 沙 or T'o 土). The language of the Shu-li(熟黎), spoken in the northern part of Hainan Island, in Linkao(临高), Chengmai (澄迈), and Ch'iungshan (琼山), belongs also here, but the Li (黎) dialects in the center and in the south of the island seem to show great divergence from the Tai languages. Their relation to this group is therefore doubtful. The languages of this group are characterized by the lack of aspirated surds, such as *p*'-, *t*'-, *k*'-, the preservation of the distinction between original *$\underline{k}$'- and *x-, * g- and * γ-; and by the preservation of an original * *hr*, as r-(in Wuming 武鸣) as *lɨ* (in Tienchow 田州)), as ð-(in Dioi of Kweichow), or as γ-(in Chienchiang 迁江), corresponding to *h*- of Shan, Siamese, Lao, Nung, etc. The development of vowels also shows many peculiar features from the following group.

b) The Southwestern group consists of some of the best known of the Tai languages and lies mostly outside of China. We may divide this group into several sub-groups: ① Ahom, once spoken in Assam, but now extinct, ② Kamti and Shan, spoken in Burma and Western Yunnan, ③Siamese and Lao spoken in Siam and French Indo-China, ④Lü spoken in Southern Yunnan, ⑤Tai Blanc, Nung, Tho, etc. spoken in French Indo-China, in the southern part of Kwangsi, and in southern part of Yunnan. This group is charaterized by the preservation of aspirated consonants such as *p*'-, *t*'-, *k*'-, by the changed original guttural spirant *x & * γ into stops, by the appearance of * *hr*- as *h*-(except Ahom where -*r*- is preserved), and by a very uniform system of vocalic correspondences among themselves.

C. MIAO-YAO —The Miao-Yao branch of the Indo-Chinese family is monosyllabic like the Chinese and Kam-Tai, and it is known to possess tones. The relationship between Miao and Yao seems to be definitely established, particularly by a study of the Yao languages in Southern Kweichow where they are not so stronly influenced by the Chinese or Tai as in Kwangtung, Kwangsi, and Indo-China. Word order resembles Kam-Tai. It is spoken by fairly primitive groups of mountaineers throughout the Southwest. Aside from the occasional use of Chinese characters there is no writing of their own.

(1) The Miao group is spoken under various names in the western mountain regions of Hunan, in a large part of Kweichow, and is found scattered here and there in Northern Kwangsi, Southern Szechuan, Yunnan, Indo-China, and Siam. It is characterized by the dropping of the final consonants, so that only *-ng* and rarely *-n* are allowed to stand in final positions. There is a distinction of palatal and velar consonants, such as *k-*, and *q-* etc., a series of pre-nasalized consonants, such as *mpr-*, *mpr'-*, *nt-*, *nt'-*, *ngk-*, *ngk'-*, etc., and consonant clusters such as *pl-*, *pr-*, *mpl-*, *mpr-*, *tl-*, *kl-*, etc., are still preserved by some dialects. The number of tones are usually eight or more. The He-Miao(黑苗) chiefly spoken in Southern Kweichow seems to form a special sub-group, it allows no consonant clusters and no prenasalized consonants, but presents a bewildering number of aspirated consonants such as *p'-*, *t'-*, *k'-*, *tɕ'-*, *q'-*, *f'-*, *s'-*, *ɕ'-*, *l'-*, *m̥'-*, *n̥'-*, *ŋ̊g'-*, etc.

(2) The Yao group is also spoken under various tribal names in the northwestern mountain regions of Kwangtung, in southern Kweichow, and is scattered here and there among the various mountain regions of Kwangsi, Yunnan, Indo-China, and Siam. It preserves the final consonants better than the Miao, as final-*m*, *-n*, *-ng*, *-p*, *-t*, *-k* are all allowable. The number of

tones varies from five to eight or more according to dialects. It is greatly influenced by the Tai and Chinese, and some have entirely adopted either the Chinese or the Tai language.

There are among the Chinese, the Kam-Tai, and the Miao-Yao groups certain fratures in common. Notably the word order of subject-verb-object stands in contrast to the Tibeto-Burman branch where we have subject-object-verb. The system of tones in Chinese and Kam-Tai consists of originally four tone classes, and this may be ultimately proved to be the case with Miao-Yao. It seems therefore possible to group them together under one branch, and it seems not improper to give it the name of Sinitic, as all the Kam-Tai and Miao-Yao languages show profound relation and close contacts with China historically, geographically, and culturally. Annamite may be possibly included in this group, although it shows strong affinities with the Mon-khmer languages.

D. TIBETO-BURMAN —This branch of Indo-Chinese family is one which presents most clearly the use of prefixes, alternations of voiced and voiceless consonants, and the use of suffixes such as revealed by classical Tibetan. Tones depend upon whether the initial is voiced or voiceless and are further influenced by the prefixes, but the system of tones seems to be much simpler than that of Chinese, Kam-Tai, or Miao-Yao. Word order is as a rule subject-object-verb. Four divisions are known:

(1) The Tibetan group is spoken principally in Tibet and Sikang, and extends into Ch'inghai and the western part of Szechwan. The earliest record of this group is dated from the ninth century, the alphabet having derived from the Devanagari form of Hindu alphabet. A great amount of literature, largely Buddhistic, exists in this form. Three main groups of dialects may be

distinguished. The Western Group, Balti, Ladak, etc. preserves more or less the prefixes, the initial clusters, and the final stops generally transcribed as *-b*, *-d*, *-g*. The Central dialect, including that of Lhasa, are characterized by the loss of prefixes, by the simplification of consonant clusters, and the dropping of final consonants. The Eastern dialects, the Khams, preserve very faithfully the prefixes and the final consonants. Belonging to this group are some Tibeto-Himalayan dialects and some north Assam dialects spoken along the southern border of Tibet and some Sifan dialects spoken in Sikang and Ch'inghai. Interesting are the Trung and Nung, called by Chinese Ch'iou-tze (俅子) and Nu-tze (怒子), in the north-eastern of Yunnan. Like some Nepalese dialects, the reduced forms of the personal pronouns are used as prefixes and suffixes of the verb to form verbal conjugations for instance in Trung:

nga ɣang dza k'ai tśia-n̥g   I food eat can,   "I can eat"
na ɣang dza k'ai ne tśia   you food eat can   "you can eat"
ɣang ɣang dza k'ai tśia   he food eat can   "he can eat"
ing ɣang dza k'ai tśia-i   we food eat can   "we can eat"
ne ning ɣang dza k'ai ne-tśia   you food eat can   "you can eat"
ɣang ning ɣang dza k'ai tśia   they food eat can   "they can eat"

(2) Kachin of the Bodo-Naga-Kachin group is spoken in the northwestern border of Yunnan.

(3) Speakers of the various languages of the Burmese group, such as Burmese, Kuki-Chin, "Old Kukik", etc. are found mostly in Burma and Assam.

(4) Among the Lolo group, the Lolo with its dialects is spoken in a large portion of Yunnan, in Northwestern Kweichow, and in Southern Sze-

chwan and Sikang. It descends into Indo-China and Siam. The Lolo has an independent syllabic writing of its own, used largely in religious texts. The Moso is spoken in the northwestern part of Yunnan and extends into Sikang. It possesses two systems of writing, one hieroglyphic and the other syllabic like the Lolo. This group is characterized by the great simplification of the phonetic system, such as the complete dropping of the final consonants and the rarity of diphthongs. Tones are usually five or six in number, and word order resembles the Tibetan. Minkia may possibly belong to this group but it shows strong Chinese influence in its vocabulary and in its word order and seems to be a mixed language.

Ⅱ. AUSTRO-ASIATIC FAMILY

Of this large family proposed by P. W. Schmidt to which the Munda, the Mon-Khmer, and according to some authers the Annamite belong, we may only mention the Mon-Khmer group of which there are representatives in China. The earliest records of this group are some Khmer inscriptions of the seventh century and a Mon inscription of the eleventh century, the alphabets being derived from the Hindu sources. The group of languages has no tones, and makes use of prefixes and infixes for the derivation of words. The stem is generally monosyllabic; the word order is subject-verb-object.

Dialects of this group spoken in China are the Palaung, the Wa and some others along the Yunnan-Burma border. We know very little about the Wa, but the Palaung is known to have no tones, and has a number of prefixes, both syllabic and asyllabical, such as *p-*, *pan-*, *ra-*, *kar-*, for example: *yam* "to die", *p-yam* "to kill", *pan-p-yam* "the killing, one who is killed". A special series of initials, *hl-*, *hr-*, *hm-*, and *hn-*, exists. This language shows close contacts with the Tai languages.

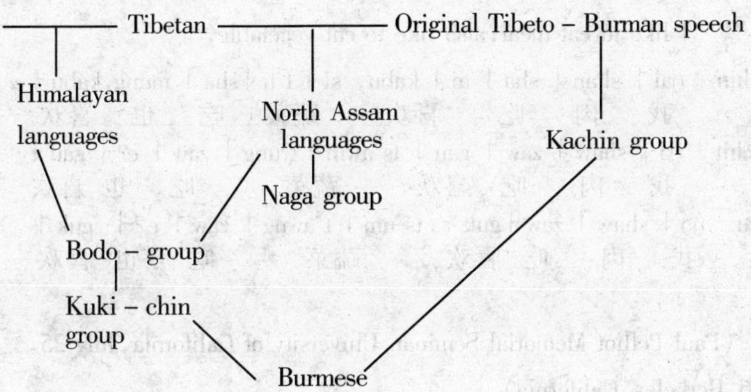

Examples:

Tai mɯ˧ ŋ˧ mi˨ ʔo˧ luk˨ dik˥ nəŋ˧ kik˨ tɕɯ˧ maːn˨ p'i˨ ti˧
时 一 有 子 小孩 一 极 是 顽皮 的,
jau˩ kiaːnʔ˨
又 懒

从前有一个小孩子非常顽皮,又懒。

Once upon a time there was a small boy who was very naughty and lazy.

Trung ŋa˨ tɹun˨ kat˥ saŋ˥
I Trung language can speak

I can speak Trung language.

ɣaŋ˥ dza˥ kăi˦
food eat

Liso ŋa˥ nũ˨˦ te˥ dɯ˨
I you beat

I beat you.

a˩ na˩ tʂ'o˥ dza˩ te˥ k'o
dog man bite

The dog bite the man.

I like to eat meat, also like to eat vegetable.

Kachin ŋai˥ shan˩ sha˥ ai˧ kabu, si˩ t'u˩ sha˥ mung kabu˧
我 肉 吃 喜欢 蔬菜 吃 也 喜欢

La-chit ŋɔ˩ shaw˥ zaw˥ gau˩ ts'awm˥ t'ung˥ zaw˥ eʔ˧ gau˩
我 肉 吃 喜欢 蔬菜 吃 也 喜欢

Maru ŋɔ˩ shaw˥ zaw˧ guk˥, ts'um˥ t'awng˥ zaw˥ eʔ˧ guk˥
我 肉 吃 喜欢 蔬菜 吃 也 喜欢

(Paul Pelliot Memorial Seminar, University of California, July 25, 1946, Berkeley, California)

Phonetic Substitutions in Chinese Loanwords from Indic

Ⅰ. Introduction

This article is a part of my recent story on "Chinese Loanwords from Indic", in which I classified the cultural borrowings into four types: (1) phonetic substitution, (2) phonetic-compound, (3) loan-translation, (4) descriptive form.

Buddhism had been introduced to China at the beginning of the Christian era. According to dependable sources, the translation of Buddhist sūtras to Chinese was started by an Arsak monk An-shih-kao in 148 A.D. From that time on, many foreign monks came from India or East Turkestan to China and many Chinese pilgrims travelled to India. The natives and foreigners on both sides co-operated from time to time and translated volumes and volumes of Buddhist books into Chinese. Up through 1287 A.D., it was recorded that there were altogether one hundred and ninety-four translators, and one thousand four hundred and eighty-six fascicles of Buddhist books translated. No doubt many Indic loanwords were taken into Chinese.

One important fact I have to mention here is that the earlier translations of Buddhist books were not entirely translated from Sanskrit but were sometimes strongly influenced by Middle Indic or other Central Asiatic languages. After 645 A. D. when Hsuen-tsang returned from India, all the Buddhist books translated by himself and his followers were directly based on Sanskrit texts or partly from Buddhist Hybrid Sanskrit. Since that time, there has been no Central Asiatic influence on Chinese Buddhist translations.

The few examples of phonetic substitution given below are merely to show how the Chinese have adapted Indic loanwords to their traditional phonetic habits.

Ⅱ. Five groups of phonetic substitution

The phonetic substitution in Chinese loanwords from Indic can be divided into five groups and arranged according to their degree of adaptation to Chinese phonetic habits:

A. Monosyllabized words which abridge the original sounds into a monosyllabic Chinese characer:

Buddha 佛陀 b'iuêt-dâ: 佛 b'iuêt

one who is awakened and the awakener

Śākya 释迦 śiäk-ka: 释 śiäk

Gautama, a family name

B. Words hybridized by their transcriptions of original sounds and their Chinese generic terms:

udumbara 优昙婆罗 iêu-d'am-b'uâ-lâ: 昙花 d'âm flower

ficus glomerata, which blooms only when Buddhism prospers

pattra 贝多罗 puậi-tâ-lâ: 贝叶 puậi leaf

a particular plant with fragrant leaves

C. Words omitting two syllables from the original sounds:

bodhisattva 菩提萨埵 b'uo-d'i-sât-tuâ: 菩萨 b'uo-sât

one who is on the way to the attainment of perfect knowledge

saṅghārāma 僧伽蓝摩 sêng-g'i̯a-lâm-mâ: 伽蓝 g'i̯a-lâm

a buddhist monastery

D. Words omitting one syllable from the original sounds:

āraṇyaka 阿兰若 ·â-lân-ńźi̯ak: 兰若 lân-ńźi̯ak

forest, monastery

samādhi 三昧地 sâm-mu̯âi-d'i: 三昧 sâm-mu̯âi

orthodox and stable

E. Words preserving each syllable of the original sounds:

bodhi	菩提	b'uo-d'iel	the supreme wisdom
maṇi	摩尼	muâ-ńji	pearl
kṣaṇa	刹那	tṣ'at-na	the shortest possible interval of time
dhūta	杜多	d'uo-t'â	"shaken off, removed, washed" one who can shake his greediness vexation and foolishness

From these few examples we can already see that in loanwords from Indic the Chinese have naturalized as many words as could be adapted to the genius of the Chinese language. The result is that *the more current the loanwords are, the more adapted they have been to Chinese phonetic habits*, witnesses the monosyllabized and hybrid words in phonetic substitution. Even though only one or two syllables of the full transcription were omitted, the result of this reduction causes them to become dissyllabic for the most part, which makes them conform admirably to the phonetic pattern of the Chinese lexicon.

Ⅲ. The phonological system

A. If a sound element is a distinct phoneme in both Sanskrit and Chinese, it is correspondingly transcribed:

Skt.	ACh.	Example		
a. p-	p-	pāramitā	波	gone to the opposite shore
ph-	p'-	sphāṭika	颇	glass
m-	m-	maṇi	摩	
b. -ai	– ai	Maitreya	梅	
c. -m	-m	udumbara	昙	
-k	-k	upāsaka	索	the male lay adherents of Buddhism

B. If two or three sound elements are distinct phonemes in Sanskrit but are only one phoneme in Ancient Chinese, they are confused in Chinese transcriptions:

Skt.	ACh.	Examples	
a. b, bh-	b'-	bodhi, bhikṣu an ordained mendicant	菩, 苾
n-, ṇ-	n-	namas; nirvāṇa reverential salutation; extinction or blowing out as of a light	那, 涅那
l-, r-	l-	tūlạ; rākṣasa cotton; an evil demon	罗, 罗

b. -a, -ā,	-a	dhāraṇī, Buddha 陀,陀 a mystical verse
-i, -ī	-i	Mañjuśrī, śarīra; sâmādhi 利,利,地 a body or a corps, relic;
c. -t, -d, -l, -r, -t		pāramitā, Buddha, pippala, udumbara

C. If two or more sound elements are distinct phonemes in Ancient Chinese but are not distinguished in Sanskrit, they are alternatively used to represent that similar phoneme in Sanskrit:

Skt.	ACh.	Example
a. kṣ-	tś-tś‘	mokṣá; dakṣina 遮,嚫 emancipation, release from wordly existence; right, on the right side, alms, done
	ṭṣ‘-	yakṣa; kṣaṇa 叉,刹 the demons of the night, and haunters of the tombs
b. -e	-iei, -iâi	caturdeśa; geya 奢,偈 four regions; a novice, the first of the monkhood
	-iĕ, -î	geya, śrāmaṇ era 祇,尼 to be sung, a song

D. Some Sanskrit intervocalic consonants were considered by ancient translators as final consonants of the preceeding syllables and at the same time as initial consonants of the following syllables:

yama-rāja	阎摩罗社,阎罗	iem-mâ-lâ-zia
samādhi	三昧地	sâm-mâ-d‘i
śākya	释迦	śiäk-ka
āraṇyaka	阿兰若	˙a-lân-ńźiak

pāramiṯā 波罗密多 pâ-lâ-mieṯ-ṯâ

E. If certain transcriptions can not be explained by their corresponding Sanskrit words, they were possibly based on some other languages:

ACh.		Skt.	Pali or Middle Indic	
比丘	bʻi-kʻi̯êu	bhikṣu	bhikkhu	
沙门	ṣa-muên	śamaṇa	samaṇa	
劫波	ki̯ɐp-pâ	kalpa	kappo	a period of 432 million years of mortals
塔婆	tʻập-bʻuâ	stūpa	thūpa	pagoda
玻璨科	pʻuâ-liei-kʻâ	sphaṭika	phalika	
目犍连	muk-gi̯en-lien	Maudgalyāyana	Moggallāna	

Ⅳ. Conclusion

It is true that, in the words of Leonard Bloomfield, "The borrowing of foreign words always entails their phonetic modification. There are sure to be foreign sounds or accentual peculiarities which do not fit the native habits. They are then so changed as to do as little violence as possible to these habits. Frequently we have phonetic compromises." In this article I have tried to demonstrate this process of phonetic compromises in Chinese loanwords derived from Sanskrit and other Middle Indic languages.

(Read before the 157th Meeting of American Oriental Society, April 17, 1947, Washington D.C.)

Review to C. P. Fitzgerald *The Tower of Five Glories: A Study of the Min-chia of Tali, Yunnan*

(Published by the Cresset Press, London, 1941. pp. 280 + 12, with thirty one illustrations and three maps.)

This book is an investigation of the Min-chia of Tali(大理), Yunnan. So far as I know, there was before no such work on the subject, "The Tower of Five Glories", called "Wu Hua Lou"(五华楼) by natives, is a tower inside the South Gate of Tali city, which was originally built in the days of Nan-chao(南诏) and reconstructed in Ming Dynasty. The author gives his book this title, perhaps to symbolize Tali city and its surroundings.

There are eleven chapters and two appendices:

Chap. 1, Assure Mountain and Ear Lake

Chap. 2, The Rice Standard

Chap. 3, The City of Great Principles

Chap. 4, The People of White Prince

Chap. 5, The Three Religions (1) Ancestor Worship

Chap. 6, The Three Religions (2) The Gods

Chap. 7, The Three Religions (3) Magic and Myth

Chap. 8, The family and the Home

Chap.9, Invitation to the Feast

Chap.10, On the Road

Chap.11, Foreign Contacts and Changes

Appendix 1, Min Chia Grammar

Appendix 11, Min Chia Vocabulary

We shall now discuss them in general.

The tribe named Min-chia by the Chinese calls itself Pai-Tsǔ(白子); it is distributed over an area around Ear Lake, vis. between long. 90°50' and 100°30' E., and lat. 25°30' and 26°48' N., stretching west as far as long. 99°30' E., along the side of Lan-ts'ang River(澜沧江) in the region of Yun-Lung(云龙) district, and northwest to lat. 27°N., in the region of Wei-si(维西) district. In the east, from the Feng-yi(凤仪) district along the Tali-Kunming highway, including Siang-Yun(祥云), Mi-tu(弥渡), Chen-nan(镇南), Yao-an(姚安), Ts'u-hsung(楚雄), Kuang-t'ung(广通), Lu-feng(禄丰), An-ning(安宁) districts, to long. 102°35'E., the region of Kunming, there are some Min-chia villages in every district, though they are not considerable in number. In the south of lat. 25°N., there are Min-chia villages only at Yuan-pa(原坝) of Yuan-kiang(元江) district along the Red River(红河), and they do not spread farther north than the Tali-Kunming line.

As to the genealogical position of the Min-chia, H.R. Davies, in his "Tribes of Yunman", appendix Ⅷ of Yunnan, supposed that they belong to the Mon-Khmer Family; Dr. V. K. Ting(丁文江) in the preface to Ts'uan-wen-ts'ung-K'an(《爨文丛刊》) suggested that they belong to the Shan, and Dr. F. K. Li(李方桂) in his "Language and Dialect" referred them to the Lolo. Mr. Ling Shun-sheng(凌纯声) agreed with Dr. Ting's theory at first, but in his latest paper "The Wu-man(乌蛮) and Pai-man (白蛮) in T'ang dynasty", made a sudden volte-face and came to the conclusion that they are kindred to the Karen tribe of the Tibeto-Burman Family. The problem is open till now. As this book is the work of an adept on the Min-Chia, although its scope is limited to Tali, I devoured it at one sitting.

According to the author's preface: "The investigation of which this book is a record was made with the assistance of a Leverhulme Fellowship for the years 1937 and 1938. As the work was carried out alone, and in a field hitherto neglected by ethnologists, I am conscious that there must be many omissions and oversights in the survey of the Min-chia culture as it is today. The lauguage barrier was certainly not wholly surmounted, for while I cannot claim to have learned to speak Min-chia with real fluency, the Min-chia of the less educated class do not speak Chinese without difficulty and cannot express all their thought in that language. The vocabulary printed as an appendix will no doubt reveal the effects of these difficulties, and the system used for Chinese nation, may not meet with the approval of all readers. My justification for this must be that I have endeavoured to readers Min-chia pronunciation as it is sunded, and that the vocabulary was made primarily for my own use when learning the language. I can only hope that this first attempt to record the Min-chia language and its grammar may prove of some interest to specialist". His wording is surely modest enough.

On the anthropological part of this book, I would not say anything as I have to confess I am not expert in anthropology. But, to my mind, the book seems, on the whole, to be nothing more than a general record of travels, and cannot be considered as the result of and accurate scientific research, because, either from the physical point of view or from the cultural one, the material collected by the author about the tribe are not adequate. As to the historical documents, such as "the Records of Ancient Yunnan"(《记古滇说》), "The Legends of Nan-chao"(《南诏野史》), "The Records of Yunnan"(《滇载记》), even the peculiar Min-chia story like "The Origin of Pai-suǔ country"(《白国因由》), none of them has been quoted by him at all. Perhaps it may be said that he was standing on the ground of modern culture and neglected the historical data on principle, but there are some common facts which have been ignored by him as well. For example, the Fire-brand Festival (火把节) on the 24th day of the sixth moon in Lunar calendar is very popular at Tali and other places of Yunnan, but he has not clearly told what it means, About another famous Festival in Tali called "going the round of Hill and forest"(绕山林), although he lavished many pages and photographs on it, he could not comprehend the exact meaning of its Min-chia term "Kwer sl-la"[①]. The remaining chapters, to be sure, have involved much thought and research, but from one who professed himself to be the student of the two famed professors B. Malinowski and C. G. Seligman, and to have spent two years on his work, we are of course disposed to expect more than these general impressions and fragmentary records and so may well be disappointed to some extent. As to his misquoting Chiu-Yuan (屈原) as Chiu-Yuan-Ming (p. 117), that may be excused as a common error of foreign scholars.

It was pointed out by the author that the linguistic part had not attained to the ideal standard. Here I want to refer to several other points. In the

① The transcriptions of Min Chai language used in this paper are Mr. Fitzgerald's.

vocabulary section (p.241—276), there are 1440 words in total. It was no means collection in quantity. Yet though he has said that this was but a rough draft for his own use in learning the Min-chia language, as it has been published, his inaccuracies are still likely to sew seeds for widespread errors. As regards the system of romanization used by him, whether the English or the Wade's type, I have only to ask if he has really succeeded in his attempt; as he said: "I have endeavoured to render Min-chia pronunciation as it is sounded?" of course, we cannot now discuss the phonetic system of the Min-chia language in detail. Confining ourselves to his record, we regret that he seems to be ignorant even of the difference between Sonant and Surd, or aspiration and unaspiration. Therefore he used g, d, b for [k] [t] [p], and k, t, p for [k'][t'][p']. For all know of the Min-chia language of Tali, there are no voiced plosives at all. In the light of this fact we may suppose that it is rather later than those other branches of Têng-chúan(邓川), Er-yuan(洱源), Chien-ch'uan(剑川), Lu-shui(泸水), Yun-lung(云龙), etc., and more influenced by Chinese. Moreover, the line and direction of the migration of the Min-chia can also be inferred from this hint. If we used voiced plosive for a voiceless one, this bare hint would be lost. Furthermore, there are eight tones in the Min-chia language of Tali; they are rather hard to discriminate but the meanings of many words which have the name initials and finals must be distinguished by the different tones. Now, the author has given up the tone-mark and neglected the classification of tones altogether, how then can he deal with so many homonyms which are the same in initials and finals but different in meaning and tone? Besides, there are certain particular sounds to give him much trouble, sounds which cannot be transcribed by romanization. For example: the Min-chia language of Tali has one back vowel which has the same position as the vowel [u] but it is pronounced with unrounded lips. The International Phonetic Alphabet renders it as inverted m[ɯ]. It also appears in the dialect of Swatow(汕头), Ch'iuan-chou (泉州) and the western part of Ho-nan(河南). The author has not only failed to make sure its sound value, but also wanted suitable symbol to represent it. Therefore it was transcribed sometime as "er" and sometime as "ur". Another case is that the open [ɛ] and closed [e] in the Min-chia language of Tali must be separated into two phonemes, but he could not distinguish them by any means and transcribed both as "ai". Hence we may conclude that the Min-chia vocabulary recorded by the author can no more be understood by the Min-chia speaking people than by those who cannot speak the language.

The grammatical section (p. 229—237) is only some fragmentary sketches not yet reduced to a complete system. The parts of speech are set in forms after the patterns of Indo-European languages, and separated into nouns, classifiers, verbs, adjectives, pronouns, prepositions and numerals. The general rule of word order is "subject-verb-object", as in Chinese. But in such cases as "vershi(rain)o(to fall)", and "piser(wind)po(to blow)", although they are similar to the English word order, they are quite unlike the Chinese idiomatic expressions such as "刮风" and "下雨". This point was considered by the author as an exception, but in my opinion, it may be the remnant trace of the original Min-chia language. Whether the adjective is to be placed before or after the noun modifier, there is no regular rule about this in the Min-chia language. The classifier is one of the linguistic traits in the Min-chia language. In the languages of Lolo, Lisu, Trung and Nung, this kind of words is very frequently used. According to the author, all the nouns of the

Min-chia language are always followed by the classifiers; and the author discovered as many as fifty odd of them. But of the fifty odd there are only twelve in accordance with the general rule. As a matter of fact, the rules drawn up by him are not quite inclusive, and cases which he regarded as irregular are not as variants with usage. If we investigate the cases more, we shall find out other rules that do cover them. The author added, "the Min-chia memorials are corrupt, Chinese form being mixed with the Min-chia. From one to thirty, Min-chia words are used, but from thirty to thirty nine, and from fifty to hundred, corrupted Chinese forms are used, with exceptions from forty to forty nine, and the numbers fifty, sixty, seventy, eighty and ninety. Over one hundred, corrupted Chinese is used except for the numbers one thousand and ten thousand". The origins of the numerals being so complicated, the genealogical development of Min-chia can not be determined by comparing its numerals.

Concerning the investigation of Min-chia, such scholars as Francis Garnier, P. Desyodins, Lefèvre-Pontalis, G. W. Clark, Henri d'Orléans, C. Madrolle, H. R. Davies, D'Ollone, P. A. Liétard, although they have discussed it here and there, are hardly to be counted as adepts. P. A. Liétard, to be sure, has written an essay entitled "Min-kia et La-ma jen au Yunnan" (Anthropos, Bd. VII, Reft4, 5, Juli-oktober 1912, pp. 677—705) and pointed out the relation between the Min-chia and La-ma peoples, but the linguistic part is also full of errors. During the war time, new books rarely come in sight. I was fortunate in coming across one book, an exclusive research on the Min-chia, it is a wonderful godsend to me! On March 23rd 1942, when I passed through Tali, Mme. J. de Beauclaire borrowed this book for me from Reverend E. D. Holmes. But the loan was restricted to a single day, and after being busy recording linguistic materials in the day time, I eagerly read it right through under the weak light of a native lamp, reading far into the night. I took down its manin points. But I was more disappointed even then I had expected: because, whether from the physical, or cultural, or linguistic point, it is not a thorough study at all, and the problem of the genealogical position of the Min-chia which I desire so much to solve is not even touched upon in it. On the whole, it is not much more valuable than a common record of travels.

(National Peking University)

Review to Yuen Ren Chao and Lien Sheng Yang' *Concise Dictionary of Spoken Chinese*

(Published for the Harvard-Yenching Institute, Cambridge, Mass.: Harvard University Press, 1947. pp. xxxix + 292.)

If one intends to study Standard Chinese, or so-called Mandarin, descriptively and scientifically, one should not miss this concise dictionary which, in certain respects, is unprecedented in the history of Chinese-European lexicography since its beginnings in the first quarter of the seventeenth century.

In the Foreword and Introduction the authors give a clear picture of the unique features of this dictionary, to some of which I should like to call the reader's special attention.

In the first place, the authors indicate the grammatical function of each word. Thus the reader will have no difficulty in distinguishing, for example, between "free" and "bound" forms, "auxiliary nouns proper", and "quasi auxiliary nouns". In addition, many new ideas about the linguistic structure of Chinese, such as the four types of complements, the "pre-transitive", the "possessive object", the "impersonal verb-object compound", etc. (see pp.

xxx-xxxi) are introduced for the first time in a Chinese dictionary. The particles and interjections, e.g., 了,啊,的,etc., have never before been described in such great detail as in the present work.

In the second place, this dictionary is not only a faithful record of current spoken Mandarin, but it also serves several other purposes: (a) In order to "channel the student's efforts in using the language to more profitable directions", the authors either mark the stylistic class of each entry by abbreviations like *lit.*, *dial.*, *epistol.*, *fig.*, *honorif.*, etc., or imply it in the translation, as 殆"well-high", but 差不多"almost". (b) As the authors incorporate the main features of ancient Chinese and modern dialect pronunciation in the Romanization by the use of a subscribed dot or by the underlining of an initial, it will be possible for students interested in Chinese opera or old-style poetry to distinguish 尖 "sharp" from 团 "rounded," or 浊音 "voiced initial" from 清音 "voiceless initial". Furthermore, the traces of the final bilabionasal *-m* and the final stops *-p*, *-t*, *-k* of the entering tone in ancient Chinese and certain modern dialects, are also indicated by the superscribed *m* and *p*, *t*, *k*. This device is very helpful to a student of Cantonese or of the Wu dialects, as well as to a student of Chinese phonology. (c) By treating all entries as morphemes rather than as characters, and by analyzing the morphemes of the language to indicate whether they are bound or free, the authors have made an attempt to give the equivalent of a dictionary of compounds within the space of a dictionary of single words. (d) For etymological purposes, the original character of the main character is given in parentheses. The entries 搬(般),撕(斯),饺(角), etc., are good examples.

In the third place, in order to aid the reader, the authors have arranged their material in the following manner: "The body of the dictionary is arranged according to the order of the commonly accepted system of 214 radicals. . . . The order of characters in each group is by the number of residual strokes." Different characters under the same number of strokes are arranged in the alphabetic order of National Romanization. The twelve most frequent radicals in their most frequent forms are given at the bottom of the pages for the reader to learn by heart. "To insure further the finding of the characters, the authors have entered each character under all its apparently possible radicals and made a cross reference to the main entry." For instance, 鲁 is entered under 72 日, with the note "See Rad. 195 鱼." If one recognizes the above arrangement and knows how to use Appendix I and Appendix Ⅲ, one will be albe to find any character included in the dictionary. As to the Romanized orthography, the National system is given parallely with the Wade-Giles system. Appendix I, Part 2, is a table of concordance of these two systems, from which the basic form of National Romanization can easily be found when the Wade-Giles form is known. The popular and cursive forms of many characters, as well as the Soochow numerals and the National Phonetic Letters, have never been included in a traditional Chinese dictionary. Beginners in Chinese are very often puzzled by such forms which no dictionary explains. By recording them as dictionary entries, the authors have removed one source of bewilderment for the foreign student of Chinese.

Finally, I wish to point out that the phonetic section in the Introduction is a handy résumé of Dr. Y. R. Chao's original findings accumulated through his continuous studies since 1916. Among these, may be mentioned the rules of tone sandhi, the two types of problems concerning the neutral tone, and the analysis of the retroflex finals. Dr. Chao first published an article on "The Problem of the Chinese Language" (*The Chinese Student's Monthly* 9[June, 1916], 572-93) advocating that the logographic Chinese characters be replaced by a new type of Romanization. In 1921 when he taught Chinese at Harvard University, he made experiments with his new system. Then, in the next year, the first draft of his National Romanization system was published in a special issue of *The National Language Monthly* ([1922]87-117), on the reformation of Chinese writing; and the twenty five principles of his new system were also announced in the same article. Thus was laid the cornerstone of National Romanization. Therefore ninety-five per cent of the official system promulgated by the Chinese Ministry of Education on September 26, 1928, and used in this dictionary, should be regarded as Dr. Chao's accomplishment. I may add that, significantly, those graduates of the Army Specialized Training Program I have talked with who were trained in Dr. Chao's orthography seem to have acquired a uniformly good command of tones.

For the benefit of the reader, a few misprints noticed by the reviewer and some points on which he differs with the authors are appended below:

Page	Line	Original	Correction or Suggestion
xxvii	3	Appendix Ⅰ	Read "Appendix Ⅲ."
45	15	打干哕	For "gagging" of preferably "retching" (without vomiting) the natives of Peiping always say 干哕 instead of 打干哕. It is different from those words for "to belch" given on p.43.
50	20	活塞	To the word indicating "a piston", a diminutive 儿 -*l* is always appended. Here

			for the character 塞儿 read *sal* (< *sai* + -*l*) for *sell*(< *seh* + -*l*).
53	15	夭折,夭亡	The character 夭 should be regarded as literary.
57	38	老 -B-*l*, 老 -B-*tz*	Besides "an old woman", it also means "a maid servant".
63	17	宝贝	When used to mean "Darling!" or "Precious!" it is frequently followed by a diminutive suffix 儿 -*l*.
91	26	织拙	It does not seem to be a popular term in the Peiping dialect. So far as I know, the natives of Peiping always say 翻鼓 instead of 织拙.
137	23	智牙	An idiomatic word for "wisdom teeth" in Peiping dialect is 尽头牙. Now and then 智齿 has been used in some textbooks of physiology, but 智牙 is very rare.
140	1	珍肝儿	The original character for "gizzard" is 肫 (p.176), pronounced ť ś ĭuěn in ancient Chinese. *Kouag-yün*, Vol.1, rime 18, 肫, 鸟藏, i.e., "bird's viscera". Therefore both 珍 on p.140 and 胗 on p.176 are borrowings, but 珍 is much less common.
141	8	⊙[1] B-*tz*	The word for "a crack" is a free form which has never been followed by the suffix -*tz*. Its AN is 道. The proverb 打破沙锅⊙到底 literally means "A cleft earthen pot cracks to the bottom." In fact, it is often used as a play on the words ⊙ and 问; therefore it has the connotation of "very inquisitive."

① This character is No.12665 in Giles *Chinese-English Dictionary*.

153	33	(ch'ih^4)	Read "(ch'i^4)".
157	15	种	In addition to being a popular form of 種^3, it is also a surname read *chung* (ch'ung^2), which even appears in the original text of the well-known novel *Shui-hu chuan*. If those rare surnames like 乜(p.5) and 笪(p.161) have all been included, why should this one be excluded?
160	33	竿 gaan	Usually written as 桿; it is the same character as that for "a penholder" and "the stock of a gun" on p.113.
251	6	□ bell	Can be identified as 倍儿. B-棒 also means "very strong". Another idiom in the Peiping dialect is 倍儿亮 which means "very brilliant" or "very bright".

(*HJAS* Ⅹ no. 3 & 4, December, 1947, Boston)

Nouvelles Remarques sur le Lien généalogique du Patronyme chez les Tribus de Langue tibéto-birmane

Dans le *Harvard Journal of Asiatic Society* (*HJAS*) 8, (1945), pp. 349—363, j'ai publié un article intitulé *Le lien généalogique du patronyme chez les tribus de langue tibéto-birmane*, dans lequel j'ai démontré l'existence d'un intéressant trait culturel de ces peuplades: le chevauchement partiel des noms du père et du fils. C'est-à-dire que la dernière ou les deux dernières syllabes du nom du père sont transmises au nom du fils et deviennent sa première ou ses deux premiéres syllabes, et cela se fait de façon continue de génération en génération. Pour plus de clarté, j'ai classé ce lien généalogique du patronyme en quatre types:

1. A B C — C D E — D E F — F G H

Ngen-heng-no No-pen-p'ei Pen-p'ei-k'o K'o-kao-lie

恩 亨 糯 糯 笨 培 笨 培 咼 咼 高 列

2. A □ B — B □ C — C □ D — D □ E

Kong-a-long Long-a-kao Kao-a-cheou Cheou-a-mei

龚 亚 陇 陇 亚 告 告 亚 守 守 亚 美

3. A B C D — C D E F — E F G H — G H I J

Yi-tsouen-lao-cho Lao-cho-tou-tsai Tou-tsai-a-tsong A-tsong-yi-k'iu

一 尊 老 勺 老 勺 渎 在 渎 在 阿 宗 阿 宗 一 衢

4. □ A □ B — □ B □ C — □ C □ D — □ D □ E

A-tsong-a-leang	A-leang-a-hou	A-hou-a-lie	A-lie-a-kia
阿琮阿良	阿良阿胡	阿胡阿烈	阿烈阿甲

Chaque type peut comporter quelques légères variations, mais en règle générale, les 4 exemples cités recouvrent tous les cas[①]

En montrant ce trait culturel, j'ai cité dans mon précédent article vingt-deux généalogies de différentes tribus telles que les Birmans, les 茶山 Atchit, les 么些 Moso, les 倮倮 Lolo et les 阿卡 A-ka[②]; j'ai également admis que les populations du 南诏 Nan-tchao et de 大理 Ta-li, et la maison de 高 Kao à 姚安 Yao-ngan faisaient toutes partie des tribus tibéto-birmanes[③].

Depuis que mon article a été publié, toute une série de nouvelles découvertes ont été faites confirmant ma théorie. En premier lieu, j'ai trouvé deux généalogies de plus dans les grandes familles Lolo de la province de 西康 Si-k'ang. La première est la généalogie de la famille 阿合 A-ho qui comprend douze générations en tout (voir figure I); l'autre est la généalogie de la famille 罗洪 Lo-hong qui comprend quatorze générations (voir figure II)[④]. Toutes, sans exception, confirment les exemples du type 3 mentionné ci-dessus.

La plus importante et la plus intéressante de toutes, est ma découverte de plusieurs généalogies 民家 Min-kia, à la lumière de laquelle on peut résoudre le problème de la position ethnique de cette tribu.

---

① Cf. *HJAS* 8(1945), 349.

② *Op. cit.*, 350—359.

③ *Op. cit.*, 361—363.

④ Pour ces deux généalogies je tiens à dire ma dette envers 傅懋勣 Fou Mao-tsi qui les a établies lui-même au mont Ta Leang dans la province de Si-k'ang.

La tribu que les Chinois appellent Min-kia se donne à elle-même le nom de 白子 Po-tseu. Elle est répartie sur une ère autour de 洱海 Eul-hai à peu près entre long. 99°55'E, et lat. 25°30'—26°48'N; atteignant à l'ouest long. 99°30'E, c'est-à-dire le long de la rivière 澜沧 Lan-ts'ang dans le district de 云龙 Yun-long; et au nord-ouest lat. 27°N. dans le district de 维西 Wei-si. A l'est, depuis le district de 凤仪 Fong-yi le long de la route de Ta-li à Kouen-ming, en passant par les districts de 祥云 Hiang-yun, 弥渡 Mi-tou, 镇南 Tchen-nan, 姚安 Yao-ngan, 楚雄 Tch'ou-hiong, 广通 Kouang-t'ong, 渌丰 Lou-fong et 安宁 Ngan-ning jusqu'à la région de 昆明 Kouen-ming (long. 112°35'E.) il y a des villages Min-kia dans tous les districts, mais de nombre peu considérable. Au sud de lat. 25°N. il n'y a de villages Min-kia qu'à 远坝 Yuan-pa dans le district de 元江 Yuan kiang, le long de la Rivière Rouge, et ils ne dépassent pas au nord la ligne Ta-li Kouen-ming①.

Quant à la situation ethnique du Min-kia, H. R. Davies, dans son livre 《Tribus du Yunnan》, Appendice VIII de *Yunnan*, croyait qu'ils appartiennent à la famille Mon-khmère ②; V. K. Ting 丁文江 dans la préface de son《爨文丛刊》*Ts'ouen-wen ts'ong-k'an* émet l'hypothèse qu'ils se rattachent aux Chan ③, tandis que 李方桂 F. K. Li dans son ouvrage, 《Langues et Dialectes》, les rattache aux Lolo ④, 凌纯声 Ling Shouen-cheng

① Voir l'article qu'écrit le Professeur 陶云逵 T'ao Yun-k'ouei (*Géographical Distribution and Tentative Census of Several Tribes in Yun-nan Provinces*, *CYYY*, 7〈1937〉fasc. 4, p. 430).

② H. R. Davies suit l'opinion de Terrien de Lacouperie. Voir *Yunnan*, *le lien entre l'Inde et le Yang-tseu*, Cambridge, 1909, pp. 343—347.

③ Publié par l'Institut d'Histoire et de philologie, Academia Sinica, 1936.

④ F.K. Li dit que《le Min-kia et quelques autres dialectes mineurs peuvent également appartenir à ce groupe (tibéto-birman).》Voir *Chinese Year Book*, Shanghai, 1938—1939, p. 49.

agrée tout d'abord à la suggestion de V. K. Ting [1], mais dans son dernier travail,《Les 乌蛮 Wou-man et les 白蛮 Pai-man sous la dynastie T'ang》, fait soudain volte-face et en vient à la conclusion qu'ils sont apparentés à la tribu Karen de la famille tibéto-birmane [2]. Cette question demeure ouverte.

Laissant de côté les caractères linguistiques que je discuterai en détails dans mon *Etude sur la langue Min-kia*, je me limite ici à la seule question de ce trait culturel: le lien généalogique du patronyme, et je me trouve soutenir l'hypothèse de Li, mais dans un sens plus large.

Dans mon premier article, j'ai cité trois généalogies de la maison des 段 Touan à Ta-li, la maison de 高 Kao qui fonda le 大中国《Ta tchong kouo》, et les descendants de Kao qui étaient héréditairement 土同知 *T'ou t'ong-tche* ou sous-préfet aborigène de Yao-ngan-fou au début de la dynastie Ts'ing[3]. Toutes ces branches Min-kia furent alors profondément marquées par les influences chinoises. Néanmoins leurs généalogies révèlaient encore beaucoup de traces de la pratique du lien onomastique. Une autre source de documents se trouve dans le《摆夷传》*Pai-yi tchouan* (Chronique de Pai-yi) dans le《云龙记往》*Yun-long Ki-wang* (Histoire du district de Yun-long). Il y est dit [4]:

"Jadis, il n'y avait pas de nom de famille dans la tribu barbare. Pour la première fois, les quatre fils de 阿苗 A-miao prirent la 2e partie du nom de leur père pour nom de famille. Il y eut Miao-nan, Miao-tan, Miao-wei et Miao-che. Le second Miao-tan, eut cinq fils: Tan-ka Tan-t'i, Tan-niao, Tan-

---

① Geographical Distribution of the Tribes in Yunnan, *Journal of Geography*, 3(1936)3.

② *Bulletin of Anthropological Studies* 1 (1938)1, Academia Sinica.

③ *HJAS*, 8(1945), pp. 362—363.

④《云南备征志》*Yun-nan pei-tcheng tche*, fasc. 19.

teng et Tan-kiang. Tan-ka seul eut un fils, appelé Ka-teng."

Il est évident, d'après ce passage, qu'ils adhéraient strictement au système du lien onomastique et qu'il n'existait pas de nom de famille ou 姓 *sing*. Nous devons signaler que le mot 摆 doit être lu 白 ou 僰. Bien que les caractères 摆 (Ancien chinois *pai*, Mandarin *pai*), 白 (Anc. ch. *b'ɒk*, *Mand. pai*) et 僰 (Anc. ch. *b'iək*, Mand. *po* ou *pai*) fussent prononcés différemment en Ancien chinois, néanmoins ils étaient interchangeables en Mandarin, particulièrement dans le dialecte du Yunnan de l'ouest. 摆夷 a été employé pour représenter les Chan, 白夷 a eté employé pour les Pertzǔ, c'est-à-dire les Min-kia, et 僰夷 l'a été de manière ambiguë pour représenter l'un ou l'autre.

Comme je l'ai mentionné plus haut. Yun-long est une des régions habitées par les Min-kia, et ce système du lien onomastique n'a rien à voir avec le peuple Chan, ce qui fait que nous devons lire 白夷 pour 摆夷.

En juillet 1944, je dirigeais un groupe de trente-trois personnes qui devait rassembler des matériaux pour le dictionnaire géographique du district de Tali. Un de mes collègues 吴乾就 Wou K'ien-tsieou trouva deux documents originaux qui sont extrêmement importants pour l'étude de l'histoire de la tribu Min-kia. L'un date de 1467 après J. C.; c'est une épitaphe de 杨胜 Yang Cheng écrite par un bouddhiste, 杨文信 Yang Wen-sin, appartenant à la Mantra-samaya, ou secte Mystique. Elle est située à 下关 Hia-kouan près de Ta-li dans la plaine 么些坪 Moso sous le 斜阳峰 Hia-yang fong ou pic du Soleil Couchant ①. L'autre date de 1462; c'est une

① Le titre original et la date sont: 善士杨胜墓志并铭,龙关习密僧杨文信撰并书呪,大明成化三年孟春三月吉日立。

préface à la généalogie de la famille 赵 Tchao à Hia-kouan, écrite par 许廷端 Hiu T'ing-touan, délégué de l'Académie Impériale de Nankin[①].

Dans le premier de ces documents nous voyons que trois générations ont la pratique du lien onomastique, ce sont:

杨贤 Yang Hien—杨贤庆 Yang Hien-k'ing—杨庆定 Yang K'ing-ting. D'après l'inscription originale de l'épitaphe, Yang Hien-k'ing est né sous le règne de l'Empereur 洪武 Hong Wou (1368—1398 après J.C.). Après que le général 蓝玉 Lan Yu et que 沐英 Mou Ying eurent conquis Ta-li en 1382, il devint le chef de son village. On s'aperçoit que durant la domination de la maison des Touan sous la dynastie Yuan, la famille Yang conservait encore la tradition tibéto-birmane du lien onomastique. Néanmoins, après la chute de la maison des Touan en 1382, les descendants des Yang tombèrent sous l'influence chinoise et abandonnèrent subitement leur trait culturel traditionel[②].

Dans le dernier document il y a également trois génératiens qui pratiquent le lien onomastique. Ce sont: 赵福祥 Tchao Fou-hiang, 赵祥顺 Tchao Hiang-chouen et 赵顺海 Tchao Chouen-hai.

Les deux dernières générations sont nées sous la dynastie Yuan. Après que 赵赐 Tchao Ts'eu (1348—1420) fut nommé *Ācārya* par la cour, la famille des Tchao s'éleva en distinction; le résultat fut la disparition à ce

① Le titre et la date sont: 太和龙关赵氏族谱叙，天顺六年二月吉旦，赐进士第南京国子监丞仰轩山人，许延端顿首拜撰。

② Je cite ici un paragraphe du texte original: "……此庆杨氏之茂族者，是大理龙关邑之贤也。高祖杨贤，元朝于知管掌方面，可行明令丛万民为乡里。曾祖杨贤庆，接任仓官，有大行之威势，祖考杨庆定，洪武年间建立苍洱府县，封为本都里长，生于三男，曰长，曰平，曰胜……"

même moment du lien onomastique.①

En me basant sur ces preuves, je me sens justifié à conclure que la tribu Min-kia, actuellement répartie autour de Eul-hai et dans d'autres régions, a probablement certaines relations ethniques avec les peuples tibéto-birmans. Après la chute du royaume de Ta-li en 1382, et la grande immigration dans la région de Tali en 1387 ②, les Min-kia eux-mêmes, au cours des temps, prirent aux Chinois beaucoup de traits de culture, et les intermariages accélérèrent aussi leur sinisation. Quant au nom de《plaine de Moso》où l'on trouva l'épitaphe, de Yang Cheng, il trahit vraisemblablement la parenté entre les Min-kia et les Moso ou Na-k'i dont J'ai donné les généalogies dans mon premier article, Item B.③Aussi, bien que les Min-kia ne fassent pas partie des Lolo en un sens strict, je maintiens qu'ils sont apparentés à une branche de la famille tibéto-birmane. Ils n'ont en aucune manière de rapport ni avec les Mon-khmer ni avec les Chan.

(*Han Hiue*, Ⅶ, fasc. 4, Pékin *Bulletin du Centre d'Etudes Sinologiques de Pékin*)

---

① Je cite ici un paragraphe du texte original:"……赵氏之先讳永牙者福应万灵不可尽述。凡几世传至赵福祥,祥顺,顺海,世居大理太和龙尾关白蟒寨……顺海生子一曰赐,赐生三子,曰寿,曰均,曰护,亦习先业,咸以德著,洪武十五年天兵克服云南取大理,赐如京款贡,均请从焉……"

② Voir Ming Che, ch. 313, 201, 明史,云南土司大理条"洪武十五年征南左将军兰玉,右将军沐英,率师攻大理,……大理悉定,因改大理路为大理府,置卫,设指挥使司……十六年命六安侯王志,安庆侯仇成,凤翔侯张龙督兵往云南品甸,缮城池,立屯堡,置邮传,安辑人民……二十年诏景川侯曹震及四川都司,选精兵二万五千人给军器农具,即云南品甸屯种,以俟征讨。"

③ Voir *HJAS*, pp. 352—354, et aussi Joseph Rock, *The Ancient Na-khi Kingdom of Southwest China*, publié par l'Institut de Harvard-Yenching, Cambridge, 1948, pp. 81—151, 377.

Tableau I

Généalogic de la Famillc 阿合 A-ho.

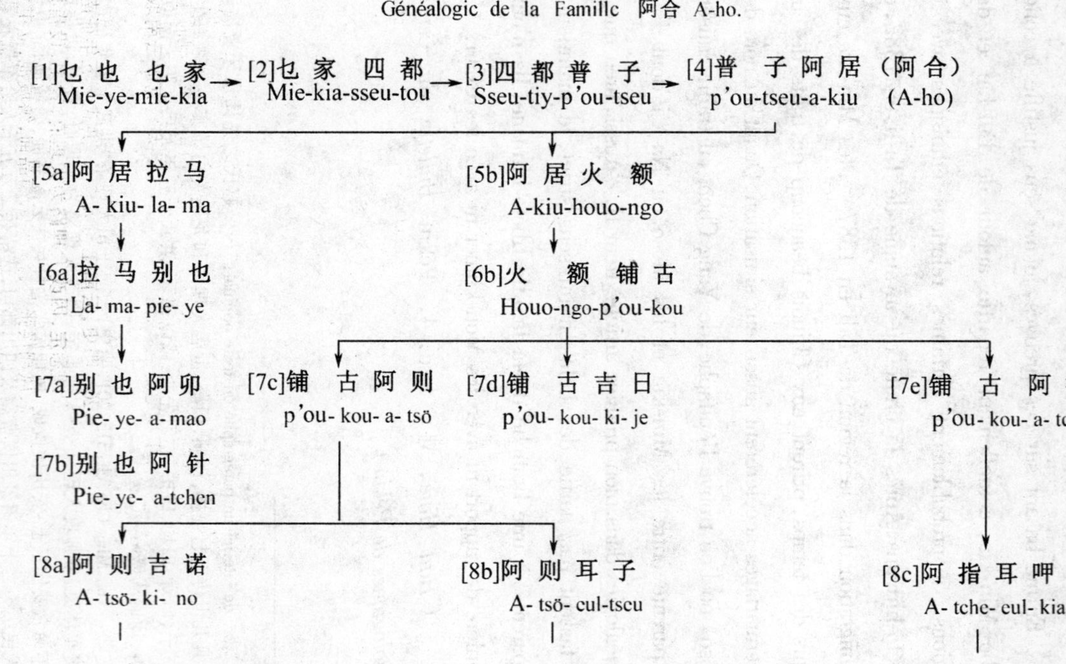

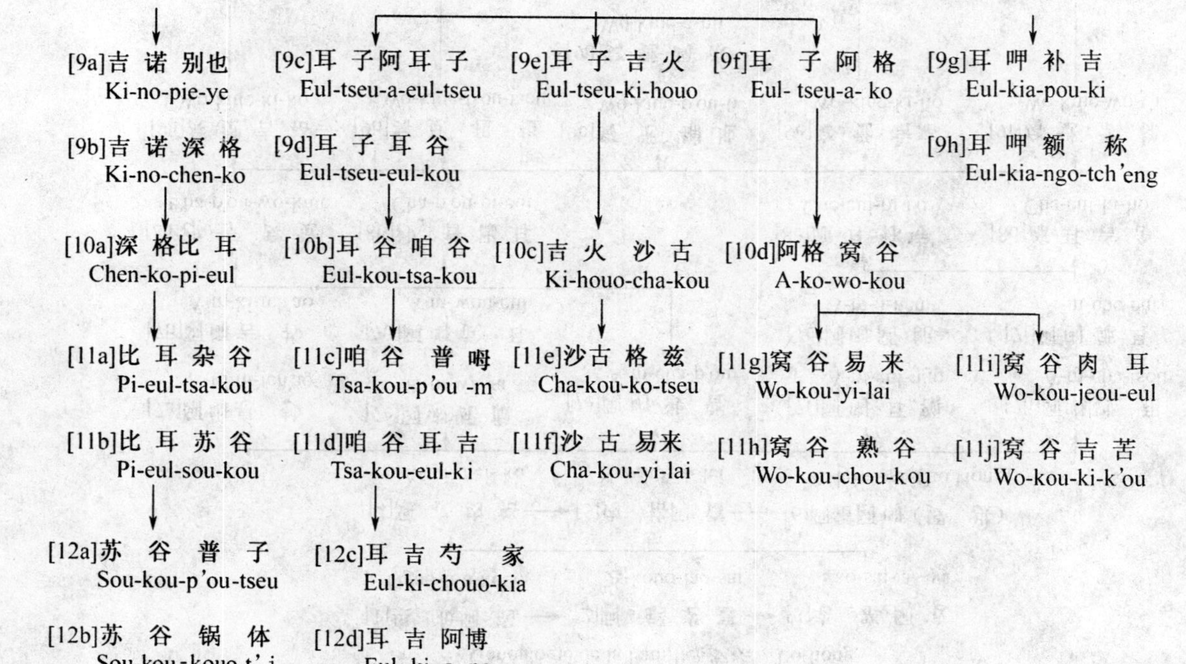
[9a]吉 诺 别也
Ki-no-pie-ye
[9b]吉 诺 深 格
Ki-no-chen-ko
[9c]耳 子阿耳 子
Eul-tseu-a-eul-tseu
[9d]耳 子 耳 谷
Eul-tseu-eul-kou
[9e]耳 子 吉 火
Eul-tseu-ki-houo
[9f]耳 子 阿 格
Eul- tseu-a- ko
[9g]耳 呷 补 吉
Eul-kia-pou-ki
[9h]耳 呷 额 称
Eul-kia-ngo-tch'eng
[10a]深 格比 耳
Chen-ko-pi-eul
[10b]耳 谷 咱 谷
Eul-kou-tsa-kou
[10c]吉 火 沙 古
Ki-houo-cha-kou
[10d]阿格 窝 谷
A-ko-wo-kou
[11a]比 耳 杂 谷
Pi-eul-tsa-kou
[11b]比 耳 苏 谷
Pi-eul-sou-kou
[11c]咱 谷 普 嗕
Tsa-kou-p'ou -m
[11d]咱 谷 耳 吉
Tsa-kou-eul-ki
[11e]沙古 格 兹
Cha-kou-ko-tseu
[11f]沙 古 易来
Cha-kou-yi-lai
[11g]窝 谷 易 来
Wo-kou-yi-lai
[11h]窝 谷 熟 谷
Wo-kou-chou-kou
[11i]窝 谷 肉 耳
Wo-kou-jeou-eul
[11j]窝 谷 吉 苦
Wo-kou-ki-k'ou
[12a]苏 谷 普 子
Sou-kou-p'ou-tseu
[12b]苏 谷 锅 体
Sou-kou-kouo-t' i
[12c]耳 吉 芍 家
Eul-ki-chouo-kia
[12d]耳 吉 阿博
Eul- ki -a -po

Tableau II

Généalogie de la Famille 罗洪 Lo-hong.

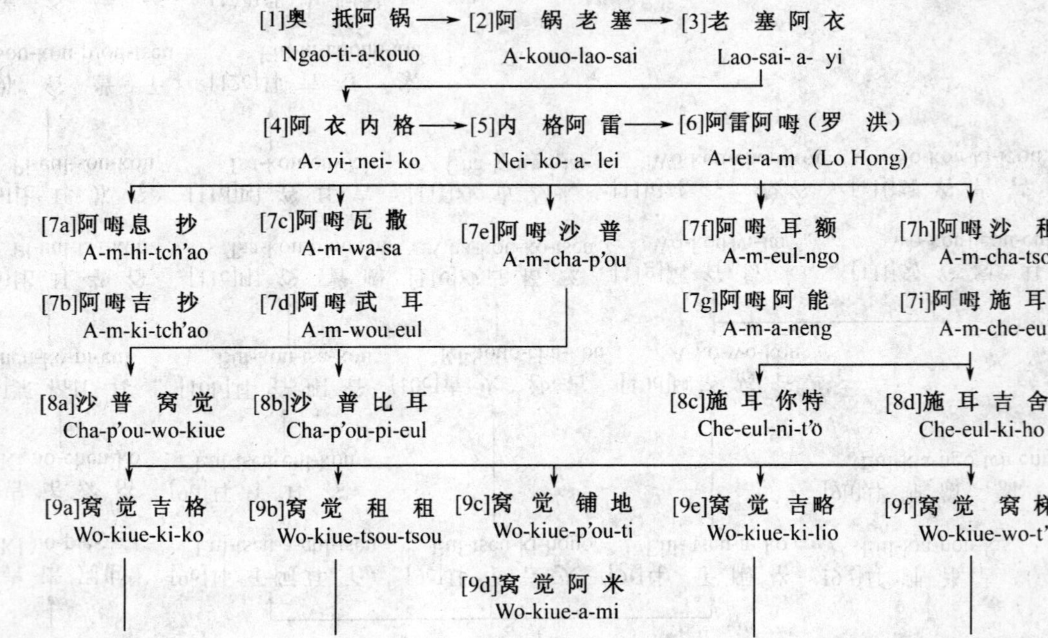

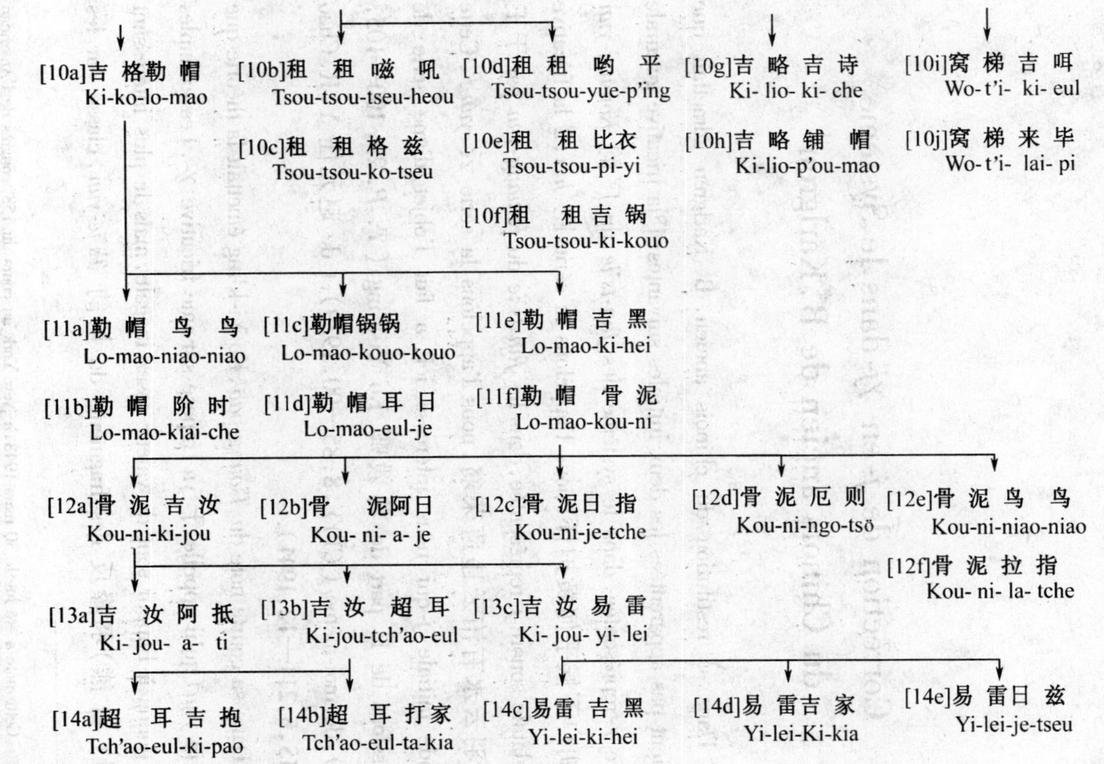

[10a]吉 格勒 帽
Ki-ko-lo-mao
[10b]租 租 嗞 吼
Tsou-tsou-tseu-heou
[10c]租 租 格 兹
Tsou-tsou-ko-tseu
[10d]租 租 哟 平
Tsou-tsou-yue-p'ing
[10e]租 租 比衣
Tsou-tsou-pi-yi
[10f]租 租吉 锅
Tsou-tsou-ki-kouo
[10g]吉 略 吉 诗
Ki- lio- ki- che
[10h]吉 略 铺 帽
Ki-lio-p'ou-mao
[10i]窝 梯 吉 咡
Wo-t'i- ki- eul
[10j]窝 梯 来 毕
Wo-t'i- lai- pi
[11a]勒 帽 鸟 鸟
Lo-mao-niao-niao
[11b]勒 帽 阶 时
Lo-mao-kiai-che
[11c]勒帽锅锅
Lo-mao-kouo-kouo
[11d]勒 帽 耳 日
Lo-mao-eul-je
[11e]勒 帽 吉 黑
Lo-mao-ki-hei
[11f]勒 帽 骨 泥
Lo-mao-kou-ni
[12a]骨 泥 吉 汝
Kou-ni-ki-jou
[12b]骨 泥阿日
Kou- ni- a- je
[12c]骨 泥日 指
Kou-ni-je-tche
[12d]骨 泥 厄 则
Kou-ni-ngo-tsö
[12e]骨 泥 鸟 鸟
Kou-ni-niao-niao
[12f]骨 泥 拉 指
Kou- ni- la- tche
[13a]吉 汝 阿 抵
Ki- jou- a- ti
[13b]吉 汝 超 耳
Ki-jou-tch'ao-eul
[13c]吉 汝 易 雷
Ki- jou- yi- lei
[14a]超 耳 吉 抱
Tch'ao-eul-ki-pao
[14b]超 耳 打家
Tch'ao-eul-ta-kia
[14c]易雷 吉 黑
Yi-lei-ki-hei
[14d]易 雷吉 家
Yi-lei-Ki-kia
[14e]易 雷日 兹
Yi-lei-je-tseu

Correction de *j*- en *γj*- dans le Système du Chinois ancien de B. Karlgren[①]

Dans sa restitution du chinois ancien, B. Karlgren admettait que n'étaient pas apparentées les deux initiales suivantes: 1°la fricative gutturale sonore *γ*- représentée, dans le système des *fan-ts'ie* du 广韵 *Kouang-yun* par 胡户下候乎何黄护怀; nous l'appelons la série 匣 *hia*; 2° la fricative prépalatale sonore *j*- représentée, dans les *fan-ts'ie* du *Kouang-yun* par 于王雨为羽云永有洧云违薳荣翁; nous l'appelons la série 云 *yun*[②]. Cette seconde initiale *j*- qui nous intéresse ici, a fait l'objet d'une série de discussions de la part de 葛毅卿 Ko Yi-k'ing (*T. P.* 29, 100—105, 1932), de moi-même (*CYYY*, 8, 85—90, 1939) et de 赵元任 Y. R. Chao (*HJAS*, 5, 211—12, 1941).

Dans sa courte note du *T'oung-pao*, Ko Yi-k'ing émettait la théorie que la série *yun* (qu'il appelle 于 *yu*) repose sur une fricative *γ*-. Les exemples qu'il donne à l'appui sont de valeur assez inégale, mais le plus intéressant est 雄 (et 熊) 羽隆反 des fragments du 切韵 *Ts'ie-yun*, classé par les

---

① Cette note a été lue le 30 mars 1948, à New York au cours du 158ᵉ congrès de l'American Oriental Society.

② Bernhard Karlgren, *Études sur la phonologie chinoise*, pp. 109—110, 111—113, 373—377, 1916.

phonéticiens postérieurs dans la série hia, laquelle est rétablie par Karlgren en *γi ung*, et que le 切韵指掌图 *Ts'ie yun tche tchang t'ou* donne explicitement comme un exemple de distribution complémentaire des séries *hia* et 喻 *yu*. Le fait le plus important est que les fragments du *Ts'ie-yun* ont:

云,户分 *jiuən* = γ(uo + p) *iuən* = *γiuən*

越,户伐 *jiwɒt* = γ(uo + p) *iwɒt* = *γiwɒt*[1]

Y.R. Chao pense que "quant à la valeur phonétique de l'initiale *yun*, la théorie de Ko ne s'écarte guère de celle de Karlgren, selon laquelle '*j*- est la fricative prépalatale sonore de l'allemand *ja*"[2]. Mais il prétend que si nous admettons que le *j*- de Karlgren représente la variante yodisée du phonème *γ*-, nous sommes alors en droit de considérer comme yodisée l'initiale 羊 *yang* (restituée par Karlgren comme une attaque vocalique laryngale douce sans yod)[3]. Nous pouvons par conséquent maintenir la théorie de "l'harmonie médiale" selon laquelle "partout où il y a *i*, il y a *yod*" sans exception[4].

A l'appui des preuves données par Ko, j'ai découvert quelques autres faits qui confirment bien sa théorie.

En premier lieu, d'après les *fan-ts'ie* du 经典释文 *King-tien che-wen* de 陆德明 Lou Tö-ming, j'ai constitué deux séries d'initiales en partant de la formule: A = B, B = C: A = C.

Le résultat est représenté par le tableau suivant:

---

① Ku Ye-ching, *On the Consonantal Value of 喻 class words*, *T. P.*, 29 (1932), 100—103.

② B. Karlgren, *Analytic Dictionary of Chinese and Sino-Japanese*, Paris, 1923, p. 6, note 5.

③ B. Karlgren, *Grammata Serica*, Stockholm, 1940, p. 49.

④ Y. R. Chao, *Distinction within Ancient Chinese*, *HJAS*, 5(1940), 3 et 4, 211—212.

Série *Hia*:

户:胡:河:何 户户胡胡何河/可我可我可可　下 户遐遐/嫁嫁稼　华 户户胡胡/花瓜瓜花 : 户胡/化化

行 户户户/诟刚康 : 户下/庚庚 : 户遐/孟孟　侯 户/豆　和 胡/戈 : 户胡/卧卧　迥 户/顶　爻 户/交 : 胡/孝　环 户/关

曷 户户何寒火/割葛末末葛　学 户户/教孝　洪 户/工　衡 华/盲　咸 行洽/缄斩　滑 胡乎于/八八八　回(洄 音胡/回恢)

遐(瑕 音户下下/遐加家加)　獲(画 音胡乎/獲麦麦)　分(鼷 音户/兮鸡)　幸(倖 音胡/幸耿)

衔(音洽行/咸斩缄)　洽(狭 音户户胡乎/洽甲夹夹夹)　乎(坏 户乎/怪怪)　寒(翰 户胡寒/旦旦半)

亥(孩 户亥/哀才)　闲(黠 户闲/八八)　黄(穫 户黄/郭郭)　贤(见 贤贤胡/遍编荐)

玄(铉 胡胡玄玄玄/犬畎犬畎典)　形刑(胫 户胡刑形/定定定定)　恨(很 户胡胡恨/垦垦恳恳)　惠(萤 户惠/扃丁)

穴(携 户穴/圭圭)　弦(cf.《广韵》弦贤並胡田切)

Série *Yun*:

于 音羽/为危　为 于/威 : 于於于于于荣/伪伪廉沾凡钳　羽(音于/雨矩)　又(有 音于/又救)

袁(援 音于/袁眷)　韦(苇 于韦/鬼鬼)　位(鲔 于位/轨轨)　往(王 于住/方方 : 于往/况况)

云韵(陨 于于云韵/敏闵敏谨)　荣(禜 为荣/命敬)　尤 有下/牛求　有

Le *King-tien che-wen* a été publié par Lou Tö-ming en 583 ap. J.-C. Il est constitué par une série de gloses sur douze des Treize classiques (Mencius est omis), sur le *Lao-tseu* et le *Tchouang-tseu*. Bien qu'il cite abondamment les lectures en *fan-ts'ie* des anciens commentateurs, son propre système de *fan-ts'ie* constitue un système homogène et n'est pas fondé sur le même dialecte que celui du *Ts'ie-yun* ①. Si nous jetons un coup d'oeil sur le tableau qui précède, les deux séries d'initiales semblent tout a fait distinctes, excepté pour les caractères 尤 et 有. Mais, en fait, elles alternent souvent. Par exemple, dans la série *hia*, le même son pour le caractère 滑 est représenté par trois différents *fan-ts'ie*: 胡八, 乎八, 于八. De même,

① Je discuterai ce point dans un autre article.

le caractère 猾 a 于 八,户 八 pour une même prononciation. Mais le 猾 de 蛮夷猾夏 dans le *Chou-king*, est prononcé 户 八 dans l'édition moderne, alors que le manuscrit de Touen-houang donne 于 八.

Ces exemples nous autorisent à dire que 户,胡,乎 de la série *hia* et 于 de la série *yun* étaient interchangeables.

Une autre preuve se trouve dans les *fan-ts'ie* du 玉 篇 *Yu-p'ien* original. Cet ancien dictionnaire publié par 顾 野 王 Kou Ye-wang(519—581 ap. J.-C.), a été révisé par 孙 强 Souen K'iang en 674, puis augmenté par 陈 彭 年 Tch'en p'eng-nien en 1013. Plusieurs manuscrits de l'édition originale sont heureusement conservés au Japon ①. De plus, 弘 法 大 师 空 海 Kobodaishi Kukai (774—835) incorpora presque tout l'ouvrage de Kou Ye-wang dans son 万 象 名 义 *Banshómeigi* ②. En 1935, 周 祖 谟 Tcheou Tsou-mo fit l'étude du système phonétique du *Yu-p'ien* original en partant de ces matériaux ③. La relation entre les séries *yun* et *hia*, comme le montre le tableau suivant, est beaucoup plus étroite que dans le *King-tien che-wen*:

胡 护徒	护 胡故	户 胡户	互 胡(故)	扈 胡古	后 胡走	侯 胡沟	黄 胡光	缓 胡节	会 胡外
奚 胡题	谐 胡階	核 胡(改)	穴 胡决	衡 胡庚	红 胡工	和 胡戈	候 胡遘	厚 胡苟	後 胡狗
华 胡瓜	嫿 胡馘	獲 胡馘	形 胡经	骇 胡骇	嵇 胡鸡	何 (胡)可	贺 何佐	遐 何加	下 遐雅
行 遐庚	杏 遐梗	荷 贺多	河 贺柯 户多	乎 户枯	悦 胡拙	尹 胡准	越 胡厥	为 胡妫	鲔 为轨
荣 为明	核 为革	解 核洒	覈 解革 械革	械	于 禹俱	迂 禹俱	竽 禹朱	尤 禹尤	王 禹方
曰 禹月	有 于九	又 有救	雄 有宫	雨 有诩	禹				

Les cinq caractères 尹 越 为 鲔 荣 qui appartiennent à la série *yun*

① 冈井慎吾 Okai Shingo, 玉篇 の研究 *Kyoku-hen no kenkyu*, Tokyo, p. 43—82.

② Yang Cheou-king, Postface au *Yu-p'ien* original (影旧钞卷子原本玉篇跋. 古逸丛书之十一), 1884.

③ Dans une dissertation du Department of Chinese Philology and Literature, National Peking University, Peiping, 1935.

dans le *Kouang-yun*, sont déjà rattachés ici à la série *hia*. De plus, dans le *Banshō-meigi*, le caractère 云 a deux *fan-ts'ie* alternants: 于勋 et 胡熏 Le caractère 属 est prononcé 胡甫, mais sa variante tardive 寓 est prononcée 于甫. Visiblement 于 et 胡 peuvent alterner librement.

La troisième preuve, la plus intéressante, se trouve dans deux poèmes allitérés, l'un de 王融 Wang Jong (468—494)① et l'autre de 庾信 Yu Sin (513—581)②, dont voici le texte:

A. 南齐 王融双声诗

园蘅眩红蘤,湖荇烨黄花。

回鹤横淮翰,远越合云霞。

B. 北周 庾信《问疾封中录》双声诗

形骸违学宦,狭巷幸为闲。

虹回或有雨,云合又含寒。

横湖韵鹤下,回溪狭猿还。

怀贤为荣卫,和缓惠绮纨。

Il n'y a pas allitération parfaite si nous lisons ces poèmes en mandarin moderne:

A. Yuan hong hiuan hong wei
hou hing yi houang houa
houei ho heng houai han
yuan yue ho yun hia.

B. hing hai wei hiue houan

① 王宁朔集 *Wang Ning-chouo tsi* p. 20, dans le 汉魏六朝一百三家集 *Han Wei Lou-tch'ao yi-pai-san kia tsi*, édité par 张溥 Tchang P'ou. Ce poème allitéré a été cité aussi par 钱大昕 Ts'ien Ta-hin dans son 十驾斋养新录 *Che kia tchai yang sin lou*, fasc. VI.

② 庾开府集 *Yu K'ai-fou tsi*, fasc. II, p. 31, dans la même *Anthologie*.

hia hiang hing wei hien
hong houei houo yeou yu
yun ho yeou han han
heng hou yun ho hia
houei hi hia yuan houan
houai hien wei jong wei
ho houan houei k'i houan.

Il n'y a pas davantage allitération parfaite si on lit d'après la reconstitution du chinois ancien de Karlgren:

A. *꜀ji̯wen ꜀γɒng γi̯wen꜄ ꜀γung ꜂jwi̯e̯*
꜀γuo ꜂γɒng i̯äk꜆ ꜀γwâng ꜀xwa
꜀γuậi γâk꜆ ꜀γwɒng ꜀γwai γân꜄
꜂ji̯wɒn ji̯wɒt꜆ γập꜆ ꜀ji̯uən ꜀γa

B. *꜀γieng ꜀γai ꜀jwe̯i γȧk꜆ γwan꜄*
γap꜆ ꜀γàng γɒng꜄ ꜀jwi e̯ ꜀γan
꜀γung ꜀γuậi γwək꜆ ꜂ji̯ əu ꜂ji̯u
꜀ji̯uən γập꜆ ji̯əu꜄ ꜀γậm ꜀γận
꜀γweng ꜀γuo ji̯uən꜄ γâk꜆ ꜂γa
꜀γuậi ꜀k' iei γap꜆ ꜀ji̯wɒn ꜀γwan
꜀γwai ꜀γien jwi̯e̯꜄ ji̯wɒng ji̯wäi꜄
꜀γuâ ꜂γuân γi̯wei꜄ ꜂k' i e̯ ꜀γuân

Mais si l'on suit notre nouvelle restitution, les allitérations apparaissent aussitôt parfaitement:

A. *꜀γi̯wen ꜀γɒng riwen꜄ ꜀γung ꜂γwi̯e̯*
꜀γuo ꜂γɒng i̯äk꜆ ꜀γwâng ꜀xwa

꜀γuậi γâk꜆ ꜀γwɒng ꜀γwai γân꜄

꜂γi̯wɒn γi̯wɒt꜆ γập꜆ ꜀γi̯uən ꜀γa

B. ꜀γieng ꜀γai ꜀γi̯we̯i γȧk꜆ γwan꜄

γap꜆ ràng꜄ γɒng꜄ ꜀γwi̯e ꜀γan

꜀γung γuậi γwək꜆ ꜂γi̯ə̯u꜄ ꜂γi̯u

꜀γi̯uən γập꜆ γi̯ə̯u꜄ ꜀γậm ꜀γân

꜀γwɒng ꜀γuo ꜀γiuən γâk꜆ ꜂γa

꜀γuậi ꜀k‘iei γap꜆ ꜀γi̯wɒn ꜀γwan

꜀γwai ꜀γien rwi̯e꜄ ꜀γi̯wɒng γi̯wäi꜄

꜀γuâ ꜂γuân γiwei꜄ ꜂k‘i̯e ꜀γuân

Excepté pour un petit nombre de mots tels que 花 *xwa*, 燡 *jäk* et 溪 *k'iei*, 绮 *k'ie*, les allitérations sont parfaites d'un bout à l'autre des deux poèmes.

Je proposerai, pour me résumer, de corriger le *j* – du chinois ancien de Karlgren en *γj* –. En d'autres termes, les séries *hia* et *yun* seraient apparentées comme deux allophones d'un même phonème. Durant la seconde moitié du Vème siècle et la première moitié du VIème, la yodisation de l'initiale *γ*- devant un *i̯*-médial n'était pas encore très avancée. C'est pourquoi le *γj*- yodisé était souvent confondu avec le *γ*- *pur*, lequel n'apparaissait jamais devant le *i̯*-médial, comme le montrent les exemples cités. Dans le dernier quart du VIème siècle, jusqu'à la période du *Ts'ie-yun* (601), la distinction entre le *γ*- pur et le *γj*- yodisé se développa peu à peu. Dans le *Ts'ie-yun*, *γ*- apparaît précisément en deux allophones, l'un pur (série *hia*) et l'autre *yodisé* (série *yun*). Cependant si nous admettons que devant *i*, il était toujours yodisé, il n'est pas nécessaire d'établir un phonème particulier pour la forme yodisée, ou de prévoir pour elle un symbole spécial (tel que *j*-).

(*Han Hiue* VIII, fasc. 3 et 4, 1948)

蜀道难

谢　序

《蜀道难》是西南联大教授罗莘田先生在 1941 年 5 月至 8 月，自云南昆明至四川东川、西川和川南旅行的游记。他的游伴有梅月涵[梅贻琦]校长和郑毅生[郑天挺]教授，行期三个月，所用的交通工具有九种，参观的学术机关十余处，会到的老友新交更是不计其数。无怪他写来洒洒七八万言，有声有色了。

我和罗莘田先生熟识，是在 1938 年秋日。那年我们自北平南下，罗太太托我们带几套寒衣，到了昆明，把寒衣送出，罗先生就同陈雪屏先生来访。文藻和罗先生是旧友重逢，当然高兴，那天谈话相当的多，我才得机会充分地领教了罗先生的言论丰采。自那时起我们过往很密，能够把罗先生加在我们知友的名单上，我觉得是非常荣幸。

罗先生是北平人，充满着燕赵的气息：诚恳、忠直、富于正义感，同时三十多年的读书，又把他造成一个纯粹的学者，恬淡洒落，霁月光风。同文藻谈起文字语言来，若非有人制止，他可以达旦不寐；和我提到诗词歌曲，也是眉飞色舞，有时还引吭高歌，大有"唾壶击缺"之概。但他也能同小孩到山下积水池边"打水漂儿"，也能同厨娘灶婢谈北方小吃。罗先生一到我们家里，真是上下腾欢，这种秋月春风般的人格，现在是不多见的。

这篇游记里，便充分地表现了罗先生的人格：三个多月困难的旅途，拖泥带水，戴月披风，逢山开路，过水搭桥，还仓皇地逃了好几次警报，历尽了抗战期中旅行的苦楚，可是他的豪兴一点不减，他研究了学术，赏玩了风景，采访了民俗，慰问了朋友。路见不平，他愤激而不颓丧；遇见了好山水人物，他又欣赏流连，乐而忘返。这篇游记，显然不是一个“回忆”，一个“心影”，而是从他精密详细的日记里扩充引申出来的，读之不厌其长，惟恐其尽！我以为将来若有人要知道抗战中期蜀道上某时某地的旅途实情、学术状况、人物动态的，这是一本必读的书籍。

承罗先生嘱为《蜀道难》写序，我真是受宠若惊。我以为人生有三大乐事：一、朋友，二、读书，三、旅行，罗先生与我有同感。假如最近的将来，罗先生在读书之余，能再出来旅行一次，使忝居友末者，又得亲其言论丰采，这不止是我一个人的希望了。

冰　心

1942 年 11 月 24 日，歌乐山，潜庐

自　序

刘彦和《文心雕龙·体性篇》说："夫情动而言形，理发而文见，盖沿隐以至显，因内而符外者也。然才有庸俊，气有刚柔，学有浅深，习有雅郑，并情性所铄，陶染所凝，是以笔区云谲，文苑波诡者矣。故辞理庸儁，莫能翻其才；风趣刚柔，宁或改其气；事义浅深，未闻乖其学；体式雅郑，鲜有反其习；各师成心，其异如面。"可见人的才性是不能强同的。生来不是文学天才，更加缺乏素养，写出文章来连自己看着都觉得不够味儿。况且人的智慧本来越用越灵，越搁越钝，十几年来把仅有的一点儿聪明才智整个地都用在搜集排比、归纳推研上面去，即或偶尔发生一点文艺的灵感也被堆积在胸里硬得消化不了的材料给压迫得一会儿就没影儿了。记得1926年住在厦门，有一回和鲁迅先生谈天，问他近来有没有创作。他说："因为要编文学史讲义不得不沉下心去搜集材料，处理材料，心思一集中在这上面，自然而然地不会胡思乱想也就写不出什么文艺作品来了。人的才智沉下去就浮不上来，浮上来也不容易沉下去。照我看创作和研究是不能同时兼顾的。"假若我要引这段话来解嘲，那么，这就是我不能成文学家的原因。

明白我的立场，那就请读者们千万别把这本小册子当文学作品看。它只是个人生活的片段记录，有什么就写什么，想怎样写就怎样写，既没深湛的寄托，更没顾虑到修辞的技巧。至于为什么要写它，却有两个原因:第一,我们去年从四川兜个大圈子回来,朋友们见面总要问:"你们在峨眉玩得痛快罢?"好像那么长的三个月,我们都优哉游哉地消磨在峨眉山里似的。为使关心我们的人明了此行的真相,我情愿花一些功夫把我们的游踪记下来。第二,回到昆明我就大病几殆,病后经医生嘱咐不许多看书,不许做繁重的工作。可是,我生平最怕空闲,尤其在这孤独的病后,假如没点儿事情消遣,说不定一病方愈,一病又起。惟一的排解方法只有住在乡下整理这一段的笔记,作为"雪泥鸿爪"的留念。由于这两个动机,我就每一礼拜写出五六千字来送给《当代评论》发表,连自己也没想到下笔不能自休地居然扯了这么长!

本来拿这样拖沓冗长的文章占了《当代评论》许多篇幅,我已经很不自安地应该向编者和读者道歉了,现在陈雪屏先生又让我把它结集起来印成单行本,格外使我有殃及手民的惭恧!有一位朋友尝说:"俗语说:'文章是自己的好,太太是人家的好。'我希望上句对,它偏不对;我盼着下句不对,它倒对了!"我对于这位朋友所说的下半句,因为太太远在天涯,已经久别五年,姑且保留不谈;对于他的上半句我却有充分的同情,深刻的自觉。说真的,我从来没有自诩文章好过,尤其是对这本东西。可是,既承雪屏的好意要把它印出来给大家看,好坏只好任读者们去估量罢。反正它也不够"藏诸名山,传之其人"的,乐得随缘流布,听它自生自灭。是为序。

1942 年 11 月 17 日,
离平五周年纪念,在昆明

蜀道难

蜀道之难难于上青天，使人听此凋朱颜！
蜀道之难难于上青天，侧身西望长咨嗟！
其险也如此，嗟尔远道之人胡为乎来哉？
——节录李白句

一 缘起

我这次虽然没经过夔门、剑阁那样艰难的"蜀道"，却在坦途中饱尝了现代蜀道的艰难！

这次的旅程经过了东川、西川和川中、川南的大部分，行期延长到三个多月。所用的交通工具一共有九种：最进步的是飞机，最原始的是鸡公车，介乎两者之间的还有小汽车、木炭汽车、酒精卡车、轮船、柏木船、黄包车、滑竿等等。行期的大部分都耗费在等车、候船、汽车抛锚、山洪冲断公路……许多想不到的事情上面，真正花费在想到的地方，想做的事，想看的朋友，乃至于想游览的山水等等上的时间，却并没有多少。

我这次的旅伴有梅月涵、郑毅生两先生。旅行的目的是为到重庆向教育部接洽西南联大的几件校务，到叙永视察分校，到李庄参观中央研究院的历史语言研究所和社会科学研究所，并且审查北大文科研究所三个毕业生的论文，到乐山、峨眉、成都各处参观武汉、四川、华西、齐鲁、金陵各大学，并且访问几位现在假期中的联大老教授，劝他们返校，顺便还看看北大、清华两校的毕业同学在各地服务的状况。自然，在公事方面他们两位是主角，我不过负着一小部分任务罢了。

二 从昆明到重庆

从5月初起就开始为定飞机票忙，连自己带朋友不知跑了多少趟中国航空公司，好容易才买到5月16日的三张票。哪知道到了那一天下午在飞机场等到4点半钟，可是“南京号”飞到后，因为载重过量，驾驶员只准上两个客人，结果只有梅先生和军事委员会一位姓施的空身走成，连一件行李都没准带，毅生和我，都被“刷”下来了！

5月22日下午5点，毅生和我又接到中航的通知，让我们当天夜里3点50分以前到公司。我们匆匆忙忙地把行装收拾好，刚想睡一会儿觉，没想到晚上10点半毅生又接到公司的通知把他一个人推延到28日。挨到夜里3点钟，我独自叫工友挑着行李，步行到宝善街。等到公司的职员慢慢地起来，把邮件和行李过完磅，天已经快亮了。5点钟到了飞机场，又候了45分，“南京号”才从腊戍飞来。那天照公司所排的座位表，我列在第一，可是，这一班的邮件因为积压了两次已经有七百多基罗①，飞机还没来，公司里的一个职员就在那儿说：“今天恐怕又只能走一两位，无论如何罗先生反正走成了。”我心里也在那么想。哪知道飞机到了以后，当真只许上两位客人，同行的里头有一位不大不小的官儿就站起来说：“我们的票是拿卢比买的，

① Kg(Kilogram)，英文公斤缩写。

难道不让我们走吗?”于是就同他的秘书带着从仰光买来的大大小小十几包舶来品,气宇轩昂地大踏步走上了飞机!公司的人既然不敢惹他,只好自己把自己所定的位次表根本推翻。当时我心里气愤非常,很想揪住他问一问:“你所花的卢比难道不是耗费的国币?你既然从腊戍买的通票,到昆明就不该下来,既然要下来就得跟别的客人一律看待。”后来一想,他虽然是贵人多忘事,至少我在南京和北平也还跟他同过几次席,说起来总算是熟人。况且他采办了那么多来路货,万一奉有上命或阃令得克期赶回重庆去交差,若是错过一班,岂不耽误了他的要公?这样一想,只好忍气吞声地仍以礼让为本。横竖秀才遇见官,有理也含冤,他们既然不尊重社会秩序,你可有什么法子?这样一扫兴,我真想根本打消到四川的意思了。

5月28日下午两点我和毅生又到了中航公司,这一天有一架容27个座位的大型机“嘉定号”飞渝,昆明可以上10个客人,4点15分我们居然走成了。同机的熟人只有高韵琇女士和林君文奎给我们介绍的一位彭碧生师长——据说他是在昆仑关立过战功的。6点40分飞机在重庆南纪门外珊瑚坝降落,我们总算安安稳稳地到了陪都。

到重庆后住在黄家垭口中央饭店,当天晚上立刻给梅先生打电话,告诉我们的住址。他住在通远门里市民医院,离我们住的地方很近,第二天早晨他就来看我们。这两个礼拜里他要办的事已经办完,在这里等得很心焦,早就托付重庆清华中学傅任敢校长替我们定舱位,只要有船,立刻就到泸州转叙永。可是这一等又是一个礼拜。直到6月4日晚上11点钟才算在朝天门外磨儿石民生公司第七囤船上了民文轮。

民文轮是民生公司前年新造的船,官舱很干净。不过这一次正赶上有一支从前方调下来的队伍,要到乐山去休息,甲板上横躺竖卧的都是武装同志,简直挤得连走道都没有了。舱里非常闷热,外面又没有回旋的余地,再加上“飞机”和“坦克”上下夹攻,这一宵压根儿没睡着。

三 从重庆到泸州

6月5日上午9点15分船开。太阳被乌云遮着,江上不时地吹来阵阵凉风,比在重庆那几天舒服多了。

下午4点半船到江津,稍停即开,8点半刚到白沙还没靠岸,在朦胧的月色下,忽然传来紧急警报的消息。事后推算,这正是重庆大隧道窒息案发生的时候。昨晚上船以前,舒舍予[老舍]、孙伏园约我们看川戏,假如船期晚一天,同时还有这个约会,说不定我们已经做了窒息鬼了。

在抗战以前凡是坐过民生轮船的,都知道它设备完全,招待周到,注意卫生,伙食适口,并且处处为旅客的方便设想,连寄信,打电报,到码头的接送全都照顾到。可是我们这两天在船上所感受的却和从前大不相同。头等舱也还设备着洗澡间和冲水马桶,不过洗澡盆变成统舱客人洗衣裳的工具,冲水马桶壅塞得涓滴不通、臭气熏天。假如你有点感冒,只要到厕所方便一下,管保不吃阿司匹灵就可以蒸得发汗,至于在这米珠薪桂的时候,伙食当然推板,那更用不着说。民文算是民生公司现在顶好的一只船,它尚且这样,其余的更可想而知了。自然,在这抗战的时候,船只缺乏,旅客拥挤,不能照太平年月那样,也是势所必至的,可是假使员司得人,管理得法,在可能的范围里也未尝不可整顿一下,好维持民生公司以往的令誉。现在听说卢作孚[卢魁先]先生要摆脱一切,仍旧整顿公司的业务,这一点很值得我们佩服。个人对于他手创的事业,无论到什么时候都得像爱惜自己子女那样的亲切。自然卢君现在的地位和声望已经超出这个初创的事业以外,不过对于这个头生爱子总得要始终爱护的。

6日晨4点半船从白沙开,下午3点半到合江。这个地方出产荔枝,每斤索价三元。听本省人说,现在还不大熟,味酸不好吃,所以没敢尝试,回想起增城的挂绿和广州的糯米糍来,真不禁馋涎欲滴。5点半到泸州,靠馆驿嘴码头,叙永分校同事黄中孚来接。上岸后他押着行李找旅馆,我们先到中平远路峨岷体育社去等他。这个地方是杨子惠做永宁道尹的时候建筑的,里面有茶社、酒家、宿舍、理发店、沐浴室、照相馆、体育场等,颇有小公园的规模。待一会儿中孚来了,一同到体育社对面的中央酒家吃晚饭。这家馆子的老板是绍兴人,堂倌是常州人,听着吴语的腔调,尝着下江的口味,真不禁有"忆江南"的感想。刚吃完饭,第七区张清源专员来看梅先生。张专员是河北定兴人,在北平的时候曾经和马伟青等合办平民中学,说起来也是同行。去年分校成立时,承他帮忙不少。9点30分,街上忽传有预行警报,店铺纷纷闭门,我们到峨岷社后面的上海快活林去喝茶,预备有空袭警报再一同到专员公署去躲避。在月色朦胧楠木高耸的露天茶座里品茗清谈,不由得想起古柏参天、朱甍碧瓦的北平中央公园来了。后来知道所传的警报是一场虚惊,我们便回到江边大来宾馆去休息。

6月7日上午9点,中孚领着我们登中山去答拜张专员,谈了半点多钟,就从三岩脑渡江搬到蓝田坝中国旅行社。这里房间清洁,招待周到,定价低廉,比旁家旅馆好得多了。经理薛卓钧,南开出身,人很精明强干。12点50分有空袭警报,我们躲在房后山上一间茅屋旁边的楠木底下,没多大工夫就解除了。

6月8日中午纳溪、泸州的清华同学会在旅行社公宴梅先生,约毅生和我作陪。饭后,梅先生报告西南联大的近况,并勉励清华同学努力做社会上的中级干部,不可想做大官。5点多才散会。承李忍涛先生答应借我们一辆小汽车，9日就可以到叙永了。

四 叙永的一周间

6月9日10点半从中国旅行社出发，顺着川滇公路南行，路旁遍种着桂圆树，绿莹莹地结实累累，颇有点儿南国的风味。这天正赶上个浓云蔽日的阴天，车开起来，风飕飕地吹动了衬衫，身上登时爽快好多。过纳溪县后，沿着永宁河纡曲前进，水转澄碧，山渐奇峭，田禾盈畴，地无隙壤。连山坡河埂都密匝匝地种满了庄稼，真正可算是善用地利了。毅生说，诸葛武侯在北伐以前，恐怕拿一隅的蜀地去抵抗中原，资源或有不济，于是先休养生息三年然后出兵，所以《蜀志·后主传》有“二年春，务农殖谷，闭关息民”的记载。地利的开发，或者从那时候起。途中经过渠坝驿、大洲驿、上马场、九鼎山等。九鼎山上有关于吴三桂的遗迹，因为要下车过河，颇费时间，我们就没能去凭吊。下午1点50分到江门，午尖，两点半继续前进。路过马岭，是前北大教授张真如的故里；兴隆场，是黄季陆[黄学典]的故里。车子都匆匆开过，没能停留。4点半到叙永车站，有联大分校庶务员罗岐生来接，他已经在中国旅行社替我们定好房间了。旅行社是就着古万寿寺改造的，清洁幽静，胜于泸州。经理虞伟如比泸州的薛卓钧还透着干练。他在院子里给我们布置了一个露天客厅，席棚虽然没遮好，可是铺着地毡，摆着藤椅，亦堂皇，也雅致，简直不像是僻处川南的内地样儿。

当晚会到杨今甫[杨振声]先生，国文系的同人也找我来谈这一年来大一国文的授课情形。夜里下了很大的雨，盖着棉被还嫌冷，这是我入川以来第一次感觉到的一点儿秋意。

“万寿朝霞”算是叙永八景之一，可是第二天起来仍然落雨，因此我们虽然住在古万寿寺的遗址也不能领略这个风景究竟有什么好看。我们因为急于想看一看分校的种种,9点钟就冒着雨进城,道路泥泞非常难走。叙永有两个城:永宁河东是旧永宁县城,河西是旧叙永厅城。关于它们建置的沿革,吴辰伯[吴晗]在《星期评论》上有一篇很详细的考证,这里就不再复述了。联大分校所占的地方一共有六处:东城两处,总办公处在县文庙,女生宿舍在帝主宫;西城四处,先修班在府城隍庙,教室和工学院宿舍在南华宫,教职员和大部分学生宿舍在春秋祠,图书馆和实验室在天上宫。春秋祠原来是陕西会馆,建筑得很宏丽,朱甍碧瓦,画栋雕梁,真有点儿像北平的几个大祠宇。其中有一座祀神的戏台,栏杆上刻着全部关羽事迹,雕工精致得很,拿它来做宿舍未免有点儿可惜。我们9点半到总办公处,由杨今甫、褚士荃领导着视察各部分,并到春秋祠拜访各位同人。下午4点钟梅先生在寓所召集分校校务委员会,报告常务委员会对于下年度分校问题考虑的经过,今甫因为突发高热没能出席。

6月11日10点40分我在县文庙里的第二十教室讲演"中国人与中国文",为的是让一般学生知道大一国文的重要性,并略述西南联大文学院中国文学系和师范学院国文学系的近况。听众约五百人,一年级的学生大部分都到了。12点20分有空袭警报,下午3点紧急,3点40分解除。这里的同人和学生对于警报看得并不十分严重,除去少数见"机"而作、不俟终日的朋友,大部分都不躲避。这种镇定是不足为训的。大凡住在一个没被轰炸过的城市里的人们,差不多都有这种态度。可是一旦遭遇空袭就会受很多无谓的牺牲。以往的嘉定、泸州便可以当做殷鉴。所以梅先生在第二天的国民月会里郑重地提出这个意思来请大家注意。4点梅先生约分校全体同人和各家眷属在中国旅行社茶会。7点中国文学系同人在四川旅行社招待我晚餐,席间就便问起讲读的进度、作文的次数、分组的标准和各组学生的程度。我很高兴本系这几位同人都能在杨今甫、彭啸咸[彭仲铎]两先生领导之下,努力合作,各尽本分。

12日上午10点冒雨进城到南华宫参加国民月会,梅先生报告总校状况,并告诫学生对于选择院系应就个人才性、学力和整个的学术前途着想,不可很短视地只注意到眼前的出路。午后3点清华同学会在南华宫招待梅先生,北大同学会在城东公园复兴亭招待毅生和我。毅生报告学校南迁以后的状况。我说学校是一个有机体,要求它的发展,得仗着每个细胞都能各尽本分。大家应当继续发扬北大的"大"处,贯彻蔡孑民[蔡元培]先生遗留给我们的"博大和坚贞"的精神,还得要不流于散漫懈怠。此外译学馆的老同学谢孜端[谢式瑾]和吴之椿、程毓淮两位教授都有演说,程先生的话尤为诚恳动人。

13日天已转晴。下午3点历史学会代表许受谔约毅生和我在二十教室演讲。毅生讲"研究历史应注意的几点",摭出叙永史地就近举例,颇为动听。我的讲题是"读书八式",共分涵泳自得、采花酿蜜、剥茧抽丝、磁石引铁、披沙拣金、郢书燕说、过眼云烟、捋摭饾饤八目。第一式为爱好文艺,或性近玄思的来说;第二式为铢积寸累,日知其所无,月无忘其所能的来说;第三式为钻研一题,逐渐深入的来说;第四式为学有重心,左右逢源的来说;第五式为信手翻检,摭拾菁华的来说;第六式为穿凿附会,自欺欺人的来说;第七式为随眼滑过,不求甚解的来说;第八式为剽窃陈言,因袭堆砌的来说。这无非想指出几种念书的方法来,好教学生知道怎样抉择。听众约三百余人。讲毕汗流浃背,辰伯在西南餐厅招待冷饮。晚6点访今甫谈总校中国文学系近况,并询问分校大一国文的各种问题。

14日决定返泸州。上午11点从中国旅行社出发,黄中孚、陈耕陶同行。下午1点半抵大洲驿,茶尖。大洲驿的对岸就是护国镇,从前叫做叙蓬溪。1916年护国之役蔡松坡[蔡锷]的司令部曾经设在这个地方,因此才改成现在的名称。在大洲驿河边的"护国岩"上面还刻着蔡松坡的题字。两点多钟到花背溪参观汪殿华主持的化验室。李忍涛、杨昌龄、姚筱端三位昨晚从古宋赶来,也在这里等候我们。这个地方楠木高耸,丛竹遍山,背岭临溪,非常幽静。6点半渡河登车,忍涛领导我们到双河场参观他所领导的一部分学生们住处,所有寝室、游艺室、讲堂、厨房等都做到纪律化、整洁化的地步。参观完了和忍涛握别,送昌龄、筱端回纳溪。8点多才赶回蓝田坝。

五 十二天的沉闷生活

回到泸州以后,原定遇着便车先到成都,转峨眉,过嘉定,然后坐船顺岷江而下到叙府,再转李庄,返重庆。可是从6月15日到26日不幸碰上八天阴雨,不单公路局的客车一律停开,连其他的运输车或商车也找不着一辆。中孚一向有"泸州通"的雅号,他走在街市上,过不了三步就得碰见一个熟人,大部分店铺对于他都有个点头的交情;而且张专员是他的老师,警察局长樊奎是他的亲戚;到了西南运输处和航空委员会,他还可以拿出客家式的广府话来叙一叙乡里。因此去年分校成立的时候,教职员学生在泸州找车,很得到他不少的帮助。——可是这一回他虽然费尽了"牛"劲,想尽了方法,结果还是急得一筹莫展。在这12天里,我们天天作走的打算,可是天天走不成功,濡滞焦灼无可如何,在我们这次旅程中算是最沉闷的一段。

6月15日早8点,吴敬直派人约梅先生和我们三个到罗汉场去玩。梅先生坐滑竿先从小道走了。我和毅生、中孚渡江到泸州,再从馆驿嘴过渡到罗汉场。刚登岸就看见"敌机入川"的黄旗,12点半接着发了空袭警报,我们赶紧步行五里多路才到了吴宅。这里门禁森严,遇到警报尤其紧张。中孚在门口给敬直打电话,打了好久,杨幼民和吴宅的佣人才把我们领进去。罗汉场是泸州最宽敞的田坝，敬直管领的一部分，占地 1800 多亩，面江环山，远离市廛，是一个可以安心工作的地方，在这里会到许多研究化学工程的朋友，大致都是由清华、北大和浙江高工三校出身的。下午淋浴一次，把几天来的黏汗和污垢都洗净了。晚间住在青冈寺新建筑的宿舍。天气闷极，电扇一直开到 12 点钟，还是热得睡不着觉。

在罗汉场的第二天，由那里的几位朋友引导，看了许多地方，得了许多知识。像我这样和理工隔离很远的人，才知道蔗糖、食盐、棉花、硫磺有那么许多妙用，颇悔自己在故纸堆里翻了半生筋斗，对于自然界许多现象却完全忽略了。

到罗汉场后曾经打过几次电话接洽车子，但是毫无结果，心里着急非常。17 日一早起来就想回蓝田坝去亲自进行。8 点半敬直和幼民冒着雨送我们到码头，大家的周身衣服都淋湿了。这时候大雨滂沱、江流汹涌，眼看着一只小船从小米滩打落到泰安场。梢公畏难，不肯开船，我们也面面相觑的略有戒心，于是敬直又挽劝我们折回他的家里。午饭后再返寓所休息。下午 3 点半幼民带着三架滑竿接我们到码头，敬直和许多朋友又都冒着雨送行。4 点 10 分船开。船上共有九名船夫：掌舵的梢公是一个将近五十岁的小老头儿，留着两撇小黑胡髭，戴着斗笠，披着蓑衣，一边把舵，一边摇橹，态度非常安闲。其余的八名都是年轻力壮的小伙子，体格健全，精神活泼，身上只穿着短裤和背心，周身的筋肉很壮美地暴露着，假使我是个画家或雕刻家，眼前便摆着几个现成的“模特儿”。这时候江水高涨，势颇险急，逆流而行，很感觉紧张吃力。沿江一共经过五个险滩，现在还叫得上名儿来的，有小米滩、黄滩、土地滩等。每到过滩的时候，梢公在后边定准舵的方向，控制着纤绳的长短，还得高声喊叫，指挥伙计。这时候他的脸部表情虽然没有平常那么安闲，可是急而不迫，忙而不乱，很够一个遇到艰难困苦时候的领袖样儿。另外一个人在船头执篙支撑着船身,不让它撞到石头上,遇到滩更险急的当儿他便跳下水去,用手来推挽。其余的七个人都上岸去拉纤,有时候全身俯伏地上,手足并用,竭尽全身的力量和梢公呼应着,才能渡过难关。过了险滩后,梢公的态度照常安闲起来,那拉纤的七个人也一齐跳到船上摇桨唱歌,其声"邪许",词意不甚可辨;每到兴至的时候,他们便"手之舞之,足之蹈之"地锐声急呼。这不过是精神发扬起来,好抵抗逆流的阻力罢了。合起这九个人的力量来,虽然尽力支撑着,可是船到了泸州的民生码头已经6点多了。梢公因为天晚流急,不肯再把我们送到蓝田坝。不得已冒雨登岸,乘车到三崖脑,匆匆忙忙地上了一个渡船。这个船上的船夫年老性贪,正赶上他渡客的"轮子",一定不肯"单推"。在江流涨得这么大,天这么黑的时候,他还不怕载重过量,极力招揽客人;而且一个人独力支撑着,闹得前后不能相顾,走了没多远就搁浅了。幸而仗着一个同船的帮他在前边摇,他在后面撑,才勉勉强强地放到金鸡渡。在黑暗中冒雨上坡,几乎失足落水。金鸡渡离蓝田坝还有五里,我们登岸后,在大雨中,上头淋着,底下趿着,暗中摸索地走了这么远的陌生的泥途,这真是生平第一次经验。8点40分到了蓝田坝,简直淋得像水鸡子一般,赶紧跑到一家北方馆子一品香去吃晚饭,喝了一点烧酒,回到中国旅行社又洗了一个热水澡,幸而算是没得了pneumonia(肺炎)。

18日、19日两天在旅行社闲待着,更觉得沉闷焦急。20日上午4点多钟起来解手,忽然觉得右脚作疼,起床以后更加厉害,用热水烫洗也不见效。10点多钟社中纷传有空袭警报,我勉强拄着手杖,一瘸一拐地走到后面的坟山里去躲避。11点果然敲了紧急警报的钟,刚过十分钟就听见机声隆隆在云层里飞向西南去。12点20分又有敌机四架从头上飞过去,过了20分钟有三架又折回来,不知究竟是敌机还是我机。下午1点半回到社里吃午饭,没有多久警报就解除了。3点,中孚催我们过江说是在那边等车比较方便。于是带着行李从蓝田坝过渡到澄溪口。我走路时右脚疼极了,上下船更感觉困难,过江后雇着一辆车才到了福来饭店。这家饭店里人声嘈杂、茶房傲慢,费了许多时候,也找不着合适房间。后来中孚托某侦缉队长向账房去谈,他们才答应在1点钟后给我们腾出三间房来,暂时先开了一间房让我们休息一下。这时候我的右脚还疼,于是跑到后面浴室去洗澡,让一个搓背的用虎骨酒揉了几下居然松快许多。晚饭以后房间仍无着落,毅生索性搬到大来宾馆去了。中孚又向柜房交涉,算是给我让出一间房来。这间房潮湿湫隘,蚊帐离着床有三尺多远,此外只有一张打牌桌和四个小凳,我因为脚疼带累得非常疲倦,急不暇择地就住了。谁知睡下以后,店中附设海国春饭馆喧嚣狂喊,简直吵得不能成眠。夜里大约1点多钟忽然有人来敲我的房门,和茶房吵着要房,我只好充耳不闻置之不理。这个饭店是当地师部某处长开的。我在民文轮上的时候,同舱一位彭参谋就介绍它是泸州第一家旅馆,我前一次过泸州还有些"心向往之",现在才知道这原来是泸州的"租界",对于我们这班过路的老实客人是不大欢迎的。

31日上午我和梅先生也搬到大来宾馆,以避喧嚣。在这里一直等了五天,到内江的车子还是渺无消息。这几天真沉闷极了。每日三餐差不多都在本地小馆子"成都味"饱尝过江豆花、甜咸烧白、麻婆豆腐、豆瓣鲢鱼等等川味。22日上午冒着雨在中央银行躲了一次警报;23日和26日两天又在新村东华建筑公司躲了两次警报,把饶辅民和唐邻岳两位工程师搅扰得不轻,而且在土人所谓"蛮子洞"(实际就是最古代的崖墓)里躲避过三个钟头。24日冒雨登白塔寺废墟,俯瞰长江、沱江汇流的状况。起初一股黄流,一股碧流,各不相混地显然分开;乍汇合的当儿,碧流还没完全汩没了它的本色,渐渐地因为黄流水大,原来的澄碧终于变成浑黄,再想分别哪是长江,哪是沱江,就很不容易了。25日好不容易碰到了晴天,我们便乘兴到三崖脑湖北茶社去临眺长江,看看不舍昼夜的滚滚江流,持续地在动,不停地在变。当它遇到滩石,碰着暗礁,也会激起些波漩,可是转瞬间还不是立即消逝吗?悟得此理,那么人生还有什么值得沾滞?

26日躲完警报以后,实在不愿意再这样不进不退地沉闷下去了,我们三个人商量的结果,决定第二天跟辅民、邻岳结伴先赴李庄。于是这12天的僵局才算打开了。

六 闷热的板栗坳

6月27日,夜里3点半,从大来宾馆赶到合众码头,上长丰轮,中孚来送行。长丰是往来泸州、叙府之间的小船,每礼拜可以往返三次。船上客人挤极了,我们把行李下舱后,勉强在尾楼找到四个位子,坐下去立刻就转动不灵无回旋的余地。5点25分开船,太阳没出来以前,江风吹得颇有寒意。沿途经过纳溪、大渡口、二龙口,并没有客人上船。到了江安突然上来不少香客,大约有廿多人,船上越发挤得连站脚的地方都没有了。这时候船身有点儿载重过量,两边的客人站得稍欠平衡便常有倾侧的现象。一个秃顶的老旅客急得打着川腔大声唤起同船人们的注意,怕是出了意外的危险!幸而下午1点25分到南溪,又过了两个半钟头就拢了李庄。船到李庄并不靠码头,仍然"开慢车"走着,只有一个小摆渡用竹篙钩住船帮,旅客先匆匆忙忙地下到小船上,然后才能拢岸。这种下船法,船上人叫做"递漂儿";乍一听起来颇有点儿担心,及至身临其境,也就平平稳稳地登岸了。

国立中央研究院历史语言研究所的所址在板栗坳,离李庄镇还有八里多。我们下船后雇了两个挑夫担着行李,慢慢地跟着他们走。离开市镇,先穿行了一大段田埂,约有半点钟的光景,到了半山的一个地方叫木鱼石,已经汗流浃背,喘得上气不接下气。躲在一棵榕树荫下休息了一会儿等汗干了,才继续登山。又拐了三个弯儿,已经看不见长江了,汗也把衬衫浸透了,还看不见一所像样儿的大房子。再往前走到了一个众峦环拱的山洼里,才算找到板栗坳的张家大院。

板栗坳的住户都姓张,他们的祖先是在张献忠乱后搬到此地的。它的区域里房子很多,史语所一共租了桂花坳、田边上、朝门口、牌坊头、戏楼院、新房子等六所。我和毅生住牌坊头的花厅院,梅先生住在朝门口的李方桂先生家里。牌坊头是清朝咸丰年间奋武校尉张繁先建造的。他的官虽然不大,房子却盖得很堂皇。只可惜当年对于通风透光的设计太不讲究,所以大部分房间差不多是既闷且暗。那天晚上温度表始终没降到90度[①] 以下,热得我通宵没睡着。

28日上午董彦堂[董作宾]先生引导我们参观戏楼院第三组办公室,他的房里遍处都是天算材料,这位甲骨文专家的兴趣,至少暂时是从乌龟壳儿跳到天文台上去了。后来又到新房子参观别藏书库和第一组办公室。下午4点,方桂领我们到田边上参观西文书库、第二组办公室和北京大学文科研究所办事处,北京大学文科研究所的学生留在李庄的有任继愈、马学良、刘念和、李孝定四个人。马、刘两君受李方桂、丁梧梓[丁声树]两先生指导,李君受董彦堂先生指导,李、董、丁三位先生对于他们都很恳切热心。据马君告诉我说,李先生常常因为和他讨论撒尼语里面的问题竟致忘记了吃饭,这真当得起"诲人不倦"四个字。任君研究的题目是《理学探源》,他在这里虽然没有指定的导师,可是治学风气的熏陶,参考图书的方便,都使他

① 指华氏度。

受了很大的益处。这一天听说有空袭警报，但是史语所同人仍然照常工作并没受影响，专从这一点来说，就比住在都市里强得多。天还是照常闷热，汗不断地在淌，中午太阳晒在背上好像火烤一样。

29日上午9点，彦堂领着我们到石崖湾社会科学研究所。毒花花的太阳在头上晒着。走了四里坑坎崎岖的小路，一只手撑着伞，一只手拄着杖，在狭窄的田埂上走的时候，虽然不至于“如临深渊，如履薄冰”那样恐惧，可是两只眼睛老得看着道儿，时常有“人莫踬于山，而踬于垤”的戒惕。这时候即使有好的风景也顾不得欣赏了。11点到社会所，会到陶孟和先生并参观汤象龙、梁方仲两君的工作室。孟和先生的住处和社会所的大部分本来在门官田，那里更偏僻难走，假定关在家里不出门，简直就可以和外界隔绝，所以社会所同人管这一个所长官舍叫做“闷官田”。我们走到石崖湾后又热又累，休息许久，还止不住出汗。幸亏这几位社会学家晓得民间疾苦，他们用凉水浸湿了手帕，换替着让我们揩汗。可是中午到镇上吃了一次饭，刚吹干了的汗衫又湿透了。10点多钟有空袭警报，11点和下午1点半听见两次很厉害的轰炸声音。据住在李庄的人说，这是轰炸重庆的回响，第二天一对报纸所记的空袭时间，果然不错，可是我们在泸州为什么反倒听不见呢？下午到羊街去看李济之[李济]、梁思永先生。思永的胃病好多了，精神也颇好；济之还像从前那么胖，在这室内温度高到106度的热天，他未免有点儿受罪。

30日，上午9点，方桂陪着我们到上坝参观中央博物院和营造学社。梁思成夫人林徽因女士搬到四川不久就患气管炎，缠绵病榻已经半年多了。我们看她去的时候，她正在院子里躺在帆布床上晒太阳，虽然脸色稍显憔悴，声音略带喑哑，可是还像好着时候一样的健谈。说起她的弟弟在成都殉国的情形来，又兴奋又伤感，在我们告辞以前简直没法儿止住她的谈锋。11点15分又听见轰炸重庆的声音，比前一次更显着清楚。当天留在济之家里并没有回板栗坳。

7月1日，上午10点，再到石崖湾访孟和先生，在极热的天气下，听梁方仲谈陕北的情形，凌纯声谈滇缅勘界的故事，好像服了清凉散一样，给我们祛除了不少的暑气。下午7点，返牌坊头，和10位北大同学谈到10点多才睡。

2日上午，约刘君念和来，评订他所作的《史记汉书文选旧音辑证》。关于中国音韵史的研究，清代几位汉学家在周秦一部分已经有过很大的贡献，汉魏以下从前还没有人注重过。顾亭林作《唐韵正》间或采取《经典释文》，洪亮吉作《汉魏音》仅只收集一些读若譬况的旧读，都不能算是系统的研究。我所从事的《经典释文》音切考和汉魏六朝韵谱，周君祖谟从《万象名义》里钩稽原本《玉篇》的音系，都是朝着这个方向走的。刘君这种工作，从前吴承仕的《经籍旧音》也收集了一部分，不过《经籍旧音》只印了《叙录》一卷，其余的究竟做到什么程度，一直到吴君已经盖棺论定我们还没看见。所以刘君不妨仍旧作他的独立研究。他这篇论文一共收了服虔、应劭、郑氏、李奇、苏林、如淳、孟康、韦昭、晋灼、郭璞、徐广、裴骃、邹诞生、萧该14家，每家各分上下两卷，上卷为音录，汇列直音和反切，下卷为音证比勘当人读音和《广韵》切语的异同。可惜各家的音切最多不过四百多条，少的才三十几条，要想把各家的音切系联成贯借以考见他的声韵系统事实上是不可能的。就大体上看来，各家和《广韵》相同的十之六七，不同的只有十之三四。不同的原因，一曰字有假借，注家以本字读之（例如，《汉书·杜周传》"因势而抵陒"服虔注"陒音羲"。按，抵陒义为击，《广韵》作㩟，与羲音同，注"击也"。《集韵》陒有虚宜一音，为擨之重文，注"毁也，通作㩟"）；一曰义有难解，注家改字读之（例如，《汉书·礼乐志》"吟青黄"服虔注"吟音含"。按，吟之音含，非拟其音，乃易其字，此与郑康成注《三礼》之"读为"例同。服盖读吟为函容之函,或含嗛之含也);一曰字具数义,注家分别其音(例如,《汉书·高帝纪》"高祖常告归之田"服虔注"告音如嗥呼之嗥"。按,《集韵》告有乎刀一音,重文有勂,注:"休谒也,《汉书》'告归之田',或从刀作韧。"休谒之告音读为嗥,服氏当时盖有此语以别于告语之告,故据以释《汉书》,此即异义异音之例);一曰人名地名随其方俗之呼(例如《汉书·地理志》"乐浪郡黏蝉"服虔注"蝉音提",按,《集韵》蝉有田奚一音,注"黏提县名,在乐浪",又《汉书·古今人表》"冷沦氏"服虔注"沦音鳏"。按,《集韵》沦有姑顽一音,注"姓也,古有冷沦氏")。凡此四类其读音之异俱不足以为推究作者当时声韵之据。刘君最初的目的,本来想"考镜汉魏六朝之音读",可是最后所得的结果只是"辑成专篇,易于省览,慎审比勘,正其讹文。世之治汉魏六朝音韵学者欲取三书旧音以为佐证,略省翻检之劳,稍减校雠之苦"罢了。本来整理史料的工作,只要能"如实地"把它胪列出来,在这门学问的本身上就是一种贡献;若是超出材料的范围牵强附会地去臆断,即使有非常可喜的意见也等于在沙漠上盖房子。因此我认为刘君的研究结果还是成功的,只批示十点意见让他依照修改。

下午看杨光先所作的《不得已》两本。去年冬天我整理昭雪汤若望文件里的罗马对音,急需参考这部书,一直到这时候才能看到,可见现在做学问的困难了。清初这场教案闹了许久,株连得很多。要判定它的是非曲直,第一牵涉历法问题。还诚如当时议政王大臣所说:"历法神微,难以遽定。"在他们争议不已的时候,康熙帝深感"己所未学,不能定其是非",于是"发愤研讨,卒能深造密微,穷极其阃奥"。可见这件事是不能凭空臆断的。关于这一点我很希望彦堂能够发表一点儿意见。第二还得明了当时的政治背景。在杨光先一方面斥天主教为妄言惑众,蓄意谋叛;在南怀仁一方面又说杨光先依附鳌拜、紊乱历法、诬陷无辜。他们的真相如何,我在这里且不多说外行话,留给研究清史的朋友去解决。我只根据何大化(R.P. Antonius de Gouvea)所印 *Innocentia Victrix* 里面的对音材料作了一篇《耶稣会士在中国音韵学上的贡献补》,为的是和我从前根据《程氏墨苑》里利玛窦的《罗马字对音》及金尼阁的《西儒耳目资》所作的那篇文章互相印证,好把清初的官话系统弄得更清楚一点儿。我所以能写成这篇文章,还得谢谢向觉明[向达]先生供给我那一批珍贵的材料。

晚上和史语所十几位老同事在牌坊头的堂前聚谈。上弦月穿过乔楠的枝叶,疏影洒在地上,大家有说,有笑,有唱,也庄,也谐,也雅。不由得想起广州东山的柏园,北平北海静心斋的叠翠楼和罨画轩,蚕坛的"董西厢",东单牌楼的洋溢胡同,上海小万柳堂的帆影枞和南京的北极阁。一晃儿又过了快十年了。

3 日,上午,约马君学良来,评订他所作的《撒尼倮语语法》。撒尼是倮倮族的一个支名,他们居住的区域以云南的路南、宜良、泸西、陆良等县和昆明近效的几个村落较多。这篇文章的材料是从路南县城东南 30 里的黑泥村得来的。前人关于撒尼语的研究当以法教士邓明德(Paul Vial)所著的 *Dictionnaire français-lolo, dialecte gni* 一书所包含的材料最为丰富,并且还收有倮倮的文字,这是研究倮倮语言文字不可少的一部书。但是这部书里关于语音的记载并没有详细的说明,有些地方还有把不同的音类混而为一的嫌疑。而且据他自己说,他的字典不是根据一个地方的方言,有时采取甲一个地方的读音,有时又拿乙一个地方的方言作标准。他为各地实用方便起见,原没有大妨碍,但在音韵系统上就未免有些混乱了。马君在 1930 年春天曾经跟着李方桂先生由昆明到路南县的尾则村去调查撒尼语言,回昆明后,李先生就让他重订 Vial 氏的字典。后来他又找到一位黑泥村的发音人把这部字典重理了一过,并且增补了许多词汇,另外又记录了五十几则故事和风俗谜语等,这些材料足够他研究撒尼语言的音韵、词汇和语法之用。现在所提出的只是音韵和语法两部分,约占论文全部的二分之一。他根据李先生研究汉藏语语法的新见解(参看《北京大学文科研究所讲演集》第一辑《汉藏系语言的研究法》)把词类分为名词、数词、谓词、助词、感叹词五类,把句法分为主要成分、附加成分、疑问句、复句、重叠语五项;完全从这种语言本身的结构去归纳各词的形式和作用。单就这一点来看,就比因袭印欧语语法去照猫画虎的强多了。李先生对我说,他这篇论文在已经出版的关于倮倮语的著作里算是顶好的。这虽然含着奖掖后学的意思,但是我看过论文初稿后,也觉得李先生的话不算是十分阿好或过誉。我一方面佩服马君钻研的辛勤,一方面更感谢李先生指导的得法。自从几个文化团体流亡到西南后,大家对于研究汉藏系的语言颇感觉浓厚的兴趣。但是我们却不想一个人包揽好些种语言,我们只想训练几个年轻的朋友各走一条路,然后汇总去作比较的研究。这几年来,除马君外,还有陈三苏女士治苗语,傅懋勣君治倮倮语和么些语,张琨君治摆夷语和民家语,邢庆兰[邢公畹]君治仲家和水户语,葛毅卿君治苗瑶语,高华年君治纳苏语和窝尼语,都有相当的成绩。当这抗战期间,图书仪器俱感缺乏的时间,这也算是我们这一行的一点儿意外的收获。

下午4时毅生约集方桂、彦堂、梧梓开北京大学文科研究所导师会议,决定任、马、刘三生的口试办法。天还是照旧热,室内温度上午92度,中午96度。

4日上午,约任君继愈来评订他所作的《理学探源》。他在论文节要里自述宗旨说:“治哲学史首在辨其异同。同者何?心也,理也。异者何?象也,迹也。凡人同具此心则同具此理,语其真际东圣西圣若合符节。万民虽众,即是一人之心;百世虽久,即是当下之理。万象森然不碍其为一本,此即所谓同。理诚一矣,然其表诠之际,其语言文字之习惯,当前所受之尘境,问题之结症,则各民族社会不尽同,各人亦异,故西洋印度各有其精神面貌,则所谓象也,迹也,此其所以异也。""既明理一分殊,则见千万变化而不离其宗。先秦诸子开后来各派之先河,虽多引而未发不若后来哲学之精析详明,而其规模大体已具,所见者大,所涉者广,此肇造之基也。先秦诸子开其规模之大,两汉诸儒绎其条目之繁,先秦众派分流,两汉杂融并收,其开拓之功亦不可忽。魏晋玄学会通儒家大易,道家老庄,超出汉儒天人感应,阴阳五行谶纬之说,由宇宙生成之研究进而究心性之要旨与宇宙之本真,旨弥远而义弥精。而佛家空宗东渐,正值此土玄风昌炽之时,不谋而合,相得益彰。无佛法之东来,玄学或将不如此之盛;无玄学之基础,佛法纵来亦不能行:此种演进,诚乃必然而自然。隋唐之际,佛教大行,东土固有学术反似暗然无光,习而不察,莫不知此为中国文化中绝时期,实则不然。隋唐时最大宗派有四:天台、华严、法相、禅宗是也。仅法相一宗极近印度宗风,故不久即消绝而不复振。其余三宗皆为中国思想,谓之为佛学影响中国,勿宁谓之为中国改造佛学,为更近理也。宋兴百年,儒家复振于五代禅宗鼎盛之后,袭魏晋之玄风,承孔孟之余绪,于理气性命心体善恶之问题,作一空前之总结束。从此内之如心性之源,外之如造化之妙,推之为修齐治平,存之为格致诚正,无不极其广大精微。此仍为一理一贯发展之迹,非自外来也。"他又说:"哲学思想发展之序莫不相反相成,迭为消长。后一时期之得,即前一时期之失,此前一时期之失,即是由于修正其以往之失误而来。先秦诸家引而未发,两汉诸儒推演其修理之极致,调和其门户之异同,自有其长;其失则流为繁芜,将哲学之理致说成科学之知解,即阴阳五行之天道观是也。强为调和门户之异同,则失之杂糅而不能融化,《吕览》、《淮南》是也。魏晋玄学救叱流失,去其固执繁琐,廓清其牵强附会,而济之以清通简易,由宇宙论进而为本体论,汉儒之蔽去矣;其失则在外世遗俗流为空谈,侈于虚胜,乃有本末夷夏之争,常现大小之辩,六家七宗各标悬解,南北两统竞立宗风。是以隋唐佛学代兴,虽不黜发义解,然其救玄学之流失故尚章句之学,重禅戒之行,立判教之义,和诸家之争,此又一修正改进之迹也。其失也,则为滞守文句,养成经生,将失蹄筌之旨;专注禅定又易流于偏枯,判教之说与义理关涉甚少,矫此流失,禅学以兴。禅学初祖菩提达摩似不能与天台之智𫖮、华严之法藏、法相之玄奘相提并论,且为魏晋文学之士所不齿,及五传之后守则蔚为大宗,风靡天下。盖其直指本源,明心见性,易简工夫正可对治前期支离之失也。然行之既久,不免走作,疑似之际则有浮光掠影之讥。一棒一喝,可作一时权教之药饵,疑不可为长久施教之法,为求解脱,反增系缚。是以宋代理学发轫,首排禅学,比之为贼仁害义之杨墨:此又为一改进发展之迹也。"最后总结道:"凡此数端皆此本文所愿阐发之义,求其考订精详则有所未遑,求其史迹纂述则力所未尽,但就问题发展为中心,各家各派为纬,以明其逐步演进之迹,沿流而求源,不以貌似而信其同,不以迹乖而信其异,就哲学思想之本身以显示吾国文化之真精神,此为本文立言宗旨。"任君在汤锡予[汤用彤]、贺自昭[贺麟]两位先生指导之下,两年的工夫居然深造自得,穷源竟委地作出这样一篇论文来,足见他很能沉潜努力。论文全稿虽然还没抄完,看过旨要和纲目也约略可以窥见一斑了。我和他谈完话觉得很满意,只对于全文结构上表示几点意见。

李君孝定今年春天才到李庄,他的研究范围是古文字学。彦堂教他先把甲骨文现有的材料编成一部字典,等完成后,再定论文题目。他能够跟着董先生看到外边罕见的材料,受到踏实谨严的训练,将来的成就应该很有可观的。一晃儿在板栗坳又住了八天。在这酷暑郁蒸的天气下,关在四面不透风的山洼里,也算把要做的事勉强办完了。要想换个地方风凉风凉，决定7月5日还搭长丰轮到叙府去。

七 叙府的三日乡居

7月5日早晨5点钟起来收束行李，7点半从牌坊头动身。史语所的同人有的送到半山茅亭，有的送到上坝，还有一直送到李庄的。下山后又看了看徽因和济之，下午1点半才到江边的轮江茶社去候船。最不敢当的，连那七十多岁的郢客老人也亲自来握手江干，表示惜别的感伤！3点长丰轮到，还用“递漂儿”的法子上船。船上并不太挤，可是好位子都被别人占完了。5点20分到叙府合江门码头，并没看见熟人来接。刚要下船，忽然有一个老头儿嘴里念念叨叨地说：“哪一位是梅校长？”原来是辅民派来接我们的。据他说，邻岳到威远包工去了；辅民和一位邓君廷法已经来接过好几次，全都扑了空。

上岸后，雇黄包车到西门外两路桥白庙子，在路上就看见“敌机入川”的黄旗，到唐家没多久，空袭警报就响了。这里的情报台就在唐家斜对面的翠屏山上，放警哨用手摇机，长短音的界限很不清楚，放哨以外还有四根挂短灯的高杆，遇到警报的时候，按照杆子的顺序，分别警报的缓急，各挂一个红灯：预行挂在第一根杆子上，空袭挂在第二根杆子上，紧急挂在第三根杆子上，解除挂在第四根杆子上。这天晚上空袭以后并没有继发紧急警报就解除了。可是在7点多钟，疏散的群众们都仰着头眼巴巴地看见第三根杆子上的红灯已经挂出来了，不过还都没露出撒腿就跑的慌张神态来，仍旧站在那儿期待着；我想他们这一刹那间的紧张情绪大概也和我差不多。不多一会儿第四根杆子上的红灯，往上一系，蓦然间就听见大家弛放的笑声了。关于这一点,我认为叙府的防空司令部还应该参照昆明或重庆的办法改良一下才好。否则既费杆子又费灯,晚上还得费蜡烛,尤其增加人民不少的紧张恐怖焦急的心情。不知在当地有什么困难没有?

警报解除后,我们和辅民、廷法、唐太太在房子外头乘凉,微风习习的比李庄舒服多了。

6日上午8点半发空袭警报,不大会儿就解除了。天气忽然又闷热起来,早晨室内88度,中午升到93度,热得无可奈何,跑到江边去看游泳,也不觉得凉快。4点多钟到两路桥附近青年服务社附设精益饭店去喝茶。一进门就看见有劈劈拍拍打得正欢的七桌麻将!参加的人物有穿黑烤绸短衫裤的,有穿军服的,有赤着膊只穿一件汗背心的。尤其引我们注意的,其中一桌有四个青年,三男一女,都穿着蓝布长衫,年纪大约在二十上下,看样子很像学生,他们的钞票虽然没有另外那些人的充裕,却也聚精会神地努力从事"上肢部运动",似乎比预备考试勤恳多了。我颇佩服这个饭店对于"青年服务"无微不至。麻将散场之后,那些穿短衣的摆了三桌酒席大吃大喝起来。酒过三巡,菜过五味,一个面带烟容的瘦汉子站起来报告新旧会员的人数和捐款的多少,报告完了,并没听见什么讨论,他们抹抹嘴儿散了,我们也就回去了。这一群人是不是所谓"袍哥儿"呢?

提到"袍哥儿",我们几乎还得借重他们弟兄们呢。5日晚上听说,民生公司到嘉定的船还照常开行。可是6日上午又听说公司里因为好几天没下雨,岷江的水落下六尺多,上行船已经停驶了。假如还继续不下雨,复航的希望简直很少。这个消息传来让我们非常焦灼。要想急着动身,只有坐滑竿走陆路的一个法子。这样不单费钱、吃苦,而且为求路上平安还得找"舵把子"写保险信。"舵把子"是四川哥老会首领的称呼,在会的弟兄叫做"袍哥儿",据说叙府的袍哥儿有仁、义、礼、信四派，下面又分36帮，以“叙荣乐”帮人数最多，它的舵把子在叙府是很站得起来的人物。每帮里有大哥、三哥、五哥，没有二哥、四哥，三哥是担任交际的，五哥是管理事务的。像我们在精益饭店看见的那个瘦汉子，大约就是五哥之流。

没想到我们在叙府会碰着抗战四周年纪念日。这个日子料想不会没警报，果然，7点50分空袭的哨子就响了。8点多听见两次轰炸的声音，据说这还是从重庆传来的回响，和我们在李庄所听到的一样。这是很奇怪的现象。我们在泸州以北从来没听见过这种回响，何以往南到了李庄、叙府反倒听得清楚了呢？这得请研究地理学、地质学、气象学、物理学的专家们给我们解释一下。

警报解除后，辅民从城里回来说，民生公司8日有民教轮上行，不过是差船，不卖客票。我们听见这个消息又喜欢，又担心，姑且拿出泸州中国旅行社经理薛卓钧的介绍信来托人去试试看。下午2点居然买到三张票，并且还饶上中央博物院夏君作铭[夏鼐]的一张。不过因为上游水浅，只到竹根滩为止，而且还没有舱位。可是，无论如何总比在毒花花的太阳底下，坐着滑竿去拜访“袍哥儿”毕竟强得多了。

下午8点钟，晚饭还没吃完，翠屏山上已经挂起一个红灯来了。9点续发空袭警报，我们一直等11点解除后，才叫唐家一个工人挑着行李，打算到洋码头附近的一家旅馆住下，为是第二天清早上船方便一些，谁想刚走过西门里的大观楼，紧急警报突然又响了。吓得我们仓皇失措地急忙花很贵的价钱雇上三辆黄包车又折回白庙子；等了好久，作铭和挑夫才走回来。到夜里1点20分警报才解除，可是时间太晚了，到城里也找不到旅馆，只好还在唐家休息到3点钟。

八 民教轮上

7月8日夜里3点起来,从白庙子步行赶到洋码头,天还没有亮。叙府是川南没经敌人破坏的一个大都市,我们虽然在这儿住了三天,可惜黄昏到来,黎明离去,走马观花简直没能瞻仰它的真面貌。到码头后船还没来,听说是昨晚开到别处避警报去了。4点半船才拢岸,上面拥挤不堪,连站脚儿的地方都没有。我们请梅先生在码头上看着行李,毅生、作铭一件一件地往船上运,我拿着几张凉席和油布去占位子。结果,好不容易挤上船,却没有方寸地被我占到。跑到船顶,看见烟突旁边有很宽敞的一片舱面,并且放着好些竹机,却阒无一人,于是自作聪明地把凉席和油布摊开,占了很大的一片领土,又搬了几张竹机把它围起来,当做"防御工事"。谁想到5点25分开船后,还没过两分钟煤灰已经布满了舱面,我的头发上、脸上和刚搬来的行李上,都洒满了黑渣子。可惜我辛辛苦苦布置的"防线",就这样轻轻易易地被突破了。幸亏曾经骑着骆驼走过撒哈拉大沙漠的田野考古家夏作铭比较机警,他和机器匠交涉,给我们匀出四张铺位来,每人得要另出35元,比票价只少10元。铺位租定,总算稍微可以喘息一下儿了,可是床窄舱矮一共挤下12个人,流品不齐,人声嘈杂,闷在里头也不大舒服。走出来,在甲板上,背着风向,眺望了许久才觉着爽快一点儿。岷江夹岸虽然没有"崇山峻岭",可是随处都可以看见"茂林修竹",满眼绿莹莹的,苍翠可爱。可惜江水仍然浑黄,对于"蜀江水碧蜀山青"那句诗只可以证实一半儿罢了。沿途经过泥溪、月波、麻柳场、么姑沱,并未遇见什么险滩。下午6点50分拢河口,这个地方离叙府260华里,再过20里就可到犍为县了。

船停后,登岸到河口街上想找点东西吃,结果只有"豆浆稀饭"可以充饥，这是岷江沿岸很普罗的食品，我颇欣赏它的物美价廉。饭后坐在江边的沙滩上望月谈天，非常凉爽，不大会儿乌云遮住月光，闪电不住地在远方晃，9点回到船上，12点就下起大雨来了。这时候，卖出铺位躲在舱顶上睡觉的机器匠，都跑进舱里来，地面上的走道全铺满了行李。舱尾的一位女客因为她铺位上的舱顶漏雨，把行李淋湿，便向一个机器匠理论，想找还票价，惹得那个机器匠用轻蔑的口吻讥笑着，好像对于她的职业有相当了解似的。

9日，早晨5点从河口开船，6点半便到了犍为。由这儿到竹根滩只剩下60里，可是沿江却有好几个著名的险滩。7点过乌角墨，江面下潜伏着不少的暗礁，波浪很大，船身有点儿颠簸，水手禁止旅客站在甲板上，一共走了15分钟才算渡过这重难关。10点20分过道士观。这个庙建在江心里的一个山崖上头，水从上游来，冲到山崖下，激起很大的波漩，所以江流非常险急。从前上水的柏木船到这儿往往出事，幸而我们的轮船却平平稳稳地渡过去了。走了一会儿又经过岷江中一个有名的险滩叫岔鱼子，不过水势并不像传闻的那样湍急。11点半就拢了竹根滩。

九　从竹根滩到嘉定

到竹根滩登岸后，因为检查行李耽搁了半点钟。12点从船码头走到“车码头”，雇黄包车到乐山，每辆价18元。竹根滩是岷江沿岸的一个大码头，市面繁荣，街道整齐，比起小县城来还显着富庶。对岸就是五通桥，可惜我们赶路太匆忙，也没能过去看看。事后听说，那里有好些人在期待着我们。沿路看见对岸有好多盐井，老远望起来，又像吸水塔，又像警钟台，恨不能叫车子停下来，过河去看看这个流传已久的制盐土法子。离开竹根滩大约二里多，车子过了一个小渡口，就一直顺着公路走。下午1点50分到牛华溪，这里比竹根滩还要繁荣。车夫领我们到“盐码头”一家叫“味腴”的小馆子去吃午饭，我们四个人随便叫了三个菜，每人要摊到六块多钱；他们几个人尽量吃“帽儿头”的大碗饭，另外还有菜有汤，每人只出两块钱；两下里的收入和消费恰成反比例，难怪有人要叹息“十年寒窗不如一辆胶皮”了。2点50分离牛华溪，3点40分过瓦场坝，茶歇；又翻两个坡就到了乐山县。

乐山是旧嘉定府的首县，城在岷江西岸，南有大渡河，北有青衣江，把它三面包围起来，颇占形胜，我们从大佛寺底下的凌云义渡坐船到对岸。因为四川旅行社没有房间，于是就住在县街的嘉林公寓。晚上武汉大学高公翰[高翰]、方芦浪[方重]、吴子馨[吴其昌]来谈。

7月10日，上午9点到文庙武汉大学去看王抚五[王星拱]、朱孟实[朱光潜]、陈通伯[陈西滢]三先生。抚五穿着一件灰色罗衫，头发全白了，脸下还有好些黑痣。回想20年前，我在北平汉花园的红楼里听他讲科学方法论的时候，他正在革履西装，精神饱满，那是何等少壮英俊！几年没见就变成这样，可见在学校里管行政事务也会让人老得快。孟实虽然两鬓斑白，精神却还焕发。那位好说“闲话”的西滢，虽然唇有黑髭，鬓杂白发，背部也稍微有些拱起，可是一穿起亮纱的蓝衫来，还依稀有点儿当年住在北平东吉祥胡同时候的风度。梅先生向抚五表示联大盼望孟实返校的意思很恳切，抚五正颜厉色地说，“武大对于朱先生比联大更需要，请你们就暂时借给我们几年罢”。于是这一场交涉就这样谈判中止。

下午1点半有空袭警报，等到两点半解除后，武大的陆凤书和桂质廷两位领着我们先到李公祠参观理学院，后来又到观斗山参观工厂，到三育中学参观工学院的实验室。这几部分的仪器和设备都是从珞珈山直接搬运来的，睹物念旧，不禁想起当年武汉大学那样宏丽的建筑,希望不久的将来这些仪器还能装设在他们原来的实验室里。工学院内附设有公路研究室,是武大和乐西公路局合办的,现在对于路面的配合已经有相当的结果。生物系在北斗山上,他们所采集的标本,有许多是别的地方所罕见的。主任张镜澄[张珽]在武大的资格最老;教授钟心煊,1926 年曾经和我在厦门大学同过事,当年是很英挺的,现在也显出老态来了。这天所遇见的几位老朋友都是我自己的镜子,我只看见别人年纪大了,若一反省自己岂不也是华发生颠,年逾不惑了吗?其实,这是不足顾虑的,最可怕的是“不学便老而衰”,只要我们发愤努力,现在正是终身事业的发轫,有几根白发又有什么关系?哪里值得感伤?胡适之[胡适]先生在美国有一首自题照像的诗说:“略有几茎白发,心情微近中年,作了过河卒子,只有努力向前!”这是我们一班中年人应该矜式的。

从北斗山下来,俯瞰大渡河的湍急水势,远远地还看见巍然坐镇在河口的大佛和绿油油一片苍翠欲滴的乌尤山。记得张船山的诗说:“凌云西岸古嘉州,江水潺潺绕郭流。绿影一堆漂不去,推窗三面看乌尤。”到此实地领略,更觉亲切有味。这时虽然汗湿重衫,反倒感觉不出炎暑来了。晚 7 点,抚五、孟实在公园路中西餐馆设宴招待。

早晨 7 点半,到嘉乐门外,去看孟实,并会到陈通伯、朱东润、徐天闵、杨人楩几位和北大中国文学系 1935 年度毕业生丁贤书。东润对于传叙文学很有兴趣,他近来所发表的几篇文章都有相当的价值。武大的中国文学系除东润、天闵以外还有刘博平[刘赜]、刘弘度[刘永济]、苏雪林、徐哲东[徐震]、黄耀先[黄焯]、李稚甫几位,因为行色匆匆,并没能一一访谈。10 点多,吴子馨、谢文炳、普施泽几位到公寓里来,领着我们从安澜门外的萧公嘴渡江到乌尤寺。船到了岷江和大渡河汇流的地方,只能看见大佛的下半身,不免有仰之弥高的缺憾。不久,“绿影一堆漂不去”的乌尤山也呈现在眼前了。走到近处一看原来在苍松翠柏的中间还夹杂一些使君子的红花，红绿相映替那岁寒后凋的孤高品格增加了不少的鲜艳。可是在我看起来，却还赶不上凌霄的可敬。关于这一点，我和李笠翁的感想相同。他在《闲情偶寄》里说："藤花之可敬者莫若凌霄。然望之如天际真人，卒急不能招致，是可敬亦可恨也。欲得此花必先蓄奇石古木以待，否则无所依附而不生，生亦不大。予年有几，能为奇石古木之先辈而蓄之乎？欲有此花非入深山不可，行当即之，以舒此恨！"这里既然有很像样儿的"奇石古木"，倘再有可敬的凌霄攀绕着翠柏苍松岂不相得益彰，更为乌尤生色？相形之下，使君子就平凡的多了。偶涉遐思，不觉在船头上痴立了许久！弃舟登岸后，一进山就看见迎面一个石碣上刻着赵熙所写的"离塠"两个大字。常听见四川的朋友说"峨眉天下秀，剑阁天下险，离塠天下奇"，可是在四川省，连这儿一共有三个"离塠"，究竟什么地方真，什么地方假，至今还是四川史地上一个聚讼的问题。不过就"奇"字来说，乌尤孤峙中流，周身都被苍翠掩盖着，天上的云影映衬着江面的波光，乔楠蔽日，修竹成林，时闻松涛，时见竹韵，虽然不是真的"离塠"，我却觉得这是入川以来第一个值得流连的地方。进了乌尤寺便到复性书院去拜访马一浮[马浮]先生。正赶上马先生在山下的乌尤坝休养没能会到，承张君立民引导我们参观图书馆、藏经阁、尔雅台和马先生讲学所在的旷怡亭，并且在客堂招待茶点，又送给我一全份讲录。寺里的方丈遍能，是北平柏林寺台源和尚的徒弟，谈起来还不俗气。我自从 1934 年在杭州见到马先生后，一晃儿已经七年，想起他的修髯道貌来，不禁心向往之；可惜我们中午必须赶到大佛寺，时间已经不允许我独自到乌尤坝去拜访他了。

12 点下乌尤山，过渡后再登凌云山到大佛顶，从顶上俯瞰，只能看见大佛的上半身，他的右颊稍微有点儿浮肿，据说这是 1935 年叔侄阋墙的内战的时候佛爷被机关枪把嘴巴扫掉，事后又用水门汀重修的。天王殿前有明永历十年重修凌云寺碑记。按,明永历十年相当于清顺治十三年(1656),就这个碑记来看,足征清朝入关十几年后,嘉定一带还在南明统治之下,人民并没奉清朝的正朔。再过五年,清兵入缅甸,永历帝被执,明朝才算完全灭亡了。下午1点嘉定清华同学会在凌云寺客堂公宴梅先生,约毅生和我作陪,主客共28人。4点才渡江返寓。

从嘉定到成都,本来天天有汽车往返,可是两天设尽方法都买不到票,我们打算先到峨眉绕一下,然后再从夹江搭车到成都。

十　峨眉四日游

7月12日上午9点,从嘉林公寓坐黄包车出嘉乐门,顺着乐西公路向峨眉进发。11点15分到青衣江(土名雅河)徐灏渡口,天忽然下起雨来。这里水势很大,公路局用铁筋洋灰修的桩子已经冲坏了好几次。过渡后,等雨稍微小一点儿又往前走。到了峨眉河(一称符文水)边,因为公路的桥梁还没修好,改走小道,经过怀苏镇,渡十七墩桥,到苏稽,12点10分午尖。怀苏镇和苏稽是因为唐朝苏颋曾经贬居在这里得的名,土人相传和东坡有关系,未免先后倒置。这一带是青衣江和峨眉河冲积的平原,沿路桑园相接,绿荫密翳,土人从事纺织的很多,所产棉绸,拿来做夏天的汗衣颇为舒适。在苏稽吃过午饭,因为车夫"打兑"(就是北平的"倒车"),延迟到下午1点20分才冒雨动身。两点半到高山铺,峨眉山的面目渐渐在烟雨迷濛里,像米家山水那样,隐隐约约地露出来了。4点40分到峨眉县城南门喝了一会儿茶,就往山里走,这时虽然斜阳欲坠,彤云半天,可是雄奇秀拔的峨眉山直立在眼前,立刻换了一番境界,不觉得胸襟开朗起来。在普贤寺前面邂逅着徐中舒和张洪沅两位,据说苇斋[沈履]已经到成都招考去了。6点半"拢"报国寺由沈太太和饶余威招待我们住在庙里的带月山房。这一天大约走了35公里。

从7月14日到17日,我们乘便逛了四天峨眉山,这是我们全部旅程中惟一的闲情逸致。因为滑竿伕子每一名一天要18元,各庙里两餐一宿也言不二价地标明20元,结果把各人荷包里所带的一点"私"钱都消耗完了。可是当年王羲之认为"登岷岭峨岭而旋,实不朽之盛事",那么我们既然来到这儿何妨附庸风雅地"不朽"一下子?好在这年头儿钱本来不值钱,花上两三百块还不够阔老们一餐盛筵,司机们几筒香烟,既然是自己血汗挣来的,并没耗费公帑,就是到峨眉绝顶站在舍身岩往下望的时候,也觉得心宁神贴,不怕亏心失足,葬身幽壑。

现在逛峨眉山有大小两条道:自从马路开辟后,山下在保宁院分歧,山中交叉的地方是清音阁,山上会合的地方是莲花石,全路的形状好像一个阿拉伯数码的"8"字。大路从伏虎寺入山,经雷音寺、纯阳殿、大峨寺、中峰寺、清音阁以至万年寺、华严顶、莲花石,再登钻天坡,经洗象池、白云寺、雷洞坪、接引殿,就可以直登金顶;小路从龙门洞,至清音阁,涉黑龙江,经洪椿坪九老洞、遇仙寺,到九岭冈和大路会合,再由莲花石以登金顶,上下一周大约有300里。逛山的人如果从洪椿坪九老洞的小道上去,先欣赏深幽的风景,然后直登绝顶,纵目满瞩,凭高俯瞰,再领略雄奇的形势,那是最理想的途径。我们原来本打算这样走,可惜连下几天大雨,黑龙江水涨不容易过去,只好还从大路上山,从小路下山。

14日上午9点,冒着小雨从报国寺动身,同游的还有方欣安[方壮猷]夫人张近芬女士。当晚住在拔海1043公尺的万年寺毗卢殿。第二天上午因雨未能登山,只看了看附近的砖殿和新殿。下午1点15分雨止,从毗卢殿出发,晚间宿在拔海2110公尺的洗象池。第三天早晨7点20分从洗象池出发,12点半就到了拔海3000公尺的卧云庵,当天下午到金顶转了一下,盼望半天佛光终于没能看见。晚上住在卧云庵里的睹光楼。这三天,我们每天升高1000公尺,算起来比昆明的马市口,已经高出1000公尺了。第四天早晨6点从卧云庵出发,到九岭冈后转入小路,下午6点15分一口气赶回报国寺;这虽然把两天的道儿并作一天走,可惜太匆促一点儿,对于后山清幽的景致没能够流连尽兴。

关于峨眉风景的描写,掌故的考证,在前人山志或今人的导游里已经有详细的记载,用不着我来说,专就游记而论,古今人也不知作过多少篇了。在这里,只拣出几项来写一写我个人的印象:

峨眉的山 大家都知道"峨眉天下秀",其实它在秀拔以外还兼着雄奇。专从奇峰怪石一点来看,它不单赶不上黄山并且还比不得阳朔;可是一提到它的雄壮伟大,我们试想一想,要是站在黄山的天都峰上看金顶那得欠着多高的脚?假如再从华严顶上俯瞰阳朔的诸峰,那不和一堆堆的小盆景差不多吗?况且在遇仙寺以上,遍山都被奇花异卉掩覆着,满眼只看见苍翠欲滴,几乎很难找到一两块没涂上青绿的岩石;假如这就可以叫做"秀",那还不算是秀到极点?明释梦觋有几句诗说:"峨眉高,高插天,百二十里烟云连,盘空鸟道千万折,奇峰朵朵开青莲",颇能写出一点它的"雄秀"样儿来。赶到晴天的时候,站在峨眉县的郊外来远望,可以看见群峰起伏有序,层次井然。劈面当前的,右边是凤凰坪,左边是伏虎山,其次是新开寺诸山;再看进去,右边是观心坡,左边是大峨诸山;更进一层,右边是华严顶,左边是九老洞诸山;倘若再望过大乘寺洗象池的几个峰头,便可以看见悬岩一列,三峰鼎峙,那就是峨眉的主峰:金顶、千佛顶和万佛顶。进山以后,若是在马鞍山过去一点的慧灯寺去凭眺,对于金顶以下的许多山也可以看得很清楚。

游山的人总喜欢住金顶,在我看还是卧云庵比较清幽。几间客室,建在悬岩的边上,小小的厅房三面都是玻璃窗,一片平台周围圈着栏杆。凭栏临眺,左边有盘陀石、印心石、睹光台,右边有象鼻石、金刚岩、舍身岩。抬头远望,还有罗汉峰、观音峰、天池峰、兔儿峰等都直立在你的面前:有的翘首云中,矫健不群;有的两峰对峙,嵯峨争秀;看着像城垣上的雉堞,又像绣成的九叠屏风。由玄武岩结成的山石,因氧化变质,微微呈现出一点赭色,在一片浓绿当中借着日光映出这一点对称的颜色来,格外显着美丽:这是我们在半山所看不到的。往下一看,陡壁悬岩夹着一眼望不见底的万仞深壑,在蔚然深秀的浓绿中间,不知什么时候几缕白云偷偷地从岩岫里溜出来,一会儿塞满了深壑,一会儿遮住了群峰,一会儿布满了平台,一会儿侵入了卧室:直闹得伸手不见掌,对面不见人,这时候才体会到古人所说"风云变幻"和"啸傲烟霞"的味道。正在云雾迷濛的当儿,天上忽然晃出太阳来,几个峰头慢慢地钻出云端,好像虚无缥缈的海上仙岛,骋目四望,只觉得白浪滔天,波涛汹涌,一会儿风吹云动,忽像滚雪,忽像翻棉,变化万千,诡谲莫测,闹得人不知道究竟是在天上?在人间?在海中?在岩际?渐渐团团的白雪又变成缕缕的流霞,五色鲜妍,光映岩谷,芒彩闪烁,好像置身琉璃世界!等到雨过天晴,抽冷子了无一物,依然现出蔚蓝的天,苍翠的峰,幽深的谷,旷远的平畴;铜河、雅河、峨眉河蜿蜒着像三条小白蛇;嘉定、峨眉两个城廓渺茫得像几个黑棋子!这时候我才觉得自己站在卧云庵的平台上,才知道,身旁还有月涵、毅生、近芬三位游侣!

晴明的早晨,站在金顶的岩头去远望,天上蓝莹莹的净无纤云,几个高峰涌现在眼前,好像刚出浴的美人披着绿绸浴衣在那里争妍斗艳一样!朝两边看,晒经山像座屏风,瓦屋山像块覆瓦,中间还有海拔 7500 公尺比峨眉高着一倍的大雪山,雪山现得最明的时候,莹澈像水晶,灿烂像琉璃,粉装玉琢,比棉堆雪球还要洁白:真可以算是峨眉绝顶的一个奇观,寺僧又指点我哪是大凉山,哪是大小蛙山,哪是火焰山,哪是大峨和二峨,说的人虽然口若悬河,如数家珍,可是在我看起来,却不免有些依稀仿佛,若隐若现。

此外使我印象很深的,还有雷洞坪和华严顶。雷洞坪建在阎王坳高头的平台上,北边是白云寺,南边是接引殿,海拔约2400公尺,离金顶还有七里。前临绝壑,悬崖万丈,沉黯不见底,左边是弓背山,右边是金顶,中间还有一列峻岭,把它三面环抱起来。每逢岩下打雷的时候,因为回响作用常常使雷声格外砰訇,于是就造出许多神话来;明万历年间还立过一个"禁声"铁碑,以警行人。其实,说破了是不值一笑的。这一带云雾很多,终年阴霾,怪木槎枒,顽石狞恶,还有鬖鬖像乱发的苔丝,长约一丈,缠挂树石间,土人叫做"普贤线",游离飘逸,倒也有点风致。

从大路上山,过了磴道凌空的上天梯,迎面有孤峰突起,高约1900公尺,那就是华严顶。在金顶没有开辟以前,它就算是峨眉山的最高峰。到了这里显然有云封岩谷、树插层霄的感觉。低头往山下瞻眺,南边有铜河,中间有峨眉,以北还有雅河,像三条白练纡曲迤逦地向下游走。由它们冲积成的平原,布满了稻田,到处都像铺着绿绒毡似的。仰天长啸,不觉心旷神怡,胸襟开朗,沉闷郁抑的情绪早就躲在一边去了。

上下山所经过的道儿,有些地方很难走,过伏虎寺刚一里多,就要爬上一个石磴险仄、高约百尺的解脱坡;到上头往下一看,真会有尘念顿消、解脱一切的思想。离毗卢殿大约十里,有一观心坡,这个坡长约二三里,既斜且陡,因为石磴太高,每登山一步磕膝盖就得顶到胸口,所以又叫做顶心坡或点心坡。过了这里再往上走,一路上怪石嶙峋,排列的像牙齿,逼窄的小道,两边都是往下溜的悬岩,形状好像鱼背一样，这就是所谓“鬼门关”。在它上头走的时候，两旁有树木翳蔽着，并不觉得怎样危险；走过去往回一看真不禁有点后怕，闯过鬼门关，越过息心所，还有一个很陡的放光坡。拐过初殿又得爬上天梯，每一级石阶差不多有一尺高，简直累得喘不过气来。快到洗象池，有一个耸立的危坡，那就是所谓“鹁鸽钻天”，一般人也叫做钻天坡，这个坡长约五里，高约二百公尺，途中有两个供人休息的亭子，本来磴道危仄，很不好走，后来有一个上海人叫顾嘉棠的，捐款二千元修筑，现在稍微宽舒一点儿。由大乘寺往左走，还得经过一个很危险的陡坡，叫做阎王堀，这个堀高约一百五十公尺，往上爬的时候，往往得拄着拐棍，攀着藤条。相传从前有一个胡僧，缚木架石，以引行人，所以又叫胡僧梯或凌云梯。到接引殿以前，先要经过八十四盘，这个地方虽然纡曲却不很难走。过了接引殿还有一个七里坡，高约三百公尺，坡顶高出海面 2800 公尺。假如坐着滑竿上山，遇到这些地方，伕子们总要求你“让坡”。照我看还是下来走好，否则不单看着他们喘息流汗有些难过，坐在上面也委实不大舒服，多少有点儿担心。由小路下山的时候，过九老洞大约八里，便到了九十九倒拐。这里本叫寿星坡，又叫冲天槽，沿着山峪往下走大约有 1800 步，53 转。朝下走比向上爬省力得多，可是步行的时候往往蹬得两腿生痛，若是坐在滑竿上，有时候一个伕子踩着一拐，另一个踩着那一拐，人就像悬在半空中一样，往下一看那万丈深壑谁都得有点儿头眩眼晕！除去上面所说的这几个地方外，虽然不能说全是坦途，大体上却没有什么险径了。

峨眉的水 从前孔子说：“智者乐水，仁者乐山。”我虽然算不得“智者”，可是总觉得水比山更可爱。峨眉的水源有两条：左边的白水，发源于莲花石，经过遇仙寺前，下流为石笋沟；右边是黑水，从九老洞绕洪椿坪而来，下流为黑龙江。这两条水到清音阁汇流为符文水,流到河口,再和发源于弓背山的黑水河汇合,到龙门洞以下叫种玉溪;从此曲屈北流,过马口,绕流峨眉城北而下,所以一般人又管它叫做峨眉河。

从小路下山,过遇仙寺,经长寿桥,才开始听见潺潺水声,由这儿到九老洞,山色得到水声的衬合,格外显着幽美。走到这里,只见流泉漱石,岩壑衔烟,雾锁丛林,云封窄径,仰头但露一隙青天,俯视便是万仞深峪,路转峰回,风景也随着变幻,两脚觉得有点儿累的时候,站下来回头一望,锅圈岩峭壁挺秀,龙桥沟瀑布三折,因境移情,立刻忘了疲乏。照我的眼光,这一段算得是峨眉山里顶秀出的。

出洪椿坪往下走,经过三道桥、二道桥和万义桥,就到黑龙江,江两旁的夹峪是栖霞灰岩构成的,峭壁对立,相距不过一丈多,却有一百多尺高。上面遮着浓荫蔽日的苍藤,下面流着莹澈见底的碧水,连一块小石头儿、一条小鱼儿都藏不了,乱石横七竖八、大大小小地堆在江心,急湍冲着它便激成了险滩。因为水大滩多,岩峭路绝,有时候非涉水不可。据滑竿伕子说,到这里得要过 24 道黑龙江,照我算起来一共只涉过 11 次水。在过第三个滩的时候,急流的力量很大,站在水里简直稳不住脚;合起四个伕子来,从满布着青苔的岩石上,一步三滑,连推带拉,才能抬过一个人来。这一刹那,心里虽然紧张,可是看着奔马似的急湍,听着澎湃震耳的滩声,在艰险中也得到说不出来的奇趣。再往前走水更大,岩更峭,峪更窄,连像上面所说的那危险道儿都找不出来;正在没法可想的当儿,幸亏前人依壁架木,修了十几丈长的七段栈道,许多游人才不至于到这儿水尽山穷,败兴而返。过栈道不远,急流冲击一块大岩石,雪白的浪花溅出多高,样子像汤沸,声音像河决,这便是黑龙江的尾流激荡成的奇观。再转一个弯,流到清音阁就和白水汇合起来了。我生平没游览过多少名山大川,不过就曾经看到的滩涧来说,西湖的九溪十八涧比不上它的险急,崂山的北九水比不上它的幽深。在我看过来,它和清音阁是峨眉山里顶值得流连的地方。

清音阁的前面有两个桥,白水从左边的桥流进来,黑水从右边的桥流进来。两条水环抱着阁的周围,日积月累,各自冲成巉岩,把急湍约束在很窄的深壑里,水势越发显着充沛有力,及至冲出岩壑,二流汇合,两股力量并在一起,其势好像强弩齐发,机枪乱射,又好像几千健儿冲锋杀敌,万匹烈马驰骋奔腾,一往直前,沛然莫御。适当其冲恰好有一块砥柱中流的牛心石,急湍冲到它的上头,激得浪花四溅声音像滂沱大雨里夹着急风迅雷一样,这就是所谓"黑白二水洗牛心",比起在桥底岩间所发的琤琮清音,显然有雅静和雄壮的不同。过了这里以后,碧流曲折,水势渐渐舒缓,河底有许多像白棋子的小石头儿,日光反射,闪烁生辉,溪水在它们上面流过,又恢复了环佩玎珰的玲玲清音,依然是雅静、幽美!再望周围一看,绿油油的苍松,翠生生的丛篁,密叶含雨,浓荫生烟,点缀着鸣泉逸韵,意味更加隽永!

从前范成大说:"闻峨眉双溪不减庐山三峡,及至龙门,则双溪又在下风。"所以游过清音阁的不可不到龙门洞。离清音后,从广福寺下坡,顺着符文水走,过清风、明月两个桥,武显、凉风两个冈,远远地看见溪水中有一条狭长横卧的黑石,好像小船一样,那就是所谓"普贤船"。再往下走,经过峪里,有几道泉水从峪壁的小孔流出,像匹练,像飞絮,像游丝,远望着又像辉煌的珠帘,这是没到龙门以前的一个奇景。过铁索桥,再走五里就到了龙门洞。上游的溪水向东流,到这儿把灰岩横穿成一个峡峪,杂树生在岩上,浓荫照得溪水绿莹莹的。岩半有一个圆龛,突出水面好几丈,当面有富春孙某钩摹苏东坡写的"龙门"两个大字。这里道路很险峻,要想细细地游览,总得坐船进峪登着梯子上去,才能欣赏峡泉的幽秀。龙门洞以东,河面渐宽,水势益缓,浅山绵亘,地势低平,慢慢地就走上出山的坦途。

山中喝的水要算洗象池、洪椿坪和神水阁三个地方最洁净。所谓“神水”就是古玉液泉,从石头缝渗出,好像经过砂滤一样,清冽适口,不愧“峨眉第一泉”。相传隋智者大师住在中峰寺的时候,常喝这个水,后来到荆州去,病中还想喝它,于是龙女就从这里取水去供养,因此现在阁下的池子里还有“神泉通楚”的石碣。这个故事虽然不可信,可是现在到峨山避暑的外国人也往往为喝“神水”的缘故,住在它附近的中峰寺或大峨寺。

早晚的两种奇观 在峨眉我遇到两种奇观,就是清晨的日出和夜晚的佛灯。我看日出不止一次,在崂山,在黄山,在南岳的祝融峰,都曾经享受过这种眼福。这次在洗象池和卧云庵又碰巧看见两回。在天刚亮的时候,站在高处远望,起初只见乌灰一片,弥漫天空,慢慢地显出鱼肚白的和淡赭两色来;待不大会儿,深赭夹着金色的光芒,从浅蓝的天边,辐射成半圆形,余辉映照出去颇远;转瞬间一轮朝暾忽然涌现出来,光芒四射,赭色顿消,这时候大地上才从黑暗转到光明。我这次所得的印象和黄山、南岳差不多,但比起在黄海边上的崂山所见却大不相同。几时才让我再到崂顶或泰山的日观峰去温习一下?

说到佛灯,那可是峨眉特有的奇观。在晴明没有云彩、没有月亮的夜晚,站在适当高度的地方,常常可以看见它。初起的时候,点点如豆,渐渐灿烂像繁星,闪烁像流萤,乍明乍灭,忽隐忽现,起先不过几点,渐渐增到万千,飘忽流动,冉冉上升,山中僧众管这种现象叫“万盏明灯朝普贤”。我15日晚在洗象池,16日晚在卧云庵,连着看见两次。所谓“佛灯”究竟是什么?到现在还没有正确的解答。有人说是山下住户所点的灯光反映上来的,有人说是由磷质发光而起的。因为这个小问题颇引起川大和武大许多朋友的争论。

佛教的掌故和法物 峨眉是佛教三大道场之一,和山西的五台、浙江的普陀齐名。据明万历三十一年癸卯(1603)傅光宅所撰《峨眉普贤金殿碑》上说:“余读《杂花经佛授记》。震旦国有大道场者三:一代州之五台,一明州之补怛,一即嘉州峨眉也。五台则文殊师祖,补怛则观世音,峨眉则普贤愿王。是三大士各与其眷属千忆菩萨常住道场,度生弘法。”因此峨眉山上关于普贤愿王的遗迹最多,各庙里的正殿几乎都供着他的像。其中比较特别一点儿的,如全山普贤像都向东,金顶的普贤像独向西。这尊像是清咸丰十一年西藏人奉达赖喇嘛命到这里铸献的,现在西藏人来朝山,单单参礼这个殿。这和峨眉县城东门外大佛寺里的带须普贤像都表现西域的特殊风格。万年寺毗卢殿的正殿有明嘉靖间所铸释迦、文殊、普贤三尊铜像,都是丈六金身,法相庄严。砖殿中间所供普贤骑象铜像,单是象就有六七尺宽,高长各一丈二尺,脚底下踏着一尺莲花,牙长五尺多,必须两个人才能合抱过来;普贤像也高丈六,像背所盖木龛,雕刻得非常精致。拿这尊像比起伏虎寺和圣积寺的普贤骑象像来,那就伟大得多了。此外,相传大乘寺是普贤和三千弟子说法处,洗象池是普贤浴象处,放光坡是蒲公见普贤现瑞处,雷洞坪一带有普贤线,龙门洞附近有普贤船,锡瓦殿和太子坪有明万历间御赐普贤愿王印,从天门石上去还有建文帝口封的“肉身普贤”……这虽不免有些依托附会,故神其说,却也可见峨眉山里关于佛教的故事是拿普贤作中心的。

关于其他方面的传说,如初殿的得名是因为汉朝的蒲公在这里采药,看见鹿的脚印儿现出莲花来,才创建的;离初殿二里还有蒲公结茅处的蒲公庵和蒲公村。砖殿也是蒲氏事佛旧址。中峰寺是北魏林淡然剃度处,现在大雄殿的左侧还供着他的遗像;宋朝的黄山谷也曾在这里作过静功。在它后面的呼应峰,相传智者大师、茂真尊者和孙思邈在此常相呼应。牛心寺即古延福院,唐孙思邈曾经在此栖隐,寺后的丹砂洞,相传是他炼丹的地方。宋朝的继业三藏从西域回来,以后也曾经在这里住过。大乘寺的木皮殿,相传是从前西域阿罗婆多尊者到峨眉来礼佛,看见山水环合和西域的化城寺相似,于是就在这里建立道场,拿木皮盖成的。此外,如华严寺是唐朝福昌达道禅师的道场,大峨寺是唐僖宗为慧通盖的,毗卢殿里的客寮是唐李白听僧广濬弹琴的地方,天门石上面的祖师殿有通天和尚的肉身,仙峰寺中供有泰庵和尚肉身,白龙洞前有别传手植的楠木。虽然真假参半,却给游山的人增加不少"思古之幽情"。

山上的碑记没有很古的;山顶的祖殿有明成化五年己丑(1469)铜碑,上铸《御制峨眉山普光殿记》;大乘寺有明嘉靖二年癸未(1523)铁碑,上铸《木皮殿记》,是嘉定州知州康浩作的,判官北徽州汪伦用篆书写的;金顶有万历三十一年癸卯(1603)的铜碑,一面铸着《峨眉普贤金殿碑》,是聊城傅光宅作的,吴郡吴士端集褚遂良书,一面铸着《大峨山永明华藏寺新建铜殿记》,是王毓宗作的,吴士端集王羲之书。此外就不足道了。

各庙里的佛像和法物,倒有不少值得留意的:四会亭有接引佛铜像一尊,高二丈一尺,是别传所铸,比接引殿供奉的那一尊还要庄严伟大。金顶的前殿有玉佛四尊,计普贤骑象像二,一高六尺,一高五尺;文殊骑犼像一,高一尺;送子观音像一,高约五尺。正殿有玉制如来像和普贤像各一尊,高一尺多。这都是1937年果迦和尚从缅甸请来的。祖殿中间供着玉佛一尊,高二尺许,毗卢殿正殿也有玉佛一尊,是清光绪间平光和尚从缅甸请来的。仙峰寺后殿的铜舍利塔,中间有小玉佛三尊,雕刻得不很精致。山下的万行庄也有玉制普贤骑象像一尊,高约五尺多,和金顶所供奉的不相上下。

在许多和尚庙里往往参杂道教的偶像,如洪椿坪后殿的楼上供着玉皇、真武、火神、灵官。极乐寺的门前有灵官楼。伏虎寺也有玉皇殿,又在祖师殿里供着"通微显化天尊三丰祖师",在两旁配享的有

"圆通祖师"和"万三祖师"……殿门口并且还挂着张三丰乩笔所书对联:"我无相,树无根,我树无根,冰心一片禅初悟;山有云,人有伴,山人有兴,道义千秋果正圆。"这还不算希奇,最可怪的是在"观音殿"里却供着"大慈大悲金光圣母"和"无惭"、"无恶"两尊者。纯阳殿总应该是道教的庙了,可是除去山门的灵官和睡"佛"殿里的吕纯阳卧像以外,其余的都是佛像。各庙里供奉川主李二郎的很多,这还可以,是本地人崇德报功的意思。此外,有许多偶像却有些莫名其妙,如白云寺供着白云祖师张良,砖殿供着红教喇嘛莲花大师,仙峰寺的阿弥陀佛作老僧装,十八罗汉里参加一位康熙皇帝:像这样释道杂糅、显密不分、古今混淆的现象,简直太乱了。我颇疑心峨眉最初也是释道对峙的,后来佛教的势力一天比一天大,许多道观便消灭了。相传中峰寺本来是晋朝的乾明观,后来明果禅师除毒蟒,道士感激他,才改观为寺。这段故事很可看出释道消长的一点儿痕迹来。九老洞所以变为仙峰寺,多少也给我们一些同样的暗示。在道观式微以后,从前所供奉的偶像一时没清除干净,便成了释道杂糅的第一个原因。再者,在一般人的心里,对于"神"和"佛"的分界本来弄不大清楚,又因为设坛扶乩的风气盛极一时,有一点儿钱的人,为祈福起见,不问原来是佛寺还是道观,只要他一高兴,就可以化俩钱儿盖一两间殿,塑几位他心目中所谓"神佛"。听说伏虎寺的祖师殿修了才五六年,是一位军官布施的,谁管张三丰邋遢不邋遢,先塑个白面长须的像,看着顺眼就得了。这就是释道杂糅的第二个原因。至于老僧装的阿弥陀佛,康熙帝变成罗汉,那完全是和尚迎合权势所致,说不定过几年后,某主席或某院长之流,在峨眉山也许取得菩萨或罗汉的地位呢。

关于法物一方面:锡瓦殿、洗象池、仙峰寺、洪椿坪、灵岩寺都有"御赐龙藏";万年寺新殿有贝叶华严经 256 张,是清光绪二十七年辉林和尚从印度请回来的;仙峰寺也有贝叶经和菩提叶经各一部,贝叶长一尺四寸余，宽二寸余，菩提叶长约二尺，宽二寸余，上面写着梵经五部。金顶正殿后面的舍身岩上有万历二十年壬辰（1592）所铸的铜舍利塔，高九尺余，凡七层，另外有一个小的，高五尺余，凡14层。仙峰寺后殿也有一个铜舍利塔，高约丈余，凡七层，外面用玻璃箱罩着，里面藏有舍利子两粒，色白略有光泽，好像珍珠似的，另外还供着三尊玉佛，好些尊小铜佛。万年寺新殿也藏有舍利子四粒，三红一白。这和砖殿所藏的迦叶佛牙一样有名。佛牙长一尺二寸，宽八寸，厚三寸，重13斤半，形状好像半只靴子，牙床作橙黄色，上面还间杂着红白两色；有人说就是象齿的化石，有空儿还得向古生物学家请教请教。毗卢殿的正殿前面有一个铜香炉铸工精巧，是明嘉靖元年造的，民国初年川督尹昌衡想把它毁了铸铜元，庙里的老和尚伏在炉上，誓以身殉，幸而才保存住。洪椿坪的藏经楼中间悬着一个千佛灯，灯柱上面都盘着云龙，刻工非常精致。据说这是1921年在重庆做的，21年才运上山，所费约五千余元，时代虽然很近，论品质倒是很可珍贵的。自从金顶屡次遭火灾，山上各庙收藏的丰富，要算洪椿坪第一，它有明破山和尚所写"悬佛日于中天光含大地，灿明珠于性海彩彻十方"长联；有清康熙帝御书《金刚经》和"忘尘虑"，"锡飞常近鹤，杯渡不惊鸥"；有雍正十三年乙卯（1735）果亲王所题"发弘四愿"横匾；有乾隆所写"性海总涵功德水，福林长涌吉祥林"对联；另外还有竹禅和尚画的读余图，张鳌的左书，奕劻的对联，海刚峰、张船山、何绍基等人的字画：这些东西在别的庙里都是很少见的。仙峰寺正殿的佛案上供着一大块水晶，长二尺余，直径约有一尺，作六棱尖柱状，庙里和尚说是从铜河买来的，这和莲花寺的莲花石可以上下媲美。莲花石有红白各一，长约一尺，宽五寸，高约六七寸，石质很润泽，颜色很莹澈，结晶的形状好像是许多莲花瓣儿拼凑成的，这个庙就因为石头得的名。

关于"陈娘娘"的传说 万年寺新殿的前楼上塑有"陈娘娘"的像,砖殿里还保存着她曾经用过的铜镜,在七里坡上面一点儿,有两棵松树遮荫着一块岩石,据说就是当年陈娘娘的梳妆台。此外,在天门石上边的沉香塔她又颁赐过珍珠繖。这件法物现在虽然遭了火灾,可是大佛寺里二丈六尺高的千手大悲观音铜像还保留着她的功德。陈娘娘究竟是谁?是什么时代的?和峨眉山有什么关系?据毗卢殿的知客果慧对我说:"她是明朝隆庆帝的皇后,万历帝的母亲,是四川内江人。她发愿心以后,和隆庆皇帝都拜峨眉临济宗的开山通天和尚明彻做老师,并且发内帑兴修万年寺、万行庵、草庵堂、报国寺、海会禅林、接引殿等处。万年寺就是因她做寿得的名。万历帝的两个弟弟都出了家,法名叫定禅、定乐。现在的太子坪就是古万行庵,这个名称是隆庆帝改的。1939年林主席[林森]又改名万历寺。里面供着皮制的太子像高一尺余,拜山求子的人们往往离开一丈多远用铜元来打他,打中的就可以生儿子。"这是从和尚嘴里所得到的关于陈娘娘的传说。案《明史·后妃传》,穆宗做裕王的时候,原配昌平李氏,生宪怀太子翊钎,嘉靖三十七年四月卒;穆宗即位后,追谥为孝懿皇后。孝安皇后陈氏,通州人,嘉靖三十七年九月选为裕王继妃,隆庆元年册为皇后,多病无子,居别宫。神宗即位上尊号曰仁圣皇太后,居慈庆宫。当神宗做太子的时候,每天早晨先到奉先殿给穆宗和他的生母请安,然后再到陈后那里定省,她听见脚步声就很欢喜。万历二十四年七月崩,谥曰孝安贞懿恭纯温惠佐天弘圣皇后。神宗的生母是孝定李太后,漷县人,侍穆宗于裕邸,隆庆元年封贵妃,生神宗,神宗即位上尊号曰慈圣皇太后,居慈宁宫。万历四十二年二月崩,谥曰孝定贞纯钦仁端肃弼天祚圣皇太后。(参看《明史》卷一百一十四)由此看来,我们可以知道陈娘娘并不是内江人,也没生过儿子,在她的列传和《穆宗本纪》里都没有提到峨眉礼佛的事。可是在

《孝定李太后传》里倒说:“顾好佛,京师内外多置梵刹,动费巨万,帝亦助施无算。张居正在日尝以为言,未能用也。”据《张江陵全集》里《敕建涿州二桥碑文》:“圣母慈圣皇太后在先帝时,梦若有神告言,宜作功德事,以福国祐民,太后意念之不忘。今上建元之首年,会(涿)州民有奏乞建桥济众者,太后忆与梦符,遂语上以欲建桥意。上曰:‘兴作,大事也。请得与辅臣计之。’出,以太后意谕臣居正。臣因言:‘时诎举嬴,古人所戒。上始即大位,一切宜与民休息。兹役太劳民,且费巨,恐有司亦未能办,奈何?’上曰:‘圣母自以宫中供奉金募工为之,一夫不役于民,一钱不取于官也。’臣顿首曰:‘幸甚!’乃发帑金五万两,诏工部以农隙鸠材,发春戒事。”又《敕建承恩寺碑文》:“皇上替僧名志善,向居龙泉寺。慈圣皇太后、今上皇帝,追念先帝及其替僧,以寺居圮坏,欲一新之;而其地湫隘,且滨于河,势难充拓。乃出帑储千金,潞王公主及诸宫眷所施数千金,命司礼监太监冯保买地于都城巽隅居贤坊故太监王成住宅,特建梵刹。”又《重修海会寺碑文》:“寺在都城之南,创于嘉靖乙未,穆宗皇帝尝受釐于此。历祀既久,栋宇弗葺,榱桷将毁,皇上即位之二年,函夏乂安,四民乐业。圣母慈圣皇太后思所以保艾圣躬,舄奕胤祚者,惟佛宝是依。乃出内帑银若干,俾即其地更建焉。既集议,慈圣皇太后暨潞王贤妃、贵人以下,咸出资助之。”又《敕修东岳庙碑文》:“今天下郡国皆有东岳庙,而京师则庙朝阳门之东,相传唐宋时已有,国朝正统中益恢崇之。……百余年来,庙寝倾圮,神将弗妥,士女兴嗟。圣母慈圣皇太后闻之,曰:‘吾甚重祠而敬祀,其一新之,然勿以烦有司。’乃捐膏沐资若干缗。皇上祗顺慈意,亦出帑储若干缗,命司礼监太监冯保择内臣廉干者董其役。”又《敕建慈寿寺碑文》:“寺在都门阜成关外八里许。先是,我圣母慈圣宣文皇太后常欲择宇内名山灵胜,特建梵宇,为穆考荐冥祉。皇上祈允,遣使旁求,皆以地远,不便瞻礼,乃命司礼监太监冯保,卜关外地营之。出宫中供奉金若干两，潞王公主暨诸宫眷助佐若干金，委太监杨辉等董其役。”又《敕建万寿寺碑文》：“今上践祚之五年，圣母慈圣宣文皇太后谕上若曰：‘创一寺，以藏经、焚修，成先帝遗意。’上若曰：‘朕时佩节用之训，事非益民者弗举。惟是皇考祈祐之地，又重之以圣母追念荐福慈意，然不可以烦有司。’乃出帑储若干缗。潞王公主暨宫御中贵亦佐若干缗，命司礼监太监冯保等卜地于西直门外七里许广源闸之西，特建梵刹，为尊藏、汉经香火院。”又《敕建五台山大宝塔寺记》：“昔阿育王获佛舍利三十余颗，各建塔藏之，散布华夷，今五台灵鹫山塔是其一也。我圣母慈圣宣文皇太后前欲创寺于此，为穆考荐福。今上所储，以道远中止，遂于都城建慈寿寺以当之。臣居正业已奉敕为之记。顾我圣母，至情精虔，不忘始愿，复遣尚衣监太监范某、李友辈，捐供奉余资，往事庄严。”由上面所引的这些材料看起来，第一可见慈圣李太后信佛的虔诚和万历一朝兴建梵宇的众多；第二可见张居正对于这种大兴土木的举动不大以为然，但也不得不将顺意旨地替皇上掩饰。——然而在这么许多记载里却没有一个字提到仁圣陈太后，金顶的铜碑上所刻王毓宗的《大峨山永明华藏寺新建铜殿记》里边虽然有“遣沙门福登赍圣母所颁龙藏至鸡足山”和“已中中使衔命宣慈旨赐尚方金钱置葺焚修常住若干”几句话，可是他所谓“圣母”和“慈旨”究竟指着仁圣陈太后还是慈圣李太后，却没有明文可考。那么，果慧所说，和山上传说的遗迹，到底有没有根据呢？这得要向熟于明代史乘或佛教掌故的朋友们请教一下。

其次要问，万历皇帝的弟弟曾否在峨眉山出家呢？据《明史·列传第八·诸王五》，穆宗共生四个儿子，考懿李皇后生宪怀太子翊釴，生五岁殇。靖悼王翊铃生下来没满一年就死了，他的母亲不可考。孝定李太后生神宗翊钧和潞王翊镠，孝安陈皇后无所出。（参看《明史》卷一百二十）那么山上传说的定禅、定乐那哥儿俩又是从哪儿来的呢？照我想这不过是替僧罢了。据张居正《敕建承恩寺碑文》上说："皇朝凡太子诸王生，率剃度幼童一人为僧，名替度。虽非雅制，而宫中率沿以为常。"穆宗的长子和次子既然都没立住，到他26岁才生的神宗，32岁才生的潞王，那么，孝定李太后对于这两个亲生的宝贝儿子，要想"保艾圣躬，舄奕胤祚"，在她想，只有"佛宝是依"是顶好的法子。她所以虔诚信佛，大兴梵刹或许都由这一点动机来的。所以我猜果慧所说的定禅、定乐就是神宗和潞王的替僧。至于太子坪的皮像也许就是她替神宗还的替身，和现在北平迷信的老太婆到妙峰山娘娘庙去"还童儿"用意一样。俗僧展转传讹，于是就造出许多神话来了。

峨眉的和尚　说到峨眉的和尚，阿弥陀佛！洒家在20年前也曾经有一度是受过三皈五戒的"优婆塞"，现在虽不信佛，怎敢违犯"绮语"、"两舌"的戒律，存心毁谤三宝弟子？可是，就我这次所得到的印象，纵然没有像某先生所说"峨眉山有峰皆秀，无僧不俗"的地步，却没有碰见几位教理宏达、戒行谨严的高僧！让我最起敬的是在毗卢殿主持护国仁王法会的能观法师。他俗名程昌祺，号芝轩，是上川东人，曾在华西大学做过11年中国文学系主任，1936年才出的家。长子绍伊，曾在日本学医，次子绍迥是清华出身再到美国学兽医的。这位老和尚童颜鹤发，道貌岸然，本来是同行，所以颇谈得来。此外，听说祖殿的传钵，禅定功夫颇深，锡瓦殿的性安，戒行很好，可惜都没会到。至于神水阁普智的和蔼，卧云庵常意的殷勤，毗卢殿妙伦的黠慧，也还不让人讨厌。另外的怎样呢？我所遇见的，有附庸风雅、借势招摇的"诗僧"；有不甘寂寞、妨害别人家庭的淫僧；有"坐，请坐，请上坐；茶，泡茶，泡好茶"，满嘴主席长、委员长短的势僧；有在游客付香资时斜睨着钞票上数码，因为下雨便留你打牌的俗僧；有把山峰的名儿背得滚瓜烂熟，比说相声的张寿臣、小蘑菇还要嘴快的贫僧；有借着经营名胜为名,实际推销茶叶的商僧:要想尽相穷形,恐怕更仆难数。冯焕章[冯玉祥]先生游峨眉归来,曾在《大公报》发表一首《救救和尚》长诗,可以替我作个佐证。我且引几句最精彩的在下面:

峨眉山,多云雾,十个和尚九糊涂;峨眉山,和尚住,穷的穷来富的富;

峨眉山,真有趣,和尚彼此生闲气;峨眉山,真好看,许多和尚抽大烟;

峨眉山,真好瞧,和尚去把女人找;峨眉山,真堂皇,个个和尚脸发黄;

峨眉山,高百里,和尚占了佃户妻;峨眉山,似座城,和尚有妻好品行;

峨眉山,有七层,和尚不妨娶女人;峨眉山,李花白,和尚娶妻有着落;

峨眉山,桃花红,娶妻省得胡闹腾;峨眉山,茶叶绿,有妻才好有约束;

峨眉山,水不死,释迦牟尼有妻子;峨眉山,石头青,和尚有妻才正经。

……

由这几句诗看起来,我们不难窥见峨眉山和尚的一斑了。他很希望有人做佛教的马丁路德,拿寺庙改学校,让和尚能够努力生产,自食其力,与其听他们掩耳盗铃的胡闹,宁可解放一点,倒省得妨害别人的家庭。我们刚到山下的那一晚,有一位很有名的和尚,听说我们从重庆来,还以为我们已经看见这首长诗了呢,他就说:“和尚也是人,要想推行佛法非改善现在的僧伽制度,调整和尚的生活不可。告诉几位檀越说,照我自己的经验,50 岁以前出家实在苦极了。”这位和尚交际很广,不过我听完这一段话,颇怀疑他曾否读过佛经,是否懂得佛法。承他很殷勤地磨了两三盘墨,让我们题字,我很想送给他一副对联,联语是:“果否通佛法,玲珑善交游。”匆匆忙忙的终于没好意思写出来。后来我在金顶上盼佛光不见,和梅先生闹着玩儿说:“假使我们能够看见佛光,我发心在50岁以后出家。”结果急得跌了一跤,佛光也没为我现出来。梅先生颇笑我不虔诚!

论起峨眉山和尚的宗派来,自从通天法师开山后,还是临济宗最发达,其次便是曹洞宗。临济宗的排行是:“清净智慧,道德圆明,真如性海,寂照普通,心源广续,本觉昌隆,能仁圣果,常衍宽宏”;曹洞宗的排行是:“广崇妙普,宏胜永昌”。现在“果”字辈在山里很占势力。曹洞宗的庙宇并没有几个。

几桩遗憾 我们上下山虽然有四天,实际上在毗卢殿和卧云庵合起来就耽搁了一整天,因此有许多地方不能久流连,有好些风景也只好割爱。其中最让我遗憾的就是没看见佛光。在峨眉绝顶,每逢山上有太阳,山下有雨,岩下编布着“兜罗云”,正当上午9点或下午3点,站在岩前和太阳成适当角度的地方,往往看见云上现出一个圆光,五色斑斓,虚明如镜,看的人的影子就收摄在圆光里头,你点头他也点头,你举手他也举手,那就是“摄身光”。此外因为云霞变幻,光度强弱,还有所谓“清现”、“金桥”、“水光”、“辟支光”、“童子光”等等名堂,据说,五光十色,非常好看。16日下午我们在金顶的观光台等了许久,因为日光不足,毫无所见。刚从金顶下山到祖殿和锡瓦殿转了一下,太阳忽然出来了;赶紧跑回卧云庵的平台上去眺望,照样没有看见什么。据一个小沙弥说:“佛光刚才现了一会儿。转眼就消灭了。”究竟是真是假,没有第二个人可以对证!反正在这儿一直等到太阳快要衔山我们始终没有和佛光结下缘。可是这半天因为我们尽在期待佛光,带累得也没有登成万佛顶和千佛顶。

洗象池前的猴群,在峨眉也是很出名的。据说在池前的石栏边或冷杉上,常常被一二百个猴子盘据着。游人如果拿包谷或其他的杂粮去喂它,就可以成天的不去。若是看不见,还可以给小和尚几个钱,让他在山门前大喊几声“猴居士”,它们就可以来了。猴群颇有组织,年老的领队,少壮的放哨。老的有三尺高,并不怕人;小猴儿只有五寸多高,毛色牙黄而润泽,常常紧附在母猴肚子上的毛里头,仅仅露出一点儿鼻子和眼睛,细看才能辨认出来。有时母猴从交错的树枝中,提溜着小猴儿扔着玩,小猴儿凌空而下,用手扶着树枝,好像打秋千一样,娇小玲珑,非常活泼生动!从游客手里取东西的时候,长幼有序,前后不紊,比重庆市民抢上汽车的秩序好得多。放哨的总得换着班儿来吃东西,遇到应该警戒的时候,它便啾啾高叫,倘若有人伤着一个猴儿,大家立刻现出一种狞恶的样儿来群起报复,很可以当得起“精神团结,共御外侮”两句口号。我们逛的时候正赶上包谷季,它们有东西可吃,就不容易喊得来,因此也未免有点儿遗憾。

我们这一回没从小路上山,我总觉得领略不够后山清幽的风景。到了九老洞,正赶上雾迷岩壑,又没能到三皇台去凭眺,尤其使我失望。据说在晴天的时候,站在三皇台上俯瞰华严顶下石笋千峰,青葱笏立,抵得一幅极美丽的画图。直到现在,我的脑子里还时常涌现这幽邃隽秀的想像。

此外,像九老洞的栱桐,白云寺以上的桫椤,因为来的时令不对,没看见它们开花,也不免有一些美中不足的情绪。

最末了儿但是不最小,还有一桩让我很失望的事,就是山里虽然有数不过来的老松,却没看见一根凌霄拿娇艳的红花点缀着它的苍翠!本来在这“高处不胜寒”的地带,具有后凋性质的松柏还勉强可以挨受,像那娇嫩的凌霄怎能禁得住一阵阵的不断吹来冷风?它早就找暖和的地方攀附在别的树上欣欣向荣去了!难怪我从乌尤寺找到峨眉山还是没有看见它!

十一 观光川大

四川大学自从疏散到峨眉后校址分散在好几个地方。7月18日上午9点承程天放校长和刘觉民、孙心磐、柯德发三位领我们到文、法学院的各部分去参观。图书馆现有中文书十万册,西文书二万册,还有一部分在成都没运来。因为地方潮湿,管理人对于书籍的保存上颇费心思。川大当局对于训育很认真,现在已经印出《训导须知》和《学生须知》两本小册子。我们参观男女学生宿舍时,柯君很仔细地把每间房的门都打开给我们看,并且告诉我们每间房住几个人,床怎样摆,下学年还要怎样重新隔断等等,足见他平时对于这一点非常注意,在他的办公室里还有画得很好看的许多图表。

17日晚上,在程校长家里,会到文学院院长向先乔先生(楚)。据他告诉我,川大中国文学系有向宗鲁[向承周]、龚向农、陈李皋、李炳英、徐中舒、殷石臞[殷孟伦]、胡芷蕃、穆济波、萧涤非、曾尔康几位。其中只有中舒和涤非本来是熟人,其余都没会过,假期中大半离开学校,所以也没有拜访的机会。先乔年近六十,容貌态度酷似顺德黄晦闻[黄节]先师。宗鲁治校雠目录学,著述颇多,北大文科研究所近两年来所收的刘念和、王叔岷、王利器诸生都是由他指导出来的。在川大图书馆里所保存的中国文学系学生毕业论文有《吕氏春秋校注》、《鹖冠子校注》、《说文段注校正》、《文选赋类异文考》、《诗经释词》、《左传引经考》、《左传地理今释》等;又藏有《四川大学国文选》二册,所收有礼记、诸子、史记、汉书、韩柳文、太炎文等:由此两部分,颇可以窥见他所提倡的风气的一斑。听说他对于教育部委托我所拟的中国文学系语言文字组课程草案,颇有批评。我这次很想会一会这个畏友,当面讨论一下。可惜不单我到峨眉没能见着他,最近中舒来信说“他已经在善觉寺病故，现尚停柩报国寺中”，从此竟自终古没有面商的机会了。

18日中午峨眉清华同学会在陈福记菜馆招待我们，约程校长夫妇作陪，主人共15位。涤非酒量很豪，我对他耿介寡合的性格非常同情，举杯对饮了两次，没想到我竟自醉了。

19日上午9点，张洪沅、郑含青、方端典三位领我们参观生物系实验室、物理化学实验室、理学院办公室。11点3刻冒雨移居山下峨眉旅行社。这里房间清洁，招待周到，饮食方便，比山上各庙强得多了。中午中舒在家里招待便饭。下午4点一同出北门，本来想到飞来殿，看一看思成所称赞的元代建筑，因为天晚路滑没能去成，只到绥山公园绕了一会儿，后来又转到东门外护国寺去看大佛。这个庙是明万历己巳建的，又叫做宝藏禅院或大佛寺。正殿供有千手大悲观音铜像，高三丈六尺，是明朝无穷大师别传募铸的。据说最初他本想把这尊大佛搬到顶上去，后来因为分量太重，难运入山，他才在万历辛卯年到北平，奏请慈宁陈太后（按，如果是陈太后尊号应该作“仁圣”，李太后曾经住过慈宁宫，但也没有“慈宁”的尊号）发帑金开建这个庙，并赐香灯田500亩。这尊大佛的帽子就有九尺高，相传起初帽子有点儿不正，后来把一个九尺高的小铜佛放在里头才正过来，现在帽缘低的地方还可以看见佛顶。佛前的木龛旁边有一口钟是明慈圣李太后所献，尚膳监苏炳监造的。后殿供文殊、普贤像都留着胡髭，相传是照西域的样子塑的，和普通的像不同。

下午6点含青、洪沅约到圣积寺。在一进门的老宝古楼前有两株大黄葛树，直径一丈多，大可十围，浓荫满地，碧色参天，在四川很少看见。旧传楼额有宋魏了翁所写的“峨山真境”四个字，现在已然看不见。楼外面还有一块石碑，刻着“古慈福院”四个篆字，是万历壬午四月分守川南道参议高任重题的。楼中间挂着一个八卦铜钟高九尺，径八尺，据说也是明朝别传和尚募铸的，每逢初一、十五的夜里敲它，声音可以直达金顶。寺里面的正殿供有铜铸普贤骑象像，象鼻子都被游人摸亮了。门外有一个铜炉，也是明朝的东西。后殿有永川万华轩施制的华严铜塔，高 20 尺，凡 14 层，铸佛 4700 尊，镌《华严经》全部，绿色斑斓，刻工精美，是很值得宝贵的。

这几天因为夹江水涨，从成都来的公共汽车不能开到峨眉，我们本打算 20 日从峨眉坐黄包车到夹江，然后再转成都。承程校长和许多朋友的好意，都怕到夹江后等不着汽车，就得坐三天黄包车，沿途还要住“海陆空并进”（“海”是外面下雨屋里立刻漏成河，“陆”是比坦克车还厉害的臭虫，“空”是赛过飞机的蚊子）的么店子，那就未免太苦了。所以他们主张打电报给武汉大学王校长［王星拱］请他替我们买成嘉公路的汽车票，先回到嘉定，再转成都。我们因为情不可却，就这样接受了他们的好意。谁想到事实演变的结果，比我们由峨眉直接坐黄包车所受的罪，竟至加了好几倍！

十二　走上了艰难的蜀道

7 月 20 日，上午 9 点 20 分，由峨眉旅行社坐黄包车，仍取道苏稽回嘉定。到了苏稽，方太太转草鞋渡搭船回家；我们一直坐车到乐山郊外的徐家塥汽车站后，又押着行李步行了七里。城里的嘉林公寓和息尘旅馆都住满了客人，好容易才在铁牛门白水街的嘉定饭店找着三个房间。当天晚上武汉大学王校长派人来通知，21 日早晨有公共汽车开成都，每张票 50 元，因为预先没有登记，得要送给司机 30 元小费，才能立刻买得票。我们想，只要少耽延几天，多花几个钱倒没什么，于是就决定托他买票。

第二天早晨 4 点半起来，6 点赶到车站，居然买到第七、第八、第九三张票，7点多，车也开来了。我们当时觉得很高兴，心里已经在盘算当天到成都后住在什么地方，先看哪几个朋友，若是像这样顺利，不出十天我们就可以回到昆明了。

车票虽然有号码，客人仍然争先恐后地自己挤上车去占座位；等到快开车了，售票员才又一个一个地喊下来叫着号码派定座位。可是最初占住后一排的几个客人，一死儿地盘据着不动，不知道预先有没有谅解，公路局的人对他们也就置之不问了。把号码叫完后，陆续还有没拿着票的客人上车，只要有一丁点缝儿他们就硬挤下去坐，也不管旁边的客人能否喘得过气来。除此之外，顶棚上还坐着四条“黄鱼”。

耗到8点20分，燃着木炭后，车总算开了。没想到刚走出20公里，到一个叫滩渡地方，就抛了锚。这个地方有一条小河，在干季本来没多深，平常只是三成水，这几天因为连下了几场大雨，立刻涨到七成水。河的对岸泊着公路局的一条大渡船，司机喊那个船上的梢公叫他把车渡过去；他借口水大流急，怕有危险，无论如何不肯解缆。司机叫了两声没人理，他也坐在一旁，不闻不问了。据几位常走蜀道的客人说：“这是两边正在要价还价的表示，大家要肯出几个钱，也许马上就可以过渡。”当时有两位热心的本地人就坐着另外的小划子到对岸去磋商，终于白费唇舌，毫无结果。就这样僵着，从10点20分一直耗到12点，司机既然不闻不问，另外也找不着公路局的人去理论。头上烈日炎炎，腹中饥肠辘辘，嘴里渴得冒烟，连一棵树荫、一块糍粑、一口开水都找不着。正在无可如何的当儿，后面忽然又开来一辆卡车，上面的客人，远望着黑乌乌的比盯在一块臭肉上的苍蝇还多。其中有兵役署的公务员，有军人，有男女学生，还有其他各色人等。最引起我注意的，有一个五十岁上下的老头儿，身材不很高，瘦瘦的，脸上略带烟容，穿着咖啡色的绸衫，戴着白草帽。紧跟在他身后还有两个身材高大的年轻人，他们在白纺绸的褂裤上罩着一件荔枝绸的长背心，脚上穿着绿丝袜黑缎鞋，毫不爱惜地就往水里踩，裆底下鼓鼓囊囊的有一个兜子。我起初还以为两个人同时害疝气呢，细一看原来每人各带着一架盒子枪。他们站在岸上喊了两声梢公，就坐划子到对岸去了。有认识他们的人说，那个老头儿是这条路上的"舵把子"，跟着他的两个人是他手下的"袍哥儿"，他们一过去也许过渡有希望了。果然待不大会儿我们车上的司机也从对岸回到这边来了，他和跟车的助手啾咕了两句，那个助手就运用"集中力量"的新名词，和每个客人勒索两元过渡费。钱收得差不多，对岸的梢公也招呼伙计，解缆执篙，立刻把船撑过来了。

过渡的办法是把船头接上两条木板，宽窄和车轮相当，距离和轮轴相等；因为水大流急，车不能直着开上去，斜着一点儿好减轻冲击的力量。费了半天事，船夫算是把木板接好了，用绳子也把船扎稳了，车上的客人都先跑到对岸眼巴巴地期待着；一会儿司机开动引擎，汽车呜呜作响，前头两个车轮已然开到木板上，大家正在高兴的当儿，没想到车后面的一个轮子已经悬了空，尽管转得怎样快，再不能把车身推进一寸。而且车身倾侧，系在顶棚上的行李晃晃荡荡的，眼看着我的箱子里那些未完成的文稿立刻就要付诸东流，怎能不急得出了一身透汗？这时候，船夫们手忙脚乱，客人们垂头丧气，司机却袖手旁观，蹲在一边儿吸香烟。忽然从离这儿八里以外的甘江铺跑来一个公路局的人员，他自告奋勇地跳下河去，指挥船夫们把那块离开车轮的木板用石头垫起一边儿来，为是让它的斜度恰好可以衔接那个落空的轮子的底下。可惜他们辛辛苦苦、"邪许"震天地工作了两三点钟，只因为力学常识不够，没把支重力三点安排妥当，板子搭好以后，车刚往上一开猛然间磕碴一声，船身动摇，石头滚落，板子滑开，车轮照旧出轨，车身倾侧的程度比前一回更厉害。

这一回大家简直的绝望了。那个自告奋勇的人也跳上岸来,拧干了衣服,躲在一边儿一筹莫展。梅先生急得皱着眉,噘着嘴,一支接着一支地吸纸烟,一句话也没有;毅生平常虽然指挥若定,不慌不忙,这时候却也满脸涨得通红,不住地拿手绢擦汗;我始终惦记着箱子里那些稿子,恐怕多少年的心血没像罗膺中[罗庸]先生那样惨遭回禄,却在路上无意中被了水灾,于是不顾一切地再渡到河那边,穿着皮鞋爬到已然向河心倾侧的车顶上去解行李,鞋底子简直滑得站不住脚。幸而在车上临时认识一位西南联大叙永分校的同学汤元森和一位乐山国立技术专门学校的同学金问瀛,仗着他们两位帮助,我和四件行李算是没有一同滚到河里去。把行李运到对岸后,嘴里渴得要命;毅生花了两块钱,托路旁一家乡下人给我烧了五大碗开水,我顾不得烫嘴不烫嘴,一口气儿喝了个干净,当时的感觉,比坐在重庆冠生园喝冰镇的鲜橘汁,或在酷暑的天气咀嚼着飞机运来的鲜哈密瓜,都似乎有味道得多。这一刹那才充分了解"渴者易为饮"的真正意义。

一直耗到下午4点半,一半陷在河里的车始终没有救起来的希望;对岸虽然从夹江开来了一辆车,可是两方面的司机没讲好交换"黄鱼"的条件,宁可对耗着也不肯"打兑"。我们恐怕这样待下去到晚上连蹲一夜的地方都没有,只得雇了两个挑夫挑着行李步行到甘江铺,找着一家么店子就歇下了。这家么店子前面是茶馆,后面有几个客房,我们住的一间有三张木床,每张上面各铺着一领草荐,地下湿得往外浸水,隔壁厕所和后院猪圈的气味,一阵阵地从那仅有的一个小窗口里吹进来,大有"熏"风恼人眠不得的味儿。我们为防御"陆""空"的侵袭,把油布铺在草荐上,又燃着好几条土制的蚊香,一切工事都布置好了,才到街上找点饮食。甘江铺地方虽小,街道倒还干净,浓绿成荫的梧桐树夹植在砖甬路的两旁,别有一种幽静的风致。我们在桐荫底下的一个街摊仅仅找到两碗豆浆稀饭聊解这一天的饥渴。当天晚上起初睡得不大好,后来忽然又下起大雨来。我想假如这一晚停到滩渡的旷野郊,上不着村,下不着店,渴了喝不到水,饿了找不到东西吃,下雨没有地方躲避,那岂不更要狼狈万分?这样退一步想,渐渐也就睡稳神安了。

22 日早晨 6 点半花八元雇黄包车到夹江。本来想到那里的汽车站去办交涉,好换车往前走。谁晓得到夹江以后,车站早把"洪水暴涨上下无车行驶"的牌子挂出来了。这样一来,夹江当真把我们"夹"在那儿了。万分无奈,只好在王家祠旅社后面匀出一张铺位来,同屋还有一个病人在那里呻吟不绝。挨到 10 点 20 分,同行的忽然有人提议从这里雇黄包车当天"拢"眉山,每辆价 55 元,我们赶路心急,也赞成和他们一起走。于是一行六辆车,向车站办了退票的手续后(手续虽然办了,可是票价至今还没有退还,结果我们每人花了 80 元只坐了 20 公里的汽车),10 点 40 分就冒雨动身,路上还遇到一阵大雨,衣服和行李全淋湿了。11 点 45 分过螺丝圈,坡陡难爬,车夫临时雇人"拉坡"才曳过去。12 点半到土门铺,车夫吃饭后,拉我的那一个忽然要补皮带,这样一耽误,同行的那三个人不耐烦多等,于是就把我们三个老搭档落在后头了,下午 2 点 40 分到张爷庙大桥,花去 20 分钟才过了渡。3 点 10 分过两路坡,比螺丝圈更难爬。过坡以后,我坐的车皮带又坏了,这样一误再误,直到 4 点 15 分才过了娴婆镇,5 点钟才到了思濛河。车夫借口天色已晚,前面到线滩还要过渡,当天无论如何不能拢眉山,极力劝我们住在这里;我们也恐怕黑天走生路,诸多不便,只好就听了他们的话了。

思濛河离乐山 61.461 公里,到成都还有 99.745 公里,我们耗费了两整天,结果才勉勉强强走了五分之二的路。思濛虽然不是什么大镇,可是听老于蜀道的人说:"成嘉公路的司机到这里总要设法抛锚,就像成渝公路的司机喜欢在来凤驿抛锚一样。他们为什么要这样呢?据说他们的'贵相知'都拿这两个地方作大本营,他们仆仆风尘,不得不找个地方消遣消遣;至于客人是否要露宿在荒郊,他们满没放在心里。"这一段话还没听完,忽然一辆汽车风驰电掣地开过思濛镇,同车的金问瀛还向我们招招手儿,说了两句话。原来他们向夹江站长交涉的结果,下午3点钟就换了这个车出发了。我当时一方面颇悔我们"欲速不达"的急性子,一方面也觉得刚才所听到的话不可尽信。

谁知道第二天早晨刚走到离开思濛不够二里的镇南桥,果然看见昨晚开过去的车抛锚在路边,车上的客人,一个个面色灰白、两眼枯涩,有的在河边洗脸,有的在车上打盹儿,显见得是一宿失眠的样儿。到这时候才把那位老江湖的话证实了。我们走出去没多远,雨越下越大。车夫简直淋得上气不接下气,勉强拉到盐水井的一个茶亭,只好暂时避一避。这个地方虽然有一家小铺儿,可是没有什么东西卖,我们尽它所有的沽了四两包谷酒,就着落满了尘土的炸麻花儿,姑且赶赶寒气,充充饥,又央告老板娘泡了一壶浑水茶,虽然苦涩不大好咽,究竟比渴着好受得多。挨到10点半,雨稍微小一点儿,又冒着雨往前走。11点45分到了线滩,没想到公路局在这里所备的渡船,从这一天早晨起,因为水涨竟自封渡了。连我们一共十几辆黄包车都堆在那儿不能过去,任凭你怎样大声喊叫,对岸管渡船的公路局人员一概置若罔闻。耗到12点多钟,大家的肚子都饿得咕噜咕噜地叫,也没地方买东西吃。幸亏毅生机警,花九块钱,让一个乡下小孩买了一升米,就托他的家里给我们煮一煮。这一家似乎很穷,几间茅屋脏得不堪,满院子黑泥和猪屎,弄得一塌糊涂,简直没有下脚的地方,我们把乐山北大同学杜高厚所送的罐头熏肉和榨菜拿出来,当珍馐美味吃,一边喝着米汤,一边嚼着半生不熟的饭。这时候有四个小孩儿,四个女人,16只眼睛都在目不转睛地注视着我们,假如我是个写生家,眼前简直是很好的一幅油画。我心里在想,四川米价这样高,绝不会"谷贱伤农"。何以这一班农人对于米饭如此希罕?后来一打听,才知道这一班佃户把所得一点谷子早已卖光,有的甚至于连包谷都吃不上。至于罐头食品在他们更是希罕物儿了。

吃完饭后,一直在河边耗到下午3点钟,幸而有一位军官的护兵向对岸放了四响盒子枪,那个渡船才算撑过来,可是那个管渡船的公路局人员公然向大家说:"现在生活高涨,连包谷都卖50元一斗,我们专靠路局一点薪水,真是连烧炭喝水都不够,所以不得不请诸位帮衬一下,黄包车过渡每辆请付五元,有钱的便过,没钱的免过。"后来开了两次船,渡过11辆车来,其中虽然也有几辆少给一两块钱,可是有五六位取巧的坐车人先空身渡过河来,打算要偷关漏税。那个管船的当真就把他们的几辆车落在河那边儿,置之不理。

4点3刻渡过线滩,车夫放足了脚力往前赶,5点3刻,才拢了眉山。预定一天的道儿,竟自走了两天,还受了这么多的罪,只好自怨命运坎坷。恐怕从夹江同行的那三位早就到成都了。当晚宿在北道旅馆,"陆""空"交袭,彻夜未能合眼。

26日早晨4点半,困眼蒙眬地起来,5点坐黄包车从眉山出发,讲明了当天拢成都,每辆价65元。8点进彭山县丽明门,刚走了20多公里,车夫在我们吃早饭的当儿,就起意"漂车"(他们管换车叫"漂车")少走路,多赚钱,为取巧自私,不惜剥削同行,充分表现了他们的劣性,同这种人真是没道理可讲的。漂车以后,9点25分继续前进,在北门外的公路旁边看见"汉张纲故里"和"晋李密故里"的石碑。11点45分过兴隆场,12点半入新津县境,下午1点40分拢邓公塘。新津是灌县下游三条河水汇归的地方,每到洪水泛滥的时候,过渡非常困难,所以俗谚有"走遍天下路,难过新津渡"的说法。我们没到这儿以前，很怕到这儿又要出什么“拐”，幸而仰仗上帝的保佑，从2点20分到3点，居然风平浪静地把我们渡过来了。当船夫把黄包车抬到船上的时候，我们虽然站着挤在人堆里没有回旋的余地，身子随着激荡的江流不住地摇晃，可是一回想起前两天在滩渡和线滩的滋味来，无论如何是轻松快活的。这一刹那回头望见邓公塘山上的修觉寺、华严寺、二郎庙、玉皇殿等许多寺观，参差错落地掩映在一片浓绿中间，居然也有闲情逸致来欣赏它的美丽了。

过渡后，在旧县稍微休息一会儿，有一辆小汽车的司机向我们兜揽生意。我们心急似箭，恨不得马上到了成都，也有意无意地和他磋商磋商，没想到因为买不到汽油没坐成汽车，结果倒被黄包车夫敲了一笔小竹杠。4点半过兴隆场，再经黄水镇，到双流县，天已经6点多了。从旧县雇来的黄包车夫又在“漂”车。我换到的一个，笨而无力，走两步歇三步，还不住地气喘如牛，在离成都南门还有四公里的地方，他简直拉不动了，我只得下车跟在他后面，细雨濛濛，漆墨乌黑的陌生路上，踽踽独行了八华里。9点半到南门后，毅生已经等了我半点多钟了。赶紧再换车到城里骡马市大川饭店新改的中国旅行社，匆匆忙忙间，很万幸的算是只丢了我一顶呢帽。

我们就在这深更半夜里到了成都。

十三 尝尝成都跑警报的滋味

到四川后所经过的城市，我最喜欢的是成都，因为它除去城圈子不很见方，街道稍嫌纡曲以外，有好些地方都像我的故乡北平。比如春熙路的繁华像王府井，玉龙街的风雅像琉璃厂，打金街像廊房头条，少城像后门里头，薛涛井和陶然亭的风格相近，草堂寺和松筠庵的规模仿佛，华西坝一带简直是具体而微的成府或清华园，只有武侯祠的地方色彩特别浓厚,在北平一时还找不出适当的对照来,美中不足的是,我们在成都只停了六天,却有四天遇见警报,“七二七”的空前大轰炸我们碰巧会躬逢其盛。

7月25日上午,因为前两天路上太辛苦了,在旅行社休息了半天,下午1点半到四圣祠医院去看寄谦[张寄谦]。她自从1939年统考取录后,教育部没能照她的第一志愿分派在西南联大,勉强在川大待了半年,肺病就发作了。一个年轻轻的孩子,独自在举目无亲的异乡害病,这是十分值得同情的,所以我到成都后第一个就去看她。她看见我,惊喜交集地喊了一声“二叔”,两行热泪立刻就淌在脸上!尽我可能地安慰了她几句,并且谈了一些昆明熟人的消息,才把她逗笑了。4点返寓,郭子杰[郭有守]和沈茀斋来访,晚7点邓锡侯先生约我们在南打金街王宅聚谈,借机会晤到朱佩弦[朱自清]、陈斠玄[陈中凡]、李幼春、李伯申[李肇甫]、刘式传、王孟甫几位和许多不大熟识的成都“文化人”。

成都在许多好处之外,值得提一下的还有小吃和市招,比如像“姑姑筵”、“哥哥传”之类,声名已经洋溢四川以外,自然用不着特别介绍了;就是像“不醉无归小酒家”、“忙休来”、“徐来”之类,先不用问它们的口味是否适口,单凭这几个招牌就够“吃饱饭,没事干”的骚人墨客流连半天的。甚至于一个卖豆浆的小铺也用“万里桥东豆乳家”七个字做招牌,未免雅得有点儿让人肉麻了。可惜我们来的时候,正赶上米珠薪桂的年头儿,“姑姑筵”一餐酒席就得四五百元,朋友们既然不敢轻易请客,我们更不敢贸然到这些地方去问津。倒是,26日中午,佩弦约我们和新从兰州回来的徐绍谷全家到名不雅而物甚美的“吴抄手”去领略本地风光,我们却非常得到实惠。不过一碗山大菰面索价三元二角,物虽美价未免欠廉了。此外,还有很著名的“黄胖鸭”和“赖汤圆”,可惜没抽出工夫去领略一下。

26日下午3点到华西坝去参观华西、齐鲁、金陵大学会到张凌高、刘式传、陈裕光、吴贻芳四位校长,高巍巍的楼房,绿莹莹的草地,看惯了我们那茅茨不翦、蒿莱不除的校舍,来到此俨然有天上人间之感。这四大学现在联而不合,校舍全借用华西的,一切开支按学生多寡的比例分配,有一位西籍的总会计专司其事。各大学中国文学系的状况,据我约略向各校当局询问所及的,华西方面,主任为庞石帚[庞俊],教授有林山腴[林思进]、钟正楙、李培甫、杜奉符、闻在宥[闻宥]、吕叔湘;齐鲁方面,主任为钱宾四[钱穆],教授有林昇平、邓子琴、胡福林[胡厚宣]、孙次舟、张维思;金陵男大方面,自余贤勋病故后,主任由文学院长刘国钧兼任,教授有高文、罗倬汉、张守义、陈延杰;金陵女大方面,主任为陈斠玄,教授有邵祖平和曾小姐等。至于三大学的中国文化研究所:齐鲁由顾颉刚主持,另外还有钱宾四、张维华、张维思、胡福林、孙次舟几位;金陵由李小缘[李国栋]主持,另外还有徐益棠、商锡永[商承祚]、刘叔遂几位;华西由闻在宥主持,另外还有吕叔湘、韩儒林两位。听说我的学生傅懋勣上学年也被在宥从华中罗致到华西做副教授兼副研究员,薪尽火传,颇为欣慰。这三个研究所的风格,大致齐鲁偏重历史,金陵偏重考古,华西偏重语言,不过中间也没有严格的分野;经费的来源都是由哈佛燕京社供给的。在这许多位中间,颉刚、斠玄、宾四、在宥、叔湘、锡永、小缘、子琴、福林本来是熟人,其余几位还都没有会过,林山腴的诗名很高,记得李审言[李祥]有一首《赠古公愚》的诗道:“雅才今日推梅县,诗派华阳起正声。文字论交半天下,平章要识此时情。”梅县指着公愚,华阳便是推崇他,他家里的肴馔也很精美,在成都,“林山公菜”和“姑姑筵”是伯仲之间的。

从华西大学出来,到后坝三大学肺病疗养院去看杨君庆惠,他是我的亲戚,曾在空军军官学校第九期毕业。当这一期毕业的时候,林徽因女士的弟弟林恒在驱逐组考第三,他在轰炸组考第三,都是那一班优秀分子,可惜一个毕业不久就壮烈地殉国,一个刚毕业就发现肺病;我真为国家养士可惜。庆惠本来是个很“棒”的小伙子,人品、志气、技术、学识都值得佩服;不幸得了这样延缠的病,看见他真让我难过,幸好他的脸色和精神都很好,大约不久,就可以康复了。我相信他一定还能替国家,替民族,建立一番功业。这个疗养院统共不到二十个人,可是有七个是空军出身的。关于这一点,我希望航空委员会和航校的负责当局对于在校或出校员生的营养卫生都得特别注意才好!

晚7点,子杰在广益学舍请我们吃饭,同座有沈蒹斋、蒙文通、吴毓明、刘式传等。8点同毓明访在宥和叔湘,华西中国文化研究所的季刊已经印出两期,可惜在内地很难看得见,这一晚在在宥那里才看见了航空寄来的样本。纸张的考究,印刷的精美,绝不是在昆明或重庆所能找到的。

在成都刚过了两天消停的日子,忽然又疲于奔命地跑起警报来了。27日早晨8点,子杰约我们和蒹斋、佩弦去游武侯祠。出南门外一里多地,老远就望见古柏参天、气象森严的一所祠宇,那便是杜工部所谓“锦官城外柏森森”的蜀相祠堂了。这个祠堂本来叫做“汉昭烈祠”,可是诸葛亮的声名和功业在一般民众心里比刘备普遍得多,结果反倒君以臣掩一变而为“武侯祠”。祠的前殿供着昭烈帝像,旁边有北地王配享,左右配殿分祀关张,两庑还塑着蜀汉二十八功臣,后殿的武侯像本来塑着丞相衣冠,可是不知道哪个受了《三国演义》的影响的俗人擅自给他披上一件八卦衣,送给他一把鹅毛扇。这和美国芝加哥博物馆根据梅兰芳《贵妃醉酒》的戏装去追摹杨玉环的遗容,可谓无独有偶的滑稽可笑。在这一层殿里,左边供着诸葛瞻,右边供着诸葛尚,壁上刻的题咏虽多,但没有超过清代以前的,其中有季刚[黄侃]先师的尊人黄云鹄先生的一首诗,倒引起我不少念旧之感。从武侯祠出来,又驱车到新西门外余家桥去凭吊"浣花溪水水西头"的草堂寺,这个地方门禁得很森严,子杰掏出一张教育厅长的官衔片子来,守门的才把我们放进去。草堂三楹,中间供着杜工部,左右分祀黄山谷和陆放翁;堂后有杜像刻石三,黄陆像刻石各一。我对着这千古诗圣的故宅虽然有无限的"思古之幽情",可是,要追慕当年"桤林碍日吟风叶,笼竹和烟滴露梢"的遗风余韵,简直一点儿都领略不到了。

当我们还没有到草堂寺以前,在路上已经看见了预行警报的黄旗,成都人因为最近几个月敌机并没有当真来过,所以大家的心里,简直不拿情报当一回事,没想到这一次敌机可当真来了——而且还来了108架!9点40分发过空袭警报后,我们还在城西四家村李幼春的家里谈天;10点45分续发紧急警报,还没有过十分钟敌机就飞到头上了。紧跟着高射炮声隆隆,投弹声轰轰,几间房子动摇得像地震,屋顶上的瓦和窗子上的玻璃被激荡得上下交响着;这一刹那的紧张情绪事后很难把它追述出来。在下午1点40分解除警报后,我们本打算到昭忠祠街赴梅东华的约会,谁知道在城里坐着车东冲西撞地盘旋了总够半点多钟,压根儿没找到一条可以通过的路。举目所见不是栋折榱崩,瓦砾遍地,就是胆断肱飞,血肉模糊!这一次灾区之广,伤人之多,打破了成都历来遭遇空袭的纪录。一直到4点我们才从城外绕到梅家吃成了午饭,这时虽然饿了半天未尝不饥肠辘辘,虽然感谢东华给我们预备下在昆明三年看不见的鲜虾和西瓜,可是一想起刚才亲眼目睹的惨状,无论有什么珍馐美味也觉得不是滋味!回到旅行社以后,看见离开我住的房子不到两丈远就中了一个大炸弹,我的房里虽然顶棚震落,尘土满地,幸而还没有直接命中,还不至于把我在滩渡辛辛苦苦从汽车顶上冒险抢救下来的那个箱子化成灰烬。

晚7点到焦家巷赴张怡荪[张煦]的约会。怡荪从离开山东大学中国文学系以后就专心去办西陲文化院的事业，当晚因为惊魂甫定没能详细询问他院务进展的情形，可是就他已经印好的《藏汉字典》，汉译耶士基《藏语文法》和《西康详图》来看，足征他在这抗战期间确乎闭户埋头地作出了一些成绩。

28日，早晨7点40分就有了敌机入川的情报，黄旗刚一挂出，全市立刻骚动，黄包车价钱飞涨，街道上挤不动的人群，各各扶老携幼，提包挑担，慌慌张张，抢抢攘攘，直着眼睛往前奔，成都市民再没有昨天以前那样镇静了。我们随着北大老同事雍克昌到西门外九里桥去躲避，好容易跑出西门，到了郊外只见疏散的群众夹在稻田中间的小道上成两条直线的样子向前蠕动着，绝不能作面的展开，一旦敌机临头这是最危险不过的。所以在成都遇到空袭，不单没有重庆那样安全的防空设备，连昆明那种跑警报的味儿都赶不上，因为第一，城市太大，从城里跑到郊外已经得费去很长的时间，走出很远的道路；第二东南北三门外各有轰炸的目标，比较上只有西路安全一点儿，因此，一遇到警报这条路上往往拥挤不堪；第三，成都郊外到处都是水田，不像昆明郊外那样空旷，要想跑出去不远就找到一个像昆明北郊的陑山、西郊的福海村、东郊的昙花寺、南郊的船房那样既有掩蔽又非常宽敞的地方，那是绝对办不到的。我们这一天，除去城里的一段路不算，来回一共走了18里，把我的皮鞋都跑绽了，结果却是一场"惩羹吹齑"的虚惊。然而因此却领略了克昌家里的田园风味，他的田庄在九里桥的道旁，周围共30亩，丛竹密翳，曲溪萦回，从外面简直不容易发现它，中午一餐便饭，承主人"自锄稀菜甲，小摘为情亲"，吃着格外香甜有味。成都坝子上的田，天干不旱，淫雨不涝，向来是很出名的，近来经"山东一人，山西一人”在那儿大量的收买，每亩已飞涨到一千四五百元。他这30亩田都交给佃户种着，每年“大春”，每亩交谷一石九斗，按四川现在谷价说，这笔收入总算很可观了。克昌是研究生物学的，现在西北师范学院任教，假如我要是他，我一定摆脱一切帮着弟弟在家经营田庄，一方面常和自然界接触也还可以不废所学，又何必仆仆风尘，一年往返两次，乃至于四次城固呢。

晚7点张岳军[张群]先生在励志社招待我们，同座有茀斋、佩弦、毓明、邓品纯、张凌高，陪席的是郭子杰、胡次威两位厅长，席间谈起白天在警报声中共有敌机150架分五批袭川，第一批炸重庆，第二批炸泸州、自流井，第三批炸内江、自流井，第四、五两批均炸自流井，损失情况还没得到详细报告。

29日早晨8点15分，预行警报的黄旗又挂出来了。本来约定这一天到宋公桥去看佩弦，被警报催逼着，索性就手儿逛了一趟东门外的望江楼。望江楼因为薛涛出的名，现在在薛涛井旁还有一块碑，刻着她暮年着女冠服的画像和清乾隆乙卯周厚辕所写的唐胡曾诗“万里桥边女校书，枇杷巷里闭门居，扫眉才子知多少，管领春风总不如”。匆匆地游览一周，便坐在吟诗楼上俯瞰锦江的碧流，从从容容地等警报，果然，9点20分笛声轰响了。我们随着茀斋到川大农学院院长王尧臣家里去躲避。12点15分忽然有机声隆隆在空中盘旋了约摸半点多钟，我们躲在防空壕里既没听见紧急警报，也没听见高射炮的声音，究竟是敌机，是我机，始终没弄明白。下午2点50分解除警报后，从农学院的后门坐鸡公车到新南门，这也是生平的第一次经验。鸡公车比北方的独轮小车子矮而小，人在上面脊背靠着一块板，两脚伸在轮子前边几乎可以擦着地，走起来，这声音吱吱吅吅的，令人发生一种不调和的、刺耳的、吵噪的感觉；我想它得名的原由，除去象形而外，这种声音也或许是可能的。

4点，在宥、叔湘约我和毅生在广益学舍里华西大学中国文学系茶叙，凌纯声、芮逸夫、马昌寿三位前一天刚到成都，颉刚从崇义桥赶进城，在这里全会着了，另外还见着三大学里许多位旧交新识的朋友。最让我高兴的是碰见了冯汉骥先生，近年来听见弄人类学的朋友提起H.K.Feng的名字来，又在*Harvard Journal of Asiatic Studies*里面看见他两篇文章，这天一见面，原来15年前我们在厦门大学就同过事了。散会后到鲁斋去看宾四，他今天才从青木关回来，我们因为还要参加清华同学会的宴会，匆匆忙忙没能多谈，约定第二天一早再去看他。

晚7点成都清华同学会在总府街涨秋餐馆欢迎梅先生，约子杰、东华、弗斋、佩弦、毅生和我作陪，饭后由主席宋涟波致词，梅先生和子杰都有演说。我一路上跟着梅先生参加好几次清华同学会，想等着机会在这里说几句答谢的话，现在约略还记得那一晚说的话大概是：

“每逢我参加清华同学会的盛宴的时候，梅先生总向大家给我介绍说：‘罗先生是我们清华的校友。’真的，在西南联大里头，假如我要巴结的话，我不单可以算是清华的校友，而且还可以算是南开的校友，可是，撇开这一层资格不提，我另外还可以找得出跟吃跟喝的好理由来。今年清华开30周年纪念会的时候，张伯苓先生打一个电报给黄子坚[黄钰生]先生说——‘清华和南开是通家之好，我们得从丰的庆祝。’当时子坚在会场上大作‘通家’的解释，最精彩的几句是：‘清华现在的校长是南开第一班的高材生，南开的教授又有好多是清华出身的，并且两校的同人还有许多叙得上姻娅的关系。’后来冯芝生[冯友兰]先生又代表北大说：‘要是叙起通家之好来，北大也并不后人，比如说，北大文学院院长胡适之先生是清华人，兄弟是北大人现在却担任着清华文学院院长，再者子坚先生说,清华同学向来穿衣服讲究"倍儿亮",北大同学总是大布之衣、大帛之冠的不修边幅,可是今天清华校友代表吴泽霖先生的衣服却充分地表现着北大的风格。'这两段颇有风趣的演说在当时非常动听,要是给他们补充几句,我还可以说:现在北大的同事有许多是清华、南开出身的,而在座的北大同学朱佩弦先生却在清华有很悠久的历史,此外像杨今甫、周枚荪[周炳琳]几位先生,乃至于兄弟个人,都在清华服务过一个时期,拿这些关系难道还叙不上'通家'吗? 既然是通家至好,诓两顿饭吃还有什么拉不下脸来的? ——"

我说完这段话,王士倬先生和一位现在叫不上名儿来的清华同学各自敬了我一杯酒,宾主才尽欢而散。

30日早晨7点45分,已经有预行警报,梅先生一起来就到茶店子拜客去了,我和毅生赶紧雇车到华西坝去找宾四,8点20分刚到广益学舍门口儿空袭警报就响了。约上宾四,随着叔湘全家,到附近一个碉堡底下去躲避;在那里碰见在宥、颉刚、斠玄、纯声、逸夫、昌寿许多熟人,后来又到小缘家里去谈天。这一天敌机虽然没来,可是听说一共有七批分别轰炸重庆等处,直耗到下午3点警报才解除。我和毅生利用这个空儿很恳切地劝宾四返校。我想像宾四这样富感情重然诺的朋友,不久一定会回到北大来的。4点,承颉刚、宾四、斠玄、在宥、王栻五位,招待我们在中西餐馆吃午饭;晚8点,又累芾斋和协和中学吴先忧校长破费,让我们在离开成都以前领略一点儿"哥哥传"的滋味。

十四 可靠的邮车居然出了"拐"!

在成都本来想多流连几天,最初还有登青城山、游都江堰的雅兴,可是住过六天反倒兴趣索然,急于想走,一则因为连续跑了几天警报,颇感力尽筋疲;二则接到蒋梦麟先生从重庆打来的电报,我们急欲会他;三则在路上出乎意外地耽误了这么多日子,自备的资斧早已告竭:所以在7月30日托东华代向邮政局定好车票后,决定第二天一早就动身。只是一件事有点儿遗憾:我们刚到成都那一天,就接到充和[张充和]寄来一封信指点游青城的途径说:"由灌县去青城山约35华里,有两路可走:一摆渡,一经索桥,来回可走不同的路,到青城即住天师洞,万不可住上清宫,因为那里的道士俗气逼人,竟有一道士满口二百五的英文,除结交要人外,又爱结识教授,琐琐麻人!天师洞主持为彭椿仙,年高德茂;另有易道士心滢者读书最多,貌甚癯雅,如有兴,可与一谈;还有一个伍知客,古风道貌潇洒出尘,可入画,不可以谈话;有一弹七弦琴道士盖与彭祉卿同派,粗慢无礼,亦无其他修养,以不听为是。天师洞正殿有一对石狮,一狮足踏一法螺,有孔可吹,音甚洪亮。青城茶有名,天师洞不如上清宫,因其居卑处下,不见阳光,上清宫则反之;山上有奇鸟,黄昏即鸣,姑名之曰知更鸟。"可惜我们匆匆忙忙的没能照她所说的去览胜寻幽,姑且记下这段话作为梦游的指南,保持着有余不尽的兴致。

在离开成都的前一天,我们已经托蓉市警察局秘书主任郭喆卿替梅先生定了31日的飞机票;可是梅先生觉得邮车只比飞机晚到一天,既可以节省去两百多块钱,三个人还可以不至于分散,所以他毅然决然地退掉了飞机票,仍然和我们一块儿坐邮车——的确,除去飞机以外这是成渝公路上最可靠的交通工具。

7月31日早晨5点,我们冒着大雨赶到西川邮政管理局,承东华和运输股吴华农股长的帮忙,把行李和座位都给我们安置"规一",同行的除去我们三个以外还有中央大学师范学院英语系杨宪益教授和他的夫人 Gladys Taylor 女士,另外还有一位到自流井供职的邮务佐林君。梅先生和杨太太坐在司机台,我们四个坐在后面。上面遮好帆布棚，下雨也不至于渗进来。司机名张培芝，北平人，看样子很老实。梅、吴两股长也替我们关照过了，7 点 25 分开车，10 点 15 分拢简阳，早餐。外面的雨虽然淅淅沥沥地下个不住，可是这 75 公里畅行无阻，一点儿问题都没发生。

没想到 11 点 10 分离开简阳，刚过了 30 分钟，走出去不到五公里，在一个叫七里碑的地方，忽然因为山洪暴发，河水漫过了公路，车便不能前进了。我困眼蒙眬地闷坐在帆布棚里，有时候幻想这是童子军的露营，有时候幻想我被困在戈壁沙漠的蒙古包中，恍恍惚惚的又焦急又难过。一会儿后面又抛锚了一辆四川公路局的木炭车，全体旅客总动员，下车来和临时雇的民夫共同推搡，费了九牛二虎的力量才把这辆车掉转头去开回了成都。经这件事一提醒，前几天我们在滩渡所遭的困厄不由得又涌现在眼前了。一直耗到 3 点 50 分，水稍微落了一点儿。司机试着把车涉水而过，慢慢地往前开，刚开到中流，水的力量把车身冲得往左歪，司机手忙心乱，一时控制不住，便把车子的一边开到公路外头的田地里，车身倾侧得很厉害，黄泥汤儿立刻流进车厢来，这时假如我们稍一张皇，起身乱动，让车子失去平衡，马上就会有翻车灭顶的危险。幸亏大家还沉得住气，从容不迫地等司机用一条粗绳子把车子系在远远的一棵树上，然后才一个一个地慢慢爬下车来。我当时只穿着衬衫和短裤，让一个乡下人领着在河里走，河水一直漫过大腿根，急流激荡得上身乱晃，这时才后悔在青岛住过一夏天却没学会泅水。等到人完全出了险，再慢慢地抢救行李，我的一个 fibre 箱子已经被水浸透，箱子毁了，衣服和稿子也全湿了。

过河后，在一个叫新市铺的小镇，找到一家么店子来安栈。我们三个住在一间七尺见方，挤下三个床铺，潮湿黑暗，空气不大流通的小房子，那位带着洋太太的杨先生也不得不暂时降低他们的“文化水准”,找到一间小屋,向毅生借了一床被单,也就勉强随遇而安。我顾不得休息睡觉,开开箱子对着一叠叠的湿稿子、一件件的湿衣服,紧皱双眉,一筹莫展。

8月1日上午,张司机赔了124元钱,雇了许多民夫,才把汽车救过河来。不过电瓶着水,非得修理好了不能再开,我趁着这个空儿就在来安栈前面的茶馆用炭盆来烘稿子。12点5分继续开车,这时跟车的邮差因为两位股长没在眼前,便不大耐烦替我们遮罩棚腾位子了,四个人挤在邮包堆里,上面太阳晒着,既没有草帽又不能撑伞,纵然昨天稍微受了一些潮湿,可是对于这么强烈的日光也着实有点儿吃不消。车开到102公里的地方,桥又被水冲坏了。幸而水已退净,路面还看得出来。司机十二分谨慎地把车子开过这重险关,大家想起昨天的情形来都不禁捏着一把汗。没想到刚渡过一重险关又碰着一块绝地。下午1点10分到了105公里的长寿桥,路面被水冲坏了三丈多长,桥梁倾圮,据说非得两礼拜不能修复,无论如何车子也开不过去了。这时司机除去盼望对面来车设法“打兑”以外,急得一点儿主意都没有。我们等到下午3点丝毫没有好消息,只得雇人挑着行李步行渡河。承资阳邮局李旭初局长招待晚餐,并且给我们找到一家紫东客栈,局面和设备比新市铺的来安栈强多了,可是我因为烘烤衣物,一直耗到夜里3点钟还没能睡觉。

8月2日早晨李局长来说,内江没有车到,恐怕前面的路也坏了,他已经替我们包了一条民船,价洋200元,走得快一点当天就可以拢内江。我们在这路费拮据的时候虽然不愿意平白多花这笔钱,可是再要等起来更觉得沉闷,只好就采纳了他的建议。10点半上船,不大会就开了。船上除去我们同车的六个难友,两个邮务人员,船夫又偷搭了两三个客人。沱江的水势很平稳,沿岸的山水远不及岷山的秀丽,在船上闲着没事洗了九件湿衣服。快到6点的时候，天上黑云浓得像锅底，忽然又下起大雨来，舱里到处都漏湿了。撑船的除去老梢公和他的侄子还有一个长工、一个短工，雨下大了，那个短工怕把衣服打湿，躲在舱里不肯出去，任凭船身在江心漂摆，梢公急得把嗓子嚷哑，他始终好像没那么一宗事。这阵雨一直下了一点半钟，就在这惊涛骇浪、急风暴雨的里头，7 点半才算脱离险境，拢了资中西门外的江岸。可是，摸着黑儿冒雨上坎，两只脚陷到泥塘里几乎没过磕膝盖。进城后，上头淋着，底下趿着，手上提着，走了半点多钟，碰见好几个客栈，结果才在中街找到一家清川旅馆，还算好，这家旅馆开张不久，床帐被褥都是新的，在紧张疲乏以后总算睡了一宿安顿觉。

资中的街道很整齐，路中间铺着大块方砖，碧绿的梧桐高耸在两旁，在雨过天晴的早晨格外显着幽静清洁。可惜我们头天晚上赶到，第二天 9 点钟又得回船，对于这个川西的大城市只有匆匆一瞥的缘分罢了。临上船的当儿又赶上一阵大雨，把到码头送行的资中邮局朱局长和李女士淋得衣服全湿了。等到 10 点 20 分雨稍稍小一点儿才开船，可是走了不到一点钟，雨又大得怕人，烟雾漫江，简直让在水上生活了四五十年的老梢公都定不准舵向。为安全起见只得泊在一个小湾子里，直到 12 点 20 分才继续开行。以后虽然浓云密布，沉黯无光，可是直到下午 4 点 20 分拢了内江，却没再下雨。

在离开资中的时候，合起我们三个人所有的钱来已经不够开发船价的了，最初我还想和宪益暂时挪借几文，没想到他在成都买完车票以后只余下刚够两天食宿的钱，拮据的情形比我们还厉害。万一下船的时候，当真凑不出钱来，我只好“为质于舟中”，请梅、郑两公上岸借钱来赎我。幸亏快到内江，那位林君把他应摊的一份拿出来，我们才算对付着下了船。这时合起我们三个和杨氏夫妇所有的全部财产只剩下六元法币，到蜀天行墅开发完拉行李的黄包车钱，五个人便都“妙手空空”了。当我们路过川陕联运处的门口儿，我们有意无意地问了一声周金台处长是否在内江，并且告诉我们住在什么地方。待一会儿金台和韩德璋都到旅馆来看我们，这样一来我们一行五个人的晚饭才有了着落。

8 月 4 日我们困在旅馆里还没唱“当锏卖马”，梅先生已经拜访内江中国银行孙祖瑞经理，通融了 500 元，除去转借给杨氏夫妇 100 元以外，假如不再遇到特别故障，我们对付着可以回到重庆了。

内江是川东、川西交通的枢纽，商业很繁盛，出产以糖和酒精为大宗，当地商人以糖业起家发财到百万以上的很多。酒精厂大小共有好几十家。酒精拿“漏水”（就是糖稀）作原料，也算是糖业的一种副产物。因为有钱的人多，所以生活程度特别高，随便吃一餐饭便得花到七八元，据说内江和自流井是四川全省生活最贵的地方。我们在这里一等车就过了三天，这期间除去上面所提到的几位朋友以外，我们还会到刘大钧先生和刘太太，大钧人更瘦了，耳朵也更重听了，刘太太是昆明明社的曲友，她的巾生和武旦都很有功夫。4 日晚在她家吃饭，因为刘先生有病，德璋临时跌了一跤，内江的两只笛子都缺了席，终于没能过成曲瘾。此外还会到清华 1932 级毕业同学李国干。

为接洽汽车的事，毅生跑了好几趟邮局。5 时听说资阳那边冲坏了的长寿桥已经搭起浮桥，那天下午成都的车才能开过来。6 日下午杨氏夫妇在邮局等了半天，结果只是杨太太一个人先走了。第二天一清早我们四个人赶到邮局，因为位子不够，又把宪益一个人落下。这样一来，我们从成都一同出发的五个人竟自分成了三班儿。

8 月 7 日，早晨 5 点半，从内江邮局出发。梅先生和一个邮局人员坐在司机台，我和毅生坐在后面邮包上。没出城的时候，我们虽然躺下，还要擦着树枝和电线过去，手里若是抓不住绳子便有滚下车去的危险，每逢遇到坑坎的地方，一颠就颠起两三尺高；假如不是亲身经验一次，我真不能想像出花钱买票坐车会受这么大的罪。5 点 50 分到挣木镇，等了 45 分钟渡船不开过来。我们的车列在第四，7 点 20 分车开到渡船上，又过了一个钟头拖船的汽划子才到，过完渡已经 9 点 15 分，司机又加了 20 分钟油，然后才开足了马力往前赶。可是车的速率越快，颠簸得也越厉害，一会儿太阳又露出来了，把周身皮肤晒得通红，直到 11 点半拢荣昌，吃了一顿午饭才稍微喘过一口气来。12 点 10 分车再开到永川，休息不到十分钟，以后就一口气儿开到青木关，看时候才不过 3 点 40 分。这一段虽然颠得骨头酸疼，晒得皮肤灼热，可是比起滩渡抛锚、新市铺翻车的情绪来，毕竟痛快得多了。

从内江开来的邮车照例在青木关换车后才继续开到重庆。这一天颠簸情形，我们都有点吃不消了，想在这里休息一晚，顺便到教育部看几个朋友，第二天再走。于是我们到邮局交涉妥当，把行李卸在第一宾馆，稍微休息一下，便上山到教育部去看吴俊升、蒋养春两位老友。恰好赶上俊升回沙坪坝，养春害病，都没见着，幸而邂逅着韩裕文、马芳若两位同学，承他们告诉了许多熟人的住址，又招待了我们晚餐，晚间到益庐访充和同到民教馆茶叙赏月，俨然又回味到当年呈贡旅居时的清兴。

十五 赶上了“疲劳的轰炸”！

我们 6 月初第一次经过重庆的时候，曾经遇到两次轰炸，6 月 1 日是在玉川别业的防空洞躲避的，6 月 2 日躲在市民医院的洞里就亲自碰见直接命中，封闭两个洞口的危机。那一次所躲的洞，假如没有四丈厚的石头,假如不是有五个洞口,结果就不堪设想了。可是,无论如何,总没有我们在青木关所遇到的警报那样频繁!

从8月8日到17日,据敌人宣称,一共轰炸了150小时,飞来一千架飞机,投过一万个炸弹,简直把陪都附近的民众搅得夜不安枕,日不得食,它们管这种恶行为叫做“疲劳的轰炸”!

在这9天里头我们几乎没有一会儿不急着要走,不过,事实上不单公共汽车完全停开,就是打电报,写快信,专人面托重庆的朋友,去打听飞机的班期,也简直得不到一点回音。15日听见西南联大被炸的消息,越发急得坐立不安,虽然马上发急电去慰问同人和同学,仍然放心不下,尤其是负着行政责任的梅先生和毅生格外焦灼万分。这样度日如年地挨过了一天,17日趁着警报稍微轻松一点儿,我们立刻搭着部里运米的卡车赶回了重庆。

在这疲于奔命的期间,我还抽着空儿好整以暇地做了两件事:第一,8月11日上午,在警报声中,承音乐师资训练班班主任杨仲子[杨祖锡,又名扬子]和教务主任李抱忱的委托,让我到彭家院子去讲演一次。那天我讲的题目是“声韵和声乐的关系”,大意想说明国字的四声阴阳对于谱曲的重要性。四声阴阳虽然随地异其调值,但是谱曲子的时候总得依照一个标准,时下的抗战歌曲把“九一八”唱成“揪尾巴”,那就是念倒了字音的实例。末了儿又附带着说了一点儿戏曲音韵的源流。当我正在高谈阔论的时候,有一阵敌机隆隆恰好从头上飞过。因为听众仍然很镇静地坐着不动,我也就不好意思“见机而作,入土为安”了。

第二,8月16日晚上,音乐师资训练班邀请教育部音乐教育委员会全体举行演奏会,我也被约参加。那一晚的精彩节目有金律声的男高音独唱,张洪岛的提琴独奏,曹安和女士用琵琶独奏“十面埋伏”,以后又唱了一段昆曲“昭君”,她还和陈振铎、杨荫浏用琵琶、二胡、笙合奏了一段节改梵音古曲的“后满庭芳”。大轴子是张充和女士唱昆曲“刺虎”里的“俺切着齿点绛唇”、“银台上煌煌的凤烛墩”、“恁道谎阳台雨云”三支。“十面”的指法纯熟，“刺虎”的珠圆玉润，是那一晚听众的公评，用不着我多恭维的。我推辞不过，勉强唱了“弹词”里的第五转“当日个那娘娘在荷亭把宫商细按”和第六转“恰正好喜孜孜霓裳歌舞”两支，大概总不免有荒腔走板不搭调的地方，辜负了撅笛的名手杨荫浏！

8月8日上午我们到教育部里拜候余次长井塘和陈泮藻两位老友。养春病后还不能到部，约我们中午到他家吃便饭。他的夫人蔡淑慎女士画法更老到了，想起1927年许多同学在杭州聚首的情形来，而今好些人风流云散，天各一方，连消息差不多都隔绝，未免不胜今昔之感！一樵[顾毓秀]是9日下午回来的，他约梅先生搬到他的新居，让我和毅生搬到部里的督学室。连续叨扰他好几次，并且听他叙述视察浙、闽、赣、桂归来的奇闻轶事，参观他从江西景德镇、福建德化所搜罗来的精致的瓷器，旅中颇得朋友之乐。俊升8月13日才回到青木关，在警报连续不断的当儿还承他招待我们一次。此外，我们在这几天里头又承部里和部外许多位朋友恳挚招待，并且领导我们到部里各部分参观，都让我们十分感谢。尤其是张充和、韩裕文、马芳若、何寿昌几位同学，从始至终地殷勤照护我们，连下防空洞的点心都替我们预备到，真是怪难为他们的。

十六 歌乐山的几天喘息

在青木关所遇到的10天空袭真让我们累得够疲劳的了。所以8月17日晚上回到重庆后，把行李安置在中央图书馆托金少英照应着，第二天忙了一天把飞机票定妥当——梅、郑两位是23日的班，我和老舍是26日的班——马上就想抽空儿到歌乐山去看孟真[傅斯年]和冰心,顺便休息几天,恢复恢复疲劳。

19日清早,一樵开车来接我们,8点30分有预行警报,我们把车停在两路口等候文藻。眼看着对面的坡上高高挂起一个红球,眼看着道旁的防空地图随时移动敌机的所在;一会儿退到恩施,一会儿又进了川境,可是文藻却杳无消息!9点40分红球变成两个,空袭的哨子也响了。司机的抱怨,恐怕车子开不出市区,我们也焦急得望眼欲穿。正在这千钧一发的紧急关头,文藻算是蹦蹦地赶到了。于是我们才叫司机开足马力往前奔,一樵的这部车年纪已经很大,早就比不上有钱机关所用的1941式了,而且前几天刚被敌机轰炸过,车棚已经炸烂,上面用油布遮着,车门用绳子系着,除去引擎没坏,几乎到处都是百孔千疮。我们飞快地往前开着,连沿路的警察都懒得拦住了盘问。刚过小龙坎,前面盖着汽缸的百叶忽然哗哗啦啦掉下一扇来,跟车的站在车头用手按住它仍旧继续往前奔;还没到新桥,车上被炸断了的电灯线又因为摩擦而燃着,假如不是发现得早一点,车上也许着了火!过山洞后,紧急警报响了,司机越发拼命往前开着,幸而路上并没发生更大的危险,我们居然在敌机没有临头以前安安全全地到了歌乐山。静下来一回想,这部车虽然破了,可是它的老福特的引擎"硬是要得"。

我们上次过重庆的时候,曾经在5月31日匆匆忙忙地到了一趟歌乐山,那时孟真正住在中央医院割扁桃腺,我们遵着医生的嘱咐并没敢和他多谈话。因为回城要赶山洞的末班车,所以在文藻和冰心的家里也只坐了不大的工夫。这次利用等飞机的空当儿,我们打算在山上和这几个老朋友多盘桓几天。

吴、谢家的潜庐在林家庙3号,和孟真所住的兔儿山中央研究院望衡对宇的只隔了一道山谷,有时两家站在廊子上就可以谈话,可是要彼此相访,假如不能飞渡的话,至少得走 20 分钟。我们因为孟真病后不便骚扰,我和毅生便住在潜庐。梅先生住在工业合作社梅贻宝先生那里。19 日下午文藻、贻宝陪着我们三个一同去看孟真。20 日一上午我和毅生去看他。梅、郑两位走后,24 日上午我一个人又去看他,他的血压已经降到 140 度,眼睛也渐渐恢复了。医生嘱咐他少见客人,少谈话,可是他在没有朋友谈天的时候反倒寂寞得起急。他爱护母校的感情还是很热烈的,有一个饮水忘源只想发展自己的同学忽然在他面前发出打倒北大的妄论,立刻气得他的血压升高了二三十度。

冰心虽然做了参政,招待朋友还是照常的殷勤。她的身体比在呈贡时稍微清减了一些,可是精神老是那么兴奋着,尤其在剪烛清谈的时候,她总是娓娓不休的越说越高兴。潜庐小而精雅,面对着嘉陵江,老远的望见星罗棋布的几堆房子,那便是沙坪坝和磁器口;兔儿山和云顶在它左右屏蔽着,一片浓绿的中间常常映衬着一块块的灰白色,那便是阔人们预备消夏或疏散的别墅;房后面还可以看得见高店子的市集,一条通磁器口的石板路,常常有坐滑竿或步行的人们像黑点般蠕动着;夜深人静的时候,除去松涛竹韵之外,往往还从隔壁的林家庙飘送过一两声发人深省的梵呗,越发显出山中清幽的趣味来。拿潜庐比呈贡三台山上的默庐,自然各有长处,不能强分好坏;不过,再要凭着默庐的窗口去眺望呈贡八景之一的"凤岭松峦",那却时过境迁比较不大容易了。不知为什么我总觉得那四个字配合得恰到好处!

合起潜庐男女主人的参事和参政的薪俸来,已经超过一千元了——可是实际上还不够山上一处开支的,每月都得亏空。他们所过的完全不是当年的"高等华人的布尔乔亚生活"了,虽然还不至于"日中一食",可是晚上往往吃稀饭,孩子们每顿饭都抱怨没有肉吃。

但是他们从丰招待朋友的老毛病却始终没改,残余的半罐 S.W. 咖啡,总等着朋友来的时候搬出那具特制的咖啡壶来,像做物理实验似的煮给你吃;快要生锈的烤箱,遇到客人来,也可借机会闻一闻鸡和猪肉的香味儿。冰心常嘲文藻是“朋友第一,书第二,女儿第三,儿子第四,太太第五”,其实她自己又何尝把朋友放在第二位呢?

今年春天,今甫从叙永给我来信,想聘老舍做北大教授,专任大一国文,赶到我把这个意思转达老舍,他的回信很简单干脆地说:“不教书!三年没念书拿什么教人家?谢谢杨大哥的好意。”6 月初我们在重庆碰见他,梅先生虽然和他初次见面,却颇喜欢他那豪爽直率的性情,守正安贫不作左右袒的品格,于是我们三人商量想约他到昆明作一次短期的讲演。他感谢梅先生知己的盛谊,就毅然答应了。这次来到歌乐山,忽然接到他从陈家桥寄来的两封信,大意说:彼此离开三个月,消息不大灵通,现在暑期已过,他已经答应朋友在陈家桥住一个时期,昆明之行拟即中止,飞机票如不能退,他愿意自己照价赔出。我们当时觉得很突兀,假如没有什么特别故障,颇不愿变更初议,于是我和梅先生各写一篇信,毅生和冰心也各附加两句,托一樵顺便带给他。信是 8 月 19 日发的,21 日黄昏他才从陈家桥步行 40 里赶到歌乐山,最初他还表示中止赴滇的意思,后来大家一致挽劝,他在酒酣情挚的当儿也就不再坚辞。第二天他回去收拾行装后,24 日晚上又同郭沫若先生一同上山来。沫若很想见我,我自从《卜辞通纂》和《金文丛考》出版后,也颇想同他当面谈一谈。可惜那一晚我正在静石湾鉴斋看沈尹默先生写字,并当面请教提顿转折的方法,沫若因为有要紧事不能久等,竟因此错过机会,使我没能看见这位仰望了很久的古文字学家!

在歌乐山一共住了六天,22 日和 23 日还遇两次空袭,那两天沙坪坝和磁器口被炸情形,在山上看得清清楚楚。在这几天里,我还会到沈士远、许季茀[许寿裳]、萧钟美、金石珊、汪旭初[汪东]、吕筑青、蒋仁宇、萧克真几位。钟美是二十多年的老同学，金先生是我在中学时的英文教员，我和这两位都好多年没见面了，异地相逢，格外觉着亲热。下山的前一晚，何容也赶到山上来，竟夕长谈，想到北平的许多往事！

十七 在天空过了生日

8月25日清早，同老舍冒雨离开了歌乐山，搭中央国库局车到重庆道门口，在新蜀报社休息半天，和周钦岳、姚蓬子谈了很久，就在那里给中国航空公司电话确定了起飞的时间和地点，午后两点到卫生局取回寄存的书籍和稿子，晚间和李季谷[李宗武]、卢吉忱[卢逮曾]、金少英、徐苏甘几位朋友在聚丰园话别。我上次过重庆的时候，吉忱正在兴高采烈地办《文史杂志》，很恳切地向各方面拉文章。这次会面才知道他已经交卸了。平心而论，他所编的八期颇博得学术界的好评，假如创办这个杂志的旨趣是在提倡学术，不羼杂别的作用，那么，就这样办下去岂不很好？为什么要顾名而不顾实，交给一个事实上不能兼顾的人去办，却牺牲了一个理想的编辑？我颇对卢君同情，并且替《文史杂志》可惜。

26日上午3时到南纪门外燕居内珊瑚坝飞机场。登记后，验完行李，天已经亮了。耗到6点半飞机才来，7点半起飞，9点40分就到了昆明。

我是1899年8月9日生的，照阴历算是清光绪二十五年己亥七月初四日，和毅生同年、同月、同日。今年8月9日在青木关，早晚两顿饭无意中都有人请我吃面；8月26日恰好和阴历七月初四相当，于是我的43岁初度就在云端里度过了。人生本来是飘忽的、渺茫的,如果能够“纵浪大化中,不喜亦不惧,应尽终须尽,何复独多虑”地活着,那么整个的一生还不就像浮沉在云海里一样?

我们这次绵延整三个月的长途旅行直到这一天才算结束。在昆明三年没出过的汗都还给四川了;辛辛苦苦吃粉笔灰余下的一点积蓄也全赔干了。而且流年不利的我,刚回到昆明不到一个星期,在路上趸来的恶性疟疾就发作了;两次反复,几天医院,八针 Quinine(奎宁),两针 Quino-Plasmoquine(扑疟喹啉),十五粒 Atebrin(阿白平),半打补血针,一磅奶粉,十几斤猪肝,几百个鸡蛋。我的天!我的两月薪俸又贴进去了。然而我却一点儿也不后悔,这种希奇的经验不是拿钱可以买得来的。

我将拿这篇信笔乱写、冗长芜杂的文章,永远纪念着这一珍贵的回忆!并且,我从四川回来就在病榻上缠绵了两个月,各方面的谢信都没有写,谨在这里对于这次旅行中一切帮助我们、招待我们的友好一总致谢!

1941 年 10 月 16 日写起,12 月 23 日写完

苍洱之间

杨　序

莘田先生这本薄薄的小册子，是游记、记载、考据甚至书评，一种兼容并包的杂文小集，也可以说是他的严肃著作之外的一种笔墨游戏。我读了不禁发生两种感想：一种可说是近乎普通的问题，另一种便是专门一点的问题。

所说普通的问题，用成语说，就是"工作与游戏"不独在教育上需要恰好的配合，在人生中，在做学问上，也都有其重要性。可是我们永远不能应用得合适，这就常会使我们的学问太死板，我们的人生太褊狭，或在另一方面，又使我们的生活太缺乏严肃性，以至流浪而无所归宿。我在这里不是去附和那种"游戏时尽力游戏，工作时拼命工作"的说法，我倒感觉这问题的重要性，是在工作与游戏的相互影响。苦丧着脸工作的人，不独自己很苦，及使看他的人或合作的人感到痛苦，我疑心他根本就做不好他的工作。他把工作变成苦恼，一定会使工作的内容，涩竭枯槁，以至窒息。因为那工作里缺少一个生动的灵魂！我甚至疑心这种人暴殄天物，他把活材料都糟蹋了。一个死灵魂压在一堆死材料下面！生动的灵魂！它是宇宙人生的锁钥，它并不需外求，它来自"不失其赤子之心"，也就是来自游戏，一种把自己糅合在宇宙万物中的游戏，一种铸山范水，嘲风笑雨，把自己分给宇宙万物，又从宇宙万物找到自己的游戏。歇！神圣的游戏，有了它盲者可以视，聋者可以听，死者可以复活，失掉它一切便都是死亡！

但道理总是两面的，这种游戏不羁的精神，必须放在严肃的工作里，才能相激相荡，琢磨生光。不然，它只是野风，是林妖，是山怪，流浪于广漠之野，消失于无有之乡。呵！那清旷流荡的野风，必穿林才激成音乐，必行水才荡为漪澜，必入云才叠成异彩；也如那游戏的灵魂，必在庄重的工作里，才能施展身手，发挥气力，放弃一切而吸纳一切，否认一切而肯定一切，破坏一切而创造一切！

离题太远了罢？不的，我在这本小册子里，窥见作者一点的游戏精神，我可以说我爱的是那份态度。作者白天游山，夜里考古，在神话造成的古庙中抄录碑文，在夕阳苍茫的山路上研究方言，这不免有些"学究的风雅"或"风雅的学究"味道，但这种味道若是配合得好，正足使那些考据文字不太死板，而放浪山水却不至流连忘返。这也正是作者的特点，而也是这本书的特点了。

另一个问题，便是游记的体裁了。单看这本书的命名《苍洱之间》可能是游记，可能是历史，也可能是地理，我猜想作者的初意，是在写游记，因为脱不了一般学者的习惯，知识笼罩一切，所以及于民俗传说，及于历史考证，及于方言研究，更为内容的广泛，不名游记而名以通名。然而作为任何旁的书看都不如作为游记看更合情理，可是一本如何奇异的游记！

说到游记，一般的总觉《徐霞客游记》是标准的游记，我对于这本名著却始终不感兴趣。我万分佩服他爬山越岭的精神，却从不觉出他对山水有心领神会的乐趣。他对于山水那种刻板式的感应（Stock Responses）因而表现为那些冗长而陈旧的刻画，只描写了山水的外形，却从未写出山水的性灵。并且，他到处只见山水而不见人，更看不见人与山水的关系。我指的是那些民俗、神话或传说。他足迹所经的地方，全无生命，因而他的山水也失掉了灵魂，他也许能成个顶好的地理学家，或是南北极探险家，但不是一个游人。

这本书的山水描写虽常是站在山水以外，却也有时融在山水之中。尤其是对于那地方民俗与神话传说的耐心研究与记载，使我们能借以窥见活动于那些山水间的初民心灵，他们的理想与情感，他们把人工的庙宇安插在山水里，也就借着代表他们理想的人格，他们的神，与他们的山水发生了不解的因缘。比我们只读一本山水的游记更能了解那些山水。所以我认为除了《五华楼》一篇太近于书评外，全书便命为《苍洱游记》也无不可。

1943 年 8 月，杨振声谨序

潘　序

莘田先生把两次苍洱之游的零星笔墨搜集在一起，行将付梓，要我在卷头说几句话，我没有法子推辞。这其间有好几个理由。第一，他和我年岁相同，前人生肖之说尽管没有根据，我们在性情兴趣上确有不少共同的地方。这一层，莘田先生在《鸡足巡礼》的《从乌龙坝到倒挂水》一段文字里也曾经提到。第二，两次的游程里，同行的朋友虽多，只有他和我两人是先后都参加了的。第三，孝通作《鸡足朝山记》后，要我做一篇小序，我不客气地做了；这番我如果坚辞，就不免见得有几分客气，而多年同学，两次偕游，甘苦共尝，无话不说，这客气是早就不存在的。

说到甘苦共尝，我又联想起一个比较有分量的理由。就是，在"鸡足巡礼"的过程里，我们两个人都几乎出过岔子，为同游诸人都增加过一些心事。我在本年2月10日的日记上说：

> 莘田今日之境遇盖与余2月6日之境遇相似。余为出游之第一日，莘田则最后一日，可云无独有偶。而今日之事，余亦负相当责任。滑竿本为余所设，余怂前毖后，执意不可，以让莘田。莘田初既徘徊于舆骑之间，终乃成李代桃僵之局。顾余亦尝自忖，设余今晨改骑为舆，则势须发生更大之僵局；二舆强弱悬殊，如余所乘者为春台之舆，则僵局之主人将为春台，春台之脚力固不逮莘田也；如所乘为莘田之舆，而亦半途而废，则前程远大，僵

局之主人即非余莫属，幸而稍获前进，亦势须独宿赵州，甚或乌龙坝矣。是则莘田之落后，从全局观之，独为不幸中之差幸。且余既演话剧于前矣，势不便再演第二次，以重累同人，同人虽不以余等之不克同进止为嫌，余则不能不以分谤者视莘田，故余于莘田实歉谢两深也。

莘田先生和我既有这一段后先媲美的因缘，我引起波澜于前，他造成曲折于后，教不平凡的鸡足之游更见得不平凡，而他所造成的曲折，我多少也要负一部分责任，如今他要我说几句话，我即明知其为画蛇添足，也何敢推却呢？

我们读游记，总遇见两种形式，一是日记的形式，二是纪事本末的形式。内容的精神也往往不出两路，一是因寄兴而多涉想像，二是因求实而多作考据。前人游记流传于今的，大抵日记体的失诸支离琐碎，或质胜于文；本末体的失诸空疏无物，或文胜于质。前者如放翁的《入蜀记》、霞客的《游记》，后者如唐宋以来古文家无数的短篇作品，其中文质彬彬的例子似乎并不太多。近来的风气不同，而不同之中显而易见可以看出几分进步。日记体的渐趋于不时髦，是一个进步的表示，本末体的力求文情并茂，可资研讨，也可供欣赏，是更进一步的表示。我们知道历史的记载很早就等于放弃了编年的体裁，传记文学中年谱的方式近来也日趋陈旧，大概都是这种演变的趋势的一部分罢！

莘田先生的这本集子和孝通的《鸡足朝山记》，无疑的都是这趋势中富有代表性的产品，文情并茂四个字，两家都可以当之无愧。不过有一点不一样，情字原可以有两个不同的意思，主观的情绪与客观的情实，孝通以前者胜，莘田先生则以后者胜，而就我个人的性格而论，我更能领会的是莘田先生的这本集子，并且认为莘田先生的做法可学，而孝通的轻易不宜学，学则易滋流弊。

我一面先后替两家写卷头语，一面却深知我自己不会写游记，我甚至于对于一切言情叙事的笔墨都存几分畏缩的心理。这大概是天分所限，无可如何的。今春从苍洱、鸡足归来，办刊物的朋友们向我索稿，我除了拿日记搪塞以外，别无长策。孝通的做法我不会，莘田先生的格调我也学不来。其实题材是一样的。人类学、民族学、历史、掌故，都是我们共同的注意范围；我于语言学虽属外行，也不能说毫无兴会。但我的情绪不够绵密，我的观察不够细到，我的文笔不够典雅，动力、资料、工具，全都不够，所以即使有些心领神会之处，也往往达不出来。

莘田先生和我虽有两次同游之雅，但他的收获要比我多得多，他于演讲、游观之外，兼事学问，特别是边疆语言的记述与分析。这是他的主要的收获，这本集子不过是一种副产品，即就这副产品而论，其中至少有一半是我耳目所未及的。去年大理之行，我们同去而没有同归，他比我多稽留一个多月；集中贰、肆、伍三篇就是这时期的产物。壹、叁、陆、柒四篇所叙的种种十九是两人共同的经验，但莘田先生到处要比我用心得多。即就《木氏家谱》一事说，我和孝通见过就算了事，莘田先生则当时既详细记录下来，事后又加以分析比较，终于成为一小篇有系统的研究文字，而在许多朋友看来，我还是对谱学极感兴趣的一个人！再就《鸡足巡礼》的别方面说，莘田先生游屐所至，至少比我多尊胜塔院和宾居大王庙两处，而这两处我因为身心与经验方面的种种限制，都是无法追随以至于根本没有追随的资格的。莘田先生口口声声要拿尊胜塔院来抵制我的“曹溪一滴”，其实这一滴是愚者千虑的一得，并且还是得之于偶然，是绝对犯不着抵制的。曹溪的一滴本来就敌不过尊胜塔院的气象万千，何况后来又加上一个宾居大王呢？我们一路谈笑，不断地喜欢算这笔得失的账，其实我口头不示弱，心里是早就认输了的，后来一到宾居，我就完全不做声了。我要借这个机会正式向莘田先生提出，我们如今一面把这笔旧账结了，一面慢慢地再寻机会，一践共游蜀西青城或滇西丽江之约如何？

1943 年 8 月，潘光旦

从滇池到洱海

假如相信星命家的话，我这一年间也许是犯“驿马”，去年夏天刚周游了几千里的蜀道，今年开春没想到又有滇西之行。

1942年1月下旬，顾一樵先生奉命来滇视察，约我一同到迤西考察边疆语言。本来去年秋天华中大学中国文学系主任游泽承[游国恩]先生就约我在寒假里到喜洲去玩，顺便调查民家的语言和生活状况。此行既然可以拿一块石头打两个鸟儿，我乐得借机会走一趟呢。

2月2日上午10点，偕梅月涵、顾一樵、潘光旦诸先生从昆明西仓坡出发，下午1点45分到禄丰。沿途所见满眼都是童山濯濯，荒草枯槁，令人只有干燥肃杀的感觉，比起去年夏天在四川所见的秀润气象来简直是别一天地。《南诏野史》引元梁王诗云“野无青草有黄尘”，确可道出这种景象。过禄丰后得要爬两个坡：头一个叫羊老哨，高度约2000公尺；第二个叫级山坡，高2140公尺，盘旋达20公里。羊老哨并不很险，级山坡既陡且弯，汽车在迂曲的崖边窄路上盘旋着，随时都会发生危险。下坡以后复见平原，田禾和树木也渐渐多起来了。下午6点到楚雄，共行192公里。承中缅运输总局余啸南总管招待我们住在滇缅公路第二工程段。晚间月色甚佳，同一樵到街头步月，信步走到荒僻无人的地方，被驻军警告才折回寓所。

第二天上午9点半从楚雄总站出发,11点15分,到250公里的地方,休息了20分钟,继续登天子庙坡。这是昆明到下关中间顶高的一个坡,高度达2600公尺,长约30公里,途中像重庆老鹰崖那样迂曲盘旋的工程就有十几处。我们走了将近一点钟,在264公里的山顶上,汽车因为油管渗漏抛了锚。车上除去司机之外还有两位工程师,但因所带的器械不够,直到下午4时还没修理好。于是一樵让我和光旦搭上一辆卡车先到山下设法寻找救济车。5点钟下山到287公里的地方,卡车把我们撂下了。这个地方叫做笠毕甸,两家么店子前面倒是停着好几辆卡车,问起来就是待修理的,没有一辆担当得起上山救济的责任。不得已,在一间么店子里找到两个有草荐的铺位,早晨在楚雄吃的一碗牛肉面,到这时候早就消化完了,肚子里饥肠辘辘的虽然一个劲儿的叫,可是看着老板娘泥手亲调的菜饭还是不敢尝试。而且心里惦记着抛锚在山顶的两个同伴,就是勉强吃也怕不能下咽。两个人轮流站在路旁望眼欲穿地仰着头向山上期待着。还算好,没过半点钟我们的车居然赶来了。休息一下继续往前赶路,7点多钟,在月亮还没上来的黑天底下看见公路两旁夹植着很茂密的树,好像西北驿路两旁的左公柳一样,不像是近年种的。果然刚到8点钟我们就拢了云南驿,这一晚享受了一次很痛快的淋浴,睡得非常酣畅。

2月4日上午8点半从云南驿出发,路上看见很大的一片湖,那便是所谓"青海",也是我们离开滇池后第一次看见的水。在祥云县南边八里有一个青华洞,《南诏野史》上说:"汉时出一鹿二首绝异"。这虽然是不经之谈,可是比起猪八戒曾经在这里洗澡的传说来,似乎还近情理一点。到祥云车站后等候汽车加油,休息一会儿,10点40分继续前进,一路上平平稳稳的,除去爬了一个红崖坡,其余都是坦途。到409公里后又走了一公里的柏油路,12点50分就到了下关。

到下关没停,即刻转上大理的支路。大理离下关 17 公里,沿路碎石满地,坎坷难行,在刚走过一段柏油路以后,相形之下,格外感觉不舒服。断断续续地下了好几次车才对付着到了县城。

大理县元明清都叫做太和,是旧大理府治的附郭首县。现在的县城在点苍山中和峰下,就是唐贞元中南诏孝桓王异牟寻所筑的阳苴咩城,也就是汉代的楪榆城。明洪武间,清康熙初,都重修过。城高两丈四尺,周围七里三分。共有四门:东名洱海,西名苍山,南名双鹤,北名三塔。背负苍山,面临洱海,以上关为龙首,下关为龙尾,城居其中,颇占形胜。县治所管辖的地方,南起下关,北至上关,西界苍山,东尽洱海,全县面积,以山水平陆合计,截盈补虚,约有 5850 方里,两关内的陆地只有 279 方里。

没到大理以前,就听见说这里有风、花、雪、月四景:风是下关的风,花是上关的花,雪是苍山的雪,月是洱海的月。下关多风的原因,据说从西南方 40 里箐所来的冷空气到下关被东山挡住,时时流到平阳地面,进到两关里面,四周也被山包围着,冷空气在里头旋转,不能腾空放散,于是互相激荡,发为狂风,声若钱塘潮涌,势若万马奔腾,每年从夏历八九月起一直到来年的二三月常常是这样。我在大理住了还不到十天,每天都刮得头昏眼花,住在楼上摇撼得像地震一样,所以我对于这一景领略得最为亲切。至于故老传说在点苍山三阳峰上有一个风孔,夏天从那里过,冷风都刺人肌肤,大理所以多风,就是由这个风孔来的,这就未免附会了。大理的气候亚于昆明,四季温暖如春,所以常有不谢之花,据《徐霞客游记》上说,龙首关二里波罗村,西山麓有蛱蝶泉,"泉上大树当四月初即发花如蛱蝶,须翅栩然,与生蝶无异。又有真蝶千万,连须钩足,自树巅倒悬而下,及于泉面,缤纷络绎,五色灿然。游人俱从此月群而观之,过五月乃已”。所谓上关的花,似乎专指着这一种。不过《大理县志稿》上说:“上关有泉从石腹涌出,旁有花一株,高丈余,夏月花开,状若蝴蝶,首尾相衔,长垂至地,盖奇观也。今不存。”现在既然不存,我们也就无从对证了。提到苍山的雪,我们一到下关已经看见峰巅岩际映射出皑皑的银辉,阮芸台《宿大理三日看点苍山》诗有云:“其一在于雪,苍山雪最大,冬春雪未奇,六月白何怪?我来六月中,夜雪积巅背,皑皑亦终日,不畏秋阳晒。”我来的时候虽在冬春之交,证以这几句诗也不难想见夏秋的景况。最后的一景,我们对它却有些美中不足。因为我们到大理的那天,已经是夏历腊月十九日,虽然还可以看见下弦月,可惜没住在洱海边上,所以对于洱海月的茫渺,正如对于上关花一样。

点苍山在县城西三里,自北而南绵亘70余里,一共有十九峰:中和峰耸峙在中央,它的南边有龙泉、玉局、马龙、圣应、佛顶、马耳、斜阳七峰;北边有光英、应乐、雪人、兰、三阳、鹤云、白云、莲花、五台、沧浪、云弄十一峰。各峰“皆如五老比肩,中坠为坑”,所以两峰中间都夹着一条溪水,合起来一共有十八溪:中溪在中和峰南,它的南边有绿玉溪、龙溪、清碧溪、莫残溪、葶萁溪、南阳溪;它的北边有梅溪、桃溪、隐仙溪、双鸳溪、白石溪、灵泉溪、锦溪、芒涌溪、阳溪、万花溪、霞移溪。阮芸台的诗里说:“峨峨点苍山,苍翠极可爱。平列十九峰,峰峰染螺黛。两峰夹一溪,十八溪为界。林樾矗浮图,岚霭罩阛阓。”颇可当做全山形势的鸟瞰。我们从下关转到大理的时候,在路上已经看见这十九叠翠屏风迤逦着遮蔽在县境的西边,它虽然没有奇峰突起,跌宕生姿,可是比肩连袂的层峦叠嶂中自然有崔嵬气象。据本地的朋友们说,苍山之奇,以清碧溪、洗马塘为最,前者是徐霞客所盛称,后者尚为霞客所未到。可惜我们来的时候正赶上风季,天气又冷,攀登绝顶,探涉寒溪,都不大容易;而且一樵行色匆匆,预备10日赶回重庆,所以只在2月6日承腾大师管区赵司令诚伯(德恒)和大理县李县长少和(世祥)的招待登了一回中和峰。

中和峰在县城的西南,和龙泉峰合为一顶,是点苍山的主峰,峰麓便作两支,中间低陷的一片叫做马蝗箐,箐中有黑泥一段,相传下有煤矿。峰下土脉硗瘠,枯黄的荒草以外,只有疏疏落落的小松,沿径所见并没有什么动人的景物。快到中和寺的时候,忽然一叠翠嶂涌现眼前,整个的峰头都被翠柏苍松遮蔽得看不见一点儿岩石的本色。回首俯瞰山下,洱海澄碧如镜,金梭、玉几、赤文三岛分峙在海中,几个"海舌"分着岔儿吐出西北海岸,海东的鸡足山绵延迤逦,一眼望不到底,迎面还有四四方方儿的大理县城,屏山镜海,市廛井然,北边的三塔,南边的一塔,危然对峙,映照得越发美丽,这一刹那我才领略出登山的乐趣来。从前杨升庵在《游点苍山记》里引李中溪的话说:"不见庐山真面目,只缘身在此山中,必须东泛洱水,卧数溪峰,庶几尽点苍之变耳。"我也觉得欲瞰洱海之胜,不能求之于海中,也不能得之于地上,只有登峰造极,俯瞰远瞩,才能一览无余,括见万象。等到傍岸临水,顶多只能看见眼前的波涛起伏,便不能欣赏到全部的汪洋万顷了。中和寺前的牌坊有清康熙帝所写的"滇云拱极"四字,寺后悬崖刻有明李中溪的"高山流水"和近人李印泉[李根源]的"磅礴排荡",寺内玉皇殿前又有李瑞清所写的"中和位育"横额,两朝三李,先后辉映,颇为这个庙生色不少。

洱海是由西洱河、洱源湖、凤羽河三个源头汇成的。北起邓川东南,南至凤仪西北,腹广约二十里,两端渐狭,长约百里,样子像上弦的月牙儿,首尾拢抱着点苍山云弄、斜阳两个峰的山麓,中虚其腹,西纳十八溪水,东纳东山老大箐水,东南纳凤仪波罗江水,东南流经下关,折西出黑龙桥,更西行出天生桥,回绕到点苍山的背后,50里至合江铺西北,纳漾濞江,南会澜沧江。海里有金梭、玉几、赤文三岛，有青莎鼻、大贯淜、鸳鸯、马帘四洲；又有九曲，皆可田可庐。我们到大理的那几天，正赶上天大有风，虽然可以登中和峰俯瞰全海，却不敢泛舟洱水卧数溪峰。2月5日早晨本打算到喜洲去参观华中大学，因为路坏不能行车，走到半路，一樵踽踽独行地跑路去了，梅先生、光旦和我折回来，乘便到才村去参观民族文化书院。才村在县城东八里的海边上，村多杨姓，在明清两代的功名很发达，村口的题名坊便是一个好证据。民族文化书院的校舍是新建筑的楼房，原系杜文秀水师营故址，院内有亭可看崇圣寺的三塔倒影，可惜时较早，风太大，我们并没看见一点影儿。书院现有教授八人，职员数人，学生九人，内分经子、历史、文学、社会四系。张君劢先生现在重庆，院务由张教务长仲友代理。从书院出来便到海边的古浩然阁去领略楪榆十六景之一的"海阁风涛"。阁凡三楹，围以石栏，临海有一牌坊，额题"龙门"两字。凭栏远眺，沧波百里，风起涛涌，像雪球一般的浪花溅起多高，大风激起狂涛，白浪助长风声，奔腾澎湃，简直分辨不出哪是风声，哪是涛声。这同中和峰上俯瞰的洱海比起来，另外是一番景象。临水亭的遗址已然找不出，只在阁对面的龙王庙里仆放着一块嘉庆十三年郡人吴光祖重修古临水亭的碑记，北墙侧还砌着一块明正德十三年的碑，碑阳砌在墙里，文字已不可辨。

2月4日，刚到大理的那一天，一樵同我到国立大理师范学校召集学生训完话，便由钟校长志鹏，贺教务主任益文，陪着去游三塔寺。三塔寺就是崇圣寺的俗称。寺在城西北点苍山小岑峰下，周围三百余亩，原来是唐开元中南诏蒙氏所创建，被灾后又经大理段氏重修。寺后面有三个塔：中间一个高三百多尺，四角一十六级，式样很像长安城外荐福寺的小雁塔；其余的两个是八角十级，比较矮一点。塔顶有款识，为唐开元元年南诏延匠人恭韬徽义造的。据本地人传说，明正统九年五月六日，地震塔裂，“旬日复合”。这种奇迹虽然不足征信，可是崇圣寺经回乱以后，法物荡然，只有三塔巍然独存，却是不可掩的事实。寺后又有雨铜观音像高二丈四尺，据徐霞客说，“铸时分三节为范，肩以下先铸就而铜已完，忽天雨铜如珠，众共掬而熔之，恰成其首，故名”。这种神话也只好姑妄听之。霞客又说：“正殿后列诸碑而中溪所勒黄华老人书四碑俱在焉”。黄华老人是金翰林王庭筠别号，现在原诗的四块碑已不存在，市上间有后人勾勒集字的对联，我看见文化书院同学王树椒替向觉明先生买到的一副，文为“梵佛一堂林宇竹窗无上地，百年千日雪山云谷更高人”。展转摹刻，字形已经走得不成样子，更勿论原书的神韵了。崇圣寺碑是元朝“翰林侍读学士知制诰同修国史受中奉大夫云南诸路行中书省参知政事李源道撰”，“真城苾芻念庵圆谟书丹”，“泰定二年岁次乙丑夏六月辛卯中顺大夫大理军民总管段信苴隆立石”。字体近李北海，绝少剥蚀，碑文仿苏子瞻表忠观碑体，借崇圣寺以表扬段氏的勋劳。其中有一段说：

段氏以三百年幅员万里之土，纳款于我。岁癸丑之后，厥祖摩诃罗瑳奉命四征不庭，至于宋境，深入邕广安南之区。上嘉之，锡以金虎符，使领旧土。公受命以来，益自奋励，抚绥蛮夷，奖练士卒。攻鄯阐，下石城，克新兴，取寻甸。挫舍利畏三十万肃集之师于滇海之上，破择多罗十余万寇抄之众于洱水之滨。有制褒之若曰：“段实款附而来，忠勤益著，庸示至优之渥，以彰同视之仁。”大哉王言，以见公之忠勋简知于上，当不在钱氏下。顾斐然之文不足以发明其蕴，惜无文忠公之笔以表扬之也。子庆番侍春官，父子并以宣慰元帅之节，继参大政，始终七觐阙庭，赏赉无算，褒大推崇，生荣死哀，以裕厥家，诸孙之为方伯连帅者又十余人。（参阅明李元阳纂《云南通志》卷十五，清黄元治修

《大理府志》卷二十九）

这一段在大理史乘上是很重要的事实，可是1912年所修的《大理县志稿》里，这篇碑文和《元世祖平云南碑》都漏而未载，当时修志的人似乎不应该连李纂《通志》和黄修《府志》都没看见，《通志》、《府志》既然把这两篇碑文一字不遗地完全载进去，何以县志里反倒没有？不知道是偶尔的疏忽，还是别抱着种族上的成见，故意删去呢？从保存文献的观点看，这两块碑在历史上都是很有价值的。《元世祖平云南碑》在城西观音市，分上下两截，剥蚀甚多。碑阴没有文字，顶上有佛像三尊，座下石赑屃颇矮，周围用砖甃着，高约一丈多。碑文是元翰林学士程文海所作。我现在根据原拓片参照李纂《通志》卷十五和黄修《府志》卷二十九所录全文，把它抄在下面（行款依照原碑），并略加校语于下：

世祖平云南碑

阙家继天立极日月所照罔有内外云南
秦汉郡县也负险弗庭乃

宪庙践祚之二年岁次壬子我

世祖圣德神功文武

皇帝以介弟亲王之重授钺专征秋九月
出师冬十二月济河明年春历盐夏四月出萧 按李志"盐"下多一"夏"字。
关驻六盘八月绝洮逾吐蕃分军为三道禁杀
掠焚庐舍先遣使大理招之道阻而还十月过
大渡河

上率劲骑由中道先进十一月渡泸所过
望风款附再使招之至其国遇害十二月薄其
都城城倚苍山西洱河为固国主段兴智及其
柄臣高太祥背城出战太败又使招之三返弗 "太"李志作"泰"，下同。

听下令攻之东西道兵亦至乃登点苍山临视城中宵溃兴智奔善阐追及太祥于姚州俘靳以殉分兵略地所向皆下惟善阐未附明年春留大将兀良合台经略之	“太败”李志作“大败”。“殉”李志作“徇”。“善”李志作“鄯”，下同。“台”李志作“觧”。
上振旅而还未几拔善阐得兴智以献释不杀进军平乌蛮部落三年七攻交趾破其都收持磨溪洞三十六金齿白彝罗鬼缅中诸蛮相继纳款云南平列为郡县凡总府三十七散府八州六十县五十甸部寨六十一见户百二十八万七千七百五十三分隶诸道立行中书省于中庆以统之大德八年平章政事也速答儿建言所领云南地居徼外历世所不能臣	“拔”黄府误作“援”。“年”李志黄志均作“十”。“彝”李志作“夷”，下同。1934年重印本删去“罗鬼”二字，“诸蛮”作“蛮国”。
先皇帝天戈一麾无思不服今其民衣被皇明同于方夏幼长少老怡怡熙熙皆自忠其往陋非我　神武不杀之恩不及此惟点苍之山尝驻跸焉若纪　圣功刻石其上使臣民永永瞻仰于事为宜中书以闻	“皇”李志作“圣”。“忠”黄志作“忘”。“及”李志讹作“反”。以上上截共30行。
翰林院臣程文海	按李志、黄志均无此行。
制曰可以命词臣程文海再拜稽首而言曰	
世祖皇帝之德大矣辟如天地之无不持载无不覆帱(而)(生)(生)(之)意恒寓于雪霜风雨寒暑变化之中物之蒙之者熏然而温洒然而濯翕然而同靡然而顺有不自知其然而然者故其功烈之(崇)基业之广贯三灵而(轶)(千)(古)以大理之昏迷旅拒虐我使人	“帱”李志作“祷”。凡字外加括弧者今皆剥蚀，据李志及黄志补入，下同。“翕”黄志讹作“翁”。“以”上李志有“夫”字。

若奋其武怒俾无遗育可也而招来绥缉终释其主弗□(诛)呜呼微天地之德孰能与于此乎(今)

陛下建中和之政凡以绳祖武厚(生)民无所不用其极中外钦承无远弗(届)是以藩方大臣于钱谷甲(兵)之外惓惓以炟昭令德为请其知为政之本也已汉世宗从事西南彝天下为之骚动蜀(民)咨怨喻之谆谆凿池莅(习)再驾而(后)(取)之(其)视今(也)孰愈(穆)(王)(周)行寓县必皆有车辙马迹焉初非(疆)(理)天下也而世犹颂之至今其视跋(履)山川洒(濯)其民而(纳)于礼义之域孰愈彼碧鸡金马与(夫)点苍皆其(山)(之)望者也汉使祭之唐季盟之夫各有畏焉耳今(也)镌未(始)(磨)(之)(崖)(纪)无能名之(绩)桓桓(烨)(烨)与世无极岂惟足以震百彝(荣)千古其余(光)所被山(川)鬼神与皆赖之呜(呼)(盛)哉臣事

先皇帝早(受)眷知今(后)待罪(禁)林(发)扬蹈(厉)职也不敢(以)(荒)(落)(辞)谨再拜稽首而系之

(以)(诗)曰

于(皇)(维)(元)载(地)(统)(天)大噫小(嘘)(日)(寒)(以)(暄)粤西南(陬)水骙山嶺(风)霆流行气交神州跋息(蠕)(蠕)(勾)(萌)鲜(鲜)(谷)(饮)巢居燕及(跕)鸢

“来”李志作“徕”。

“诛”上仍蚀一字，李志及黄志均脱。“此”李志作“斯”。

“建”李志作“达”。

“炟”半蚀，李志及黄志均作“光”。

“颂”李志作“诵”。

李志“畏”上有“所”字。

“烨烨”据李志补，黄志作“弈弈”。“被”黄志作“著”，“皆”李志作“嘉”，“哉”上多一“矣”字。

黄志无“以”字。

“骙”黄志作“驶”，“勾”黄志作“上”，“行”李志作“形”。

繄谁之恩(圣)祖神(孙)(武)烈文谟湔祓生
存既有典常被之服章我吏(我)(民)(我)工
我商(万)(国)一家孰为要荒点苍(苍)(苍)
禹迹尧(墙)(井)(钺)(参)旗(终)夜有光威
不违颜作善降(祥)嗟尔耄倪视(此)勿忘

□宪二年仲春月黄□□吉□　　按李志、黄志均无此行。

以上下截,共38行。

这个碑文的上截保存得还好,下截现在剥蚀得不能卒读,假使李中溪也存着成见,那么这一段文献岂不就掩湮没了吗?我希望将来重修大理县志的时候,应该抱着历史家的态度,换一副眼光,把这些有关系的文献搜补进去才好!

2月5日一清早,一樵在赴喜洲以前又约我同游了一趟一塔寺。一塔寺是宏圣寺的俗称,寺在城西南一里许,塔为方形,凡十六级,高约二十余丈,和崇圣寺中间的那个塔高度式样都差不多,相传是周昭王时阿育王所造,又有人说造于隋文帝,都不知道根据什么来的。自从明吴鹏《重修崇圣寺记》把三塔顶上的款识"唐开元元年南诏延匠人恭韬徽义造"误作"贞观六年尉迟敬德监造",杨升庵的记文也跟着错下来。辗转传讹又有人以为这一个塔也是尉迟敬德监修的,那就越发无稽了。宏圣寺为唐时蒙诏所建,明嘉靖间李中溪重修过一次,一塔和三塔也是李氏在那时捐资重修的,在一塔的座下有嘉靖二十五年"监察御史荆州知府郡人李元阳大观堂修改记",杨升庵篆额,生员秦世贤集赵松雪字。寺前有嘉靖丁酉杨升庵勒的岣嵝碑,又有张思叔座右铭碑,末有题识云"万历庚辰江陵刘维写于武定使署属太和令孔宗海刻石点苍山之报功祠"。所谓"报功祠"不知是否指着嘉靖二十一年佥事王维贤所建的武侯祠说。祠毁于清咸丰丙辰的乱事,1912年拿旁边的玉皇阁改祀武侯,现在当地人就把它认为一塔寺。

祠前有石坊，横额前刻“望重南阳”，后刻“名留西蜀”，这是唯一可供后人凭吊的一点儿遗迹。国立大理师范学校的附属小学就设在一塔寺，现在由俞君思敬主持之。

到大理以后，梅、顾、潘三先生本来想约我一同回去，可是我一则发现大理师范的学生里有许多来自边地的，可以供给我许多语言材料，二则想践泽承之约，所以决定把寒假在大理消磨过。2 月 6 日晚，送他们到下关，7 日早晨，承严燮臣先生招待到温泉洗完澡，又游览一回天生桥。温泉离下关五公里，属凤仪县，水比安宁的热，但所含的硫磺质也不多，设备还清洁。天生桥离下关四公里，是洱河西流处。绝壑深堑，中间有一石梁，像人字形，凭虚凌空，仅仅可度一人，所以叫做天生桥。桥的西边约百步，洱水出桥外石崖悬泻数百尺急湍激石乱，浪花飞溅，沫泡成珠，好像初绽的梅花，四季一样，所以相传叫做“不谢梅”。桥上路旁的石崖侧，有清光绪丙午赵州牧武昌□□□所立“汉诸葛武侯擒孟获处”石碑，近内政部次长张维翰视察迤西，因为和史实不合，已经派人用石灰涂去。其旁有宣统元年邑人所立“蒋壮勤公立功处”石碑，蒋名宗汉，鹤庆人。左侧还有隆庆□年李元阳《天生桥石表记》，因为时间匆促，未及细读。当天下午 1 点半送梅、顾、潘东返后，就承中缅运输处下关总站薛文蔚总管自己开车把我和马希良师长一同送回大理了。

1942 年 2 月 14 日，夏历辛巳除夕，写于点苍山麓

苍洱之间

从滇池到洱海的旅程，我已另有短文记述。因为边地族语材料的吸引，一晃儿我在大理又住了一个多月。在这一个月里，我记录了傈僳、俅子、怒子、拉吗、民家五种族语，对于民家我还注意到大理、喜洲、邓川、宾川、洱源、鹤庆、泸水、云龙各地的方言差别。在工作进行上，我应该感谢国立大理师范学校钟志鹏校长，华中大学中国文学系游泽承、包渔庄两先生和五台中学的教导主任王树森，给我很多的便利。

工作的情形相当的紧张，大概除去夏历辛巳除夕、壬午元旦和往返喜洲的途中，很少空闲。为恢复疲劳只抽出两三天来登山临水，访古寻幽。虽然到处都是走马观花的一瞥，却也有不少值得记述的，现在就把它点点滴滴地写出来。

一　大理的新年

大理过年的情形没有什么特别的。除夕的下午各店铺大都闭起门来，大街上有好多人当真拿着笤帚实行扫除。元旦街上很冷静，除去看见三个一群五个一伙穿着新衣服的拜年人，还听见道旁关着门的铺子里透出清脆的掷骰子声。人类学者许烺光为研究祖先崇拜问题很想深入民间，后来听说此间大规模的祭祖在七月不在正月，也就没有什么收获。正月初五日在三塔寺后边有所谓“葛根会”，本地人很踊跃地参加,红男绿女们都在游罢归来的时候,购得葛根和甘蔗。这个会的来源不可考,想来许是在初春吃一点清凉的药品可以免疫解渴。初九日中和寺还有所谓"圣诞会",听说有许多民家去唱调子,我因为那天赴喜洲,没能去观光,所以也没领略到"哀而伤"的韵味。

二 杨玉科祠和杜文秀府

杨玉科和杜文秀是清咸丰丙辰迤西事变中最有关系的人物。杨祠在省立大理中学内,就是原来西云书院故址。玉科字云阶,丽江人。由劳绩洊膺提督,二等男爵。初隶张正泰部下,正泰被戕后,集有义勇数十,往来中甸、维西间。乙丑冬率敢死百余,夺取鹤庆。后随巡抚岑毓英克复大理,底定迤西。越南之役连败法兵,光绪乙酉正月初九日阵亡于谅山,予谥武愍。西云书院即取迤西杨云阶创设的意思。祠中一小龛内供着一个高约一尺的塑像,着清代衣冠,眉宇颇生动,但姿态不大好。导游的朋友说是杜文秀像,我想就是玉科本人。假若是杜文秀就不该供在杨祠内,更不该穿着清代衣冠。后来在观音堂看见杨玉科的另一塑像才证实我的怀疑是不错的。祠前有光绪十七年八月所刻三次御赐祭文的石表。书院曾经刘安科重修,花木繁盛,亭榭曲折,颇能脱俗。有石碑一,上刻宋湘嘉庆丁丑所作《洱海行》及道光二年所作《种松三绝句》。宋湘字芷湾,嘉应州人,道光间官大理府知府。尤其别致的是在大理石的花池边上刻有安化贺宗章所作的《湛园八咏》。

杜文秀的帅府就是清代的提督衙门。据《大理县志稿》说:"提督署在城内五华街。清咸丰六年大理城陷,回首领杜文秀并署北民人屋产,加造内城,改称帅府。同治十年乱平,巡抚岑毓英堕其城垣。光绪元年提督杨玉科中军李锦昌,请款修复甬壁大门。七年提督黄武贤、中军黄河洲请款重修。”自从1913年裁撤提督后,曾经做过陆军步兵旅司令部、迤西道尹公署、迤西镇守使署、现在是腾大师管区司令部,赵司令诚伯(德恒)即驻节于此。诚伯腾冲人,日本士官学校骑兵科毕业,1920年曾任大元帅府参议,博闻强识,健谈工诗,每逢茶余酒后,谈笑风生,四座叹服,几乎不容旁人有插嘴的机会,近所作《无题八律》、《怀人八绝》,很得李玉溪的韵味。又有《大理绝句》32首,风格情韵超轶杨升庵、宋芷湾之上,把这个南诏故都渲染得生色不少。部内的大堂颇轩敞,地下铺遍大理石,堂后可望苍山,且有绿蕉翠竹交相辉映,极为幽静。有坐椅四张,雕工很精致,背上刻着麒麟,相传是杜文秀的遗物。堂前有明弘治三年大理卫所铸铁炮四尊,俗称作“铁桶江山”,“桶”或由“铳”音转。此外别无杜文秀的遗迹可考。

三 关于喜洲

喜洲就是南诏时候的大厘城,或因隋将史万岁曾驻兵于此,管它叫做史城,现在当地的民家话呼做 ha chie, chie 即是“脸”或“睑”的对音。唐樊绰《蛮书·六赕第五》云:“大厘谓之史赕。……太和城、大厘城、阳苴咩城,本皆河蛮所居之地也。开元二十五年蒙归义逐河蛮据太和城,后数月又袭破苴咩。盛罗皮取大厘城,仍筑龙口城为保障。阁罗凤多由太和、大厘、邆川来往。蒙归义男等初立太和城以为不安,遂改创阳苴咩城。”又云:“大厘城南去阳苴咩城四十里,北去龙口城二十五里,邑居人户尤众。盛罗皮多在此城,并阳苴咩,并邆川,今并南诏往来所居也。家室共守,五处如一。”《新唐书·南蛮列传》云:“大厘睑亦曰史睑。”又明弘治八年杨谟《重修大慈寺记》云:“蒙氏九代孙孝桓王迁都五峰下‘国号’史城。”明李元阳《云南通志》卷十六《羁縻志》云:“异牟寻以唐代宗大历十四年嗣立,先居史城。”原注“史城,今喜洲也”。可见喜洲在唐代同现在的大理城(就是那个时候的阳苴咩城),是一样重要的。现在从表面上看起来,喜洲比大理整齐得多。镇里的殷实大户有杨、董、赵、李、尹、张、严诸姓,各家的宅第都是画栋雕梁,轮奂可颂。最近新建筑的一所大宅子,听说花了二百万,澡盆、恭桶、发电机,色色俱全。镇里绅士捐资兴建的苍逸图书馆和五台中学,在抗战时候看起来,都觉得堂皇富丽,颇堪羡慕。当地有“穷大理,富喜洲”的俗谚,大概不算是夸张。美中不足的就是苍蝇太多。听说到夏天更厉害,说话时若不用手掏着,往往有飞到嘴里去的危险!

喜洲在明清两代科第也颇发达。明朝的给事中杨弘山(士云)就是此地人,客家门首悬着“进士第”、“甲科第”、“大夫第”的不一而足,在四方街的通衢还竖立着题名坊和翰林院给事中的石牌坊。市面三天一街,每天早晨还有邻村妇女聚到街上卖布,颇有古代“抱布贸丝”的遗风。在街上通用民家话,有时候外来人买东西,间或遇到“我不懂汉话”的回答。本地人管汉话叫做“汉”,管民家话叫做“白”。假如立志研究民家话,我想在这个环境里住上半年就可以有相当的成就了。

四 华中大学

抗战以后,华中大学起初从武昌搬到桂林,后来又由桂林搬到喜洲,到现在差不多快三年了。校址在喜洲镇的东南,是由大慈寺、张公祠和文庙三处合成的。大慈寺是南诏时建的,明成化乙酉和弘治八年两度重修,寺中现有明洪武戊寅沙门无极《宝莲殿记》和弘治八年杨谟《重修大慈寺记》两个碑。据元张道宗《记古滇说》云:“时六诏之渠帅曰蒙舍诏、越嶲诏、越柏诏、浪穷诏、施浪诏、邓赕诏,国相张建成始服五诏。又三十年王(蒙诏威成王乐诚)遣张建成朝唐。建成乃喜洲人也,入觐过成都大慈寺,适寺初铸神钟已成,寺僧戒曰'击钟一声施金一两'。时建成连叩八十声。僧惊问曰:'汝何人,连叩如此?'曰:'吾云南使张建成也。'僧乃易其名曰'化成'。成曰:'佛法南矣。'遂学佛书,归授滇人。成至京朝唐,时玄宗在位,厚礼待之,赐以浮屠像而归。王崇事佛教,自兹而启。"这一段传说和大慈寺创建的历史颇有关系。张公祠是已故司法总长张榕西先生(耀曾)的家祠。他的始迁祖也叫张建成,和上面所说的南诏国相同名。据《张氏宗谱》上说:"始祖张建成'直隶凤阳人',元时官滇通海路古桥州。负奇好义,仗义倜傥。榆段高其名,迎至礼遇,遂卜居喜洲。"自明以来,以甲第显者凡三人:张洪文,明嘉靖乙未进士,号桂城先生,曾创建桂香书院;张云鹏,明弘治壬戌进士;张士铿,清光绪庚辰进士。到榕西为第二十六代。文庙也是元时创建,下祀唐御史杜光庭神主。这三个地方联接起来恰好够华中大学三院的教室和办公处之用。

华中从韦卓成校长接办以来已经有 18 年的历史,平时不求闻达,却独自关起门来苦干。比如理学院卞彭年[卞彭]、万绳武、萧之的各教授在物理、化学、生物方面都有自己的贡献;熊子璥教授利用迁校的旧汽车发动电流,除去供给实验外,还可以烧燃全校几十盏电灯。最初每晚开灯 4 小时只需国币 10 元,现在虽然物价高涨所费也不过 30 元上下。就这一桩来讲,就可以看出华中同人利用现有设备一点一滴去做的精神!教育学院在黄秋浦(溥)院长领导之下颇注意于英语和音乐师资的训练,三、四年级学生都借五台中学去实习。文学院里除去中国文学系的几位老朋友外,我还会到历史社会系的许烺光,经济系的唐炳亮、张祖尧各教授。中国文学系的研究室由游泽承、包渔庄两教授领导,从 1938 年以来,每年都有研究报告寄给美国哈佛燕京社,因为大家的努力,每年协款递有增加。他们所写的论文,据我看到的,如游泽承的《说蛮》、《西南夷语考》、《火把节考》、《说洱河》,包渔庄的《释僰》、《民家非白国后裔考》,傅懋勣的《昆明倮倮语研究》、《利波语研究》等等。本年新聘葛毅卿任副教授,葛君在教育部时,曾到滇、黔、川、康一带调查,所得边疆语言材料甚多。许烺光教授是著名人类学者马利诺斯基的高足,他最近作 *The Differential Functions of Relationship Terms* 颇有独到的见解。他现在的计划是研究上关到下关一带的祖先崇拜问题。

五 圣源寺和罗刹阁

在昆明看到《白国因由》和《苍洱碑》已经久仰圣源寺的大名了。3 月 8 日我在五台中学记音告一段落,承该校教师王树森先生和邱钟棠女士招待我去游圣源寺和罗刹阁,同伴还有一个初中一年级学生名叫李月超。圣源寺离喜洲约七里,寺里大殿旁边的清光绪间杨泰山《重建圣源寺碑记》云:"蒙氏建寺名圣源。由唐至宋真宗时段氏重修。炎宗壬子年寺毁,平国公高顺贞复建之,纪大士一十八化世,传为白国因由,绘影图形洋洋如在。及元有元帅杨智公,明则中溪李太史、桂楼杨先生,相因而修饰润色,极庄严。近迄清康熙时,寺遭水患,仅存大殿。有先觉、大龄、含宏、省机等……结志修补,积十六春秋而修还如故。……自丙辰兵兴,贼分兵驻寺堵御,同治壬申京兵大发,贼竟束手无策,放火而逃,将千百年古迹化为乌有矣。……光绪壬午邑人重兴土木,戊子而大殿告成。"那么,现在的大殿只是清光绪间重修的罢了。殿中供着三世佛,前面的 20 张隔扇,上面刻着《白国因由》,下面刻着《观音圣迹》图像。第一到第七述观音降罗刹事,第八到第十一述白国来源,第十二到第十六述观音降诸夷,第十七到第十八述大理起源,第十九"示梦岑宫保绘图擒贼"和第二十"杨总戎扫穴擒渠"两章是今本《白国因由》所没有的,这显然是光绪重修时为纪念岑毓英、杨玉科而追加上去的。南偏院另有殿三间,殿廊左壁嵌着杨黼所作汉字白音的《苍洱碑》,右壁嵌着清康熙五十四年董学祖所撰《省机禅师实行碑》。殿里边,南有康熙三十一年《圣元寺开山大师中和尚实行碑》,北有康熙三十三年《圣元寺常住碑记》。中祀观音化身之老僧,左祀文昌,右祀火神。香火并不发达。苍洱上面的民家话现在已然没人能通其读。喜洲有两位会念它的音,但不会解释它的意义。前年傅君懋勣曾经指导华中中国文学系学生萧雷南把它的音记下来,并略考杨黼的事迹。按,杨黼大理下羊溪村人,别号存诚道人。"素好学。读五经皆百遍。训诲乡里子弟,口不言人过,兼好释典。口绝膻味。工书善篆籀。人劝其应举,必当有获。笑曰:'性命不理,而理外物乎?'庭前有大桂树,缚板其上,题曰桂楼,日夕偃仰其中,咏歌自得。尝以方言著《竹枝词》数十首,皆发明无极之旨。每出游,遇林泉会意,辄留连不能去。然以父母在堂,不欲远离。家虽贫,躬耕数亩,以为养亲甘旨,但求亲悦,不愿余也。父母殁为佣以营葬,葬毕入鸡足山,栖于罗汉壁之石窟中,十余年,寿八十,子孙迎归,无疾而终。"(节采李元阳《存诚道人杨黼传》)。由此看来,他在《苍洱碑》以外还有用民家话所写的数十首《竹枝词》,可惜我在仓卒中没有找到。

到圣源寺后,忽然赶上急风骤雨并且夹着冰雹。可是我们并不因为天气变了就失望。我仍旧拿着小本子东抄西写,李月超去买柴,王先生帮着烧火,邱女士把带来预备野餐的菜烹调起来,居然也凑成四菜一汤。其中有一味是麂脯,就着升酒细细咀嚼,别有一番滋味。假如不下雨,大家坐在山坡上去吃更当有趣了。王、邱两位同是学艺术的,所以生活懂得艺术化。三八妇女节是他们俩的结婚纪念日,顺便约我同游,随后才知道我无意之中夹了一回萝卜干儿。

吃过午饭,雨过天晴,太阳又出来了。下午1点半钟由圣源寺出发,从从容容地顺着小路走,约摸有五六里的光景,王、邱两位用手指给我看,在莲花峰的山腰,从一片苍翠中映现出一段红墙,那便是罗刹阁。上阳溪的水从峰际流下来,分散成几条小溪随处澄澈见底。我们循着溪流,冲着红墙的方向走,经过上阳溪村尽头的一片草坪,登上72级石磴,便到了遗爱寺。寺前有万年青两株,高约三四丈,大可两三围。北殿祀清平景帝,有神主云:"大圣祐祚皇基清平景帝三四五爷新王太子神位",后院西殿祀玄坛,南院的里殿中间供着释迦、孔子,左边供着关岳,右边供着文昌,可谓"文武圣神"(用原匾语),同冶一炉。出寺穿小径上行约百步,在两峰环抱间,乃见罗刹阁。阁下有大石约两丈许,宽亦相称。中有罅漏,用砖密密地砌起来。相传观音把罗刹封闭在这块石头里边。罗刹译言邪龙。本地传说唐以前罗刹为害大理,唐初观音大士制服罗刹,才建立了白国。这不过是一种开辟的神话罢了。罗刹阁就建在大石头上,所供观音也作老人装,二指上翘,貌颇慈祥。站在阁前远眺洱海澄静如镜,沃野百余里,稻田和菜花交映,黄绿相衬,好像是王、邱两位有意替我这位客人安排好了的图案!阁前有大树四五株,高约三四丈,下无枝叶,只在顶际如张绿伞,在山上许多疏林中间它确可以秀出众表。寺后拿莲花峰作屏障,上阳溪的水声不舍昼夜地在潺潺响着,难怪罗刹当年被观音引诱到这个地方就舍不得出来了。我们因为苍山顶上浓云又起,不敢尽兴流连,匆匆赶下山去,刚到上阳溪村里,大雨夹着冰雹果然下起来了。王君找着一个五台中学学生的住家暂避一会儿,承他们几个学伴会合起来勤勤恳恳地享先生以酒食。可惜我们午饭吃得太饱,只能接受他的好意,却没有下咽的胃口。4点半雨止后同着几个学生一块儿返喜洲,沿途同他们温习着民家话,并不觉得疲乏。

六 洱海之滨

自从2月5日在才村的临水亭望过一回洱海，这一个月里我并没有再到过一次海滨。3月9日记音工作停止后，包、游两君留我多盘桓两天，那天下午我们三个便溜达到海滨去聊天儿。由城北到海滨有两条小路：偏南的一条，垂柳夹径，风不扬尘，走到尽头便是所谓龙湖。湖周遍绕着水杨，在一个好像镶着绿边的镜子中间漂出一座宛在水中央的楼房来，那就是苍逸老人严子珍（镇圭）的别墅海心亭，因为怕风没敢泛舟容与湖心，但在岸边凝视，已然让我想起暌违已久的西湖阮公墩、湖心亭和北平的北海、什刹海来了。偏北的一条，一直可以走到海边的沙村。杨柳荫下铺着茸茸的草地，海东的山上反映出落日的斜晖照在从沙村横吐出的一条沙洲上，站在远处一望，依稀像是青岛的栈桥。几个水鸟在无拘无束地任意翱翔着，两三匹啃青的小马很驯顺地低着头找它们要吃的草。幽谧的背景恰好和澄静的湖面得到调谐，它和我在才村所见的“海阁观涛”，完全是两般景象！附近有一个小庙叫做顺则庵，难道就是从“不识不知顺帝之则”取意吗？

七 中央皇帝庙和三灵庙

在大慈寺的对面有一座中央皇帝庙，大概就是喜洲的本主庙。迤西所谓“本主”各村镇都不相同。这里所祀的中央皇帝，像高丈六，貌颇狰狞，赤须环眼，贯甲顶盔，横剑危坐，向西南怒目而视，看起来略有点儿毛骨悚然！土人相传是元世祖忽必烈的像，不知有何根据。在我看来，倒和下文所记三灵庙里的福景灵帝有些相似。本主庙两旁的配像是些判官、小鬼、马童之流，和别处的城隍庙里的配像相同。那么本主的地位也许和别处的城隍相当。

三灵庙在喜洲西五里许凤阳村外，背沧浪峰，临霞移溪，竹树森蔚，溪水萦回，登高凭眺，亦可俯览洱海之胜。庙里有殿三楹，中间供着"大圣元祖重光鼎祚皇帝"、"大圣圣德兴邦皇帝"、"大圣镇子福景灵帝"、"大圣妙感玄机洱河灵帝"四位塑像，还有"沧浪峰霞移涧得道有感龙神"牌位。关于"三灵"的来源，庙的北庑有明景泰元年《三灵庙记》碑，记述得很详细，兹录原碑全文如下：

三灵庙记　五峰兰雪道人杨安道书　并篆额

窃闻三灵者，其来尚矣。按白史自唐天宝壬辰蒙诏阁罗凤神武王时肇兴神迹，至灵至圣。其一灵乃吐蕃之酋长，二灵乃唐之大将，三灵乃蒙诏神武王偏妃之子也。厥诞生时，中宫无出，阴谋以猴儿易而弃废，埋于太和城之道旁。密遣侍女夙夜视之。冢生一苇而畅茂。群牸往复，有一牸牯先来爱护。一旦斑牸忽食之。女遂报于中宫。宰牸剖腹，出一男子，被戴金盔甲，执剑恨指，腾空而北往吐蕃。后率兵伐太和，至德源城，蒙诏乞和而归。后同二将复举兵至摩用，大战弗克，回至喜脸，赤佛堂前三将殒命。乃托梦院塝耆老曰：若立庙祀享，能通水利，除灾害。遂定星揆日，不月而庙宇成焉。由是雨旸时若，五谷丰稔。每于四月十九日阖郡祈告。迄异牟寻孝桓王追封，号曰元祖重光鼎祚皇帝、圣德兴邦皇帝、镇子福景灵帝。院塝有一长者，乏嗣，默祷。其圃种一李树，结一大颗，坠地现一女子，姿禀非凡。长者爱育，号曰白姐阿妹。蒙清平官段宝瑺聘为夫人，浴濯霞移江，见木一段逆流，触阿妹足，知元祖重光化为龙，感而有孕。将段木培于庙庭之右，吐木莲二枝。生思平、思胄，号先帝、先王。思平丁酉立位，国号大理。建灵会寺。追封母曰天应景星懿慈圣母。重创三灵庙。世传三十五代,凡三百九十一载。迨我圣朝洪武壬戌,大理臣伏。胤子段名赴京,见任湖广武昌卫镇抚。有宪椽院塝杨赐等施舍田亩。城南善士杨正等曰:三灵庙者一乡香火祈福之所,寂然不动,感而遂通,岂可不思补报乎?是以征言刻石,以彰厥德。予不揆疏谫,述其梗概而词曰:

三灵圣帝　天性正中　生前为将　殁后祀崇　阴翊治化
威德惟隆　雨旸顺序　祈祷必从　阖郡瞻仰　沛泽感通
黎民获福　于变时雍　西山苍苍　东海溶溶　纪德贝石
垂祐无穷

景泰元年岁次庚午秋菊月下浣　城南村　院塝村　江度村

这段传说虽然荒诞不经,但是同蒙氏起源的传说也相仿佛。《记古滇说》、《南诏野史》、《滇小纪》等都没有提到它,《大理县志稿》也没有收入,所以我把它抄下来供研究蒙段历史的人们参考。在庙中抄录的时候颇为辛苦,泽承站在碑前用临川腔的国语一句句地念,渔庄和我伏在一个灶台上各抄一半,回到喜洲又托万先法君誊清,这么一段东西也包含着四个人的劳作呢。碑里所引白史,应该就是《白古通》。《白古通》或疑杨升庵所伪托,不过李元阳的《云南通志》引它的地方很多,清乾隆时人陈鼎所作《蛇谱》也记着在剑川何氏家见到《西南列国志》,似乎当时是真有这部书的。在喜洲时会到一位宾川丁石僧[丁怀瑾]君,他说光绪初年还有人看见过《白古通》的残叶,究竟是假是真,实在无从悬揣。向觉明先生对于这部书一向抱着当年刘继庄"悬金而求,募贼以窃"的态度,我到大理以前他谆谆托我找寻它的下落,结果我所能答复他的还是"杳无消息"。

1942 年 3 月 12 日写于点苍山麓

八 无为寺与下鸡邑

3月24日，我把云龙、泸水、剑川的民家语记完，又访大理县立中学赵绍普(继曾)校长审正过民家语的声调，此行的主要工作，总算告一段落了。赵诚伯司令和马希良师长曾经允许替我接洽回昆明的交通工具，所以我访他们去辞行。谁知这一来，惹得他们异口同声地强留我多住了一个礼拜。这时徐悲鸿先生由保山开完劳军画展，路过大理，要到鸡足山去览胜，也被诚伯留在他的“帅府”下榻。在这一周间，他们除去料理紧急公务以外，大部分时间都费在招待这两个“酸秀才”上头。

25日李县长约游无为寺。寺在大理城西北八里许，点苍山兰峰的半腰，双鸢溪和白石溪分流于南北，原来是明朝永乐八年建造的。我同诚伯、悲鸿从城里出发，一边走，一边谈，健步直前，乐而忘倦，三乘滑竿跟在后面几乎赶不上。直到过了五里桥，拐上崎岖的小路，才想起让滑竿代了一段步，悲鸿还不时地跳下来流连风景，给抬他的黑籍伕子节省了不少的劳力。快到无为寺以前，第一惹起我们注意的，便是在迎面的一垛粉壁上镶嵌着用大理石刻就的“南诏胜迹”四个大绿字，那就是“月含桥”的遗址。转过粉壁，老远便看见那三棵驰名的唐杉耸矗在寺前了。三棵树都高约十几丈，周约四五围，各有各的姿态，一点儿都不相同。中间的一棵从主干旁分出一枝细干来，离地一丈多高，便枝叶扶疏，左右匀称，看着虽然茂密，姿态却不免平凡。北边的一棵主干之外分出三枝细干，经苍山的西风吹了一千多年，所有的枝子都向东指着，比中间的那一棵显着好看多了；可是我顶喜欢的还是南边那一棵。它是一棵独干，在离地五丈许才有枝叶，四条虬枝矫健地向东北指着，另有两枝却指向反对的方向，牵掣作势。远望起来,像几条小龙儿腾空的在云中搏斗;又像一个和巨无霸一样高的拳师金鸡独立般斜撑开两膀在那儿比着奇俏的势子! 寺的位置,据明汝南王朱有勋的游记说:“由溪而入,榛莽蒙翳。路若穷然,思欲回履,忽闻绝壁峭岩之间有人声,知为幽胜之所。遂披藤扪萝,且歇且进,历幽峦,蹑石磴,倏然若飘浮骞腾,则身已在万顷云上矣。流盼容与,愈进愈佳,松涛响空,兰气袭人,乃忘其向之疲也。”可是,照我这次登临的印象来说,这种幽深奇险的境界,已经和寺里刻着这篇游记的“玉磬碑”一样看不见了。寺里正在翻修的翠华楼,是元世祖忽必烈的驻跸台遗址。相传明建文帝也曾在这里住过。大殿的廊子上有一口大铁钟,是明正统十年乙丑四月二十五日铸的。寺门的南边有明崇祯九年的石碑,正面刻着慈溪冯补衮《榆郡唐梅诗序》,碑阴刻着段藻云《衢山房碑记》。此外在大殿前还悬着清光绪二十一年刘安科所题“清净无为”和光绪二十五年李瑞清所题“无为寺”两块匾;翠华楼下的右壁嵌着李根源所写的沐璘、杨慎、李崇阶、杨仲琼、刘谦诸人的《游无为寺》诗。大殿的楹柱上有1935年邑人杨荣升所作长联云:“日晒经坡风敲玉磬趁日暖风和快过月桥登驻跸;泉名救疫树列香杉爱泉清树古闲邀阁老步华楼”,寺僧大乘说这副对联包括“无为八景”,实际上已然大半湮没不存了。晒经坡在寺对面的东北方,相传唐玄奘曾晒经于此,坡上终年不生青草。这个传说,不单上半是无稽之谈,就是下半也和事实不符。不过站在坡上向东眺,洱海澄碧如镜,鸡山迤逦如屏,拿望远镜来细看,连鸡山顶上的楞严塔都清清楚楚地摆在眼前。回首西顾,三棵唐杉的雄姿,掩覆在苍山的底下,因为光线、方向的变换,和进山时所领略的景象又不同了。在坡上凝望了许久,天风虚岚,牵衣萦发。跑回寺门前,悲鸿正在替三棵唐树写生。他先用木炭起稿,再用铅笔墨笔勾勒,对于光线的向背,皴纹的稀疏,丝毫都不肯草率。从前听见一位朋友说:“没成名的人卖力,成了名的人卖名。”照我自己的经验,再参证许多当真成名的人的实例,处处都可以证明这句话是自暴自弃的。离寺下山,大约4点多了。转过月含桥,便见缕缕的浓云像炊烟般从山谷间冒出来,一会儿弥漫了山腰,一会儿笼锁住古寺,慢慢的连苍山的几个峰头也迷失了本来面目。煦日的光辉刚刚隐匿起来,无情的西风便凛冽地吹着,坐在滑竿上摇摇欲坠,雨星儿不时地刮上了面庞,眼看着大雨就要下起来了。悲鸿为到五里桥挖一块玉带石,放开了脚步在地下走着,我们坐着滑竿都赶不上他。下山刚三里许,果然下起雨来,我和诚伯躲在一家水碓房的门前,等着雨小一点儿,又跑到一家民房里去歇息。幸而这一阵急风骤雨不大会儿就过去了,我们慢慢地在地下走着,各自谈了一两件可歌可泣的回忆,不知不觉地便回到了北门。

27日中午,悲鸿和周军凯、李立柏来邀,同应杨杏村(时芳)团长的约会,到下鸡邑去看打鱼。下鸡邑在大理城的东北八里许,是才村迤北洱海边上的一个村子。到北门和诚伯、希良、志鹏诸人会齐,15骑马鱼贯地络绎前进。我虽生长北方,却从小儿没学过骑射,在马上东摇西晃的始终稳不住重心,更不用说控纵急徐的骑术了。所骑的一匹小马,据说是相当骏良的,可惜所驮非人,丝毫不能伸展它的才能,羁勒在缰索之下,俯首帖耳地慢慢走着,有时回过头来长嘶一声,宣泄它的郁积,似乎在表示所遇不谐的哀怨。据骑兵科的先进赵诚伯说:“会骑的人骑马,不会骑的马驮人。”马不幸而不能驰骋无羁的任性发展,它总愿被一个控制有方的人骑着,却不甘于庸庸碌碌地驮着一个随风飘摆坐不稳雕鞍的懦夫!所以我这一天虽然幸而没从马上滚下来,却对于这一匹小马十分的抱歉!

到下鸡邑杨宅休息片刻,便坐着两只小艇容与在洱海间。风不很大,海里吹不起波浪来,顺风向南驶着,走得很快。天上布满了乌云,太阳避匿在云的后边,可是隐藏不住的光芒又偷偷地从云缝儿里钻出来,辐射下几道霞光,映衬着黯黮的天空越发显着明丽。等到日光的斜度超越出乌云掩蔽的范围,便成片地洒满在海东的山上,因此一水的间隔就有阴晴的不同。小船泛过龙王庙的时候,风涛并不像我2月初在岸上所看见的那样险恶。到了才村渔人已经下过大网了。我们虽然没能看见洱海渔民的捕鱼生活,可是顺风泛舟,浮沉在水色山光中也觉得不虚此行。回来的时候,风浪较大,小船吃水颇深,心里未免有点儿害怕。杏村素来好客,款待得很殷勤,并且坚留我们在下鸡邑多盘桓两天,直到黄昏的时候还不肯放行。我们趁着他带有七成醉意,不得已留下诚伯殿后,不辞而别,快马加鞭地逃出了下鸡邑。一气儿跑了五六里,我和马渐渐和谐,两膝和臀部的控制,自己也觉得有点儿把握,不过刚在骑得稍有趣味的当儿已经回到大理城的东门了。

九 "挂彩"归来

经过一番酬酢,3月30日诚伯、希良、军凯、立柏才送我到下关。承中缅运输总局下关总站薛凤章总管(文蔚)和陈车务长(昆书)的关照,第二天一清早我便搭7636号GMC车从下关出发,司机傅某,湖南人,人还老实,沿路总算顺适。当天没赶到楚雄,在沙桥过夜。4月1日早晨6点从沙桥起身,走出去不到十公里,汽车撞在一块大石头上,断了两块钢板,虽然还能对付着往前走,可是车身向左侧倾很多。我恐怕过级山坡的时候发生危险,一到楚雄总站便托余啸南总管设法。承他和黄车务长帮忙,把原车立刻发厂修理。黄车务长恐怕修理耽误时间,当天赶不到昆明,又给我换了一辆9688号新Dodge车,机器和座位都比原车好得多,司机蔡某,湖北人。8点30分开出总站后,蔡司机下车去买米,直等到9点钟,我原来坐的那辆7636号车已经修理好了开过去，他还没有来。又等了好半天，他同队的一位贵州人才跳上车来，替他开走。大约11点钟左右，开到152公里的地方，离级山坡下坎还有两公里的光景，突然被昆明总站派出来的一辆稽查车给拦住。几个广东口音的稽查其势汹汹地先向我盘问，幸而我有薛总管填发的乘车证，算是没被他们捉作“黄鱼”。后来好像预先知道这辆车上有私货似的，就七手八脚地仔细检查。结果在车底下前后轮子中间的铁梁里搜出64罐味王，两匹法兰绒，又在车箱下层搜出肥皂三箱。检查过后，因为司机的是替工，没法被带走，可是他沮丧极了，似乎这一批货里他也有相当的股份。我因为车上的罩棚没扣好，恐怕行李遗失，站在车旁边帮助司机扣罩棚，那辆稽查车竟自没看见车旁边站着人，猛然间从对面开过来，一下子就把我撞倒了！当时，我右额上皮破血流，右肩头和右膝都很疼痛，衣服也撕烂了。幸而是竖着躺下的，假如横着倒下，那便会受了腰斩的惨刑！在刚一撞倒的那一刹那，我心里很清明，我惦记我那18个单位的语言记录，我可惜我两个月来昼夜不息的辛勤，尤其怕20年来的学养就这么糊里糊涂地断送在卤莽的司机的手里！况且4月1日是万愚节，即便昆明或大理的朋友接到我的凶信，还许当做闹着玩儿呢！及至同车的一个广东小孩把我扶到车上去，扎住伤口，宁神休息了好久，我知道不会死了，可是又担心有血毒或破伤风的危险。下午3点到了禄丰，赶紧到卫生站去检查。站上的一位周大夫，是上海医学院出身，曾经在呈贡见过。据他说伤势不大严重，他替我仔细地消过毒，让我安心了好多。过禄丰后，车开得很快，6点10分就赶到昆明西郊的黑林铺。因为汽车不进城，我便换了一辆马车，拉着行李慢慢地走，回到青园还不到7点钟。

将养了两个多礼拜，伤势渐渐平复了。到现在，只是右肩胛骨有一小部分稍微突出，右额上也残余着一个小疤。没想到在40岁以后竟自留下这么一点儿小小的创痕！恐怕遇到阴天下雨，它还会不时地犯疼呢！

1942年5月4日补记于昆明青园

清碧溪记游

去年春天我将要离开大理的时候，诚伯坚留我同游清碧溪。他说："到大理而不登洗马塘，临清碧溪，探波罗崖，未免辜负了苍洱胜境！三月杪春寒未杀！雪风时起，纵登洗马塘也见不到杜鹃遍山的奇景，畏难而止，犹有可说。但是无论如何必须玩过清碧溪和波罗崖才算不枉此行。"说罢，便长吟他和志希酬唱的诗，又朗诵他所作《约友人游清碧溪书》里的警句："郡西有清碧溪，颇可游。溪上下两叠，为潭者三。夏涨为溪，秋竭为潭，水色晶莹，直视见底。两岸飞崖无数，上与天接。高峰绿树，倒植横生。山寒不鸟，水冷无鱼。呼喧不至，静如太古。理柱调弦，引吭便歌，峰青曲罢，相对寂然。视舆佳丽，负姣童，挟弓佩弹，围绕驺从者，又如何乎？"豪兴四溢，旁若无人。当时我虽心焉向往，终以校电促归，有愿未偿！

今年2月初，我应印老[李根源]和荫国之约重到大理讲学，总算跟苍山洱海有缘，居然有再度登临的机会。那么，这次游览第一不能忘怀的当然就是清碧溪。

2月4日，恰值夏历壬午岁除，中午诚伯在他的官邸欢宴讲学同人。看见诚伯，看见这古老的杜文秀府，越发引起去年未阑的游兴来。没等终席，便约光旦、春台同游。出赵邸，坐小汽车到七里桥圣麓公园，改乘仲笣给我们预备的滑竿朝着马龙峰的方向西进。约三四里，见流水穿石滩间，那便是清碧溪下游了。涉滩，缘溪北行，再里许,马龙、圣应两峰的余脉形成了巉峻对峙的山峡,骈突如门,上耸下削,溪水就从这里破门而出。从此以内,崖夹于上,溪嵌于下,石皴如画,流水成音,崖际的杂树遮翳住已向西转的日光,格外透出深窅清幽的情韵。进峡后,靠着马龙峰这一边走,逼仄的小径盘纡在崖端,越往里越曲折,而层峦叠翠也越显着奇秀,又一里许,崖端径断,滑竿不能前进,乃溯溪行乱滩中,屡涉其南北。这时我和春台已然有点儿勉强支持,但是光旦贾其余勇,叫一个滑竿夫搀着,仍然高高兴兴地向前跋涉。大家正在腿酸汗流的当儿,偶一抬头,突然看见西面两峰耸矗,中劈仅如一线,另外一个高峰掩映在这劈开的小门后面,积雪中垂,如匹练界青山,五彩的望夫云从峰际流出来,烘托得苍松黛峦分外显着奇丽!这时我已神凝形释,俨然陶镕在大自然的炉冶中,刚才那一点疲乏,早不知什么时候从峰巅云际飞过点苍山,抛到漾濞江心去了。

清碧溪的源头就在双峰底下,水从源出,先汇为上中下三潭,然后下流成溪,曲折以趋洱海。峰麓有一片广坪,坪际崖穴间数有炊爨痕迹。不肯攀峻涉险的游人们,往往在此止息,置酒雅集,只能坐览峰色水声之胜,而不能亲赏潭影波光的幽异,虽说兴尽而止,终不免辜负了溪山。我虽孱弱,岂肯与若辈为伍?于是,披榛除莽,更向前行。自坪西下复与涧遇,涧源有一泓清水,澄冽莹澈,细石布底,累累可数,拿它的部位推度,这或者就是所谓下潭?

从此穿行丛莽间,沿南峰西进,约半里许,仰见右崖凿"禹穴"二大字,相传是明太守杨邛崃所刻。再前即直逼夹门下,水从门中突崖下坠,高约丈余,宛如倒挂珠帘,和后峰积雪争洁比白。这条白练倾泻而下,蓄为澄潭,广两丈余,水作纯绿色,深不可测,这大概就是所谓中潭。对岸北峰的旁边有一斜阪,高约丈余,逼仄无级可登,冰雪未消,滑腻不可着足。但由它登崖,便可望见上潭。春台抖擞精神,踏两潭间的溪中乱石,爬上对岸的斜阪,猿行而上,蛇退而下。据他告诉我和光旦说:“上潭就在中潭的崖上,稍偏北一点儿,形状像一个钵盂,水色益较深碧。盂满水溢,便从崖缘流下来注入中潭。崖端阪上积雪极滑,稍一失足,就有坠崖的危险。但盂边有冰柱倒垂,好像石钟乳一样,颇为美观,能见此奇,总算没有枉冒这一番危险。”在我们这次旅行的全程中,这一举可算是春台顶勇敢的表演,事后追想,我还佩服不置!

听罢春台的描写,我和光旦面面相觑的默然许久。起初光旦颇想手足并用地尝试一下,从者侯君遵荫国、仲�的嘱咐极力劝阻,他也只得罢了。但他还怕我受他牵累不能尽兴,劝我还得努力攀登上潭。其实我呢?想起李中溪所说:“水出山石间,涌沸为潭,深丈许,明莹不可藏针。小石布底,累累如卵如珠,青绿白黑,丽于宝玉,错如霞绮。上有坠叶,鸟随衔去”,“下潭水光深青色,中潭鸦碧色,上潭鹦绿色。水石相因,水光愈浮,石色愈丽”,杨升庵所说:“垒崿承流,水色莹澈。其中石子粼粼,青碧璀璨,丽如宝玉”,还有徐霞客所说:“再逾西崖,下觑其内有潭,方广各二丈余。其色纯绿,漾光浮黛,照耀崖谷。午日射其中,金碧交荡,光怪得未曾有。……踞石坐潭上,不特影空人心,觉一毫一孔无不莹澈”,心里未尝不跃跃欲试地想身临其境,一探究竟。继而一转念,想起霞客当年“蹑峰槽与水争道,为石滑足,与水俱下,倾注潭中,水及其项”的险状,不觉不寒而栗,惴惴而止。况且“青碧璀璨,丽如宝玉”,“漾光浮黛……金碧交荡”,“水光愈浮,石色愈丽”等等景象,主要的条件必得有“午日射其中”,才能显现出来。即使像光旦所设想的“峰头彩云为此间常事。云影在潭,则潭水与水底石丸皆呈缤纷与骀荡之象,余等虽未见云影,已见射影之云,而所见独多,且于此得悟潭中水光石色所由幻化之理,亦慰情胜无矣”,那也得在烈日当头的时候去临瞰才有法子证实。我们到中潭太阳已经隐匿到岭的西边去了，即使冒险爬到上潭，暮色已快笼罩下来，哪里还看得见水色的幻化？更哪里窥得到水底诸色斑斓的石丸？不如适可而止，反倒永远留存一个有余不尽的想像——大凡想像中的境界总比现实的美丽得多！光旦又告诉我：庐山的三叠水和南岳的水帘洞也是跟这里差不多的玩艺儿。那两个地方我都没到过，惟其没到过，也许比到过更美一些？

兴尽缘溪下山，到七里桥已然星斗满天了。

归来重检《徐霞客游记》，颇疑我们所看到的中潭、下潭，乃至于春台登临的上潭，并不能叫做第一潭、第二潭、第三潭。因为《游记》中在霞客落水曝衣后明明说：

> 披衣复登崖端，从其上复西逼峡门。……余欲从其内再穷门内二潭，以登悬雪之峰。……遂转北崖中垂处西向直上。一里，得东来之道，自高穹之坪来，遵之曲折西上，甚峻。一里余，逾峡门北顶，复平行而西半里，其内两崖石壁复高骈夹起。门内上流之涧仍下嵌深底。路旁北崖，削壁无痕，不能前度。乃以石条缘崖架空，度为栈道者四五丈，是名阳桥，亦名仙桥。桥之下正门内第二潭所汇，为石所亏蔽不及见。度桥北，有叠石贴壁间。稍北叠石复北断，乃趁其级南坠涧底。底有小水，蛇行块石间，乃西自第一潭注第二潭者。时第二潭已过而不知。只望涧中西去，两崖又骈对如门，门下又两巨石夹峙，上有石平覆如屋而塞其后。覆屋之下，又水潴其中，亦澄碧渊渟，而大不及外潭之半。其后塞壁之上，水从上涧垂下，其声潺潺不绝，而前从块石间东注二潭矣。

他从此历涧中石块西上，更从北崖转陟密箐中，路断无痕，再去巾解服，攀竹为绖，最后因为壑底之涧又环转而北，跟垂雪后峰，界为两重，终于爬不上去，他才想转回来：

> 时已下午,腹馁甚,乃亟下。……遂从旧道五里过第一潭。随水而前,观第二潭。其潭当夹门逼束之内。左崖即阳桥高横于上。乃从潭左攀磴隙,上阳桥逾东岭而下。四里,至高穹之坪,望西涧之潭已无人迹。亟东下沿溪出。

从这两段看来,可知霞客所谓第一潭、第二潭是指着峡门里面的说,和我们所见到的上、中、下三潭有分别。照他所说那样险仄,即使我们到中潭时天光还早,恐怕也没有那么矫健的脚力去探胜寻幽了。叔伟[曾昭抡]的兴趣、胆气、脚力比我都强,不知他的游记里提到这两个潭没有?

归结我对于这峡内的二潭,也正像洗马塘和波罗崖一样,愿意常常留存一个隽永、美妙、余味无穷的想像!

1943 年 5 月 15 日深夜 4 时追记

大理的几种民间传说

一　观音降罗刹

相传大理古时候是泽国,洪水一直浸到山腰,人民居住在山上靠着打野兽采果实来过生活。后来黑龙和黄龙打仗,把下关那里打倒了,洪水一下儿落下去,才显出这一片坝子来,在隋末唐初的时候,为罗刹所据。罗刹译言邪龙,性情暴虐,喜欢剜人眼,食人肉,百姓受害,困苦不堪。贞观三年癸丑(?)观音大士从西天来,至苍山五台峰下化做一个老人,到附近村子里探访罗刹和罗刹"希老"张敬的事实。人民一见老人恺悌慈祥的样子都很敬爱他,把罗刹虐害人民的情况从头到尾地诉说了一遍。老人很和蔼地安慰他们,告诉他们罗刹多行不义渐渐要恶贯满盈,大家只要静心期待着,不久就可以过安乐的日子了。

后来观音大士探知罗刹的希老张敬是阿育王后代张仁果的苗裔,为人仁而不智,知道罗刹的暴虐,却没法子规谏他。不过当时同罗刹往来最密的只有张敬一个人,观音打算靠他介绍去接近罗刹,于是就化做一个梵僧住在张敬的家里。过了十几天,由张敬荐他见罗刹,罗刹一见梵僧,心生敬爱,款待甚恭,问他喜欢什么东西。梵僧但求一块安静的地方可以结茅藏修,地方的大小仅够袈裟一展、犬跳四步就行了。罗刹慨然许之。梵僧即请立券,并当众宣誓。一切手续都办妥当，梵僧当将袈裟一铺，覆满苍洱之境，白犬四跳，占尽两关之地。罗刹一见大惊，后悔不迭。这时有五百青兵和天龙八部在云端拥护，大作鉴证，罗刹枉自悔恨，也无可如何，乃善告梵僧曰："我国土人民都属你管了！闹得我们父子连住的地方都没有了，可怎么好呢？"梵僧说："这倒好办。我另有一个天堂胜境可以给大王住。"于是他在上阳溪涧内碌瓮摩出一洞，化为金楼宝殿，白玉为阶，黄金为地，化螺蛳为人眼，化水为酒，化沙为食，美味珍馐，陈设器具，种种俱备。罗刹到这里面一看，觉得比旧时的国土还好，居然乐而忘返，并要求梵僧把他的眷属搬来。梵僧等他的眷属搬进去以后，大显神通，用一块大石头塞住洞门，自己化做黄蜂飞出来。又叫铁匠李子行拿铁汁浇它，并且造了一个塔，镇在洞上，叫他父子永远不能出来。现在大理上阳溪苍山山麓的罗刹阁，就是这段传说的遗迹。

观音降罗刹以后，又授记细奴罗为大理国王。时张乐进求为云南诏酋长，具九鼎牺牲，请细奴罗诣铁柱庙祭天卜吉。忽有金谷鸟，一名金汉王，飞在细奴罗右肩，连鸣"天命细奴罗"三次，众皆惊服，细奴罗遂登位，称奇王，遂进贡朝唐，子孙累世封王，传至舜化真共13代，凡237年。（王崧本《南诏野史》作247年，注云："蒙自唐高宗永徽四年癸丑至昭宗天复二年壬戌实250年，《滇载记》作310年，亦误。"）

这段传说，除去起首的一小节录自当地人的口说外，大部分见于《白国因由》(第一章到第六章)。《白国因由》是清康熙四十五年丙戌大理圣元寺主持寂裕刊行的，现在书版还存在庙里。据寂裕的跋语，此书盖本于《僰古通》，"逐段缘由原是僰语，但僰字难认，故译僰音为汉语，俾阅者一见了然，虽未见《僰古通》而大概不外于斯"。按，《僰古通》亦称《白古通》或《白古通玄峰年运志》，也有人管它叫做《白古记》或《白史》，杨慎的《滇载记》就是从它删正而成的，李元阳的《云南通志》引它的地方也很多,大概当时确有其书。其中的记载当然不能当做信史,可是从民间传说里却反映出不少历史上的暗示。就拿这段故事来说,咱们一看就知道它神话的意味多,历史的意味少,传说的成分多,事实的成分少。可是假定咱们能够不拘泥字句去活看,便可得到许多有趣味的启示:(一)可以看出大理在佛教史上的地位。大理古称"灵鹫山",亦名"妙香国",从这种移山倒海的借名,就可见出这地方接受印度文化之早。说到白国和蒙氏的祖先,也有人推溯到西天摩竭国的阿育王。据《南诏野史》"南诏历代源流"条引《白古记》说:

> 三皇之后,西天摩竭国阿育王第三子骠苴低(案《白国因由》作次子骠信苴)娶大蒙亏为妻;生低蒙苴(《滇载记》作低牟苴),苴生九子,名九龙(《滇载记》作九隆)氏:五子蒙苴笃,生十二子,七圣五贤蒙氏之祖;八子蒙苴颂,白子国仁果之祖(此据胡蔚本,王崧本作"白崖张乐进求之祖")。

这里把白子国和蒙氏推溯到同一祖先,固然和《白国因由》不同,可是《白国因由》卷首说到白子国的来源,佛教的色彩更为浓厚。据它说:阿育王听他老师优婆毱多的话,认为白国是释迦如来为法勇菩萨时,观音为常提菩萨时修行的地方,遂封仲子骠信苴于白国,号神明天子,即五百神王。传至十七代孙仁果,汉诸葛亮入滇场,予姓张,至三十六代孙张乐进求朝觐,上封云(云下疑脱南字)镇守将军。我们明白这种崇奉佛教、向望印度的心理,那么,推溯大理的开辟和蒙氏的建国而抬出一位观音大士来是没有什么奇怪的。(二)可以看出古代对于龙的崇拜。在汉族和许多邻近部族的神话里有许多关于龙的传说,最近闻一多先生所讲《伏羲的传说》已经引证了不少,这里不能一一列举。这个故事的开始就说到黑龙和黄龙打仗的话,又所谓罗刹其实就是邪龙,蒙氏建国始祖细奴罗据说也是黄龙之子(详下文)。那么,所谓观音降罗刹的传说,里面隐含着以黑龙或邪龙作图腾的部族和以黄龙作图腾的部族互相争霸的事实。后来黄龙一支战胜了,为安抚黑龙或邪龙的部族才造出这个神话来。所谓金谷鸟连鸣"天命细奴罗"三次也正是蒙氏造出来的"篝火狐鸣"的把戏。在初民社会里要想得到人民的信服,非玩这一套伎俩不可。(三)观音大士的降临大理何以在贞观三年癸丑呢?这是为和蒙奇王细奴罗建国年月衔接的缘故。按,贞观三年(629)的干支应该是己丑,不是癸丑,而在这以后的第一个癸丑恰好是唐高宗永徽四年(653),也就是细奴罗建蒙国受唐封的一年,这在张道宗《记古滇说》和王崧本《南诏野史》都无异词。(惟胡蔚本《南诏野史》谓细奴罗于唐太宗贞观二十三年己酉代张氏立国,自称奇嘉王,建号大蒙国,又称南诏。)造传说的人本来为给蒙氏建国找出一个"天命细奴罗"的根据来,事实的造端原是永徽四年癸丑。要想推得早一点,所以倒溯24年假托是贞观三年,可惜无意中把真的干支"癸丑"写出来,不觉得就露出马脚来了!

由这三个观点看,咱们对于故事的发展便可以了解许多。可是清康熙二十九年黄元治所修《大理府志》卷三十《杂异志》也记载"神制罗刹"的传说道:

> 俗传大理旧为泽国,邪龙居之,是为罗刹,好食人,有老僧自西方来,托言欲求片地藏修。罗刹问所欲,僧曰:"但欲吾袈裟一展,犬一跳之地。"罗刹许诺。僧曰:"合立符券。"遂就水岸上画券石间。于是袈裟一展,犬一跳,已尽其地。罗刹欲背盟,僧以神力制之曰:"别有胜地居汝。"因于苍山上阳溪神化金屋一区,罗刹喜,移其属入焉,而山闭矣。僧乃凿河尾泄水,是为天生桥。至今人以洱水赤文岛为大士地券云。

此段所记和《白国因由》详略不同,黄志纂修的年月比《白国因由》的刊行较早,大概也是从《白古通》一类的书转载下来的。黄氏对于这些“怪诞诡僻之事”,认为“智者守其理,愚者溺所闻。溺而不返,则百端邪说遂乘人心之所溺者,而愈造其理之所必无,君子所以滋惧也”。可是他持之不坚,态度颇为模棱。他在这一段传说的后面自注道:

> 俗以大士泄水,未有居民,故双鹤引之。然相传大士以唐永徽四年始现身大理,而楪榆县则自汉时已置,若谓至唐始有居民,则蒙氏取河蛮太和城、大厘城,又于何所哉?鹤拓事或在古初,迨邪龙作祟,大士制之,使不敢为民害,则有然耳。

我觉得对于民间传说应该透过它的背后去看,万不可拘执故事的本身去考究先后,争论信否。像黄氏这种疑信参半、两面都不彻底的态度,是不足为训的。

二　南诏始祖的感生说

在帝政时代,一般老百姓觉得皇帝是至高无上、神圣不可侵犯的。皇帝本身,尤其是开国皇帝,也总想把自己烘托得不是“常”人,甚至于不是“人”,才觉得可以高居人上,于是就发生了历史上的“感生”说。咱们只要一翻开每个朝代的“太祖高皇帝”本纪大半就可以找到这一类的记载。先从荒渺难稽的远古来看:

> 黄帝母曰附宝,之郊野,见太电绕北斗枢星,感而怀孕,二十四月而生黄帝于寿丘。颛顼母曰昌仆,亦谓之女枢。《河图》云:“瑶光如蜺,贯月正白,感女枢于幽房之宫,生颛顼。舜父瞽叟姓妫,妻曰握登,见大虹,意感而生舜于姚墟,故姓姚。”(以上并见《史记·五帝本纪》正义)

> 禹帝王纪云:父鲧妻修己,见流星贯昂,梦接意感,又吞神珠薏苡,胸坼而生禹。名文命字密。(《史记·夏本纪》正义)

契母曰简狄，有娀氏之女，为帝喾次妃。三人行浴，见玄鸟堕其卵，简狄取吞之，因孕生契。(《史记·殷本纪》)

后稷名弃，其母有邰氏女，曰姜原，为帝喾元妃。姜原出野见巨人迹，心忻然，欲践之，践之而身动如孕者。居期而生子，以为不祥，弃之隘巷，马牛过者皆辟不践。徙置之林中，适会山林多人。迁之而弃渠中冰上，飞鸟以其翼覆荐之，姜原以为神，遂收养长之，初欲弃之，因名曰弃。(《史记·周本纪》)

大业秦之先帝，颛顼之苗裔，孙曰女脩，女脩织玄鸟陨卵，女脩吞之，生子大业。(《史记·秦本纪》)

这都是战国以前的例。至于汉以后，更多得不可胜举了。为节省题外的篇幅，姑举汉朝为例：

汉高祖之母刘媪，尝息大泽之陂，梦与神遇，是时雷电晦冥，太公往视，则见蛟龙于其上，已而有身，遂产高祖。(《史记·高祖本纪》)

这种传说在中国历史上既然还普遍流行着，何况那宗教情绪较浓的初民社会呢？刚才最后举的一个例提到龙，恰好底下我所要讲的南诏和大理的始祖感生说都和龙有关系。

据《白国因由》上说：金齿龙泉寺下有易罗丛村，村女名茉莉娩，貌端美异常，有蒙迦独娶为妻。后蒙迦独因捕鱼溺死江中。茉莉娩往寻之，见江中有木一根逆流而上，遂惊迷若梦，见一美貌男子与之语，既醒，痛哭而回，后常往龙泉池洗菜浣衣，于池边又见前日梦中男子，是夜忽至房中，因而怀孕。父母责之，茉莉娩诉其故，父母相语曰：此乃池中黄龙也。后生九子。九子既皆长大，一夜黄龙又至茉莉娩家，见其子，与子相戏。茉莉娩因多子为累，拟将诸子送还黄龙。黄龙嘱其送至初会之池侧芭蕉竹林茂密处。一日茉莉娩如约送往，八子皆驾云而起，茉莉娩携幼子仰望云中，见八子皆现龙形。蒙迦独

亦化为黄龙,帅其八子俯视茉莉�大吼三声,山川震动,竟飘然而去。茉莉娆携其幼子归,取名细奴罗。

细奴罗幼时即举止异众。其母见邻居不可与共处,移居哀牢山下。又有豪邻名三和者图谋之,有仆波细负幼子避难东迁,开南城居之。及长躬耕养母,娶蒙欻为妻,生子罗晟,娶寻弥脚。一日细奴罗父子往大巍山下耕田,观音至其家化斋,因授记细奴罗使为白国王。事已见前。(节取《白国因由》第七章至第九章)

这段传说完全是从哀牢沙壹的故事演变出来的。《后汉书》卷一百十六《西南夷列传》说:

> 哀牢夷者,其先有妇人名沙壹,居于牢山。尝捕鱼水中,触沉木,若有感,因怀妊。十月产子男十人。后沉木化为龙,出水上。沙壹忽闻龙语曰:若为我生子,今悉何在?九子见龙惊走,独小子不能去,背龙而坐,龙因舐之。其母鸟语,谓背为九,谓坐为隆,因名子曰九隆。及后长大,诸兄以九隆能为父所舐而黠,遂共推以为王。后牢山下,有一夫一妇,复生十女子,九隆兄弟皆娶以为妻,后渐相滋长。

常璩《华阳国志》卷四《南中志·永昌郡》下记载这故事便和《后汉书》稍有出入:

> 永昌郡古哀牢国。哀牢山名也。其先有一妇人名曰沙壶,依哀牢山下居,以捕鱼自给。忽于水中触有一沉木,遂感而有娠。度十月产子男十人。后沉木化为龙,出谓沙壶曰:若为我生子,今在乎?而九子惊走,惟一小子不能去,陪龙坐,龙就而舐之。沙壶与言语,以龙与陪坐,因名曰元隆,犹汉言陪坐也。沙壶将元隆居龙山下。元隆长大才武,后九兄曰:元隆能与龙言,而黠有智,天之贵也,共推以为王。时哀牢山下复有一夫一妇产十女,元隆兄弟妻之,由是始有人民。

在这里面,“沙壹”变成“沙壶”,“九隆”变成“元隆”,也许是传写的错误。到了元张道宗《记古滇说》、明杨慎的《滇载记》和阮元声的《南诏野史》里,故事的内容就变相多了。《记古滇说》云:

哀牢国永昌郡人蒙迦独娶摩梨羌,名沙壹,居哀牢山。蒙迦独捕鱼,死哀牢山下水中,沙壹往哭,忽见一木浮来,坐其上,平稳不动,遂常浣絮其上,若有感,因生九子,是为九隆。后又产一子,即习农乐。

《滇载记》云:

滇域未通中国之先有低牟苴者,居永昌哀牢之山麓,有妇曰沙壹,浣絮水中,触沉木,若有感,是生九男,曰九隆族。种类滋长,支裔蔓衍,窃据土地,散居溪谷,分为九十九部。……蒙氏始兴,曰细奴罗,九隆五族牟苴笃之三十六世孙也。代张氏立国,号曰封民。蒙氏伪称南诏,实唐贞观三年也。

《南诏野史》云:

按哀牢夷传古传有妇名沙壶因捕鱼触一沉木,感而生十子。后木化为龙,九子惊走,一子背坐,名曰九隆。又云:哀牢有一妇名奴波息,生十女,九隆兄弟各娶之,立为十姓,曰董、洪、段、施、何、王、张、杨、李、赵。九隆死,子孙繁衍,各居一方,而南诏出焉,故诸葛为其国谱也。(王崧本“南诏历代源流”条)

归纳这几条记载来看,咱们可以指出这个故事的几种演变:(一)在《后汉书》和《华阳国志》里沙壹本来是没有丈夫的,到《记古滇说》里便有蒙迦独做她的丈夫,到《滇载记》里便有个低牟苴做她的丈夫,而且和《白古记》“阿育王第三子骠苴低娶大蒙亏为妻;生低蒙苴,苴生九子,名九龙氏”的传说发生关系。加上蒙迦独就可牵扯到南诏,加上低牟苴就连白国的血缘也找到了。(二)照《后汉书》和《华阳国志》“九隆”原为“背坐”或“陪坐”的意义,《记古滇说》和《滇载记》都以九为数字，所以改“十子”为“九子”以迁就九龙氏之说。但《记古滇说》要和南诏拉上关系，所以在九子之外又添上一个习农乐。（三）《记古滇说》以习农乐为蒙迦独和沙壹直接所生，《滇载记》以细奴罗为低牟苴和沙壹的三十七世孙。两者的世次相差很远。（四）《记古滇说》所谓“蒙迦独娶摩梨羌，名沙壹”，似乎拿摩梨羌当做沙壹的族名。（五）《南诏野史》的记载大致和《后汉书》、《华阳国志》相同，只有奴波息的名字和董、洪、段、施、何、王、张、杨、李、赵十姓是从前各书里所没有的。

照这样推寻下来，可以看出这个故事越演变越和《白国因由》接近了，只有“天命细奴罗”的祥异还没加上去。黄元治《大理府志·杂异志》恰好填补了这个空当儿：

> 哀牢蛮蒙迦独捕鱼溺死，妻沙壹往江上哭之。触沉木，若有感而娠，生十子。后沙壹至水涯，沉木化为龙，作人语曰：尔为我生子安在？九子见龙惊走，独少子背龙而坐，龙舐其背。蛮语谓背为“九”，谓坐为“隆”，遂名曰九隆。哀牢山有夫妇，生十女，九隆兄弟皆娶之。自是种人滋长，散居溪谷，分为九十九部。后有细农罗者，九隆裔也。当唐贞观年耕于巍山，数有祥异。会白国主张乐进求以诸葛亮所立铁柱岁久剥落，重铸之，因社会祭柱。有大鸟飞细农罗肩上，久之不去。众骇异，谓天意有属。张乐进求因以国让之，遂立为奇王，是为南诏。

到了这里，《白国因由》所记的故事几乎完成了，不过其中还有一个很大的漏洞。细奴罗的建国受封，《记古滇说》和王崧本《南诏野史》都说是唐高宗永徽四年，但张道宗自己却把后汉时代的沙壹当做他的母亲，时代悬隔，岂不自相矛盾？关于这一点杨慎和黄元治把细奴罗的世次推后，总算可以弥缝了，可是还不如《白国因由》索性根据同一“母题”(motif)另造故事，更较妥当。在本节开始所引的故事里，哀牢山变成“金齿龙泉寺下的易罗丛村”，沙壹变成“茉莉姣”，九隆变成九条龙，既然没有时代的限制，那么，就把幼子当做细奴罗也就不至于发生问题了。全篇故事里除去开首的“金齿”两个字和第七章末尾所说的“移居哀牢山下”及“永昌城西有九龙冈”以外，丝毫没有牵涉到哀牢的话。

咱们由这里可以悟出传说的流变性，可以了然传说和历史不同。反过来说，历史上许多冲突矛盾的记载也未尝不可以用传说或神话的观点去解释它。明白这一点，那么，张道宗、杨慎、黄元治把南诏的感龙诞生说附会到哀牢的沙壹身上去，已经多事，若再因为这个附会硬把南诏和哀牢拉上血统，那就更辗转曲解了。关于这一层，凌纯声先生在《唐代云南的白蛮与乌蛮考》、包鹭宾先生在《民家非白国后裔考》里已经有详细的辨正，这里恕不多谈。

感龙诞生的传说并不限于哀牢有，也不限于南诏有，就近取譬来说，像前文所举的汉高祖，后文所述的段思平，岂不都是从一个“母题”孳衍出来的？况且专就南诏而论，感龙诞生的传说也不限于细奴罗一人。《旧唐书·南诏传》谓细奴罗之父名蒙舍龙，“蒙舍龙者，盖谓蒙舍之龙耳”(用包鹭宾语)。胡蔚本《南诏野史》把蒙迦独改作龙迦独也就是这个意思。又《南诏野史》“景庄皇帝世隆”条云：

> 按成王(昭成王晟丰祐)妃乃渔家女，浴于江，金龙与交，生世隆。七岁开掌，中有“通番打汉”四字。唐武宗发兵四十万取西南，自建昌入。世隆迎于古宗，杀唐兵二十万，于交界处立铜柱。先是唐惧世隆(按，原作“隆舜”，据下文隆舜条“父为唐患”句校改)为患，妻以公主，察其所为。公主以年庚送唐，武宗命太史推之，知其为龙也。(据王崧本)

由此看来，世隆也可以和他的建国始祖细奴罗先后媲美了。

三　大理始祖的感生说

感龙诞生的传说既然从哀牢流转到南诏，那么，大理国的段氏要想把他的建国始祖造成一个奉天承运的真龙天子，也非得依样画葫芦地抄袭这一套把戏不可。《南诏野史》“大理国”条记段思平之生云：

其母因过江水汛，触浮木，若有感，而娠，生思平，并其弟思良。（据胡蔚本）

大理喜洲镇凤阳村（土名晨登村）三圣灵宫内有明景泰元年庚午（1450）的《三灵庙记》碑，记载这个传说尤其详细，那上面说：

院塝有一长者，乏嗣，默祷。其囿种一李树，结一大颗，坠地现一女子，姿禀非凡。长者爱育，号曰白姐阿妹。蒙清平官段宝璁（包鹭宾疑即《新唐书·南蛮传》之段娩宝，见《民家非白国后裔考》14、15两页）聘为夫人，浴濯霞移江，见木一段逆流，触阿妹足，知元祖重光（按，碑文上半蒙诏阁罗凤之子死后显灵，追封元祖重光鼎祚皇帝）化为龙，感而有孕。将段木培于庙庭之右，吐木莲二枝。生思平、思胄（按，原碑如此，不知何字。诸书皆作思良），号先帝、先王。思平丁酉立位，国号大理。建灵会寺。追封母曰天应景星懿慈圣母。重创三灵庙。世传三十五代，凡三百九十一载。[按，《南诏野史》“晋天福二年（937）段思平开国至宋理宗宝祐，元年（1253）元世祖灭段氏，段氏据云南共二十二主三百十六年”。王崧注“按，自后晋高祖天福二年丁酉至宋理宗淳祐十三年癸丑改元宝祐，共三百十六年。《滇载记》作三百五十年误。大理作三百十五年，盖除见灭之年不计耳”。计自思平至兴智凡二十四传，自段实至段明又十一传，则碑文所谓三十五代不误，惟自宝祐元年至明洪武十五年壬戌(1382)段氏亡，应为一百二十九年，并前三百十六年计之共为四百四十五年，碑文所谓三百九十一载，不知何据。]

照这段记载来看，不单整个的传说和细奴罗的诞生出于同"母题"，甚至把段氏的血统也和蒙氏拉上关系了。

四　猴儿换太子

在《三灵庙记》上面另外还载着一个有趣的故事说：

按白史自唐天宝壬辰(752)蒙诏阁罗凤神武王时肇兴神迹，至灵至圣。其一灵乃吐蕃之酋长，二灵乃唐之大将，三灵乃蒙诏神武王偏妃之子也。厥诞生时，中宫无出，阴谋以猴儿易而废弃，埋于太和城之道旁。密遣侍女夙夜视之。冢生一苇而畅茂。群毕往复，有一犌牯先来爱护。一旦斑牸忽食之。女遂报于中宫。宰牸剖腹，出一男子，被戴金盔甲，执剑恨指，腾空而北往吐蕃。后率兵伐太和，至德源城，蒙诏乞和而归。后同二将复举兵至摩用，大战弗克，回至喜洲，赤佛堂前三将殒命。乃托梦院塝耆老曰：若立庙祀享，能通水利，除灾害。遂定星揆日，不月而庙宇成焉。由是雨旸时若，五谷丰稔。每于四月十九日阖郡祈告。迄异牟寻孝桓王追封，号曰元祖重光鼎祚皇帝、圣德兴邦皇帝、镇子福景灵帝。

这件事《记古滇说》、《滇载记》、《南诏野史》、《白国因由》等书都没有记载，所谓《白史》大概也就是《白古通》。按，《南诏野史》阁罗凤的儿子叫做凤伽异，曾与段俭魏败唐将鲜于仲通兵于洱河，又筑省城，破曲靖，未立而死，另外就没有什么事迹了。这个传说和狸猫换太子的故事出于同一"母题"。狸猫换太子的故事，在元人所作《金水桥陈琳抱妆盒》杂剧里只说：宋真宗的李美人生了太子后，刘皇后怕夺了她的宠，秘遣宫女寇承御将太子诓出西宫，害死后丢在金水桥下。承御抱太子至金水桥侧，不忍下此毒手，正踌躇间，恰好穿宫内使陈琳奉敕抱黄封妆盒过此，欲到后花园采取时新果品，给楚王赵德芳上寿。二人遂设计藏太子在妆盒里，救之出宫，隐藏于楚王府。十年后，太子继真宗登极，是即宋仁宗，这时寇承御已被刘皇后拷毙了，仁宗询陈琳，备得其情，乃奉李美人为纯圣皇太后，封陈琳为保定公，追封寇承御为忠烈夫人。这个故事演变到《龙图公案》和石玉昆原本《三侠五义》里，便加入拿狸猫剥皮掉换太子，诬李妃产生妖怪一段，再变到海派的胡闹戏，越发乱七八糟不知所云了。论故事的时代是猴儿换太子在前，可是，论它们发生的先后，也许狸猫换太子的传说已经深入民间，这段故事才模仿着孳衍出来的。这一点还得靠继续获得新材料来证实。

五 望夫云

这是一段很香艳的传说。据黄元治《大理府志》卷三十《杂异志》云：

> 俗传昔有人贫困，遇苍山神授以异术，忽生肉翅，能飞。一日至南诏宫，摄其女入玉局峰为夫妇，凡饮食器用皆能致之。后问女，安否？女曰：太寒耳。其人闻河东高僧有七宝袈裟，飞取之。及还，僧觉，以法力制之，遂溺死水中。女望夫不至，忧郁死，精气化为云，倏起倏落，若探望之状。此云起，洱河即有云应之，飓风大作，舟不敢行，人皆呼为望夫云，又呼为无渡云。

又周宗麟《大理县志稿》卷三十二杂志部古迹类，也记载这个故事说：

俗传蒙氏时有怪，摄宫中女，居于玉局峰巅。女所欲饮食，怪给之不绝。因山高候冷，女苦之，与索衣。怪慰之曰：河东高僧有一袈裟，夏凉冬暖，可立致。遂夜至洱河之东罗筌寺，将袈裟盗出，僧觉之，以咒压怪，溺死寺西水中，化一大石坪，俗称石骡子。女望之不归，遂郁死，精气化为云，名望夫云。每每岁冬云现，即大风狂荡，有不将海中之石吹出不止之势。航渡者皆苦之。非情非理不经之谈也。

这段传说姑且不管它有没有情理，单就故事的本身说却颇有文学的韵味，所以文人墨客往往喜欢形诸吟咏。例如邑人沙琛《颠风频日望夫云起七古》云：

缫车圜转丝抽水，雌龙梦断云窝靡。俯身东望喔天鸡，曈曈日射贝宫紫。呲蓝噫气云乱呼，直撇涛山见海底。黄姑织女河东西，盈盈咫尺甘分携。嗔痴小婢情凄迷，望夫云起青天低。一声响应石龙子，扬沙走砾无端倪。点苍濛濛青弄色，冰封雪沍藏花密。园林桃李满空飞，星斗朱幡遮不得。喈喈危巢望岁氛，知风知雨不知云。吹花擘桃曾何惜，懊恼停舟欲济人。（《大理县志》稿卷三十艺文部）

又赵廷玉《咏望夫云七律》云：

一缕浮云几度秋，坚心常注海中沤。浪沧涛打蛟龙窟，绰约神明水月楼。卷地难平千古恨，回峰又锁百重忧。可怜夫婿无消息，空抱情根护石头。（同上）

最近腾越赵诚伯欲谱此事为望夫云传奇，儒将风流，颇有骚人的情致。

如果分析故事的来源，咱们可以说："河东高僧有七宝袈裟"和"河东高僧有一袈裟，夏凉冬暖"云云，是从"饮光迦叶守佛衣以俟弥勒"的佛教故事演变来的（事见《白国因由》卷首和李元阳《鸡足山记》）。现在鸡足山上的传衣寺和袈裟殿,都和迦叶传衣的掌故有关。至于望夫云起何以紧跟着就飓风大作呢?这从气象上也可以得到解释,因为在苍山顶上如果有云作探望之状,那就可以表现隔山的冷空气渐渐侵过来了,两方面空气的冷热既然不平衡,当然会因交流而起大风。这种现象,常在洱海弄舟的渔夫或梢公都可以凭经验知道它的因果关系,正如常人知道"月晕而风,础润而雨"一样。不过他们只能知道当然而不能知道所以然,勉强要找到一种解释,在初民社会里充斥着泛灵的(Animistic)思想,自然而然地就构成这个怪异的传说了。

六 余论

除去这几桩故事以外,像火把节传说里关于曼阿娜妻阿南和宁北妃慈善的故事,都是很有趣的,因为游国恩先生已经有一篇详细考证,这里就不再赘叙了。总之,我们研究民间故事和传说,应该注意它发生的背景、反映的事实和孳衍的转变,然后才不至于沾滞拘泥被故事给束缚住。像上文所引黄元治争论观音现身大理的年月先后那一段话,就是不能了解传说性质的一个例。至于他对于"龙子九隆"所提出的疑问,那就更可笑了。他说:

> 感龙生子,古今有之。然岂能一乳生十子乎?或是沙壹先后生十子,独九隆一人是龙种耳,故曰少子也。否则哀牢十女,亦岂触龙而产于一乳,遂年纪之相匹乎?(《大理府志》卷三十《杂异志》"龙子九隆"条自注)

像这样的怀疑,我觉得还不如老老实实地保持"知之为知之,不知为不知"的态度比较好得多!

1942年12月6日写于昆明青园

五 华 楼

C.P.Fitzgerald *The Tower of Five Glories*:

A Study of the Min-Chia of Tali, *Yunnan*

London, the Cresset Press, 1941.

这是一部最新出版的研究云南大理的民家的著作。全书共280页,另加序目12页,还有31幅插图、3张地图。

五华楼在大理南门里的五华街(旧名鼓楼街)。据康熙时范承勋所修《大理府志》说:"五华楼废址在今郡城中央,世传南诏丰祐建,方广五里,高百尺,上可容万人,下可建五丈旗。元世祖征大理,驻兵楼前,重修。明兵燹始废。今城中谯楼曰五华。姑存其名云。"著者拿它当做书名,大概是象征着大理城和它的附近的意思。

全书分11章,另外有两个附录:

第一章　苍山和洱海

第二章　米是主要的食粮

第三章　大理城

第四章　白国的人民

第五章　三种宗教(一)祖先崇拜

第六章　三种宗教(二)神

第七章　三种宗教(三)迷忌和神话

第八章　家族和家庭

第九章　宴会

第十章　在途中

第十一章　和外国人的接触与变迁

附录一　民家语法

附录二　民家词汇

民家的现代分布区域是在滇西环洱海各地方，就是东经99度50分到100度30分，北纬25度30分到26度48分之间，可是西边远到东经99度30分云龙县境的澜沧江沿岸各地，西北远到北纬27度维西县境。东边从凤仪县起沿大理到昆明的交通大道上祥云、弥渡、镇南、姚安、楚雄、广通、禄丰、安宁各县，以达于东经102度35分昆明县境，每县都有民家的村落，不过数量不很多。在北纬25度以南只在红河流域元江县境的远坝有民家，他们分布的北界也没有超越昆明大理路线的。他们分布之广几乎和云南迤东的罗罗，西南边缘的摆夷，有鼎足而三之势，可以算是云南省内一个很大的部族。关于他们的系属问题，英人戴维斯(H.R.Davies)认为是属于孟吉蔑系(Mon-Khmer Family)，丁文江认为属于摆夷，李方桂认为属于罗罗，凌纯声起初赞成丁文江的说法，最近在《唐代云南的白蛮与乌蛮考》那篇文章里又认为和藏缅的卡伦(Karen)接近。因为中外学人对这个部族始终还没系统的研究，所以有许多问题都还悬而未决。这部书既然是专门研究民家的著作，纵然它的范围只以大理一地方为限，我也不禁不由得很渴望地把它一气读完。

据著者的自序说，这部书是1937和1938两年他受Leverhulme奖学金补助时所作的调查报告。因为这个工作是他独做的，而且这块田野向来为民族学家所漠视，他自己觉得对于现代民家文化的调查难免有许多省略和疏漏的地方。关于语言的障碍他自认实在没有完全克服，因为在那时候他还不能说很流利的民家话，同时那些没受过多少教育的民家人也不能毫无困难地把他们所有的思想都用汉话表达出来。附录的词汇无疑地显示着这些困难的结果。至于他为记录民家话所采用的罗马字拼音,是根据英文的而不是根据中国人习用的威妥玛式(T.F.Wade's System)。他恐怕这一点不能得到所有读者们的赞许,于是辩解说,他只打算把民家的读音像他们所念的那样转写过来,那一些词汇也是为他自己学语言时应用的初稿。他只能希望这初次记录民家词汇和语法的尝试,可以引起专家的一点儿兴趣。像这样的措词总算是够谦虚的了。

这部书里的人类学部分,我自己承认是个门外汉不愿意多说什么话。不过,就我粗浅的观察,我觉得这只是一个普通的旅行记录,算不得精密的科学研究。因为无论从体质人类学和文化人类学的观点来讲,他所搜集的材料都嫌不够味儿!关于文献上的材料像《记古滇说》、《南诏野史》、《滇载记》,乃至于专讲民家来源的《白国因由》,他简直的没引用过。这还可以说,他的立场专在研究现代文化,无妨忽略历史的考证,可是有些眼前的事实,他也没能考察得精密。例如6月24日的火把节,在大理乃至于云南别的地方几乎是家喻户晓的,却没能说清楚是怎么一回事;又如4月间的"绕山林",在大理也算是一个很热闹的节令,他虽然费了许多篇幅和好几片照相去记载它,却不能了解民家话"Kwer sa la"的真正意思。此外的几章,他自然也费了不少的心思,搜集了相当的材料,然而一个自认是马利诺斯基(B. Malinowski)和西里格曼(C.G.Seligman)两位名教授的学生,费了两年的功夫,所得的只是些泛常的印象,片段的记载,从责备贤者的观点讲,我总不免有点儿失望。至于他把屈原误作Chu-Yuan-Ming(117页)那是一般外国人常犯的毛病,倒无须对他单独地苛责。

语言一部分的不够好,著者已然很客气地交代过了,在我看还有几点得要声明一下。词汇一部分(241~276页)一共收了1440个词,数量并不算少。他虽然说这只是为自己学话用的初稿，可是既然印出来公诸当世，如果记录得不够精确，就难免有人以讹传讹辗转误会。他所用的罗马字，我先不管它是英文式还是威妥玛式，我只问他是否能够如他所说的"I have endeavoured to render Min Chia pronunciation as it is sounded"？咱们现在自然还不便谈到民家音系的细微地方，单就他所记的音来讲，他似乎连清浊音和送气不送气都分不清楚。所以他拿 g、d、b 来代表(k)、(t)、(p)，拿 k、t、p 来代表(k')、(t')、(p')。照我亲自听到的大理民家话并没有浊塞音，从这一点正可以推断它比邓川、洱源、剑川、泸水、云龙等处的民家话较晚，汉化的程度较深，还可以推测出民家迁徙的路线和方向。若像费氏这样以浊代清，岂不把这一点儿启示给淹没了吗？再说：大理民家话一共有 8 个声调，听起来相当复杂，有许多声韵相同的字专靠调类的不同来区别意义。现在著者根本不标调号，不分调类，试问他怎样处理那一大些同声韵不同意义的字呢？此外还有些不是罗马字所能转写下来的特别音，他也感到相当的麻烦。例如：大理民家话有一个和 u 同部位的不圆唇的舌后元音，国际音标用倒 m(ɯ)来代表它，在中国汕头、泉州和河南西部也有这个类似的音。著者既然捉摸不住它的音值，又没有适当的符号来记它，于是有时候写作(er)，有时候写作(ur)。又如大理民家话的 e 音应该分作侈弇两个音位，他没有法子分别，就只好一律写作(ai)。因此我说他所记的民家词汇，不会说民家话的固然看不懂，会说民家话的尤是看不懂！

语法一部分(229～237 页)只是一些零碎的札记，还没能构成系统。关于词性的区分仍然沿袭印欧语的形式，分作名词、量词、动词、状词、代词、介词、数词几类。语词的顺序普通是"主词——动词——宾词"。可是像"刮风"、"下雨"一类的句子，"刮"和"下"也可以放在"风"、"雨"的后头。关于这一点，著者把它当做例外，我却觉得这也许是原始民家语序的遗迹。至于状词放在所状者的前边或后边,在民家话里并没有一定的规律。量词(Classifier)是藏缅系语言的一个特点。在罗罗、傈僳、栗子、怒子等语言里,这一类词都很发达。据著者说,民家话在所有名词的后边都随着量词,他所发现的一共有50多个,可是只有12个按照普通的规律。其实他所提出的几条规律并不能赅括,他认为不照规律的也不见得全是随便乱用,只要看到的例子多了,自然可以找出它们的条理来。数词混合汉话和民家话而成,颇多讹误。宜从1到30用民家语词;从31到39,从50到100用辗转传讹的汉话;可是其中的40到49,还有50、60、70、80、90几个数目,又是例外。100以上的数目除去一千和一万以外,也用辗转传讹的汉语。像这样糅杂的情形就无从拿数词的比较,断定它的系属了。

关于民家的研究,从前有 Francis Garnier, P. Desyodins, Lefèvre-Pontalis, G. W. Clark, Henri d'Orléans, C. Madrolle, H. R. Davies, D'Ollone, P.A. Liétard 几个人虽曾零星涉及,却都不是专门的著作。P.A. Liétard 固然指出了民家和那马人的关系,但是他所记录的语言部分也是错误百出的。现在居然得到一部专门研究民家的著作,在书籍邮递困难的时候真算是空谷足音了。1942年3月23日我住在大理的时候,承鲍克兰夫人(J. de Beauclaire)从 E. D. Holmes 牧师那里,替我借到这本书,但借期只限一天。那天白日里我忙着记音,没得空儿看,晚上在荧荧如豆的菜油灯底下,一直到夜里1点多钟才把它看完,并且摘记下些要点来。不过因为我希望太切,结果却不免失望!因为它无论在体质、文化、语言三方面都没有彻底的研究,我渴望着要解决的民家系属问题,它简直的没有提到!所得的效果和读一本旅行记差不多!

1942年5月16日即壬午四月十二日写于昆明宝台山

鸡足巡礼

一　不肯低头便挂冠

壬午的元旦，一个人在点苍山麓的凄风苦雨里度过了，谁料到癸未的元旦我又睡在洱海边上才村的渔船里？然而，鸡足巡礼的愿却终于达到了。

一觉醒来，已经是第二天早晨，人还没起身，船已启碇好久，顺风扬帆，不到两个钟头就拢了挖色镇。从挖色朝鸡足，有两条路可达：前山路远而好走，百多里地须走两天；后山路近而荒僻，约七十余里，午前动身，当晚就可赶到金顶。我们仗着人多势众，决定取道后山。

上午11点钟离挖色，经过官邑村、小长曲、大长曲，再翻过玉亮山，便到了一片积雪的鸡足后山。昨晚在船上刚同小弟弟学会了执缰控送的姿势，今天居然也骑在一匹高大的古宗马上，随众跑了三四十里，并且翻了一道高岭，虽然戒慎恐惧地正襟危坐，透着有点儿紧张，毕竟很侥幸地还没翻鞍落马。

可是，一到后山，那种正襟危坐的姿势就不适用了。一片洁白耀眼的琼崖玉谷，晃得人闪烁迷离；冰雪铺成的石径，滑得马蹄三步一蹶；遍山丛生着蔷薇、杜鹃，青枫的枯枝，杈桠窝刺，也并不因为这批游客而自甘躲避。这在常骑马的人们只要抱住马头，信马由缰地往前走，什么问题都不会发生的。我呢？因为不懂这个诀窍，顾到下头就顾不了上头，权衡轻重，只要不掉下马，滚到山涧里去，纵然上面挂得头破血出，帽飞衣烂，也没功夫管那么许多了。就这样不肯低头地昂踞马上，果然那些交互纷歧的乱枝不容我强项不屈，竟自毫不容情地把我那顶旧帽子挂掉了三次，并且额角手背也都蹭有微伤。最后，左眼突然像被云雾蒙蔽起来一般，感觉一阵模糊，急忙用手一摸，原来一片眼镜不知被树枝弹到哪里去了！可怜它伴着我二十多年，不料在万里以外葬送在冰天雪地里，那样薄脆的东西岂能像迦叶所守的那件金缕衣一般的点缀名山呢？

峰回路转，居然看见金顶上的华严塔了。催马赶到桃花箐，先到的同伴们已经在茶棚里煮好咸菜饵饫汤在等着。大家看见我那半副丧偶的眼镜都笑不可仰。可是眼镜虽然丢了，“不肯低头便挂冠”的滋味也尝着了，总算比教我骑术的小弟弟还强，的确连一次马都没落过。谓余不信，山灵其共鉴之！

夜幕渐渐笼罩下来，夔公[潘光旦]还杳无消息，再等下去大家都要摸不着路了，于是偏劳一位更年轻的小弟弟在茶棚里同两个弟兄守候着，我们便打马上山。一颗晶莹的亮星斜挂在眉月上向我们眨眼欢送，落日的余晖烘托得晚霞泛出几种调谐的色彩来，也似乎献给游子流连，但刚刚转过两个山头，前途已经黯沉沉的，除去白雪的反照，全山几乎一片昏黑。马行生路，趑趄不前，这时我也不敢骑在马上逞英雄了。起初还牵着马走，偏偏那刚刚丧偶的独光眼镜不肯帮忙，在雪埋冰封的山上懵懵懂懂的，深一脚浅一脚的，简直辨不出哪里是悬崖，哪里是深壑，哪里是平路，哪里是山坡，稍一失足，就会抱恨千古！幸亏小弟弟连搀带拉地扶着我，才不至于舍身崖际，伴佛长眠！这时的两手除去帮助支持自己，哪里还有牵马的空儿？因为这么一蹭蹬，便和前面的同伴失掉联系，暗中摸索，越发迷失了登山的正途。陈完后人走过夷方，曾经有过迷路的经验，一路上“哈……呜……哈……呜……”地喊着，虽然博得前进者的应声，依然辨不清登山的方向。好容易转了几个弯，蓦地看见石壁上像有字迹。小弟弟划根火柴一照，原来已到“曹溪一滴”。这时上面的接应也到了，几个人鼓勇续登，没多久，隐隐约约地已然望见华严塔。在桃花箐时，本来想在迦叶殿过夜的，谁想误投误撞地会爬到金顶呢？可是，假使有人问我：“从桃花箐到金顶的风景怎样？”我的感觉是昏暗、紧张、恐怖、险阻，除此以外，一概茫然！

山顶风大得很，熊熊炭火，不解严寒，盼夔公不至，盼行李不来，虽然个个困眼蒙眬，却有谁酣然熟睡？这一宵便在焦急、盼望、寒冷、疲倦、寂寞里度过了。

1942年2月6日，癸未正月初二日

二　走马下山兴未阑

鸡足山的得名，由于全山形势好像一个前纾三距后申一趾的鸡脚。昨晚在昏冥中爬上金顶，连方向还辨不清，哪里顾得到全山形胜？清晨绝早起来，披上查阜西[查夷平]兄惠借的皮外氅，冒着刺面的寒风，爬上了华严塔的第三级。凭高俯瞰，所谓“趾”“距”所在，也仿佛得之。然而，我最注意的还是“峰顶四观”。

所谓四观是日观、云观、海观、雪观。日观是东望日出，和泰山日观峰的意思相同；云观是南望祥云县的彩云；海观是西望苍山洱海；雪观是北望丽江县的玉龙雪山。为争取时间，第一当然先看日出，可惜雾气太重，朝霞黯然，不免失望，比起在崂山、黄山、南岳、峨眉所经历来的殊为减色！再转到北边看雪山，远远地倒似乎有两个白堆，恐怕新丧偶的眼镜欺哄我，赶紧再用望远镜看，仿佛稍微清楚一点儿，但也不觉得怎样奇丽。明人王士性的《游鸡足山记》说:“入庙西北指则云间见丽江雪山。余从峨眉望大雪山,在印度万余里,然旭日刺雪,光犹仿佛上余衣袂。此去丽水不千里,乃黯然无色。或云此白石堆成,意近之。”可惜我在峨眉绝顶望贡嘎雪山时,恰好赶上日光不足,和此无从比较。至于士性所说“在印度万余里”和“或云此白石堆成”云云固然荒唐,可是“此去丽水不千里,乃黯然无色”的印象,却和我当时的感觉相同。至于西望洱海远不及在苍山中和峰上所见的清晰,南望彩云尤其是可遇而不可求的机会,若云奇观,则愧无眼福!

除去峰顶四观,我还想会会大错和尚所称赏的“鸡足四友”。四友者华首门为奇友,玉龙瀑为清友,传衣寺古松为老友,华藏洞为奥友。耗到10点左右,夔公欢欢喜喜地步行到顶,大家不禁欢呼起来。他眉飞色舞地谈露宿“打火”的奇遇,餐风吞雪的清福,滑竿伕积瘾过深的老态,清晨独赏我们在昏冥中茫无所见的后山奥景,一宿所得竟自兼备奇、清、老、奥四绝,那么,偕此友而同访四友,岂不更增游兴?可惜老友、奥友非我们游踪所及,清友被导者所误,当面错过,幸而和奇友有缘,还算勉强瞻仰到它的丰采。

华首门在铜佛殿西太子阁后,悬崖飞矗二十余丈,上如穷阙环覆,中如双扉紧掩,下则户阈宛然。相传这里就是迦叶守衣入定的地方。它的上面是绝顶观海门下的危崖,崇崇隆隆莫见其巅;下面是舍身岩侧的百仞深壑,窅窅冥冥莫究其底。站在这里俯仰瞻眺,雄奇渊奥的感觉同时并起。凝神默化,又好像置身在一幅万仞苍崖图中,恍恍惚惚地连自己究竟在哪里都似乎辨别不出来!钱邦芑拿它当做奇友,可谓善于品题了。举一反三,那么,老、清、奥三友一定也该名副其实,虽然没缘面晤,想来大错和尚还不至于欺哄咱们。

在鸡足山的鼎盛时代,据说全山共有三百六十几座庙宇,现在所剩的大小不过24座,其中要算石钟、大觉、祝圣、寂光、悉檀、传衣、华严七个寺比较大。我们从金顶下来，沿途看见观音阁、大悲阁、铜佛殿、太子阁、迦叶殿几座，都没什么可称述的。从慧灯庵以下走马看山，越发没有从容礼佛的机会了。就我们所看到的说，大觉、石钟、祝圣、悉檀四个庙的模范毕竟宏大。

大觉寺，明万历间无心禅师奉密旨把华严寺的藏经搬到这个庙里来，但现在的庙宇却是新翻修的。门前有桫椤两株，左边的六丈多高，右边一株稍小。中间还有一棵很大的黄桷树。附近有万寿寺、兴元寺、大智庵三个小庙。玉龙瀑便在大觉寺后面一里多地的寂光寺，听怀空说，那里还有元朝的公主坟，可惜导游者地理不熟，竟自让我们把这个清友交臂失之！

石钟寺，相传因为从楼下掘出一块钟形的石头得名；也有人说，当初建寺的时候，侧崖有石，风吹如钟声：这都是姑妄言之的传说，找不到什么凭据。庙宇也是最近翻修的，现在还没竣工。山门后有小西天，塑工尚不恶。韦陀殿上有1913年中山先生所书“坛云性海”的匾，这在佛寺中颇少见。山门前也有桫椤三株，比大觉寺的还要大些。住持亚琋，云南盐兴人，据云治法相宗，但谈话未涉教理。庙里藏有担当、大错、许鸿和临济宗第七十一代中峰和尚的墨迹。许鸿的名字有三分之二和徐宏祖的声音近似，难怪口耳相传，竟会被人误认做徐霞客了。

祝圣寺在钵盂峰下，众峰环拱，形势极佳。从前本来是钵盂庵的遗址，民国初年，当代禅宗大师虚云和尚才创建了这个庙。住持怀空字满照，虚云弟子，盐城人，俗姓李。他的伯父李鹤宁，字湘谷，是咸丰时候的进士。庙里的龙藏阁有龙藏一部，频伽精舍藏一部。阁下悬有李霞所绘罗汉数幅，神采奕奕，颇为生动，但怀空不肯轻易示人的“镇山之宝”却是清乾隆间屈尔泰所画的墨龙。全幅宽约八尺，长亦如之，头部昂举，右爪前攫，姿态极为雄健，其余半匿云中，若隐若现，惟其见首不见尾，才格外蕴蓄着神奇莫测的韵味。据画上赵藩的题跋，尔泰是提督董芳的幕府，死后葬在丽江。从龙藏阁东边的静室遥望对面的塔盘院，林木深秀中，白塔巍然高峙。彼此映照起来，越发显得祝圣寺占取了很好的形势。

在祝圣寺住了一宿，第二天早晨步行到观瀑亭去看响鼓坡下的瀑布。可惜天干水少，瀑布很微，涓涓细流，无可欣赏。对面的牟尼庵里有三会柏一株，系由刺柏、扁柏、圆柏三种合成，这倒可以供给研究植物合种的人们采做标本。由牟尼庵曲折东行约二里许，就到了悉檀寺。

悉檀寺是鸡足山最东的丛林，后倚九重崖，前临黑龙潭，是明朝万历间古德本无创建的。丽江木土司世为护法檀越，现在寺里的和尚大部分还是丽江人，所以在客堂待茶的时候，我们能够尝到富有丽江土风的油炸糯米粑粑和胡麻酥油茶。寺内有大佛一尊，是从西藏运来的，弥勒殿前的横匾也是藏文，古宗的气味虽重，但门前又有万历己未年“悉檀禅寺”的匾，因为没有跟和尚详谈，还不敢断定现在的宗派是显是密。最早的碑文有万历四十八年谢肇淛所撰和天启间蔡毅中所撰。几个庙比较起来，悉檀寺的世家气派比较重一点儿，连和尚都不大有暴发的味道。庙里藏有木氏宦谱和图像，谱前有嘉靖二十四年杨升庵所作序文，我另外有一篇文章专论它，这里不再多赘。

从悉檀寺东南行约三里许，登一小坡就到了尊胜塔院。尊胜塔院俗称塔盘寺，寺后有一个印度式的白塔，跟北平白塔寺和北海里的样式完全相似。黄克强夫人拟在这里办一个保育院，现在虽然添盖了许多平房，但还没有开始收容儿童。

站在塔盘寺前面，隔着一道深谷向北远眺，可以综览金顶天柱峰以下的全景，恰好像峨眉慧灯庵的地势一样。我们这次随着一大帮游侣匆匆地走马下山，既没经历猢狲梯的险仄，也没流连罗汉壁的奇峻,至于袈裟石、虎跳涧、八功德水等等古迹,更是白白放过,丝毫没能徘徊凭吊!在快要离开这座名山以前,幸亏能在塔盘寺前有这一会儿流连,我才领会到崖壁插天盘云、松杉森蔚郁翳的鸡足山何以在四周许多童冈荒阜中秀出众表!可惜夔公不良于行,小弟弟懒病复发,他们都在悉檀寺里休息,竟自牺牲了这一幕胜景。夔公动不动就夸耀他喝过曹溪一滴水,在光天化日之下看见过后山,得此抵制,我也有反攻的武器了。至于小弟弟那篇笔姿生动、想像丰富的《朝山记》,只欠在塔盘寺前多挹取一些灵感,也未尝不是遗憾!

1943 年 2 月 7 日至 8 日

三 人莫踬于山而踬于垤

离开石钟寺差不多将近 3 点钟,骑马下山,时常戒慎恐惧地顾到前踹后仰的姿势,并没有多少优游的余裕来欣赏山水。有时走在平坦的路上,偶一回顾,那巍峨的苍崖翠嶂上,一塔危耸,越往下走越显出它的雄秀来,这时对于鸡足不禁有点儿恋恋不舍的情绪。前年游峨眉,我深悔没有取道后山,先欣赏它的清幽,再由前山下来领略它的雄秀。可是,这次游鸡足,却恰好有相反的感觉,因为鸡足的好处只有从前山进来才可以领略到的。假使把我的归程改作进路的话,那么,一过"灵山一会"牌坊便时时有高山仰止的向往心,对于这当前的胜景,迎头瞻仰总比回首顾盼好得多。至于后山呢?那 70 里路只碰见三个人的冷僻,姑且不必管它;单就地形而论,快到桃花箐才峰回路转地望见金顶,一看它的高度并不比自己所在地崇巍许多,那景仰心不由得就减低了大半。再说,遍山积雪,举目都是肃杀衰飒的气象,哪里有前山那一片苍翠的秀色可以涤荡人的胸襟?假如我再度登临，我一定由前山上去，然后找一条不重复的路仍旧由前山下来。这完全从欣赏自然的方便着想，后山的路纵然当年徐霞客两次都没走着，我也不能因为好奇而称赞它比前山好。

这一天我骑的还是那匹古宗马，下山时特别小心，一路上倒还平稳。到了沙子街，赶上香市旺盛，人很拥挤，我渐渐就有点儿控制不住了。过“灵山一会”牌坊时，本应该绕亭子下边走，但是，这匹马既然总想尾随着那匹领队的英国白马走，我又不能得心应手地把皮缰拉转到该走的方向，只好听天由命地任它性儿往前闯。同伙的十几匹都绕道儿走平地了，单单这两匹马偏要从四五尺高没有台阶的亭座上一跃而下。这一来连白马的鞦头都扯断了，而我却仍旧骑在古宗马上安然无恙，同伴们对我这种奇迹怎能不交口夸奖呢？哪知赞声未绝，这一帮马忽然随着领队的白马成群打伙地跑起来，我骑在马上就像狂风吹弱柳般的东摆西摇，跑出去还不到两箭远，身不由己地便从马后面甩下来！幸而皮短衣里还衬着很厚的毛衫，两脚褪镫以后赶紧拿肉粗衣厚的地方着地，好像戏台上武花脸穿着胖袄摔“踝子”似的，跌得响声虽大，皮肉却毫无伤损。

经过这番波折，“陈完后人”忙把他骑的那匹“老爷马”换给我。这匹马保重极了，走三步歇一歇，打两鞭子跳一跳，犯起性来还有时停住不走，因此走出不远就离群落伍，踽踽独行了。当天晚上我们原定在炼洞镇过夜的，从沙子街到炼洞大约有三十五里，若像这样磨蹭，岂不又得一个人摸黑儿？可是，心里越起急，越觉着马走得慢，任凭你鞭打腿夹，它还是丝毫无所动于中地慢慢儿走着。正在束手无策的时候，忽然经过一个小水沟，一下子精神没贯注到，没把皮缰带顺，马的前腿陷在泥塘里，我便整个又从马头上栽下来！这一回是先拿右肩头着地，好像杨延辉过关探母时摔的那个“抢背”似的。不过，戏台上是铺着绒毡的，尽管作一次这样的“身段”，衣服上也许粘不着一点儿尘土。烂泥的功用固然和运动场里的砂土相同，但它对于衣服却没有绒毡那样客气。所以当我从泥塘里爬起来的时候，毫没感到伤筋动骨、皮破血出的苦痛，只是右半身"胡为乎泥中"的狼狈现象，是无论如何也掩饰不住的。

走了不远，赶上了骑术比我仅胜一筹的"陈完后人"和"绍兴老倌"。他们看见我这副仪容，一边嘲笑，一边同情，三个人结伙慢慢儿走着，胆子便壮了许多。可是，当我6点半蹭到炼洞的时候，连这两位缓进同志都没追得及。他们像先遣部队一般的把我落难的情形报告给主人，俊陶衔命来迎，我才找到了镇公所。

当晚我在宿舍的烛光底下一边洗涤衣服上的污泥，一边想起《淮南子·人间训》所引的尧戒来：

战战栗栗，日谨一日！人莫踬于山而踬于垤！

这次破天荒骑了二百多里地的马，只在平地上栽了两个筋斗，格外觉着古人这两句话值得回味。

1943年2月8日

四　记宾居大王庙

到宾居，红日已快衔山了。

那一天早晨骑着一匹牵着不走、打着倒退的瘦马跟在"绍兴老倌"后面走。老倌自从脸上挂彩以后，鼻头虽然肿大，胆子可格外小了。假使他骑在马上不动，那巴黎绅士式的小胡髭，映衬着方方的大脸，青青的两腮，剪裁合度的深藏青色外氅很飘洒地披拂在马背上，从后边一望，谁不觉得有点儿唐·吉诃德的神秘？可是，马刚一迈步，他那两只手立刻作一个凤凰展翅式把马鞍的前后紧紧地抓牢，每逢上下坡,更加惴惴焉有临深履薄的恐惧。抓得越紧,马尾巴掀得越疼,起先它还如怒如诉地嘘呖呖哀鸣,后来索性尥着蹶子转弯儿,无论如何不肯往前进。直到毫没办法的当儿,他只得下马步行,让马在后头跟着。像我这样一个不懂骑术的人,骑着那么一匹瘦马,跟在这样一个前驱者的后头,难怪离开炼洞还不到一里,我们早就落伍了。

这样一直磨蹭到晌午才到了牛井街,大队已经过去好久了。替老倌雇到一乘滑竿,因为自己没铺垫,他也只好委身于白虱蠕蠕然的伕子被褥里,我换乘那匹尥蹶子的马跟着三个四川小马伕走,那马居然变得很驯顺,在平坦的公路上有时还能跑两下。下午2点40分赶到宾川城,并没比滑竿迟到一步。

在宾川会上大队,我仍然骑着那匹不愿意驮"绍兴老倌"的马,随着几位能征惯战、驰骋自如的朋友走。这匹马随上群以后,颇想显两手儿给我瞧。它总想和那匹领队的英国白马并驾齐驱。及至抢到前头,它又故意放缓了脚步,等到落后两三丈远,然后再一口气疾驰上前。一路上总是这样乍前乍后、忽疾忽徐地随着大队走,好像表示它的脚力绰绰有余,尽管让别的马暂时抢一下先,只要它一努劲儿就没有赶不上的。果然,后来那匹白马撒腿一跑,它也施展出蕴蓄着的能力,四蹄翻飞地赶上前去。这么一来不要紧,只吓得我紧勒皮缰,夹住两腿,目不邪视,两耳生风,若飘浮云中,若随惊涛漩涌,不知是真是幻是我非我,两三里地的工夫,虽然显得臀部作疼,幸而还没再堕马。昨天从鸡山到炼洞途中,表演一次"踝子"、一次"抢背"的羞惭,纵然还没掬得西江之水,似乎多少也洗刷下去一点儿了。

趁着领队者下马打猎的当儿,我却等到夔公领导的一批缓进派。毕竟研究过社会学再读十三经诸子百家(爱丽丝的名著还没算在里头)的人,修养胜我许多,见面后,他虽然对我伸一伸大拇指紧接着却提出"知足不辱,知止不殆"的意思,劝我加入他们一帮。也就因为我接受他的善言,到宾居以前才保持住没再堕马的令名。

找到寓所以后,真是人困马乏,不想动弹。可是,一听说镇西一里许有一座大王庙,是当地的名胜,不由得又兴奋起来了。恰好王三公子和"一代完人"扛着猎枪要到大王海子的边上去打野鸭,"陈完后人"也愿意陪着我去,于是我们便在一群本地小孩子前呼后拥之下,鼓起余勇去逛庙。路上却在想:"宾居大王","宾居大王"……为什么那样似曾相识的耳熟?在哪里听见过他的故事?看见过关于他的记载?……正在想着,突然两个顽童逞能地说:

"你知道大王姓什么吗?"

"我怎么不知道!姓张,有什么希罕!"

呕!想起来了。两年前我看一本叫做《白国因由》的小书,是讲大理开辟的神话和传说的。那本书里说:大王名叫张敬,是阿育王后人张仁果的裔孙。隋末唐初做大理暴主罗刹的"希老",曾助观音大士降服罗刹,以除民害。后来因为天命归细奴罗,观音乃授意张乐进求把大理的土地人民交细奴罗掌管,这就是南诏的始祖蒙奇王。传到舜化真共13代,凡337年。观音又因为张敬有帮助伏罗刹的功劳,乃封他为宾居大王。分点苍山中峰桃溪水一派,自洱河东山涌出宾居地界,灌溉一方,着彼处人民一年供奉牺牲360副。又赐庙前金井玉栏杆,并与敬香附子一种,以消宿食。所以他虽僻处宾居享受却不亚于蒙奇王,也就欣然接受了。这段故事当年本来很熟悉的,怎么事隔两年就会渺茫起来了?

既然引起这段回忆,更渴望着瞻仰这位大王的丰采了。走过大王海子,暮色已然笼罩下来,顺着海子的西堤走进庙门借着落日的余晖,影影绰绰地看见迎面的石牌坊上刻有"仁慈庙"的立额和"仁风慈雨"之类的许多横匾。正殿中间有一位王者衣冠的神道,长须秉笏,身高丈余,虽然也还慈祥庄严,但在昏暗光线底下,不由人起了一种恐怖的感觉！神座下，供桌上，摆着不少小型的大王像，这大概是本地农民供养的。再看见殿前那些“泽沾广被”、“永镇山川”、“太和元气”、“神威远庇”等等横匾，似乎当地生长在农业社会的老百姓竟把这位仁慈大王当做龙王看待了，照规从“仁慈”两个字上着想，我觉得还和《白国因由》里的传说有关。他为大理人民的福利牺牲了罗刹，为尊重天命所属听凭张乐进求把王位让给细奴罗；宁可把眷恋故主的悲哀深埋在心底，大理人民却得救了；为而不有，利万物而不争，自己情愿僻处宾居，却成全了蒙氏13代337年的南诏国。若不是赋性仁慈，岂肯这样豁达大度？假使我是大理或宾居人，我也愿意馨香俎豆地崇祀这位仁慈大王！

从正殿往东走，两股泉水，流成清冽的池塘，曲桥迂回，有亭半圮。旁有三间配殿，中间塑着一位女神，两个侍者。左边的三尊像都赤裸裸地围着树叶，好像传说中的三皇。右边的两尊像，一个虎头，一个多臂，貌颇狰狞。这些究竟是什么神道，也无暇去考证，但在庙门前的一个碑上模模糊糊看见有“灵泽园三教堂”的字样，大概就是这里了？

关于大王海子另外还有一段传说。相传从前洱海上有一个渔夫，一天他看见海东的山脚下有一个窟窿，海水不断地向里面流。他异想天开地在猜：“海水会不会从这个窟窿流到隔山的宾居地界呢？”于是好奇心鼓励他拿一片破鱼网拴着一段木头做标识塞进窟窿里。过两天他假装到宾居的大王海子去打鱼，果然看见那段拴着破鱼网的木头在水面飘浮着。他发现这桩秘密后，赶快回来用一口大铁锅把那个窟窿堵起来。没几天，大王海子里的水就干了。于是宾居的人心慌慌，旱象已成。那个渔夫便跑了来，假装会求龙王发水，但须祈祷祭祀的银子若干两。银子收足了，他就跑回去把铁锅一揭，海子里的水立刻就涨满了。这样不止一次，宾居的老百姓虽然觉得他的神通广大,可是疑心也一次比一次地增加。最后一次,当他回去的时候,便派了几个人暗中尾随着。果然,他们发现他又去揭铁锅,这才恍然大悟他一向玩的是什么把戏!一赌气子把他往窟窿里一塞,从此这个黑心的渔夫才永远不会再做这样损人利己的勾当了。

这个传说又是从《白国因由》演变来的。拿黑心渔夫和仁慈大王对照岂不更显着相映成趣吗?

1943 年 2 月 9 日

五 从乌龙坝到倒挂水

到宾居的那晚,有两位识途的人都说,第二天要翻乌龙坝,下倒挂水,山路崎岖,乱石坑坎,没有骑马经验的人恐怕不大好走,于是商量给我们三个骑术欠佳的雇滑竿。在鸡山香火正旺的几天,滑竿是不好找的。我表示如果找不到三乘,应尽先让给夔公和"绍兴老倌"。夔公鉴于后山露宿吞雪的惨剧打定主意不蹈覆辙;老倌却当仁不让,斩钉截铁地表示,就是雇到一乘,他也得坐。

第二天早晨,两乘滑竿雇到了。临出发时,夔公毅然决然地昂坐"老总马"上,老倌也很机警地把两个壮丁抓住,老早盘据在滑竿上。剩下两个已过兵役年龄、烟容满面的伕子守着一架毫无铺垫的滑竿,等我去坐。我因为预备骑马,行李已交给驮伕,这时难却主人的好意,便借了一身雨衣垫着,勉强随队出发。赶了一里多地才从驮马上撤出一床铺盖来换上。乍在平地上抬着走的时候,也觉得没有骑马那么紧张,心境稍一舒展,哪知走出还不到五里,情形就大变了!两个伕子中比较年轻的一个,脚底下开始像拌蒜般的东摇西晃,脸色惨白,汗珠子像黄豆粒那样大,嘴里呻吟不止,还不停地爹妈乱叫。我坐在上面又是可怜,又是可气,心想今天大概要与夔公同一命运了,我们的生肖既然相同,造物岂肯不一视同仁呢?……正在想着,那个伕子的情形更狼狈了,拿出一个烧好的烟泡子用舌头乱舔,也解救不了他的燃眉之急。后面的老伕子被他拖累得不轻,嘴里也不干不净地骂着。我看他实在支持不住,只得下来步行。这时大队已经走得看不见影儿了。勉强走到白头坡,我恐怕上面的坡更陡,落伍太远,时间晚了诸多不便,赶紧让那个烟鬼跑到前面去喊同伴给我留下一匹马。哪知他有气无力地喊了两声以后,忽然无影无踪地"开小差"了!这一下真坑人不浅!我不单没有马骑,没有杖拄,而且还添了一份行李累赘着,在荒山旷野、不见人烟的地方,叫我怎么办呢?不得已,只好咬定牙关,挺起胸膛,叫老伕子扔下滑竿,背上行李,领着我迈开大步,走上前去。一起头儿,仗着自力更生的精神,脚步也还矫健。不过,毕竟人已经有几十岁年纪了,再加上75基罗的体重,越走越觉着有"勇士不能自举其身"的感想。爬上二台坡的时候,汗流浃背,气喘心跳,口渴头昏,差不多也快赶上刚才开小差的那个黑籍伕子了。正在无可如何,幸而挑橘子的担子在眼前休息,赶紧吃了两个橘子,又揣起几个,歇了好一会儿才往前走。翻过梁子上便看见乌龙坝的一片平原,这时天已经正晌午了。平坦的土地上印着许多马蹄痕迹,但同伙却没有留在后面的。在坝子上一家民房里讨了三大碗开水吃,喉咙里润泽了许多,疲劳也稍微恢复了一些。继续在丛莽和泥塘中前进,约摸又走了一个钟头才到了倒挂水。

到倒挂水便开始下坡。不过这七里多的下坡路,却完全是怪石嶙峋、溪涧萦回的泥泞曲径。下来时需要半涉半走,没有手杖颇为吃力。然而在疲惫艰苦之余,还可以振奋起我的游兴来的,就是这里有变幻无方的许多溪水供我流连。几乎每转一个弯儿都有银练珠帘一般的瀑布从陡壁悬崖上垂下来,激在乱石堆上滚起雪白的浪花,然后在涧底莹澈地流着。底下的小石子被阳光从水里折映上来，五色斑斓，光彩夺目，和溪里涵泳自适的小鱼一样的可爱。这比起西湖的九溪十八涧，崂山的北九水，峨眉后山的黑龙江来，格外清幽孤峭。假使我骑在马上战战兢兢，或坐在滑竿上转动不能自如，哪里会有这种从容欣赏、畅饱眼福的机会？所以，无论怎样辛苦，我总算勉勉强强地做了半天的徐霞客！

下完倒挂水，山口外边一片碧绿的凤羽坝子便涌现在眼前。走了五十几里路，历尽险途，到这里才算赶上掉在后方休息的病马，赶紧找了一匹骑上，顿觉精神百倍，舒适异常，再有多"棒"的滑竿伕来引诱，我也不肯上当了。

赶到凤仪县城已近黄昏，同伴都先回下关去了，只留下几个人守着待运的行李。客人中惟我一人落后，不久俊陶便衔命乘吉普车(Jeep)来接。比起同行的几位来，除去没来得及到温泉洗尘，我也一样安安全全地在当晚9点多钟返回大理的敷文书院。

1943年2月10日

记鸡山悉檀寺的《木氏宦谱》

我，和费孝通先生不同，比较是有历史癖和考据癖的。我写不出像他那样笔姿生动、想像丰富、情趣盎然的《朝山记》；我也写不出像曾昭抡先生那样时间准确，里程精详，宛然和在化学实验室称量药品一样谨严的游记。假如我要写的话，尽管怎样事先有意避免，写出来的结果多多少少总有些像胡适之先生《庐山游记》那一类的玩艺儿。这也是才分所限，无可如何！

可是，这次鸡足巡礼归来，我却不能贯彻我的考据癖了。因为我对于这座颇有佛教掌故的名山，事前既没有翻检志乘，事后也无暇参考前人的游记，除去入山迷路的那一晚，曾经在金顶僧寮围炉瑟缩、眼倦神昏地翻检了一会儿《鸡足山志》以外，再没有对这名山胜迹有所考究。两天半在山上走马观花所得，实在很少可以称述的。祝圣寺的墨龙，怀空和尚认为是"镇山之宝"，它是清乾隆间屈尔泰所绘，屈为提督董芳幕府，死后葬丽江。石钟寺有担当、大错、许鸿和临济71代中峰和尚等人的墨迹，许鸿竟被谈锋甚健、交际圆融的老和尚当做徐霞客，这种音近而讹的错误，叫我这研究韵学的人当时也不好意思矫正。入山以前，李印老[李根源]对光旦兄说，鸡山有永历帝的衣冠和李定国的告示。可是，在我们所经过的几个庙里都没找到这一点儿南明史迹。山上看见的东西比较可以引起我的探索兴趣的，只有悉檀寺所藏的《丽江木氏宦谱》罢了。

悉檀寺在鸡山最东的丛林中，后倚九重崖，前临黑龙潭，是明朝万历间古德本无所创建的。丽江的木土司世为护法檀越，现在寺里的和尚大部分还是丽江人，所以在客堂待茶的时候，我们能够尝到富有丽江风味的油炸糯米粑粑和胡麻酥油茶。寺内有大佛一尊，是从西藏运来的，弥勒殿前的横匾亦为藏文，古宗气味虽重，但未与寺僧详谈，不知宗派是显是密。最早的碑文是万历四十八年谢肇淛所撰和天启间蔡毅中所撰。

《木氏宦谱》长约一尺六寸，宽半之，装裱甚为讲究。前有嘉靖二十四年杨慎所作序文。底下自第一世“爷爷”起，至第二十四世木钟止，各有图像和世系说明，自第九世以下，装裱次序稍有凌乱，且缺第十。按，木氏属藏缅系么些族（自称纳西），第一世“爷爷”宋徽宗时来雪山。第三世阿琮阿良入元。第七世阿甲阿得入明，洪武十五年赐姓木氏，改名木得。第二十世木懿顺治十六年降清。此谱修至第二十四世木钟，时当清雍正间。现在把他们的简单世系列在后面：

1 爷爷——2 年保阿琮——3 阿琮阿良——4 阿良阿胡——5 阿胡阿烈——6 阿烈阿甲——7 阿甲阿得——8 木初——9 木土——10“木森”[①] ——11 木嵚——12 木泰——13 木定——14 木公——15 木高——16 木东——17 木旺——18 木青——19 木增——20 木懿——21 木櫾——22 木尧——23 木兴——24 木钟

据陶云逵先生说：《木氏宗谱》共有四种：（一）《木氏历代宗谱碑》，在今丽江县治东南十里蛇山木氏坟地，清道光二十二年所立。（二）杨慎《木氏宦谱序》，藏丽江木府。（三）《续云南通志稿》南蛮志么些诏附注之《木氏宗谱》，《志稿》系光绪二十七年修成。（四）《木氏

---

① 原缺，据《木氏历代宗谱碑》校补。

宦谱图像世系考》。图谱前有道光二十年海南陈钊钟所题"木氏归命求世之图",今藏木府与杨序合装一册,但杨氏所序的谱并没有图像而且世代也不同。[①] 这四种里当然要算第一种的史料价值最高。碑上说:自汉代至唐武德间之叶古年,凡17世,又6世乃至秋阳。从秋阳以下至清乾隆间之木仁,共39世,皆有名爵可考。原碑是陶氏1935年从丽江为中央研究院历史语言研究所拓来的。1937年董作宾先生作《爨人谱系新证》(以下简称董文),1938年凌纯声先生作《唐代云南的乌蛮与白蛮考》(以下简称凌文)均曾引用。现在我把它重列一下,以便和悉檀寺的《木氏宦谱》比较:

1 秋阳(唐高宗上元时为三甸总管)——2 阳音都谷(唐玄宗天宝时,南诏阁罗凤授为总督元帅)——3 都谷剌具——4 剌具普蒙——5 普蒙普王——6 普王剌完——7 剌完西内——8 西内西可——9 西可剌土——10 剌土俄均——11 俄均牟具——12 牟具牟西——13 牟西牟磋——14 牟磋牟乐——15 牟乐牟保——16 牟保阿琮——17 阿琮阿良(元世祖亲征大理,以功升茶罕章宣慰司)——18 阿良阿胡——19 阿胡阿烈——20 阿烈阿甲——21 阿甲阿得(明洪武十五年赐姓木,故又名木得)——22 阿得阿初(木初)——23 阿初阿土(木土)——24 阿土阿地(木森)——25 阿地阿寺(木嵚)——26 阿寺阿牙(木泰)——27 阿牙阿秋(木定)——28 阿秋阿公(木公)——29 阿公阿目(木高)——30 阿目阿都(木东)——31 阿都阿胜(木旺)——32 阿胜阿宅(木青)——33 阿宅阿寺(木增)——34 阿寺阿春(木懿)——35 木樱(清康熙时)——36 木松——37 木润——38 木

① 见陶云逵《关于么些之名称分布与迁移》一文后所附《丽江木氏宦谱比较表》,《中央研究院历史语言研究所集刊》第七本第一分第135页后,1938年出版。

楫——39 木仁(乾隆时)

这两种材料的不同之点有五:(一)《宦谱》的第一世相当于《宗谱碑》的第十五世,惟所谓“爷爷”是否就是牟乐牟保,尚有疑问。杨序和宗谱碑都没有“爷爷”这个名称,而《世系考》上说“爷爷”是“西域蒙古异人,乘大香树,浮入金沙江,至北浪沧,夷人望而异之,率众迎之登陆。时有白沙,羡陶阿古为夷人长,妻以女,生一子曰阿琮。牟乐牟保抚以为嗣”。那么不单“爷爷”和牟乐牟保是两个人,牟保阿琮也是牟乐牟保的养子而不是亲子了。(二)《宦谱》的第二世年保阿琮应据《宗谱碑》校改作牟保阿琮。(三)《宦谱》自第八世木初以下均改赐姓,《宗谱碑》则并列么些原名,直到清康熙时才不复列。(四)《宦谱》的第二十一世至二十四世和《宗谱碑》的第三十五世至第三十八世命名不同。(五)《宦谱》没有和《宗谱碑》第三十九世相当的一代。由此可见《宦谱》是从阿琮的本生父修起,现存鸡山悉檀寺的一部,从清雍正以后就没有续修。

杨慎的《宦谱序》也托始于叶古年,以下所列相当于《宗谱碑》的第一世秋阳至第二十八世阿秋阿公。《续云南通志稿》列有 18 代,除叶古年外,相当于《宗谱碑》的第一世秋阳至第十七世阿琮阿良。这两个本子所列各代名氏都是简称,而且译音用字也不全同,详见陶氏的《比较表》。《木氏宦谱图像世系考列》有 29 代,自《宗谱碑》的第十五世起至第三十九世木仁止,又增加木秀、木睿、木汉、木景四世,但把牟乐牟保改作“爷爷”,把第二十二世阿得阿初改称木初,以下皆从木姓,不列原名。这最后的一种,我认为和悉檀寺所藏的同出一源,不过从木仁起续修过五代罢了。

在这《宦谱》里顶惹人注意的，就是“父子连名制”[①]。例如：牟保阿琮的儿子阿琮阿良，用父名的下两字作己名的上两字，而他的儿子阿良阿胡，又把他的下两个字用作上两个字，好像文字游戏中的“顶针续麻”似的。这种制度在么些族里很早就有。在丽江流传的么些多巴字经典里，也载有洪水后的六代宗祖名氏，那六代是：

1 宗争利恩——2 恩亨糯——3 糯本培——4 本培呙——5 呙高劣——6 高劣趣……[②]

可见这种制度的起源是很远的。余庆远的《维西见闻录》上说：么些族“无姓氏，以祖名末一字，父名末一字，加一字为名递承而下，以志亲疏”。照他的说法应该得出下列的公式来：

祖父　　父亲　　自身　　儿子　　孙子

甲乙丙——乙丙丁——丙丁戊——丁戊己——戊己庚

但事实上并不如此。且拿洪水后的六代做例，便可得出下列的公式：

宗争利恩（甲乙丙）——恩亨糯（丙丁戊）——糯本培（戊己庚）——本培呙（己庚辛）——呙高劣（辛壬癸）——高劣趣（壬癸子）

这只是拿父名的末一字或末二字作子名的首一字或首二字，并不承袭祖名。就是在《木氏宗谱碑》的39代里也没发现过这种现象。余氏的话似是而非，不可不辨。

父子连名制并不专行于么些族，在所谓爨族，乃至于其他藏缅系的各部族，都有这种文化特征。据胡蔚本《南诏野史》引《白古记》所载南诏历代源流，当得下列的谱系。

---

① 此名采凌纯声说，见《唐代云南的乌蛮与白蛮考》，《中央研究院历史语言研究所人类学集刊》第一卷第一期，第66页。董作宾称此作“以父名为子姓的制度”尚待商酌。例如，皮罗阁与阁罗凤皆属蒙氏，皮与阁都不是姓。

② 见董作宾《爨人谱系新证》，中山文化教育馆《民族学研究集刊》第二期，第183页，第192页。

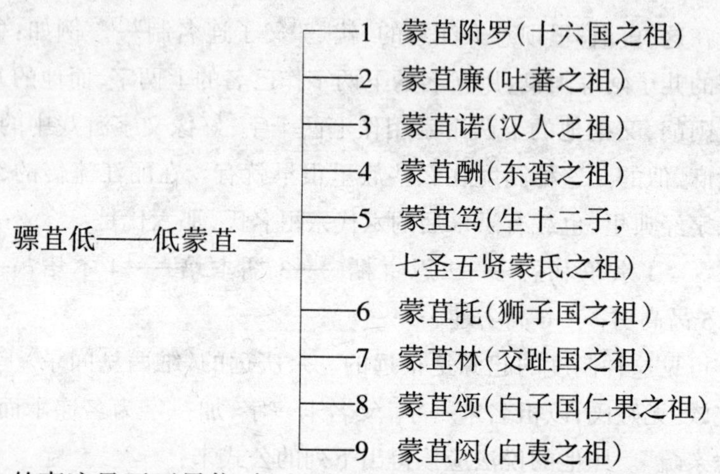

其中的事迹虽不可尽信，但由骠苴低到低蒙苴，再到蒙苴附罗等 9 人的连名制却是显然无疑的。又据樊绰《蛮书》、《新唐书·南蛮传》、阮元声《南诏野史》、杨慎《滇载记》等所载六诏世系也可以和上面所说的互相发明，兹再谱列于下：

(甲)蒙舍诏世系　自细奴罗至舜化真十有三世，立三百十年：

1 细奴罗——2 罗晟——3 晟罗皮——4 皮罗阁——5 阁罗凤——6 凤伽异——7 异牟寻——8 寻阁劝——9 劝龙晟

劝利晟——10 晟丰佑——11 世隆——12 隆舜——13 舜化真

(乙)蒙巂诏世系　凡四世为南诏所灭：

1 巂辅首

2 佉阳照——3 照原——4 原罗

(丙)浪穹诏世系　凡六世为南诏所灭：

1 丰时——2 罗铎——3 铎罗望——4 望偏——5 偏罗矣——6 矣罗君(一作罗君)

(丁)邆赕诏世系　立五世为南诏所灭：

1 丰咩——2 咩罗皮——3 皮罗邃——4 邃罗颠——5 颠文托(一作颠之托)

(戊)施浪诏世系　立三世为南诏所灭：

1 望木

望千——2 千傍——3 傍罗颠(《新唐书》合二、三两代为千旁罗颠)

(己)越析诏世系　或称么些诏，立仅二世，为南诏所灭：

1 波冲

□□——2 于赠(波冲兄子)

照这六诏的世系看起来，除去蒙舍诏的世隆、浪穹诏的罗铎二人尚待考订外，其余都没有违背父子连名制的。专就这一点文化特征来讲，我们就可以断定六诏应该属于藏缅系而不属于台系。

这种制度后来在倮倮和窝泥族中仍旧保存着。据毛奇龄《蛮司合志》卷八中说："诸甸本土，罗罗和泥人好相杀，死则偿以财。家无姓名，其有名者或递承其父名之末字，顾无姓。弘治中知府陈晟以百家姓首八字，司分一字加于各名之上，诸甸皆受，惟纳楼不受。"① 又丁在君[丁文江]先生所编的《爨文丛刻》里有《帝王世纪》一种(或称人类历史)，内容是记载贵州水西倮倮安家的世系。书中从宇宙开辟、人类始祖讲起，到吴三桂灭安氏为止，共 114 世，世代相承，都是父子连名。兹列表于下：

(甲)水西倮倮安氏世系一

1 希母遮——2 遮道公——3 公竹诗——4 诗亚立——5 立亚明——6 明长夬——7 长夬作——8 作阿切——9 切亚宗——10 宗亚仪——11 仪亚祭——12 祭迫能——13 迫能道——14 道母仪——15 母

---

① 见前引凌文 6 项。

仪尺——16 尺亚素——17 素亚得——18 得洗所——19 洗所多——20 多必益——21 必益堵——22 堵洗仙——23 洗仙佗——24 佗阿大——25 大阿武——26 阿武懦——27 懦侏渎——28 渎侏武——29 武老撮[①] ——30 撮朱渎

(乙)水西倮倮安氏世系二

1 渎母吾——2 母齐齐[②] ——3 齐亚红——4 红亚得——5 得古沙——6 沙古母——7 古母龚——8 龚亚陇——9 陇亚告——10 告亚守——11 守亚美——12 美阿得——13 得阿诗——14 诗美武——15 美武梦——16 梦蝶多——17 多亚质——18 质吾勺——19 吾勺必——20 必一梅——21 梅阿亮——22 亮阿宗——23 宗亚补——24 补亚勺——25 勺亚讨——26 讨阿常——27 阿常必——28 必益孟——29 孟吾守——30 守亚典——31 典亚法——32 法一宜——33 一宜尺——34 尺亚主——35 主亚典——36 典亚即——37 即亚登——38 登亚堵——39 堵阿达——40 阿达多——41 多阿榻——42 榻阿期——84 期阿否——44 否那知——45 那知渎——46 渎阿更——47 阿更阿文——48 阿文洛南——49 洛南阿搕——50 阿搕一典——51 一典即期——52 即期忍一——53 忍一卜野——54 卜野一尊——55 一尊老勺——56 老勺渎在——57 渎在阿宗——58 阿宗一衢——59 一衢下宜——60 下宜阿义——61 阿义阿洛——62 阿洛阿冬——63 阿冬大屋——64 大屋老乃——65 老乃老在——66 老在阿期——67 阿期老帝——68 老帝下直——69 下直那考——70 那考崩在——71 崩在老知——72 老知老铺——73 老铺不足——74 不足直巴——75 直巴安

① 武老撮,兄弟共 12 人;(1)武朱只,(2)武朱佗,(3)武朱仪,(4)武朱帝,(5)武朱义,(6)武朱明,(7)武朱觉,(8)武朱朋,(9)武朱通,(10)武朱替,(11)武朱执,(12)武老撮。

② 母齐齐兄弟共 6 人:(1)母亚考,(2)母亚怯,(3)母亚奢,(4)母亚卧,(5)母客客,(6)母齐齐。

作——76安作直吾——77直吾老成——78老成洛西——79洛西非说——80非说老古——81老古老得——82老得老颠——83老颠一分——84一分明宗(即阿客安昆)

得到这一批材料参证,咱们更可以相信这种制度在倮倮族中是很通行的了。并且它不单通行于贵族,也还通行于民间。凌纯声先生1935年在云南遇到一个四川大凉山附近的倮倮青年曲木藏明,据说他的父亲能背家谱,上下世连名,数十代相承,丝毫不爽,凌先生曾托他回去笔录一份,可惜后来并没有寄到。①

不过,这种民间口传的倮倮家谱,凌先生虽没得到,我最近却无意中得到两份茶山人的家谱。今年2月间我从大理回昆明,带来两位茶山青年,一个住在片马的叫董昌绍,一个住在噬戛的叫孔科郎。他俩都在密支那英国人所办的中学念过书,能说茶山、浪速、山头三种语言,兼通缅文,略懂英文。有一次我请他们讲茶山的故事或历史,孔科郎毫不费事地很快就写出他自己的46代家谱来。我当时喜出望外,颇为惊讶。再问董昌绍,他也背出9代来。这两份家谱完全是父子连名的。现在分别抄在后面:

(甲)孔科郎世系

1. Ya be Bawm
2. Mashaw Bawm(弟)
3. Bawm Shaw Chung
4. Chung Shi Nin
5. Shi Nin Hkying
6. Hkying da ək
7. Da ək Saw

① 见前引凌文70页。

8. Saw Yaw Chu
9. Chu Fu Fek
10. Fu Fek Hkum
11. Hkum Kwe Zik
12. Zik Hku Lam
13. Hku Lam Pe
14. Shaw Gyaw La Xang
15. Xang Zaw Byu
16. Byu Zaw Te
17. Te Mau Yau
18. Rau Yau Hpyau
19. Hpyau Byaw Yang
20. Yang Lawm Lik
21. Lik Ding Chit
22. Chit Kang Yau
23. Kang Yau Gwi
24. Gwi Chung Chik
25. Chung Chik Yaw
26. Yaw au Ding
27. Ding Law Waw
28. Waw Law Jang
29. Jang Law Bawm
30. Bawm Law Nu
31. Nu Kyang
32. Kyang Bau
33. Bau Myaw

34. Myaw Htuk

35. Htuk Bawm

36. Bawm Zing

37. Zing Yaw

38. Yaw Bawm

39. Bawm Hkaw

40. Hkaw Ying

41. Ying Sau

42. Sau Ying

43. Ying Yaw

44. Yaw Ying

45. Ying Hkaw

46. Khaw Lang (孔科郎)

据他自己说,第十三代以上还没真变成人,他们和牛、狗、草、木都可以讲话,第十四代起才是人。

(乙)董昌绍世系

1. Yawn Sau

2. Sau Chang

3. Chang Lang

4. Lang Bau; Lang Gying

5. Bau Zung; Bau Ying; Bau taik

6. Zung Ying

7. Ying Sau

8. Sau Chang

9. Chang Sau(董昌绍)

据他自己说,约在400年前第一代初来片马,披榛莽,启山林,现在下片马有他的坟和碑,碑上刻着他的像和汉字;第四代的坟在下片马 Gyung Gyang 山上,没有碑;第五代的坟在下片马 Aw Yaw Bau,也没有碑。孔、董两个人比较起来,董的先人似乎搬来的晚多了。

茶山和么些、傈傈不同,他们自己没有文字,现在借用的罗马拼音还是韩森(O. Hanson)给山头人造的。然而他们把家谱记得这样熟,那就可见父子连名制的构成,恐怕就是帮助没有文字的部族记忆世系的。

茶山人属于藏缅族的缅人支,足征父子连名制并不以么些、傈傈为限。凌纯声先生根据 Phayre 的《缅甸历史》(*History of Burma*)第 279 页说:"在二世纪至四世纪的时候,缅甸有孔雀王朝 Moriya,其王亦父子连名,如 Pyo－so－ti, Ti－min－yi, Yi－min－baik, Baik－then－li, Then－li－jong, Jong－du－yit 等名。所以父子连名的文化也可以说是广义的藏缅族的文化特征。"① 现在我既得到茶山的两种新材料更可以给凌说添一个佐证了。又据陶云逵先生说:他曾亲见傈傈、阿卡老人,背诵他们祖先的名字可以到四五十代之远②。我企望他赶快把材料拿出来,供我们比较参证的资助。

大凡人一有了癖好总是没法子救药的。朝山拜庙不知流连风景,欣赏自然,看见人家一本断烂的家谱有什么希奇?然而竟自下笔不能自休地,小题大做地扯了 6000 多字,岂不是那点儿考据癖在作祟吗?话又说回来了,既然费了那么大的劲,跑了那么远的野马,还得勒住丝缰,有个交代。于是总结上文,得出以下的结论:

(一)鸡山悉檀寺所藏的《木氏宦谱》从牟保阿琮的本生父"爷爷"修起,和《木氏宦谱图像世系考》同出一源,但缺修木仁、木秀、木睿、

① 见前引凌文 73 页。
② 见前引陶文 125 页。

木汉、木景5代；比丽江蛇山的《木氏历代宗谱碑》上面少了14代，下面缺了1代。

（二）父子连名制是广义的藏缅族的文化特征，就我们已经得到的材料来讲，在唐代的乌蛮或爨人、么些、倮倮、窝泥、阿卡、傈僳、茶山、缅甸都是通行的。

（三）这种顶针续麻式的父子连名制是帮助没有文字的部族，乃至于有文字的部族，记忆他们自己的世系的。

至于费孝通先生是否嫌我积癖太深，当代的文学家是否骂我给名山减色，且自由他，何暇计及。

1943年5月4日，昆明青园

跋

罗常培先生写下十多部语言学专著，一百来篇语言学论文。而且，他教出许多学生，分布在全国各地，也有的在国外，从事语言工作，卓然成家。他继往开来，不断开拓，是我国现代语言学奠基人之一。这些，大家都知道，都认可。除了语言学之外，他还写过两本文艺性的游记——《蜀道难》和《苍洱之间》。这方面，许多人都不知道，一些谈罗先生一生业绩的文章也没提起。这也难怪，这两本书印数少，又是在抗战期间的后方印的，流传不广，连当年给《蜀道难》写序的“世纪老人”冰心都说：“如今这本书也找不到了。”她说这话是1979年12月（《罗常培纪念论文集》401页，1984，商务）。我保存的一本还是解放前在一个学生手里偶然见到，向她要来的。《苍洱之间》似乎流传更少。

罗先生在《蜀道难》自序里说：“生来不是文学天才，更加缺乏素养”，认为自己即使有点文艺“灵气”，也被积年的研究语言的辛勤工作给窒息了，并引鲁迅当年亲自对他说的“创造和研究是不能同时兼顾的”自身经验为证。是的，罗先生不以文学创作名世，但只要读过他写的《中国音韵学导论》和《汉魏六朝文研究》（整理刘申叔遗说）这两本书，就会知道他用文言说理叙事是何等严整精练，音节和美。他写的许多通俗性谈论语言文学问题的文章晓畅明白，举重若轻，口语化的程度又完全像他平日的谈话或讲演

(有些本来是演讲的笔录)。罗先生有深厚的文学修养,驾驭文字有匠心独运的功力,在研究典重的语言问题之余,给我们留下这两本文学著作,特觉珍贵。

其实,这两本书也都跟罗先生的学术研究相关,是他学术研究的投影,不是单纯的游山玩水的记录,只要一读就清楚了。《蜀道难》固然写了旅途的艰难曲折,写了峨眉胜景等等,也写了抗日战争大后方学术界的许多事,文化界的许多人。如果要了解抗战期间我们学术文化界的情况,其中有不少第一手的难得材料。罗先生 40 年代初期曾三次从昆明去苍山洱海之间的大理小城(最后一次是 1944 年夏秋之间,同去的众人中有我),主要目的是调研少数民族语言和汉语方言。那里秀丽的自然景物,独特的风土民情,动人的民间传说,丰富的历史遗迹,触发了他因搞研究而并未窒息的文艺"灵气",给这现如今成为举世闻名的旅游胜地写下一份半世纪前的人文写照。

罗先生自小有写日记的习惯。我看过他十六七岁时的整本日记,也看过他 40 年代日记的散页,都是用墨笔工整书写的,记叙详尽,兼有笔记性质。因此,他写这些游记性的文章不光凭记忆,而是从日记里生发、演绎、扩充而成,所以写来头头是道,有凭有据,却又不是干巴巴的流水账,而是文质交映,挥洒自如,真所谓"超以象外,得其环中",使人读来不觉终卷。

我们常说"文如其人"。罗先生为人朗爽耿直,胸无城府,曾有"文直公"之称。他写文章不故作高深,不矫揉作态,不玩弄辞藻,正如他自己说的,"有什么就写什么,想怎样写就怎样写"。说到底,这是对读者的真诚,是品德的体现。相形之下,现在常见报刊有特别标出"散文"的,其中不少以扭曲语言为创新,以故弄玄虚为深奥,有似梦呓,不知所云。这是"文心"不诚,"文德"不直,把假冒伪劣货色混入精神产品领域,说到底,也是作者品德的体现。

罗先生逝世快40年了,读其文,想见其人。他的风范令人深切怀念。

周定一

1996年6月于北京

零星文章

自　传

1899年8月9日(清光绪二十五年己亥七月初四日)我生在一个没落的满族家庭。本族源出吉林宁古塔的萨克达氏,后裔分罗、老、苍三姓。有人因为我姓罗,怀疑我是爱新觉罗氏,其实我本是寒门衰族,和"胜朝贵胄"毫无关系。

我的出生地在北京西直门内曹公观后西井胡同租赁的三间南屋里。这个地方后来被"陆军大学校"圈入,现在是华北中学的一部分。我家都隶属正黄旗军籍,三代以内并没有做大官的。父亲靠他月饷和季米的收入养活我们一家六口,生活的艰苦可以想见。宣统末父亲选拔做宣武门的"城门吏",那是一个七品小官,哥哥也挑补了步军统领衙门的游缉队,这时家里的生活比较松动了一点儿。家庭经济状况除维持家人生活外勉强可以供给我一人上中学。从当年直到现在,父兄和我自己始终是"房无一间,地无一垄",主要的生活来源完全是靠月薪收入的。

我5岁开始在家里识字。父亲和哥哥都没念过多少书,母亲是文盲。但父亲很聪明,办事尤其精明能干。他们看我还不笨,8岁就把我送进一家私立小学。念了不到一年,因为先生改就公立学校教员,我也转在一家远亲的专馆里做外附生。这家专馆只有本家学生和我两个人。先生是个村学究,学问平常而且专门哄着本家学生,对我是漠视的。在我幼稚的心灵里第一次发现贫富的不平。没到两个月就转在另外一家私塾。那个私塾的先生很好,我跟他念了《孟子》、《诗经》、《书经》的全部和《左传》的一部分,并且开始练习作文和讲书。

1910年投考"京师公立第二两等小学堂",因为念过一些旧书,会作文,略懂算术,就编入高小第二年级。刚一编级的时候,随班听讲感觉有点儿躐等。经过短时期的努力,不单跟得上班,而且"崭然露头角",每次考试都名列第一。当时的同学现在还保持友谊的只有老舍(舒庆春)一个人。

辛亥革命以后,各学校短期停顿,曾经利用这个空当儿补习国文、英文、算术,兼学蒙语。1912年春天第二两等小学堂解散,我报考第二小学,不久又被归并到第四小学,当年毕业。次年春,升入市立第三中学,因为英文成绩较好,提升一学期。这个中学是由八旗右翼中学改组的,同学大多数是八旗子弟,家境大都贫寒,但生活自由散漫,不肯刻苦努力。能够彼此砥砺黾勉上进四十年如一日的,只有董鲁安(董璠,于力)和我两个人。那时,我们两个人努力的方向,除去学校课业以外,喜欢读康有为主办的《不忍》杂志,梁启超《饮冰室文集》和宋明人的语录,只是暗中摸索着找道儿。校长昆明夏瑞庚(筱琅)是个面貌很凶恶而心肠很慈善的人,非常同情贫寒的学生,对我尤其特别奖掖。我一生的转捩,他实在是一个重要的关键人物(详下文)。1915年秋天,北京学务局举办了一次全市各中学四年级学生观摩会考,我校的同班学生吃了数学和英文的亏,都考得很坏,只有我考取了甲等第三名。当时谣传考取前三名的毕业后可以选派日本留学。这个谣传增加了我无限的幻想和奢望。父亲因为家境日落,人口日多,虽也盼望儿子深造,但苦于经济力量不够,一心只想我毕业后马上可以找到一个"打现钟"(就是只顾眼前的生活)的事儿,好贴补家用。恰好蔡锷主办的经界局正在招生,目的在训练一批经界人员，经过 3 个月短期训练后，就可以派出去测量全国没有“升科”的黑地。父亲极力督促我去报考。我自己一方面体谅父亲的苦衷，一方面却为中学毕业后到东洋留学的幻想所引诱，心里十分不愿意考中。当时曾经给哥哥写了一封长信，说明自己不甘小就的志向，请他替我向爸爸说情。哥哥很感动地回了一封信答应我的要求，鼓励我深造的志向，并且说爸爸如果不肯供给我时，他情愿帮助我，成全我的志愿。后来虽然考取了经界局，父亲经哥哥劝说的结果，并没坚执我必去。过了不久，速记传习所招生，父亲又让我投考。这个传习所是龙溪蔡璋办的，从清末资政院，以至 1913 年的国会跟其他一些会议机关，所有速记人员都是由他训练组织的。父亲让我报考的本意是想 6 个月毕业可以找个事做；我自己却想，学会速记，听讲时笔记作得特别详细，而且是夜班不妨碍中学课业，所以就欣然答应了。每月现洋 6 元，加上往返车费，非十几元不够，在当时的确够老父撑持的了。同班同学多半是各机关派送的，自费生很少。有几个纨袴子弟混进来，只是花钱消遣。我年纪小，学生气味重，跟他们随不上群，每天只是勤恳学习。学期终了时，因为我一分钟能记 140 字，速率最快，交的练习最多，考试成绩 97.5 名冠全班，慢慢儿地被人注意起来了。可是从此以后便增加了骄傲心，学习也不如从前努力，毕业考试的第一名竟被法院派来的一位老学生王念恒给争了去。这一段生活，使我学会了一种技能。那时袁世凯正在酝酿帝制，我学会速记已经达到记好笔记的志愿，又把精力集中到中学课程上，准备毕业考试，并没想钻在污浊的政治圈中拿速记挣饭吃。当时虽辜负了老父的期望，事后追想起来，亏得父亲给我搭了这个梯子，才使我后来有半工半读自学上进的机会。

1916 年夏天，父亲得“血蛇瘟”（一名丹毒）急症，患了 9 天的病就去世了！那时我还不满 17 岁，离中学毕业还有一个月。乍经这样非常事变,真是无所措手足。幸亏哥哥帮助把父亲发丧得相当风光。一个没有恒产的家庭,打肿嘴巴充胖子,结果我们哥儿俩闹得“一屁股两肋的债”——这就是我独立生活开始时所承受的全部遗产。

父亲下葬后,离我的中学毕业考试只差两星期,连闷郁带着急,脖颈后生了一个很大的疮,俗名叫“砍头疮”。这时心理的痛苦比生理的痛苦更厉害。忍痛准备考试,疮痛实在难受;不忍痛准备考试,则四年的功夫废于一旦,何况在“无父何怙”的关头,学业是不容拖延呢。无奈何,咬着牙关,顶着绷带,把考试应付下来。校长、教员和同学都替我掉了几点同情泪。这时,我的出洋幻想和考清华、北大的迷梦不由得不醒了。哥哥不单娶了亲,而且已经是两个孩子的父亲,即使有心帮助我,委实没这份力量。何况父丧之后,欠债还没法儿偿还呢!但是,我上进的心并没完全泯灭,只打算投考官费的北京高等师范学校或天津陆军军医学校,好使读书和吃饭都有个着落。

这时袁世凯死了,83天的洪宪烟消云散。黎元洪按临时约法继任大总统,下令恢复旧国会。我的速记老师蔡璋奉命组织众议院秘书厅的速记科。有一天,我正在家里准备升学的功课,哥哥忽然满头大汗地跑回家来,拿着一张报纸指给我这个消息,并且马上叫我去拜访蔡科长。他的心境我很明白,但是,我一则不愿意干求,二则不愿意变更我的升学计划,实在不大起劲儿,当时不肯扫了哥哥的兴,终于去了。幸喜,那天我所拜访的蔡科长并没在家,于是留了个名片,匆匆完成了哥哥的使命。不料,第二天蔡科长居然根据名片上的住址写了一张明信片来约我即日面谈。我觉得约谈和干谒不同,便如约前往。见面后,他问我愿不愿担任众议院秘书厅速记科的二等技士。我想到当时家庭经济情况和个人升学前途的渺茫,便答应了。从此之后,我就靠自己的技术,每月挣80元大洋,不单可以维持自己的生活,贴补家用,而且可以偿还父亲的丧葬费了。

我一进去的时候，本来派定在委员会工作，后来因为大会需要人，没几天就调在大会。大会照例每周开会三次，另外有时还加开宪法会议或两院会合会。每次开会时两名速记技士一班，每班担任30分钟记录，下会场后还得花四倍的时间去翻译整理。如果当天的会议时间不超过8班240分钟，那么，每人的工作不过就这样了。待遇优，工作轻，速记员大多数又是很年轻的。年轻的人处在有钱、有闲的环境，又受了议员不良作风的影响，难免把金钱精力专注在吃、喝、嫖、赌、穿上面去。我在同事里年纪最轻，刚一入社会就陷在这样一个圈子里，简直危险极了。正在坐着这一叶扁舟在惊涛骇浪里找不着方向的时候，眼前忽然现出一座灯塔——那就是我的中学校长夏瑞庚先生。

在父丧之后，家庭经济正陷绝境的当儿，我忽然得着这样好的职位，不单哥嫂欢喜，亲友羡慕，我自己不由得也有一点儿少年得意、踌躇满志的气概。有一天我去拜访夏瑞庚校长，他一见面就对我说："你不要觉着得意，其实现在正是你的危险关头！"随后他又劝我不要住进同事的宿舍，不要同流合污，应该在工作余暇多念些书，积蓄一些学费，准备考文科大学。这一次当头棒喝，使我又警觉起来。同事里边也有对我正言规劝的，同时又看见同科中有的同事公余在点读《说文》，这都在不同的角度上给我很大影响。就在那年秋天，我受同事马世诚的鼓励，同他一起报考了北京大学文科中国文学门。

我所以报考中国文学门，并不是因为夏校长夸奖我的文章像王临川，也不是因为我的国学根底好，不过因为大学预科和别的部门功课太繁重，不适合我半工半读的要求，并且那时中国文学门和西洋文学门只要英文、国文特别好的，不管是否预科毕业，就可拿同等学历的资格投考本科。我的国文虽然不特别好，可是直接进本科的引诱力却很大，这样我就贸然报了名。在考试的时候，除了别的功课以外,国文出了三道题:(一)九流皆六艺支与流裔论;(二)附辞会义务总纲领说;(三)尔雅以观于古说。事后知道这几个题目都是黄季刚(侃)先生出的。当时我不知怎样糊里糊涂地就完了卷,过两天发榜居然考中了第四名,从此便走进了半工半读的大学生活时代。

那时北京大学的校长是胡仁源,教授大都是保守分子,同学大多数是资产阶级或地主的子弟,念书的目的是想做官的多,想研究学术的少。直到1917年蔡元培先生做校长,请了许多新进教授,学校的风气才为之大变。我刚一进大学的时候,因为跳了两年预科,听见什么,都觉得闻所未闻,看见哪个同学,都觉得学问比我高。况且一个星期我至少得有三个半天到众议院去做事,又不熟悉大学的读书方法,只知道听讲,写笔记,而不知多念参考书。像这样,即使用功,又怎么能和其他同学比呢?学年考试的结果,平均虽然得到81分,可是因为缺席扣分太多,只剩下68分,列入丙等。黎元洪被督军团逼迫解散国会后,我失业了一年,但读书反倒专心多了。我在中国旧文学上的一点根柢就是在这一年内打下的。1918年春天,大病后又结了婚,后来由蔡璋援引再进临时参议院的速记科工作。一方面由于半工半读的分心,一方面受新旧思潮的波荡,直到1919年"五四"后,我在中国文学系毕业的时候,思想上虽然起了转变的萌芽,业务上却没有显著的进步。

在中国文学系的三年间,我的思想是懵懂的,做学问也漫无方向。第一学年时,对钱玄同先生的音韵学感兴趣,可是也没走对了路。那时要找陈澧的《切韵考》,都不知道到琉璃厂买一部《东塾丛书》。白天到图书馆用铅笔抄几页,晚上回家再用墨笔誊清,到如今我还保存那本没完成的愚蠢抄件!第二学年时,用功的重心放在刘师培先生的中古文学和中古文学史上面。在讲堂把他的"口义"用速记记录,回家又逐字逐句地翻译成文言。现在我虽然保留一部最完整的笔记,预备编成《左盦全集》所没收入的《左盦文论》四卷,可是在当年真不知道花了多少冤枉工夫。第三学年是我思想转变的开始。转变的主要动因,是《新青年》和"蔡元培先生给林纾的信"对我起了很大的作用。我的思想完全以蔡先生的思想自由和学术自由做骨干。在解放前的二十多年里,我一直拿他那博大而坚贞的精神做我理想的人格。我赞成他的"兼容并包"的态度;我崇拜他的"临大节而不可夺"的气节;我服膺他那"富贵不能淫,贫贱不能移,威武不能屈"的精神!在他死后第二天我作了《博大和坚贞》一文来哀悼他,就是发挥这种思想。三十年来我所以能做到"大德不逾闲"的地步,完全靠这种"北大精神"的帮助!但是,我固然受了它的好处,同时也没能超出它作进一步的发展。那时我在行动上的具体表现,就是在中国文学系毕业后,又半工半读地转入了哲学系。

"五四"前后,我在思想上发生了很大的矛盾:学习的是旧文学,而又有对新知识的要求;吃的是安福系国会的饭,而又有浓厚的反政府的情绪。每逢从众议院回学校宿舍的时候,穿着一件华丽衣服都觉得惭愧,必须罩上一件蓝布大褂,才觉着还了我的学生本色。那时北大哲学系在思想上占全校的领导地位,我认为要解决我的思想矛盾,非进哲学系不可。对于当时的出版品,只要是"新"的,不问它属于哪党哪派的,都本着蔡先生"兼容并包"的态度尽量搜集。对于西洋哲学名著,只要先生介绍过的,就设法托日本的丸善书店代订。我从政府挣来的薪金,除维持家人和自己的生活外,大部分用在买书订报上面。"五四"后的两年,正是北大哲学系如日中天的时候。外来的杜威、罗素先后讲学;本校的胡适、梁漱溟分庭抗礼。两年间我在治学方法上颇受实验逻辑"思维术"的影响,在人生哲学上很被《东西文化及其哲学》所倾倒,对于形而上学和纯唯心论反倒不大感觉兴趣。

1921年夏,山东教育厅约请杜威、黄炎培、梁漱溟等到济南去讲学,梁先生约我去记录他的讲演。后来出版的《东西文化及其哲学》,就是根据我那次的记录由陈政整理成的。我应用速记术在学术上的贡献,除了前面所说的《左盦文论》外,还有这部《东西文化及其哲学》。

同一年的夏天,我接受了天津南开中学国文教员的聘书。这时安福国会已经闭会,生活费用没有来源,必须找个职业才能维持家用,所以就不能在北大哲学系第三学年继续求学了。我在南开中学共教两班国文,一班四年级,一班二年级;所用的教材完全改变了古文释义派"臣密言"、"臣亮言"的旧作风,加选了许多语体作品。就是所选的文言文,也注意到思想内容,例如黄梨洲的《原君》,邓牧《伯牙琴》里的《君道》、《臣道》等篇。那时南开教务课组织得很严密,教员在班上的言论行动,教务干事随时都会报告教务主任。我选了一篇李大钊的《今》,没过一个星期,教务主任就来检查我了。

直奉战争后,奉派所支持的徐世昌伪总统被推翻,黎元洪被直系军人拥戴,二次上台,召集民六被解散的旧国会。于是我又恢复了众议院秘书厅的速记技士职务。这次国会刚一开会,就引起民六"北京法统"和民八"广州法统"的纠纷,党派的争执比从前更厉害。不久,又闹出曹锟贿选总统的丑剧。这时我除去挣钱吃饭以外,实在痛苦万分。恰好董鲁安约我到京师公立第一中学教一班国文和修身,我想教书是我的正当职业,就答应了。鲁安在北京教育界是第一个教语体文的;修身一课也不"讲道德、说仁义",而是拿"社会学"及"社会问题"做课本。我接手之后,"萧规曹随",在当时就被认为是崭新的人物了。论薪水数目说,众议院的收入比一中多着六七倍,可是我的工作重心却在一中而不在众议院。后来一中发生换校长的风潮,继任校长仍旧挽留我教书兼任总务长。不久这位新校长又出国了,他委托的代理人被学生驱逐,风潮闹得不可开交。那时顾孟余担任北京教育会会长,他和学务局局长商量约我做代理校长,来平息风潮。我接任后的办法:第一,实行财政公开;第二,聘请好教员,但绝不任用私人;第三,聘请教育界名流讲演;第四,因为我当时还兼任众议院的职务,就把校长的全部薪水捐购新图书。这样做了一年,跟学生相处得很好,可是却因此遭受了校长私人的嫉妒。那位校长刚一回国,就叫学务局撤销了我的代理校长职务。我在三天之内办完了交代,并且登报声明:在我任内经手款项,保管的图书、仪器和其他校产完全交代清楚,同时就应西北大学的邀请,到西安去做国学专修科主任兼教授。我走了没几天,学生不满意那位校长,风潮再起。他的党羽怀疑我从中鼓动,给我扣上一顶"反帝国主义大同盟领袖"的帽子。假如我不去西安,或许真到卫戍司令部坐几天监牢呢。其实,在当时我真不配戴这顶荣誉的帽子,可是,到后来,这个给我扣帽子的校长却做了地地道道无耻下流的汉奸。

我初到西北大学教书的时候,刚 26 岁,学生有许多比我岁数大的,程度也很不齐。我所教的功课里面,有一门文字学,开始讲音韵的部分完全应用钱玄同先生的学说,可是自己心里发生了一大串的问题。又因为我在国会做过几年事,无形中受到听写各地方言的训练,从此就打下我后来研究语言学的基础。在西安住了一年,跟学生处得倒很好,但是在军阀混战的局面下,陇海路时常不通,不单外边的书报杂志看不见,有好几个月连家信都接不到,精神苦闷万分。到 1924 年夏天,我就脱离了西大,从风陵渡过河绕道太原才回到北京。假如我晚走一年,也许赶上刘镇华围城的厄运了!

离开西北大学之后,河南中州大学请我做中国文学系教授兼主任,我因为军阀混战的局面还没终止,决定辞谢,留在北京。那时奉皖两系联合把直系打垮,吴佩孚惨败,曹锟被囚在中南海的延庆楼。

段祺瑞被推为临时执政；孙中山改组国民党，实行联俄、联共、扶助农工三大政策，又北上和段联合。我当时认为国势或者有好转的希望；同时段祺瑞又召开各种会议，需要速记人材，有五个机关约我帮忙，于是我又整天忙得头昏眼花地吃起“旧锅粥”来了。谁知过了几个月，这班军阀还是换汤不换药地胡作非为，“三一八”首都革命，段祺瑞露出了狰狞的面目，惨杀了许多学生！我实在不能再在这种政府底下敷衍鬼混了。恰好厦门大学托林语堂邀请北京许多学者到厦大去讲学，于是我便追随鲁迅先生、沈兼士先生等到了厦门，起初很想暂时躲避北洋军阀黑暗势力的压迫，找一块清静的地方做学问，谁知道一到厦门，立刻发现那种气氛简直和我们所想的不对。不到一年我们大家就同时离开了。我到上海住了几个星期，马叙伦先生就约我到浙江省政府民政厅去服务。做了不到三个月，接到广州中山大学的聘书，于是又恢复了我的教书生活。从此之后，我就再没离开学术界。

我在中山大学中国语文系教书，所任的功课，大多数属于音韵学的范围。后来赵元任先生调查两广方言，我把积下来的疑问没日没夜地和他讨论了一个星期，这才把语音学打下了根基。前中央研究院历史语言研究所成立后，我又转到这个研究所做语言组的专任研究员，一待就是七年。

在研究所的七年里，业务的确有了发展，思想却非常停滞。在学术上，赵元任、陈寅恪、李方桂都给我很多启发；傅斯年对于我专业的成就也不能说没有帮助。七年间，我一共做了 4 部专书、14 篇论文（详目见《中国音韵学导论》附录），又调查了徽州 6 县 46 单位的方言，编好《汉魏六朝韵谱》和《经典释文》的反切长篇。同事们恭维我是多产的著者，其实，现在检讨起来，并没有什么特殊贡献。

1934 年秋天刘复病逝后，北京大学约我回母校服务。前三年还算由中央研究院借聘，从 1937 年就专任北大教职，中央研究院改为通讯研究员。中间除去旅美三年半外，直到现在没有离开过我的岗位。北京沦陷后，我感觉到环境的胁迫，决定赶快离开北京。承许多同事的帮忙，把我没完成的稿件和长编加速地赶完（详情见《七七事变后的北大残局》）。1937 年 10 月 14 日我就离开北京从香港绕道梧州到达长沙临时大学设在南岳的文学院。

到南岳后，南京已经沦陷了，学校又在筹备往昆明搬家。我把那学期的课程结束后，就从长沙坐火车到广州，再从香港搭船到海防，转滇越铁路直达昆明。到昆明那天是 1938 年 2 月 26 日。长沙临时大学迁到昆明后，改名为西南联合大学。因为校舍不够，文、法两学院一度搬到蒙自，后来又搬回昆明。在这种搬来搬去的情况下，经过一年，业务才渐渐就绪。在昆明的六年内，起初还是为教书、处理中国文学系系务和自己的研究工作忙，后来因为敌机轰炸的次数加多，校外人事关系复杂，一天从早忙到晚，仍旧做不了多少事。在业务一方面的成就除了在联大中国文学系和北大文科研究所培植出些个学生外，就是旅行大理三次，调查了十几种西南少数民族语言。

我第一次到大理主要的目的是为调查少数民族语言。我因为发现的活材料很多，就在大理师范住了三星期，在喜洲住了两星期，然后才回到昆明，路上过楚雄不远的地方，不幸被汽车撞伤，几乎丧命（详细经过看我所作的《苍洱之间》）。

第二次到大理是 1943 年 2 月。我这次的收获是得到了相当丰富的茶山、浪速、山头的语言材料。

第三次到大理是在 1944 年夏天。我的任务是编《大理方言志》，顺便得了许多民家话的材料。

我在昆明六年，从汪精卫的叛国艳电和蒋介石压迫新四军的事件发生后，对国事甚为悲观。中间曾为视察叙永分校到四川巡行一遭;又为国语推行委员会和中国语言学会开会到过两次重庆,眼见许多稗政和四大家族的贪婪,深恨国民党对不起人民。对于联大的学生,我却不论何党何派都一视同仁地爱护,有了错误当面诃责,有了困难也尽量帮助。因此学生送了我两个绰号,一个是“长官”,一个是“罗文直公”。“长官”的来源并不是骂我官僚作风,因为1939年一级的毕业生有大部分是我给介绍的职业。有些进步的学生我是掩护的,因此而不致被捕的大有人在。因此1944年5月8日在西南联大新校舍草坪上所开的文艺晚会,由我和闻一多的号召,竟到了3000多人。我在那天开会时所致的开幕词(见《中国人与中国文》第50~56页),现在检讨起来,始终没离开“五四”以来的自由主义作风,顶多希望作到调和、妥协的统一战线。

这几年里的经济生活是很困窘的。我的老婆带着两个小女孩留在北京尤其艰苦。在日本投降前两个月她曾经在被服厂做工,来维持母女三人最低的生活。但是我在南方除去薪水和稿费外,并没有接受一文不义之财;她在北京固穷也没求亲告友。当我的两个大孩子逃难到宝鸡时,来电告急。我不得已曾向出版社卖了三部稿子,得到几千元法币才把他们接到昆明。所幸我的稿子是两部游记(《蜀道难》、《苍洱之间》),一部《汉魏六朝专家文研究》,都和政治全不相干。

1944年夏天,北大蒋梦麟(孟邻)校长突然接到美国朴茂纳大学(Pomona College)请我去担任人文科学的访问教授。接到电报后,我曾经考虑了很久。当时反蒋的斗争已然尖锐化。一多、光旦等也劝我不要远离祖国。可是,我从中学时代就梦想出洋,因为经济压迫和家庭牵缠,直到45岁才得到这个机会,如何肯失掉呢! 所以我终于应聘了。那时想要得到官员护照,非得先到中央训练团受训不可。我宁可领普通护照坐三等舱,也不愿意受那种法西斯的训练。朴茂纳大学答应到达后再付旅费,我出国前,只得把存在昆明的书全部卖掉,换了一点外汇,才勉强成行。刚到美国,除去教六小时书外,全部时间都用在学习英文和了解美国人的风俗习惯方面。"客来而忙"是个小城,人口不过四千多,环境很优美。朴茂纳大学的前任校长晏文思,在岭南大学做过13年校长,对中国人感情很好。这个小城的居民也不像别的地方那样歧视黄脸人。我当时全工全读,忙得没有一会儿闲暇。我所以把Claremont译作"客来而忙",足以代表我那时生活情况的一斑。这个小大学有两件出名的事:一件是在学生里出了一个电影名星罗勃泰勒;一件是送了梅兰芳一个名誉博士。

我在"客来而忙"住了一年半,除去英文达到能听、能说、能写的程度以外,对于本行的学问很少进步。1946年在伯克利(Berkeley)加里福尼亚大学住了两个月,整天关在图书馆里,对于本行学问才开始作进一步的探讨。当年8月移教耶鲁大学,每周只担任四小时的研究讨论班,指导两个研究生作博士论文,其余的时间都在自己的办公室里工作。周围环绕着许多成名的老教授,他们那种自朝至暮、孜孜不倦的治学精神,对我起了很大的作用。1947年暑假又在安树镇密西根大学举办的语言研究所住了八个星期,会见了全美国的著名语言学者,并且选修了三种课程,对于美国语言学界的情形总算有了相当的认识。

在美三年半,听到闻一多被刺的消息,非常愤慨,激发了我热爱祖国的民族意识,于是毅然决然地在1948年7月3日离美返国。到达北京那天恰好是"八一九",就是伪金圆券发行和国民党特务包围北大的日子!一进都门就碰上这两件倒霉的事,感觉非常悲观。

回国后看见国民党的倒行逆施比在昆明、重庆所见所闻的更加深了千百倍,对于各方面的民主运动却也失掉了联系,不由得又回到"学术第一"的躲避现实的世界,把自己关闭在东斋的斗室和文科研究所的语音乐律实验室里,谢绝各方面的活动,除了广播一次"对于想到美国留学的人说几句话”外，也没发表任何言论或文字。起初只是整理12年来散在各地方的书籍稿件，直到北京围城的前一个星期，承查夷平同志帮忙，才把存在南京历史语言研究所的25大包重要书籍稿件都替我航运到京。还有一大部分时间消耗在筹备北大50周年校庆。到了12月16日，西郊已经解放，胡适已经走了三天，解放军的炮声已经清晰可闻的时候，我还为校史和已故教师遗著两种展览忙碌了两整天。校庆那天接到南京的电报要用飞机接一批人南下，我毫不犹豫地立刻谢绝了。

围城的50天内，我一心只想把未完成的著作赶成一两部，万一北京解放后，北大不能存在，研究工作不能继续，我也可以达到“殉校”、“殉学”的志愿。志向一定，炮声和冷弹都对我毫无影响。我居然在旧历戊子除夕，1949年1月28日，完成《语言与文化》初稿，重订《经典释文中的徐邈音》，并且在油灯底下把《恬庵五十自订年谱》写到16岁。

北京城内守军和平解除武装后的第四天，北大汪子嵩同志找我来，问我对于大学教育的意见，并且希望我能做一点领导青年的工作。我对他说：“我过去固然没有革命的成绩，同时也没有反革命的记录。我是一个做研究工作的人，过去怎样，现在和将来还希望怎样。我只希望有研究学术的自由。至于领导青年的事情，自己觉得有些过时了。”“五四”返校节那天，我坐在台下听别人演说；“五四”文艺晚会，我站在民主广场听着一位一位介绍新文艺理论，想起当年我和一多发起第一个“五四”文艺晚会的盛况来，觉得我现在落伍了！我应该努力学习，赶上大时代！5月5日和5月9日，听了两次周恩来同志的讲演，第一次他说：共产党人应该避免骄傲与急躁。第二次他颇推崇学术研究的地位。6月11日在北京市委举行的一次座谈上，彭真同志说：“凡是从事脑力劳动、依靠薪金生活的人都属于工人阶级,教育工作者也属于工人阶级。"这句话对我起了重大作用。我很高兴。因为我认识到我不是革命对象而是革命动力的一部分。从教授研究员联合会扩大为教职联,再进一步筹备北大工会和北京市教育工作者工会,我都做了积极分子之一。跟我一块儿参加筹备工作的许多青年同志都以行动影响了我。我从闭门研究变为接近群众。

谢谢群众的鼓励,又让我参加了北京市第一、二两届各界代表会议,中国人民政治协商会议第一届全体会议和亚洲澳洲工会代表会议:这一切更给了我从实际学习的机会。

1952 年春北京人民医院病榻

我怎样进的大学

小的时候跟着母亲到东城去探亲戚，路过马神庙，我扒着轿车上的玻璃窗往外瞧，看见路北一座府第的朱红大门里映衬着一段很好看的绿竹花障，好奇心驱策我问道：

“妈！这是什么地方？”

母亲说：

“这是从前的四公主府，后来改作大学堂。在里边念书的，有的是中过举人进士的，有的是做过大人老爷的。盼望你长大了也可以进这个门。”

自从懂得念书，就时常惦记着母亲那几句话，时常憧憬着一个未来的幻境。

1916年一个初夏的黄昏，骄阳的余威还在火炽着，路上的尘土干得像香灰一般，呛得人透不过气来，街头的几个野狗热得搭拉着舌头流涎喘气，偶尔传来一阵卖酸梅汤的清脆的冰盏声，也还不能把人镇得清凉一会儿。几个顽皮的中学生放学出来，跳跳蹦蹦、说说笑笑地走着，一个个满头汗津津的，脸上红得像刚开的玫瑰花，可是这暑热的火焰丝毫灼不着这些青年们充沛的活力。这时候我们都快毕业了。我一边儿跟同学们说笑，一边儿在想不久怎样实现儿时由母亲所启示的绮梦，无穷的希望摆在眼前，郁蒸的炎夏立刻就变成和煦的阳春了。抽冷子家里的一个老妈子拦住我喊道：

“二少爷！还不快点儿回家？老爷病得很厉害！”

这一嗓子简直像晴天霹雳般的把我吓呆了，赶紧三步并作两步地跑回家去，看见爸爸躺在床上，脸上烧得像火炭一样，并且浮肿起来，神志已经不大清醒了。一个 17 岁的孩子哪里禁得住这么大刺激！急得眼泪在眼圈儿里乱转，一点主意没有，只得一边儿给哥哥打电话，一边儿赶紧请医生。

第一次请来的是一个西医，他诊断后说：

“你父亲得的这种病叫血蛇瘟，俗名大头瘟或丹毒，死亡率虽不很高，却也相当的危险。治疗的方法得要内外并进，外敷药和内服药都得用。”

我跟着他去取药，他又翻出内科诊断学来给我看，他的处方和治法都算按部就班的，照我的意思就该信任他到底。可是一个孩子怎能当得了家？哥哥是个没准主意的，庶母和堂兄被传统的思想笼罩着，都觉着西药只能治外科，时令瘟疫还得请教中医，“胳臂扭不过大腿来”，到底儿还是依着他们了。

三天后，请来一个很有名的大夫。他穿着蓝亮纱袍子、青实纱马褂，脚下用双梁儿福字履，迈着方步，一步三摇地扭进来，把镶在小帽中间的一块桃红璧玺都摆得闪烁放光，等到“望、闻、问、切”后，不慌不忙地理着乌黑的八字须，点头咂嘴地说：

“府上老爷的贵恙俗名叫痄腮，照医书上说应该叫做瘟毒发颐。不要紧，吃两剂药就好了。诸位尽管万安！”

“脸上的浮肿，怎样才能消呢？”我问。

“这是上焦火盛，外感时邪，吃药后消解一下，内热退尽，外面的浮肿自然会消的。”他很有把握地回答。

“病人大便秘结已经快五天了，请先生给想想法子。”我又说。

“好的！先吃这一剂药往下行一行看。万一不见效，兄弟还略通西医，再服一点儿特效的西洋泻药，自然就没妨碍了。”他仍然满口地应承着。

这样挨延了三四天，不单浮肿未消，病没有起色，连大便秘结的毛病都没减除。到束手无策的当儿，他才拿出一包泻盐来。我知道这位大夫已然技穷，毅然决然地主张再把那位西医请回来。这样一折腾，病人当然很吃亏。那位西医深感病家拿不定主意，中西杂投的难办，颇有“敬谢不敏”的神气，经我再三哀告，他才答应竭力挽救。哪知再服西药后，刚有一点儿通便的希望，我那位自作聪明的堂兄恐怕病人支持几天中气不足，异想天开地烧了一口鸦片烟给他老人家吸。这样一来把毒气完全锁住，大便照常秘结，头部肿得更加厉害，到阴历丙辰四月二十那一天我就永抱终天之恨了！

母亲故去的那一年，我刚 14 岁。当她病重的时候，看见她不能躺下睡觉，看见她喘得上气不接下气，看见她咯血，我就自恨没有医学常识，找不出“病灶”所在，不知道对症下药的治疗法。才过了四年，又不幸守了九天父亲的病。在这九天里我忽略了晨昏，忘却了饥渴，整个的精神都集注在病人身上，心里老像有一块大石头压着似的，病轻一点儿它就挪挪窝儿让我喘一口气，病重一点儿就把我压得闭闷要死，可是，对于医理上的愚昧还跟四年前一样。假使我的医学常识进步一点儿，怎能听凭家里人的中西杂投？怎能让顶亲爱的父亲受庸医的摆布？

父亲的丧事，仗着哥哥东挪西借地勉强办完了。我们不敢铺张，但也没有委曲了父亲 52 岁艰苦自振的生活。那时我只是一个未成丁、不成器的孩子，大责任都加在哥哥的肩膀上。事情办完，我们所分得的遗产只是一身债，父亲辛勤挣来的一些动产和不动产都给庶母抓在手里去了。

中学的毕业考试离父亲死后只有两星期光景。在那当儿，我因为悲闷郁积的结果,在脖颈后面生了一个大痱子,俗名叫做“砍头疮”,据说溃烂化脓以后,要是闹得厉害的话,打个嚏喷脑袋就会掉下来。顾名思义虽然惴惴自危,可是四年的光阴怎肯废于一旦?只得头上缠着绷带,咬牙忍痛地去应付考试。幸而在校的时候还懂得用功,知道我的身世的老师们都十分同情我。勉勉强强渡过这个难关,疮也渐渐平复,还算没有真个“砍头”。不过,“毕业等于失业”,在我这新近丧父的孩子格外感觉莫大的威胁!究竟升学?找事?让我踌躇得连夜失眠,愁眉不展。

哥哥是个小军官,饷糈所入只够自赡妻子,哪有余力供给我升学?他虽然真挚地愿意帮助我,我怎忍颟顸地累赘他?即或要升学也只能选择那有膏火、有饭吃,不需要家庭供给的学校。一想起马神庙的朱红大门和绿竹花障来,不由得跑到父亲的新坟上对着死去的父母痛哭一场!

父亲弃养的前一年,北平学务局举行过一次中学观摩会考,据说考在前三名的可以派送出洋。因为这个希望惹起我很大的妄想,发榜以后就欢天喜地地跑去告诉父亲说:

“爸爸!我这次考了个甲等第三,大家都恭喜我毕业后可以出洋呢!”

父亲慢吞吞地叹口气道:

“孩子,我哪里能不愿意后辈发达呢!不过,我已经过五十了,这么大的家庭负担已经压得我够疲倦的了。出洋虽好,只是远水解不了近渴,怕是我支持不下去了!”

我沉默了一会儿,答不出话来。父亲接着说:

“你不要失望!一个人只要有志向,随时随地都有上进的机会。我愿意你先找个事做,等到可以自立,再继续求学也还不晚。俗语常说‘天助自助者’,古来有些能够成就的人往往不是承袭父兄余荫长大的。”

当时我怕惹老父伤心也就不敢再谈下去了。过不多久,袁世凯为羁縻蔡松坡起见,曾经创办了一个经界局,想在短期里训练出一批测量人员,好去清丈全国没有升科的黑地。父亲听说毕业后出路还不坏,就督促我去投考。那一次投考的人很多,连我们中学里一位数学教员也跟我同场做考生。录取以后,我还迷恋着出洋的幻想,不甘心去做一个经界局员,便写了一封信给哥哥,表明我的志愿,求他在父亲面前给我讲情。哥哥回了我一封很恳切热诚的信,一口答应帮助我,勉励我继续求学。经他的解劝父亲也打消原意了。

不久,父亲又叫我投考速记传习所。中国速记学是龙溪蔡毅若(锡勇)老先生发明的。他采取美国毕德曼(Pitman)的方式,融会中国的等韵系统,用弧矢圈点等符号错综配合,创造了 22 个声符,32 个韵符。前清末年召集资政院,需用记录人材,那时蔡老先生已经去世了,他的儿子蔡子英(璋)先生就奉命到北平组织速记传习所,并办理资政院的记录事务。由资政院递变到 1913 年的参众两院,所有记录人员没有不出自蔡氏之门的,到我学习的时候已经是第六班了。因为是夜班,只有六个月毕业,不至于妨碍我的中学功课,所以我也乐得多学一种技术。不过父亲仍然希望我靠它找到一个职业,我却只想拿它当做升学后记录讲义的工具。没想到父亲死后,我痴心妄想的灿烂的幻梦整个的惊醒了!他老人家勉强我学得的一技之长,竟然会给他这孤苦无依的孩子做了一生中一张很好的梯子!

洪宪帝制失败,袁世凯急死了。黎宋卿[黎元洪]继任总统,恢复国会,汤济武[汤化龙]复任众议院议长,刘放园组织秘书厅,蔡子英仍任速记科科长。这时候我正关在家里忙得连报纸都没功夫看地埋头预备应考北平高等师范和天津陆军军医学校的功课。忽然有一天,哥哥满头大汗地跑回来,拿着一张当天的报纸给我看:

“你瞧！这是众议院秘书厅的名单，你们蔡老师做了秘书兼科长了。你何妨找找他去呢？”

我很踌躇地说：

“怪难为情的！毕业一年多了，连一封信都没通过。怎好贸然去找他？”

“可是……嗳！”

哥哥吞吞吐吐地把话又咽回去了。我很了解他的苦衷，我知道我和他共同负着还债的责任，我感念他一向对我的热诚，我明白他目前对我希望的迫切，我委实地鼓不起勇气，想不出法子来拒绝他的提议。可是叫一个初出茅庐、生性腼腆的孩子去见官，岂不是一个大难题？

车子雇在门口儿等着，只得硬着头皮跳上去。到了蔡家恰好主人不在家，像奉了大赦一般的留了个名片就跑回家来。没想到蔡先生看见名片居然想起那个一分钟能记140字的学生来了，他马上写信约我面谈。接到信后我又去看他。他很和蔼地和我对答着：

“一年多没看见你了，你毕业后做什么来着？”

“我继续在中学念书。”

“现在毕业了没有？”

“已经毕业了。”

“你打算做事不？”

“本打算考大学或盼望学务局保送出洋的。现在家父弃养，家庭环境骤变，能有个适当的事做也好。”

“那么，我想约你到众议院秘书厅去帮忙，你肯吗？”

“先生如肯提拔，我是很感谢的。”

这样三言两语事情就成功了，跟着发下委任状来，官衔是众议院秘书厅技士兼宪法会议秘书，从此就穿上马褂，挂起徽章，夹着皮包，做起小官儿来了。

刚进众议院,月薪是80元,若拿物价指数计算,比我现在阔得多了。每周的工作只是出席大会三次,每次两个人一班,共同记录30分钟,每班的稿子总得花四五倍的时间才翻译得出来。乍一进议场,看见济济一堂的五百“罗汉”,听着南腔北调的各地方言,脑子里新装进“赞成”、“反对”、“弹劾”、“建议”、“表决”、“通过”、“三读”、“审查”、“临时”、“动议”、“讨论终局”……等等的名词,简直有点儿莫名其妙,过了两个星期也就慢慢地习惯下来了。后来我对于方言学的兴趣和“民次初步”的训练都是这时候不知不觉地在下意识里潜伏下了萌芽。

同事的一班少年,年纪小,收入多,多少都沾染点儿纨袴气息。工作余暇,耳朵里灌满了四头、同花、三番、满贯、素娟、翠喜、文弟、香妃。讲究起吃来,你说瑞记的叉烧宣腿和红烧羊肚菌做得好,他说致美斋的醋浇半片比酱汁中段味儿鲜,吃腻了酒席时常还尝尝全聚德烤鸭子或撷英铁扒鱼的特别滋味。若是单单喜欢到戏馆子捧捧刘喜奎、张小仙,逛游艺园给良小楼、陈来喜“戳几个火儿”,在同辈里还得算是道学先生呢。穿得朴素一点大家就骂你是阿木林,在青缎子小坎肩儿上排着水钻的纽扣却没人嫌你像戏子。脱了寒羊若是不换灰鼠,就得像没到数九老早穿上狐皮一般的被人讥笑。一个刚刚跳进社会的孩子这样日积月累地耳濡目染着,好像独自驾着小船儿糊里糊涂地在惊涛骇浪里行驶一样。正在要触礁的当儿,幸亏一个管理灯塔的老人把那盏明灯对我照得亮亮的,才算没翻下去!

我的中学校长夏筱琅先生,名叫瑞庚,云南昆明人,是两榜出身,因为字写得坏,没能点上翰林,所以在科甲班里有“丑字夏筱琅”的绰号。他生得身材魁梧,透着有点儿凶相,可是在严肃的外貌里却蕴藏着恺悌的内心。对于学生管得虽严,爱得也切,清寒子弟尤其得到他好多慈惠,我是他特别垂青的学生,四年中间只有一次因为在休息室大声唱二簧受过他的申斥,此外并没有挨过骂。在我进国会以后,有一天他特别派人把我找到学校里,一见面就问答起来:

“你近来忙不忙?还有工夫念书吗?”

“忙倒不太忙,只是刚一到差,诸事还没就绪,所以眼下还没工夫念书。”

“咱们学校里总算有几个好学生,可惜受家境的限制大部分不能升学,你就是其中的一个。你不要因为有个小差事就自己满足,照我看这是你的厄运,不是你的幸运,稍一不慎就会随波逐流地坠落下去。”

“先生的教训我一辈子不会忘记的。不过我的身世先生完全清楚,照我的环境看,您觉得我现在的出处进退究竟应该怎样好?”

“一个人应该善于利用自己的机会。你现在所做的事,收入多,工作轻,不善于利用它,就会饱暖生欲荒嬉废学;善于利用它,也可以把握时间,半工半读。这样一来,不单能够继续念书,连无味的酒食征逐都可以避免了。”

“假如我能够升学,先生看投考哪个学校好?”

“以你的才性论,我看还是投考北京大学文科国文门合适。你的文章有点儿像王临川,升学后可以用心揣摩一下。”

经过这一番训诲和鼓励,那个马神庙朱红大门里的绿竹花障又在我心里隐约出现了。于是我才下了投考北京大学的决心。可是直到现在我还不知道我的文章哪点儿像王临川呢。

夏先生是1918年在北平故去的。在他死后20年我避地到昆明来,一听见丢掉韵尾鼻音的昆明话,想起当年他把校役王宽喊作“蛙夸”的腔调,不由得追念起这盏在我的生命海里的指路明灯来了。

1916年蔡孑民先生没到北京大学以前,文科国文门和英文门有一个特例:凡是国文或英文特别优良的可以不经预科的阶段直接投考本科。那时候我的国文程度并不出色,不过,预科必修学程多,时间比较呆板,对于我半工半读的学生不大适宜;本科的学程有选择的余地,伸缩性较大,时间支配得当就不至于旷课太多。为迁就自己的缺陷,我就不嫌躐等地投考本科了。我记得那一次的英文题是 *The Seaside Holiday*,国文题有"尔雅以观于古说"、"九流皆六艺支与流裔论"、"附辞会义务总纲领说"等七八道,投考国文门的至少得做三题才算完卷。幸亏有几个题还把握得住,总算勉强终场了。邻座有一位投考法科的,不知道"附辞会义,务总纲领"两句出在刘勰《文心雕龙》的《附会》篇,硬把上句末尾的"义"跟下句起头见的"务"字接搭起来,权利义务的扯了一大阵。到发榜时,我的名字徼倖还没跟他同落孙山。

自从入了大学,我的生活才整个的得到一个转捩。虽然躐等而进耽误了许多基本的训练,虽然兼任技士消耗了许多有用的脑筋,虽然一曝十寒旷废了许多宝贵的光阴,可是我无时无地不想在缺陷中努力!我生平最服膺《周易》"既济"之后终之以"未济"的道理,我认为宇宙如果可以圆满具足,进化且将停止,宇宙所以有进化,正因为它有缺陷,不满足。从缺陷求完全,从不满求圆满,然后才会有"天行健,君子以自强不息"的人生观。所以我不诅咒我的坎坷,我倒讴歌我的坎坷;我不因为不如人而自馁,我反因为不如人而自励。惟其这样,生命才永远是动的,不是呆的;是活的,不是死的。

在我进学校办注册手续那天,跨进了马神庙那座朱红大门,便在那一段绿竹花障底下徘徊了许久,儿时的绮梦果然实现了,可是,引起我的企图的母亲呢?替我买梯子的父亲呢?

1942 年 8 月 9 日初稿,27 日重订,昆明。

(原刊《中国青年》第 6 期,1942 年,署名罗莘田)

七七事变后的北大残局

当七七事变发生时蒋校长梦麟正在南方，法学院院长周枚荪(炳琳)已经改任教育部次长。那时北大重要负责人留在北平的只有文学院院长胡适之先生(他6月22日刚从南京回来)、理学院院长饶树人(毓泰)、秘书长郑毅生(天挺)和教务长樊逵羽(际昌)。

事变发生的第二天，我到米粮库4号去看胡先生。在他那里遇见了徐森玉(鸿宝)、张奚若、陈之迈、张佛泉、沈仲章五位。大家询问胡先生对于时局的意见，他当时以为卢沟桥只是局部事件，或者不至于扩大。他原定8日下午6时赴南京开会。正在我们坐着的当儿，中国旅行社来电话说津浦通车仍旧照常开行。于是胡先生便照他预定的时间离开了北平。那天晚上杨今甫(振声)本来预备在他的新居——旧那王府——约我们几个朋友吃饭，临时因为同和居不肯出来“打发”，于是他也把我们“打发”了！那时今甫正和沈从文专心编辑中小学校教科书，还没正式加入北大。可是他不久离平赴京，对于后来长沙临时大学的成立尽了很大的力量。

当时各院系的秩序还没完全被卢沟桥的炮火轰散。举几件小事来说：那一年北大和清华联合招生，7月10日我和两校考试委员会的负责人，从上午8时到下午7时半在红楼地下室监印了新生试题12000份；13日接着又监印北大研究院的试题，并且评阅文科研究所研究生高庆赐的初试卷。16日中国文学系的新旧助教办交待，我还给新聘的助教吴晓铃、杨佩铭规定了约法十二章。19日又和魏建功、唐立庵(兰)、卢吉忱(逮曾)、李晓宇(续祖),在文科研究所会商北大所藏甲骨卜辞付印事。其他各院系和行政部分也都照常进行着。

从7月15日到月底教职员一共在松公府大厅(现在的孑民纪念堂)集了三次会:第一次是15日下午4时,议决通电表明态度,公推我和建功草拟电稿。第二次是20日下午6时,公推钱端升、曾昭抡和我起草宣言,大意约分三点:(一)申述我国国民素爱和平的本性,(二)指出现在的情形,(三)预测将来的责任。陈援安先生(垣)并提议多发表在国际间有利于我们的新闻。于是又公推张子缨(忠绂)、叶公超、钱端升联络各方面,组织对外宣传团体。那晚一直延到9时才散会。在我们开会的期间,四郊的炮声一个劲儿地隆隆响着!第三次是31日下午3时,那时北平沦陷已经三天了。大家在凄凉惨痛的氛围中仍旧主张镇静应变,共维残局。

但是自从“七二九”以后大家的精神实在已经逐渐涣散了。城陷的那天,逵羽就避入了德国医院。上午10时我到第二院巡视只碰见了郑毅生、章矛尘(廷谦)、梁实秋和潘光旦。11时到第一院,听说卢吉忱曾经来过一会儿,后来连工友的影儿都不见了。到了8月7日平津试行通车,海道可航,于是逵羽便首先离开了北平。第二天河边率日军入城,分驻天坛、旃坛寺和铁狮子胡同等处,人心更加浮动。8月9日毅生、树人、公超、端升和我在欧美同学会晤谈,一部分同人便主张早离危城。于是11日清晨公超、树人、实秋和姚从吾就陪同胡适之太太离平赴津。在张皇失措中从吾还给胡太太丢了一只箱子。

同人既然纷纷南下,北大的重担几乎完全压在毅生一人的肩头。还没走的同人更觉得常常交换意见共撑残局的必要。我自己曾经参加过的聚会一共有三次:

8月13日上午9时由我约集马幼渔[马裕藻]先生、孟心史[孟森]先生、汤锡予(用彤)、邱大年(椿)、毛子水、陈雪屏、魏建功、李晓宇、卢吉忱等在第二院校长室商量怎样维持校务。结果仍决定于未离平以前协助毅生共同支撑,低薪职员暂发维持费30元。

9月13日毅生、雪屏、大年和赵廉澄(迺抟)借灵境7号林宅约幼渔、心史、锡予、子水、建功、冯汉叔(祖荀)、谢季骅(家荣)、罗膺中(庸)、刘云浦和我聚餐,并商讨最近学校发生的事情。在这次聚会以前有几件值得记的事:自从北平陷落以后市内报纸完全登载日人所办同盟社的消息。市民只赖着无线电和英文《北平时事日报》(*Peiping Chronicle*)稍微窥察一点儿真实战况。8月24日《时事日报》被封,消息更加闭塞。我们除去从唧唧啦啦被搅乱的电波里偷听一点南京的广播,几乎完全和自由中国隔绝了!8月25日日本宪兵四人到第二院校长室检查,由毅生独自支应,后来周作人闻讯赶到,用日语和日宪兵驳辩,那时他还站在北大同人的立场说话。过了两天日人又到图书馆索取三多时中俄画界地图并且请孟心史先生给他们解释。这时的情势已经越逼越紧了。8月25日汉奸所组织的地方维持会约各校负责人谈话,北大派顾亚德参加。27日又函约各校负责人在第二天下午到南海丰泽园会商保管办法。经同人商定派包尹辅参加。并且校方自动先入保管状态,每部分各留一二人负责。30日尹辅报告参加地方维持会谈话情形。该会决定先请各校将保管各项加封,然后再由该会派人查核。9月3日日军进驻第一院和灰楼新宿舍。据最后和红楼告别的吴晓铃报告,中国文学系门外的标志是"𠃊小队附属将校室しょうこうしつ";文学院院长室门外的标志是"南队长室たいちようしつ"。他对于自己的岗位总算恪守到最后一刹那了!

在那一天建功突然接到地方维持会文化组的通知约他到丰泽园开会,他为避免纠缠,曾经到我家避了两天。到9月9日建功得到长沙临时大学就要成立的消息。同时蒋校长也有电报来，对于结束北平残局的办法有所指示。这些重要的消息我们都在13日的聚餐会里交互报告了。那天到会的14个人里廉澄是8月30日才从上海回来的，他对于"八一三"前后的情形，叙述颇详。

9月23日留平同人在王府井大街承华园聚餐，约略交换近日所得消息。

9月29日上午再集会于灵境7号林宅，参加者10人，对于沈肃文信中传来的结束办法有所讨论，公推建功、膺中用留平全体同人口气函蒋校长陈述平方情况，结尾有"总期四十年辛苦经营之学校，不致成为无人顾视之堕甑；三十余坐幽待旦之同人，不致终虚卫校存学之初愿。至于私人餔啜，当此之际，非所敢闻"等语。在我们这次聚会的前两天，毅生突然接到胡先生9月9日从九江轮船中所发一封署名"臧晖"的信，这的确给我们大家打了不少的气。原信照片已在校史部分展览，我现在还愿在这儿节录下来：

> 久不通问，时切遐思，此虽套语，今日用之，最切当也。弟前夜与孟（蒋孟邻校长）、枚（周枚荪）诸公分别，携大儿子西行，明日可到汉口……弟与端（钱端升）、缨（张子缨）两弟拟自汉南行，到港搭船，往国外经营商业，明知时势不利，姑尽人事而已。……台君（台静农）见访，知兄与莘（罗常培）、建（魏建功）诸公皆决心居留，此是最可佩服之事。鄙意以为诸兄定能在此时期埋头著述，完成年来未能完成之著作。人生最不易得的是闲暇，更不易得的是患难——今诸兄兼有此两难，此真千载一时，不可不充分利用，用作学术上的埋头闭户著作。弟常与诸兄说及，羡慕陈仲子匍匐食残李时多暇可以著述；及其脱离苦厄，反不能安心著作，深以为不如前者苦中之乐也。弟自愧不能有诸兄的清福，故半途出家，暂做买卖人，谋蝇头之利，定为诸兄所笑。然寒门

人口众多,皆沦于困苦,亦实不忍坐视其冻馁,故不能不为一家糊口之计也。弟唯一希望诸兄能忍痛维持松公府内的故纸堆,维持一点研究工作。将来居者之成绩,必远过于行者,可断言也。弟与孟兄已托兴业兄(浙江兴业银行)为诸兄留一方之地,以后当继续如此办理。船中无事,早起草此,问讯诸兄安好,并告行,不尽所欲言,伏维鉴察。弟臧晖敬上。

这封信使同人都振奋起来,在幽居沉闷的当儿,得到无限安慰和鼓励!

10月8日中午同人又在锡拉胡同景福阁集会,参加者28人,对于致蒋校长信自由签名者20人,由孟心史先生和董康领衔。其余的除刘志扬、何作霖早退外,幼渔先生、毅生、矛尘、吉忱、周作人和徐祖正都没有签名。

10月28日下午4时在灵境7号林宅开茶话会。这时长沙临大的消息渐渐明朗起来。在这次聚会以前10月18日裘开明从长沙回到北平,告诉我们不少眼见的事实。同天又接到逵羽9月27日从香港所发的信,又过了四天他本人也到了天津。10月26日建功又得到吴俊升的促行电。这时日人的统制逐渐加强,学校一天比一天难维持,同人再待下去,难免拖泥带水。于是留平的36人除幼渔、心史、汉叔、缪金源、周作人、董康和徐祖正外都决定分批南下。这次开会后两天,从吾又从长沙来电催我和子水、锡予、建功、钱宾四(穆)、齐思和等快走。11月3日孟邻先生的陷电也到了,其中特别提明"国文、经济两系需人,盼莘、廉两兄即来,莘兄工作可与中研院合作"。于是同人遂陆续南下。最后在11月17日离开北平,21日同乘湖北轮从天津去香港的有我和毅生、雪屏、膺中、建功、大年、廉澄、王霖之(烈)、周濯生(作仁)和包尹辅诸人。北平沦陷后的北大残局就这样暂时结束了!

在这四个多月中间最值得佩服的是郑毅生。自从“七二九”以后北大三院两处的重责都丛集在他一个人的身上。他除去支应敌寇汉奸的压迫外还得筹划员工的生活、校产的保管和教授们的安全。别人都替他担心焦急，他却始终指挥若定，沉着应变。一班老朋友戏比他为诸葛武侯，他虽逊谢不遑，实际上绝不是过分的推崇。由“七二九”到10月18日他每天都到学校办公，并且绝不避地隐匿。到10月18日那天，地方维持会把保管北京大学的布告挂在第二院门口，他才和在平全体职员合摄一影，又在第二院门前地方维持会的布告底下单独拍了一张小照（见校史展览），以后就不再到校。可是他对于留平教授的集会每次都去参加（见前），对于校产的保管也组织得很严密。

留平的诸人中有一老一少最值得怀念：年老的是孟心史先生，年少的是缪金源同学。

心史先生从北平沦陷后便日夜忧思，晚间必听中央广播，白天还不辞劳苦地翻着字典看 *Peiping Chronicle*，他那时的心境在我所抄录的《孟心史先生的遗诗》（载《治史杂志》第二期，北大史学系在昆明所印行）里完全可以暴露出来。可是他在忧患中还没废弃研究，8月20日送给我一篇《海宁陈家》论文稿，我马上编入《国学季刊》第六卷第三号，24日就交给晓宇付印。现在那一期季刊虽然夭折，孟先生的手稿却幸而保存。我们这次把它影印，编入50周年纪念论文集里以纪念先生！他因困处危城，劳瘁忧煎，以致得了很重的胃病。经协和医生诊察，断定是胃癌，他自己还不相信（见《10月18日病中作七律三首》），后来经朋友婉劝终于11月4日进了协和医院。11月14日，我离平的前三天，到协和医院向先生辞行，他给我看他近作三首讽刺郑孝胥的诗，我当时就在病榻旁边把它们抄下来：

郑氏兄弟父子昨来寓拟寄二律

1937 年 11 月 11 日

七载参商迹两歧，合并仍恐见无期。兵间始识生离苦，病里曾裁死别诗。扫径开门惭废阁，挥毫落纸忆风仪。悬知二老兼尊幼，同迓高轩一过时。

宿瘤丑已取憎多，况踞胸中作臼窠。刚值乱离思节缩，竟缘危惙费搜罗。病才创见身先试，家纵全倾奈命何！为报故人消息恶，膏肓攻达窘医和。

枕上作有赠

1937 年 11 月 13 日

城郭人民旧乡国，令威归来一叹息。事变何须岁月深，潮流只觉年时激。天生磊落人中豪，意气上薄青云高。纲常大义一手绾，天地杀机只目蒿。乾旋坤转我何有，进退绰然仍敛手。天道难堪只侮亡，人生长策惟邱首。呜呼！郏鄏灵长鼎旋迁，宅京最久是幽燕，即论人海藏家世，规矩高曾越百年。君不见贵由赵孟何如贱，况有春秋夷夏辨！一世犹难与俗论，万流何况由天演。弃我去者锁国年中旧是非，逼我来者横流日后新知见。噫吁嘻！锁国原无大是非，横流自有真知见！

那天临别的时候，先生握着我的手说："这三首诗希望莘田兄带给南方的朋友们看看，以见我心境的一斑。我们这次分别恐怕就成永诀了！"我当时答道："望先生安心养病！最近的将来我们一定还会在我们心爱的北平共同治学的！"于是先生泣，我亦泣！这一段印象让我深刻记忆在脑子里永久不会忘掉。谁想这位“卅年襞积前朝史，天假成书意尚殷”的老少年，竟自赍志以殁，真个和我们永诀了呢？

金源耿介孤僻，落落寡合。但是从北平沦陷后，他却始终抱定“誓饿死不失节”的气骨。当我们南下时，他因体弱累重，事实上不能离开北平，于是1937年度一整年就隐居却聘，食贫自守，直到1938年秋天才到辅仁大学哲学系和司铎书院教几点钟书，月入130元，后来因发“非宗教”的言论得罪了天主教神父，第二年就没有续聘。他在战前，自奉相当丰厚，每食非鱼肉不饱，但在辅仁教书时因为入不敷出已经减到每天一粥一饭。离开辅仁，生活更加困难。他在1941年4月25日给建功和夏卓如[夏德义]的信片里说：“弟自离辅大后，生事良苦。岁杪又举1男(共5男1女)，牛乳竟月费二三十金。诸儿量甚宏，每日食十斤(玉米或小米一餐)。且全家长幼均多病……以贫困故，概不服药。老父因仰食者众，且季弟营小医院于沪，两年来亏耗血本万金，今年不复能相济。然誓饿死不失节！……”自此以后，他从每天一粥一饭减到每天两顿粥，到最困苦的时候，全家只落得日食一粥了！经这样冻馁折磨，便饿死了一个傲骨嶙峋、临大节而不可夺的朋友！过了两三个月他的夫人也因贫病交迫追随金源于泉下了！

我自己从七七事变后，悲愤中只好借辛勤工作来排遣愁烦，由7月16日起，每天除去为维持学校残局来开会和晚间听中央广播电台报告战况外，每天总花去5小时去写我的《临川音系》，直到9月25日才把前三章的全稿写定，第四章的表格完成，就在30日交给周殿福、谭志中、吴永祺三位分别赶抄，10月27日先把这一部分清稿托锡予带交傅孟真和赵元任。在这期间，工作虽然紧张，心境却异常难过！故都沦陷之后，是否还应该每天关在屋里埋头伏案地去做这种纯粹学术研究？这件事的是非功罪颇不容易回答。可是当时我在想,我既不能立刻投笔从戎,效命疆场;也没机会杀身成仁,以死报国,那么,与其成天的楚囚对泣,一筹莫展,何如努力从事自己未完成的工作,藉以镇压激昂慷慨的悲怀?假如能在危城中奋勉写成几本书,以无负国家若干年养士的厚惠,那么,就是敌人把刀放在我的脖子上,也会含笑而逝,自觉对得起自己,对得起学校,对得起国家!

9月25日那一天,忽然接到元任9月8日从长沙铁佛东街25号寄给我的一封信,信里完全用亲戚间问讯的口气,全篇不加标点符号。上款称"莘田二哥",和平常惯用的"迪呀莘田"迥然不同,下面署名"赵重远",也是由废弃已久的别号"宣重"引申出来的。他用隐语告诉我中央研究院迁湘后的近况和经费的情形,劝我立刻南下。末了儿又用反切语说"匣姥,照线,状齐去志,尚,帮合入没,匣合去快",影射着"沪战事尚不坏"六字。居然没被敌谍侦查追究,也可算是奇迹了。过了两天毅生又接到前面所引胡先生从九江轮中寄来的那封信。我自从接到赵、胡的两封信以后,好像注射了两针强心剂,越发地紧张工作起来,除去把临川方言的特别词汇和不规则的读音摘记出来以外,又和周祖谟、郁泰然合作,依照时地编订《汉魏六朝韵谱》,和周殿福、谭志中、吴晓铃、吴永祺合作分类重抄《经典释文》的卡片。到10月中我离开北平时,居然能把有关《经典释文》反切的材料交太平洋行(Pacific Storage and Packing Coorporation)运到青岛,再转香港。我真不能不感谢我这些患难相依的伙伴儿了!然而11年后我又回到北平,才知道泰然从昆明回来没几天就因癌症长逝,志中在敌伪盘踞的期间也因贫病交迫早已夭亡!永祺的下落不明,殿福又因不足自赡而改业!这都是很可痛惜的。我愿意拿我这些工作永远纪念着他们!

1948年12月9日,为北大50周年纪念作。

(原刊《北京大学50周年纪念特刊》,1948年12月)

在大时代中生长的北京大学

北大从诞生到现在的50年中可谓饱经忧患！她建立的那一年正赶上戊戌政变，前五年是甲午战争，后三年是义和团。辛亥革命时她刚刚23岁。民国以来，在国内则经过洪宪帝制、张勋复辟、军阀混战和日寇侵陵；在国际间则经历了两次世界大战。抗战八年间，北大转徙流离，自湘而滇，师生们受尽了艰辛，却始终没忘了蔡孑民先生倡导下的北大精神和马神庙汉花园、译学馆的旧日生活。胜利以后，这个忧患的余生回到故都，稍微喘过一口气儿来，原打算多少作些补充和复元的工夫，可是内战的烽火又完全粉碎了这种企图，让一班渴想北大发展的人从希望中感觉到失望！

从另一观点看，在过去50年间，不单中国的政治发生了空前的变动，就是世界的思潮也在奔腾澎湃地流向不同的出路。当北大建校时马克思的全部《资本论》刚刚发表了六年，而孙中山先生就在那一年首倡“三民主义”。过了四年克鲁泡特金的《互助论》出版了；再过五年甘地的《印度自治论》也出版了。最巧不过是在北大校史上最光荣一页的五四运动发生的那一年（1919），世界上的政治思潮也五光十色地放出了不同的光芒。举其重要的来说：那一年孙中山先生在上海发表《孙文学说》和《建国方略》，改中华革命党为中国国民党；第三国际开成立大会于莫斯科，而同时意大利的法西斯蒂也组织就绪。此后四年苏联正式成立，又四年而中国国民党北伐成功。照历史的推演来看，这一段的思想错综是第一次世界大战的结果，也是第二次世界大战的起因。第二次大战后哲学思想的自由发展远不及第一次大战后那样热闹，可是三年来世界局面的不安，中国内战的扰攘，实际上还是两种理想的冲突。北大过去的50年就正是在这世界思想纷歧的情境下生长的。

在这艰辛忧患的环境中又遭逢着思想纷歧的现象，北大应该怎样自处呢？从史实上看，已往的50年间大致经过了四次演变：

从戊戌到清末，大学刚在草创时期，教员和学生对于大学的观念，并没超过“翰林院”或“进士馆”。这期间的学生后来虽然也有不少变成学术领袖或革命先进的，可是大多数却拿着丰盛的膏火，沿用“大人”或“老爷”的称呼，把学校当做了仕进的阶梯。民国以来，“虽逐渐演变，而官僚习气不能洗尽。学生对于专任教员不甚欢迎，较为认真的且被反对。对于行政司法界官吏兼任的特别欢迎，虽时时请假，年年发旧讲义，也不讨厌。因有此师生关系，毕业后可为奥援。所以学生于讲堂上领受讲义及当学期学年考试时要求题目范围特别预备外，对于学术并没何等兴会。讲堂以外，又没有高尚的娱乐与自动的组织，遂不得不于学校以外，竞为不正当的消遣。”（语见蔡孑民先生《我在教育界的经验》）他们对于国内的政治情形和世界学术潮流大半是茫昧的。这是北大生长的第一个阶段。

1917年蔡孑民先生长校以后，首先揭破的就是“大学生当以研究学术为天职，不当以大学为升官发财的阶梯”。他认真想把北大办成一个近代的大学，以提起学生研究学问的兴会。当时学校的组织尽量发挥民治精神。“对于各家学说，依各国大学通例，循思想自由原则兼容并包。无论何种学派，苟其言之成理，持之有故，尚不达自然淘汰之运命，即使彼此相反，也听他们自由发展。”（语见前引文）这种态度正和第一次大战后的世界潮流相配合。当时国内的政治情形黑暗已极,而北大却能在蔡先生领导之下奠定了自由主义的学风。当时虽然不断地和恶势力奋斗,可是这种学风并没受了实际政治的摧残。从此以后北大乃更形成其"大"。这是她生长的第二个阶段。

从北伐成功以后,前一时期还在流行的许多学说,有些已经自生自灭地渐渐被淘汰了。然而北大却还始终维持自由主义的学风,并没受一党一派的统制。在国民党刚统一的时候,有一派人很想利用政治势力把北大吞并了。结果由于北大师生的共同奋斗,这个自由主义的壁垒幸而没被他们攻破,遂了他们"包而不办"的志愿。在抗战八年间,北大流亡滇南和清华、南开组成西南联合大学。三校同人本着互让互谅的精神共体时艰,开诚合作,一方面拥护政府抗战到底,信念决不动摇,一方面仍旧贯彻自由主义的学风,没受"党化教育"的波及。当时想得联大而甘心的,曾把它比作第二次大战前半的列宁格勒。无论如何,联大最后挨到胜利的来临,三校仍然回到马神庙、清华园和八里台恢复了各自的阵地。北大虽在艰难困苦、颠沛流离中,却始终没改变了学风,丧失了自由。这是她生长的第三个阶段。

胜利后的三年多,北大受时局的影响,虽然没能像理想的发展,专从思想自由来讲,却勉强算是五四运动后的第二次曙光。教职员学生主办或撰稿的刊物,在这纸张昂贵、印刷困难的现状之下,仍然像雨后春笋般地生长着。他们的思想和主张不尽相同,可是都能并行不悖地各自发抒所见:这正是蔡先生所倡导的北大学风,30年来一贯的自由空气。也就是北大生长的第四个阶段。

假如有人问我,这50年来北大最大的成功是什么,我毫不犹豫地回答:就是自由主义的学风。在这50年间政治是动荡的,思想是纷歧的,翻开历史来看,它的确是空前的大时代。大学是思想的领导者,在这大时代中,她惟一的态度只有不管政治的压迫,任着各派思想自由发展。至于实际的政治如何演变那另外是一个问题，不可和研究真理的大学教育混为一谈。

假如再有人问我“自由”的定义是什么？我愿意还引蔡先生一句话作本文的结束：“自由者，富贵不能淫，贫贱不能移，威武不能屈，是也；古盖谓之义！”（见1912年教育部所定《公民教育纲领》）

为北大50周年纪念作，1948.12.14

我是如何走上研究语言学之路的？

编者按：本文是莘田先生于1954年2月20日下午在语言研究所（当时所址在东城太平胡同3号）给青年研究人员作的报告。语言研究所成立初期，陆续有青年研究人员参加工作，大家都很愿意知道莘田先生的治学经过和方法。先生应同志们的要求，作了这一次报告。由于时间很短，先生只谈了1934年以前研究汉语音韵、汉语方音的经过，而且也只谈到很少几种著作。先生作报告时态度非常谦虚，对青年寄予很大的希望，勉励青年人努力学习，为社会主义革命和社会主义建设而工作。我们这些亲身受过先生教诲的人今天重温这个报告，对每句话都感到特别亲切，好像先生就在我们面前和我们讲话，不禁使我们又回忆起先生的面貌和声音，倍增对先生的怀念。报告是王辅世同志根据记录整理的，记得不全，只是先生报告的大意。

我半生没有什么成就，即使说有一些成就，也是微不足道的。不过，我觉得半生以来我的治学精神，有可供青年同志学习的地方。我心里常有几个字，就是“在缺陷中努力”。我总是感到知识不够，不如别人，因此要求自己要加倍努力。另外，我有一股子知其不可而为之的劲儿，明明知道自己的力量不够做某一件事，但勇于担负起做那件事的责任，不怕困难，不怕辛苦。我总觉得人人都可以做自己的老师。如果说我有什么长处,这就是我的一点长处。

我也有不可学习的一面,这就是我没有把力量放在革命事业上。在我做学问的时期,正是中国反帝、反封建的大革命时期。我做研究工作,没有跟革命配合,而是努力争个人的名利;没有发扬革命英雄主义,而是发展了个人英雄主义。希望大家不要学我,应当把研究工作跟革命事业结合起来,为社会主义革命和建设贡献力量。

下面我谈一谈我是怎么走上研究语言学这条路的。

一、根基薄弱　我家不是地主、资本家或官僚家庭,而是一个没落的封建家庭。我的父兄都不是读书人。我小时候读私塾,到 9 岁上小学。魏(建功)先生 14 岁就能读《说文》,我到 20 岁还不知道有《说文》这么一部书。所以说我的根基薄,不是家学渊源的。旧书我只读了《四书》、《诗经》、《书经》和半部《左传》。中学毕业以后,没有上预科就考入北大文科本科。我是躐等生,程度比同班同学都差,傅斯年能背半部《文选》,能读英、法、德文的书。我在中学上学时,英文还不错,上大学不要求学外文,我选了丁班外文,读 *Royal Reader* 第四册,教师教得不好,我也没有好好学。现在有的同志觉得在大学时期没有能够认真读书,没有学到什么东西,这不要紧,假如及时努力,仍可以学到所要学的东西。

二、我研究语言学的萌芽　我研究语言学并不是没有原因的。我在中学读书时,利用业余时间跟人学习速记,学会了 22 个声母、32 个韵母的记法。本来我是想要用速记来记笔记的。正赶上 1917 年黎元洪当大总统,恢复旧国会,我的速记老师约我到国会用速记作记录,每月工资大洋 80 元。我每次记 30 分钟,会后要用 4 个小时整理。我学会了声、韵母符号,并用来作会议记录,记音就有了训练。另外,国会里有各省的人,他们说各种不同的方言,我很喜欢听外省人讲话,也愿意学他们的话,我记得当时我学会了汤化龙的湖北话。

后来,我学习了王照的《官话字母》,又学习了注音字母,我对拼音、记音发生了很大的兴趣,打下了研究语言学的基础。

三、在上大学时期的暗中摸索　我的基础不好,旧学问、洋学问都不够。当时我的大学同学都比我强。朱希祖讲文学史,我听不懂,夏锡祺讲课,我也听不懂。只有钱玄同(名夏,字仲季,号玄同,后改“疑古老爹”)年轻,讲话清楚。文字学,一部为音韵篇,钱玄同著,一部为形义篇,朱宗莱著,因为我有记音训练,我对他讲的东西有了兴趣。当时我对古书知道的很少,先生和同学们提到的书名我都不知道。那时我手中有国会给的薪水,他们说一部,我就去买一部。只有陈澧的《切韵考》买不到,这书是广东木刻版,木版烧了,所以不易买到,我只好到理学院去抄。后来我到广东教书时,才买到了《切韵考》。大学时期我听刘师培的课,用速记记笔记。由于我不是书香门第,不会做学问,尽管有著名的学者做老师,我未能提纲挈领地去找参考书,发现问题向老师求教,我只是暗中摸索。

四、教书以后的锻炼　1924 年我虚岁 26 岁,大学毕业后在西北大学做教授,校址在西安。我兼国学专修科主任,前任是胡光炜[胡小石],很难接,我的确有点心虚。但我打定主意埋头苦干,还是接下来了。我教的课是文字学,兼教中国文学史、修辞学。课程多,备课很苦。文字学没有教完,只教了一年,因军阀刘镇华和胡景翼打仗,我回到北京。谈到教书,起初我想什么都可以教,只要好好备课,写出讲义就行了,但事后证明,教书不能专凭讲义。因为上课时,学生要提问,超出讲义所讲的范围,就回答不上来了,所以自己必须把问题都弄清楚,才能教学生。举一个例子:钱玄同讲音韵学时引劳乃宣《等韵一得》上的话说戛音作戛击之势,透音作透出之势,轹音作轹过之势,捺音作按捺之势,我自己并不明白是怎么回事,我给学生也这么讲,学生怎么能懂?不能以其昏昏使人昭昭。后来我看高元的《国音学》，才给我解决了问题。高元引用 Henry Sweet 的话给端、透、来、泥作了形象的描写，我对劳乃宣的戛、透、轹、捺就明白多了。所以，我觉得遇到问题应当多找几本书，看各家是怎么讲的，这非常重要。从这时起，我就开始摸索语音学了。我的头一本语音学的书是从丸善株式会社买的。这是 1924 年的事。

就在这个时候，陈嘉庚请鲁迅、张星烺、顾颉刚、陈万里到厦门大学去教书，我也被请去了。到那里以后，听当地人说“去哪里?”是 k‘ito lo，我觉得厦门方音很有意思，我就存心要学厦门话。当时我开的课有经学通论、中国音韵学史，课余之暇，请人给我发厦门音。

1927 年，我到广东中山大学任教，开声韵学、等韵研究、声韵学史等课，搜集材料很多，现在还保留着一些讲义。在广州，我为了研究《广韵》，每月出 30 元港币跟人学广州话。因为我对劳乃宣把音分为戛、透、轹、捺四组有很多疑问，看了高元的《国音学》，也只是明白了一些，并不是彻底明白。1928 年赵元任先生到广州调查方言，我就向赵请教戛、透、轹、捺的问题，赵先生在三天之内把我三年的疑问都解决了。赵和我的关系是介于师友之间的。赵记音的时候，我也记，记完以后，如果发现自己记的和赵记的相同，就非常高兴，增加了记音的自信心；如果自己记的和赵记的不相同，知道自己记得差，应当向赵学习。

五、在中研院七年　在中山大学教书的过程中，我觉得自己的学问不充实，应当先充实自己再去教书。于是我辞去中山大学中文系主任的职务，进了中央研究院历史语言研究所。那时研究所只是一个筹备处，设在广州东山，傅斯年任所长。我主要想整理音韵学史，我想把汉语发展史全部列入计划。我又想研究广州话的虚词，又想学瑶语，东西乱抓，不知道先搞什么好。后来有人说我的坏话，我就打定主意发愤努力。我记得在 1929 年元旦我有意保险 20 年，我要玩儿命,非干出个名堂来不可。那时候我的文章都不离开汉语音韵发展史,第一篇文章是《耶稣会士在音韵学上的贡献》。写这篇文章,我是先整理《西儒耳目资》和《程氏墨苑》,我手边没有《西儒耳目资》,托人到东方图书馆把《西儒耳目资》中的音韵部分抄录出来,每日苦干,废寝忘食。

不久研究所搬到北京。我想写《厦门音系》,请林藜光发音半年。我手边还有 1927 年在厦门记的材料,我利用那些材料作了一个字表,请发音人校正。厦门话文言与白话相差很远,我只问文言的音,请发音人把音灌在蜡筒上。我先把灌的音用国际音标记出来,然后请赵元任先生听蜡筒上的音,给我校正。赵先生记音非常有经验。特别是声调,赵先生记得最准确,经常改正我的错误。后来,我考学生也是在蜡筒上灌音,让他们记音,然后评定正确与否。《厦门音系》这本书我自己并不太满意。现在苏联要翻译我的《厦门音系》、《临川音系》和《唐五代西北方音》这三本书,我认为只有《唐五代西北方音》写得较好,可以翻译。

我写的第二本书是《唐五代西北方音》。写这本书,完全出于偶然,同时觉得导师非常重要。有一天我到团城古籁堂去找罗庸,在他那里我见到《敦煌遗书》,其中有羽田亨搜集的被伯希和拿走的《藏汉对译千字文》(伯希和《敦煌文件》第 3419 号),我正在研究汉语语音演变史,就向罗庸借了这本书,把每个字都抄在卡片上。当时陈寅恪先生在北京,我得到他很大的帮助。他指导我读参考书,找其他材料。我埋头钻研,以三个月的时间完成了这一本书。当时正是长城战役猛烈进行,北京可以听到炮声的时候!

第三本书是《临川音系》。1933 年我到青岛去讲演,见到游国恩,他是临川人,我觉得他说的话很有特点,我就记了他的音。回到北京以后我又找辅仁大学的黄森梁记音。我认为如果把江西客家话研究清楚，可以解决民族迁徙的一些问题。

第四本书是《徽州方言调查》，共调查了 6 个县 46 个点的材料，稿子尚未整理。

另外还有几件未完成的工作：

1.《两汉三国南北朝韵谱》，1933 年已开始作，参加工作的有丁声树、周殿福、严学宭、吴晓铃，后来交给周祖谟整理。昨天周把稿子交来，但第二、三、四章没有写完，如何校对很成问题。

2.《经典释文音切考》，声韵类已有百分之八十完成。

3.《唐五代宋金元词韵谱》。

4.《韵镜校释》，共搜集了二三十个本子。

我在中国音韵学方面的底子不是在上大学时期打的，而是在中央研究院摸到的门。我不是读好了书再写书，而是用剥茧抽丝法和磁石吸铁法为写书而搜集材料，材料越集越多，1928 年至 1934 年这七年间写了一些文章。大家如果把自我培植和工作结合起来，在工作中磨炼，就会随时有所发现，引出问题，设法解决这些问题，就是你们的成就。

悼念陶云逵教授

云逵，你记得吗？23年前，在南开中学大礼堂北侧的一间小楼上，时常有一个广额浓眉、目光炯炯、年方17岁的学生，去找一个比他只大6岁、曾仅替他本班老师代过一两星期课的青年国文教员去谈天。所谈的题材，上自宇宙人生，下至修辞造句，说者毫无顾忌地信口开合，听者也凝眸注意地心领神会，那就是咱们认识的开始。

隔了12年，在上海曹家渡小万柳堂的帆影楼上，一位衣冠齐楚、仪表堂堂、刚从德意志学成回国的青年学者，同着李济之[李济]先生来看我，寒暄才罢，就大谈华欧混血种的问题。此后在工作余暇，有时我陪他到兆丰公园散步，有时他跟我回杭州，一同到九溪十八涧去洗足，那便是咱们同事的开始。

抗战五年后，你从云大转入联大，并主持南开大学文科研究所的边疆人文研究室，因为兴趣的接近，你找我来谈天的次数更多，同时庆兰[邢庆兰]、华年[高华年]也变成这研究室的一员，逐渐奠下了沟通人类学和语言学的桥基，这是咱们友谊加切、情感加深的开始。

去年春天咱们同去大理，你劝我增订民家语的材料，同时你趁着大家朝鸡足山、登中和峰的当儿，独自去调查民家捕鱼和过年的风俗。回来路过天子庙坡谈到这种计划的进行，彼此都高兴得了不得，在爬过这个高达2600公尺的高坡时，几乎把咱们所会的昆曲和皮簧都唱光了，这是咱们学术合作的开始。

在广漠的人海里，咱们居然有这么几次的遇合，能够说没有缘吗？你受过严格的科学训练，同时又禀赋着艺术的天才，具有丰富的热情，也有急遽傲慢的脾气。可是你对于我这差有数年之长的人，从做中学生一直到大学教授，并不因为我学殖天分抵不上你而失掉应有的敬意。因此我对于柳漪[冯文潜]先生和你艰辛缔造埋头苦干的研究室，愿进最大的努力保持合作互助的态度，以酬知己。

这个刚在滋生的嫩芽，耐过了一年半的风吹雨打，已经逐渐有欣欣向荣的气象了。谁料到晴天一声霹雳竟自击死了一个天天灌溉这嫩芽的主要园丁呢？

云逵，你是不该死的。虽然尧尧殇折伤了你心，因为研究室事任劳任怨地费了你的力，因为生活窘促逼得你从手到口地写文章，消耗了你的血，可是，你有结实的体魄，充沛的活力，坚强的意志，饱满的精神，一切都抵挡住，无论如何，你是不该死的。况且，你不是有伉俪甚笃的年青太太和还在襁褓的女儿吗？你不是有未完成的著作和刚发轫的事业吗？你不是有合作互助的朋友和追步后尘的学生吗？你怎能撒手不管，然而你竟死了！为什么？为咱们贫苦的生活已经到了极限？为没钱治病耽误了症候？为初民思想弥漫社会？为医术医德尚待改良？究竟为什么？请你告诉我。

去年12月30日你约我和伯蕃[刘晋年]、秉壁[郑昕]提前去吃夜饭，那时亭玉[林亭玉]生产后还未满月；三样馅儿的几百个饺子，都是你亲手包的，老实说，那些饺子真不够味儿，也不像样儿，可是它们因为充满着情谊，所以我吃着特别香。尤其是你能欣赏我的母校里许多朋友，格外使我增加了无限的知己之感，谁想到这一餐竟成了散场饭呢？

我最近所写的《藏缅族的父子连名制》，远不及你那两篇《大寨黑夷的家族与图腾》和《西南部族的鸡骨卜》。然而，承你阿其所好地一定让我去沾边疆人文的篇幅，直到你被回归热的螺旋侵袭到第九天，已经谵语神昏的时候还念念不忘这篇文章，叫亭玉到处乱翻，直到我亲笔写信告诉你尚未交出，你才放心。云逵，冲着你忠于事业、忠于朋友这一念，我愿意从旁协助柳漪、庆兰、华年、才澄[赖才澄]等让你亲手灌溉出来的那一点嫩芽永生着，请你瞑目吧！

最后，我想拿两副联语来概括我的哀思，其一："武林访胜，苍洱寻幽，时忆旧游增怅惘；津市谈文，沪滇论学，忍披遗著理丛残。"其二："谵语病帏间，念念不忘连名制；痛心遗笥里，孜孜方竟卜骨篇。"

（原载《边政公论》第3卷第9期，1944年，署名罗莘田）

第一个五四文艺晚会的回忆并怀一多、佩弦

1944年的“五四”，昆明西南联大的同学发起了一个文艺晚会，约请一多、佩弦、今甫[杨振声]、从文、君培[冯至]、广田[李广田]和我担任讲演。会场是在联大新校舍南区10号——那是我们常常举行学术讲演的一个较大的教室。那天晚上我和一多、佩弦从福照街冠英[余冠英]家里赶到，会场已经挤得满满的，外面还围绕着好几层。另外还有更多的学生跑到北区的广场上要求改到那里开会。可是已经在第十教室占了两点钟座儿的热心听众坚决反对。我和一多百般劝导无效，加上三青团的分子又乘机捣乱，于是这个大家渴望的晚会，竟至没有开成！

经过这番挫折，我们更觉得这个晚会非开不可。于是由我和一多领导，改在8日晚间在新校舍北区的草坪上补开。讲演的人除了上面所举的几位以外又添邀了卞之琳、闻家驷和孙毓棠三位。“那天在傍晚的时候，昆北道上公路两头，就像潮涌般的人都向着新校舍奔去。真的他们有着远道朝山的行脚僧一般的虔诚与热望。而这晚会真也可以比喻做一座香火旺盛的圣地。过去有人说，联大像一潭止水，而现在则是止水扬波，汹涌壮阔！”（语见当年5月9日《云南日报》）

那天由我开场，并讲“五四前后新旧文体的辩争”；君培讲“新文艺中诗歌的收获”；佩弦讲“新文艺中散文的收获”；毓棠讲“谈中国的

戏剧”；从文讲“五四以来小说的发展及其与社会的关系”；之琳讲“新文艺与西洋文学的关系”；家驷讲“中国新诗与法国文学”；广田讲“新文艺中杂文的收获”；一多讲“新文艺与文学遗产”；最后今甫讲“新文艺的前途”。从下午7点钟起，在月光底下连续开了5小时的会，从始至终，一直在肃静、宁谧、热烈、渴望的氛围里进行着。席地而坐的盘得脚麻，环场而立的站得腿酸，可是压根儿没听见一丁点儿不耐烦的反应或无意识的浮嚣！

我的“开场白”大意说：我们在广场上举行这个晚会有三种意义：第一，广场没有墙壁的间隔，象征着联大是一个没有隔阂的整体。第二，皎洁的月光底下开会可以使每个人的心地越发洁白光明。第三，在广场上可以尽量吸收自由的空气免得闭闷在小屋里窒息得难过。这完全是针对当时反动派的压迫而发的。晚会开过后十多天，我又在5月21日的《云南日报》上发表了一篇《从文艺晚会说起》的星期论文。在那篇短文里我提出了三个口号：(一)“中西合流，文语分系”；(二)“文艺离不开生活，要想把握住当前的大时代，有远大抱负的作家应该踊跃地下乡或入伍”；(三)“要拿历史的眼光重新估定中国文学的价值，还它一个在当时当地应有的地位”。其中的第一个口号，当1946年联大分家后，清华大学商量院系计划，一多发挥这个意见，要把它见诸实行。后来佩弦替他整理遗稿，又缀辑起来作成一篇《调整大学文学院中国文学、外国语文二系机构刍议》(《国文月刊》63期)。当时虽然没能实现，可是解放以后又有好些人旧事重提起来。没料到我偶然的一个理想，竟得到两位亡友和一些时贤的欣赏！至于第二、第三个口号，我到现在还继续维持着，而且自信并不违反时代精神。我们只要翻开毛泽东《在延安文艺座谈会上的讲话》(结论第二节论“人民生活中本来存在着文学艺术的矿藏”和“我们决不可拒绝借鉴古人与外国人”等)和《新民主主义论》(第十五节论“清理古代文化的发展过程,剔除其封建性的糟粕,吸收其民主性的精华,是发展民族新文化提高民族自信心的必要条件”等),对于我所提出的后两个口号当然不会否认的。这两本小册子虽然都是在1944年以前发表的,可是当我写那篇短文的时候的确没有寓目的机会!

那晚参加讲演的十个人除了一多被民贼戕害,佩弦因为忧愤和贫病交迫以致早死外,其余的八个人倒都好好地活着,并且还都留在北京。可是尽管离我们长逝的只有一多、佩弦两个人,而这个缺憾是没法儿弥补的。我在联大和一多、佩弦共事七年,一多是诤友,佩弦是良友。我们三个轮替着主持中国文学系,始终本着互让互谅的精神共谋系务的发展,我和一多都是直性人,遇有公事上的争执佩弦总以温柔敦厚的性格来调融其间。所以联大虽由三校组成,中文系人数又较多,却始终能和衷共济地团结成一个整体。每当“五四”纪念日回忆往事,缅怀亡友,都使我有无限的伤感!我们要想永远纪念着闻、朱两位先生,应该努力参加革命阵线,彻底铲除反动残余,好给两位先生报仇;北大、清华、南开三大学的中国文学系师生们,尤其应该持续我们在第一个“五四”文艺晚会所领导的精神,好让一多、佩弦永远不死!

此文原系“五四”三十周年为中国语言文学系壁报而作,未曾正式发表。今年《光明日报》为“五四”纪念索稿,即以之塞责。由今检讨,用第一身口气太多,个人主义包袱较现在更重也。

1950年5月7日莘田记。

(原刊《光明日报》,1950年5月7日)

忆佩弦

去年8月13日,我刚在上海登岸,仲瑜[陈政]就告诉我:“佩弦昨天死了!”当时好像晴天霹雳一般,不由得愣住了!这真是我回国后第一个不幸的消息!

我和佩弦在北大同学的时候并不太熟,起初只在马神庙一带看见一位短小精干,目光炯炯,春秋喜欢穿紫呢夹袍的少年,后来才知道他就是朱自清。1930、1931两年我俩在清华中文系同过两年事,彼此才算熟识了。记得我每次下课后,很少到教员休息室,经常是到图书馆地下室的中文系办公室找他聊天,一则因为他蔼然可亲的风度吸引着我;再则因为那间屋里插架都是有关新文艺的书报杂志,也很掀动我的兴趣。

佩弦搜集这些新文艺的书报杂志,不单由于自己的爱好,而且足以表现他敬事负责的态度。那时他正担任一门“新文艺思潮”的功课。这在有些不大负责的教师,只要找几本“关于书的书”,挦扯饾饤,东拼西凑,就可以到班上对学生吹牛了。然而佩弦却绝不出此。他几乎每章每节都是从直接材料里抽出意见,然后再用批判的精神组织成的。他这一部书虽没写成,可是我这次打开沦陷北平12年的书箱却侥幸保存了一份纲要,纵然只是一鳞一爪,而故人的遗风余韵竟稍赖以保存。

佩弦治学的精神,一向是实事求是,“敏而好学,不耻下问”的。

他的本行是哲学,但因天才、夙养、勤学好问和忠于职业的关系,二十几年来,不单把他造就成独具风格的散文家,专以旧诗而论,他的宋诗也可算是升堂入室了。文学以外,他的求知欲也很浓厚,一事不知马上登记在小本儿或卡片上,逢人便问,绝没有强不知以为知的态度。这种谦谦君子的作风真是难得可贵。

抗日期间,从衡岳而蒙自,而昆明,我们又在西南联大同了七年的事。这七年患难的经历格外增进了我俩的友谊。他一向秉着温柔敦厚的诗人性格,从来不闹宗派,出风头,争名位,摆架子。我和一多都是直性人,遇有公事上的争执,佩弦总拿他的诗人性格来调融其间。所以西南联大的中文系虽由三校组成,人数又较多,可是七年中间大家却始终本着互让互谅的精神,团结成一个整体,以共谋系务的发展。事过追忆,不禁让我缅怀故人!

过去四年间,我不在国内,同佩弦也不断有书札往还。自从一多被民贼戕害后,他的思想越发前进了。当时流行他的名言有"向青年学习,同时代看齐"两句。我乍一听起来,颇不以上半段为然。因为我那时心目中所谓学习,只执着在"业务"一方面。一年来的改进,使我深切体验到这两句话的意味,可惜佩弦骨灰已寒,已经来不及向他商讨了!

去年8月25日北平教育界同人在清华园给佩弦举行追悼会,在场的人多半眼泪不干。我被推勉强讲了几句话,竟至泣不成声,不能毕其词!今年北平解放后,圣陶、西谛诸友来到北平,故人欢聚之余,一想到他,举座立时黯然,圣陶竟至号啕不止!佩弦——你何尝死呢?你的影子将永远在我们这一班故人和崇爱你的青年们的记忆中!

(原刊《进步》,1949年8月12日)

戴望舒先生在中国小说戏曲上的贡献

13 年前,我就经吴晓铃先生介绍认识了戴望舒先生,不过,一向"神交",直到去年夏天才会到面,并且在北大文科研究所语音室,给望舒先生录过音。如果我今天把那套录音设备带来,那么我们不单可以瞻仰他的遗容,而且可以听见他的遗音了。为悼念望舒先生,我今天以他的一个朋友资格来说一说他在创作和翻译的贡献以外的另一方面的成就,那就是古典文学中的小说和戏剧的研究。远在 15 年前他就开始了这个艰巨的工作——我说"艰巨"两个字,是有理由的,因为:(一)在古典文学里这是一个被人鄙视的冷门,说是"引车卖浆"者流所喜欢的玩意儿,虽然有像鲁迅先生那样的先驱者筚路蓝缕地做了好的带头,可是,仍旧是"能为者不为",很少有人做傻子。(二)搞这套东西的人需要具备许多条件,比如说:语言、声韵、训诂、版本、目录、历史、民俗学、社会学和人类学,都多少要知道一些,对于专门搞创作的朋友们等于一种苛求。(三)当时的政府处处疑心我们,你弄一点和广大的人民接近的东西或是广大人民所喜欢的东西,他就说你想造反,加以迫害。所以,望舒在破天荒地编一个提倡这种研究的周刊的时候,还只能拿"俗文学"那样自贬身价的招牌做烟雾,不能公然提出"大众文艺"的名字。他的苦衷也就等于当年研究小说戏曲的专家马隅卿先生(廉)自称他的书斋做"不登大雅之堂"!比比看!现在我们搞"大众文艺"的朋友们该多自由、痛快!

望舒在这一方面的工作,可以归纳做四个部门:

一、校点

例如:明席浪仙的《石点头》,清初艾衲居士的《豆棚闲话》。

二、搜集

这是继续鲁迅先生《小说旧闻钞》的工作。

三、辑佚

这是继续鲁迅先生《唐宋传奇集》和《古小说钩沉》的工作。

望舒在二、三两方面的成绩最大。

四、考订

这是独立的专题研究。代表的作品如《袁无涯本水浒传的真伪》,一破别人的误见,得到不能移动的正确结论;《读〈李娃传〉从小说里看唐代的社会》,和历史印证,解决了大家一向读这篇小说所无法讲通的问题;《说张山人》找出"相声"最古的形式,均能道前人所未道,表现出他的深湛的学力和聪明的判断力。

从前面所举出望舒的工作里,我们还可以看得出来,他所做的,都是"为人之学",都是在建筑工程中的烧砖瓦的工作。拿他这样一个兼通古今中外的聪明人而去做所谓拙笨的、费力不讨俏的工夫,这是不自私的表现,是为大众服务的表现,最值得我们学习。

听到整理望舒遗稿的朋友们说,差不多有一半是关于这方面的著作,这真让人吃惊!望舒在这一方面的成绩被他的诗名所掩,连他很近的朋友,都有不知道的。他在12年前编《俗文学》的时候,曾经发表过我的《北平俗曲百种摘韵序》。在这方面总算"知己",所以我愿意提出来讲一下。

最后,就学术研究来说,现在,我们经过学习,纠正了观点,正应该开始写一部新的中国小说史,我们要建筑一座坚固的大厦,望舒所烧的砖瓦一定会发挥它们所具备的效能,希望他的同道们,能够快快地把稿子整理出来，编印出来，这是我们在望舒死后应该负的责任，这也是望舒为人民、为学术最后一次的服务，他一定高兴我们这么做。

（原载《光明日报》，1950年3月6日）

赵元任小传

赵元任原字宣重,后来废去,始终名号一致,也不喜欢用笔名,在国外发表论著用 Yuen Ren Chao 或 Y.R.Chao 署名。1892 年 11 月 25 日生在中国江苏省的武进县。1910 年考取第一届清华学校官费留学生,赴美国康奈尔(Cornell)大学学数学,1914 年得学士学位,再入哲学院研究一年。1915 年转入哈佛(Harvard)大学,1918 年得哲学博士学位。1924 ~ 1925 年又赴法国入法国学院和莎娜学院研究语言学。

他半生都在文化教育界活动,并没做过其他职业。历任美国康奈尔大学物理学讲师(1919 ~ 1920),清华大学数学讲师(1920 ~ 1921),美国哈佛大学中文哲学讲师(1921 ~ 1924),清华大学教授(1925 ~ 1929),美国耶鲁(Yale)大学访问教授(1939 ~ 1941),美国哈佛燕京社汉英大字典编辑(1941 ~ 1946),海外语言特训班中文主任(1943 ~ 1944),美国加州(California)大学教授(1947 到现在),美国密西根语言学研究所教授(1946 ~ 1947);前中央研究院历史语言研究所研究员兼语言组主任(1929 ~ 1948)等职务。在社会活动一方面,他做过中国科学社的理事、美国语言学会会长(1945 年度)、美国声学社社员。

他学问的基础是数学、物理学和数理逻辑,可是对于语言学的贡献特别大。从 1922 年到 1948 年,他一共发表了语言学专著约 14 种,论文约 21 篇。近二十年来科学的中国语言学研究可以说由他才奠立了基石,因此年轻的一辈都管他叫做"中国语言学之父"("Father of Chinese Philology")。

音乐是他的癖好,可是因为他秉赋音乐天才,又经过严格训练,所以也有很大的成就。在1911年到1931年"九一八"之间,中国的新音乐发生了很大的变动。1911年前后,中国受了西洋音乐的影响,开始创作新的歌曲。这种新型歌曲全部采了西乐的形式和方法,但歌词仍用旧诗词小令的体裁。五四运动并不曾影响到音乐,直到赵元任、陈田鹤等才开始用新诗做歌词,开始用新型的歌曲来唱新诗。这样,新歌曲才真正有了新气象。赵元任所作的曲,最得意的当然是抒情歌,例如,《上山》、《海韵》、《茶花女中的饮酒歌》,所谱的是徐志摩、刘半农、胡适的白话诗。他作曲的技术是够好的,可以跟后来的黄自媲美。他的作品也带有浓厚的中国风格,并且善于运用民谣体。在思想感情上,他也比以前的作曲家稍能接近现实生活。例如,他的《劳动歌》、《织布谣》、《卖布谣》,都对贫苦的人寄有温暖的同情。但是空有这种温和善良的人道主义的同情怜悯,并不能追溯人民痛苦的基本来源,而且有一些幻想对于受苦难的人民并没有多大好处。因此他的歌曲也就流传不广,不能给斗争者多少鼓励。他所作的曲大部分都收在《新诗歌集》(上海商务印书馆出版,1926年)和《儿童节歌曲集》(商务印书馆,1935年)两部书里。另外还有一篇论中国音乐的文章收在陈衡哲主编的《中国文化讨论集》(*Symposium on Chinese Culture*,1931, Shanghai.)第四章(pp.82~96);琼斯主编(D. Jones)的《语音学杂志》(*Le Maître Phonétique*)也收了他一篇论中国歌曲的短文(第3集第39期,1924年4~6月份,9~10页)。

歌曲比较流行的有下列各种:

一、《小诗》,胡适词。

二、《卖布谣》,刘大白词。

三、《劳动歌》,词见《星期评论》。

四、《过印度洋》,周若无词。

五、《织布谣》,刘半农词。

六、《也是微云》,胡适词。

七、《教我如何不想他》,刘半农词。

八、《茶花女中的饮酒歌》,刘半农译词。

九、《海韵》,徐志摩词。

十、《上山》,胡适词。

十一、《尽力中华》,自作词。

十二、《注音符号歌》,自作词。

十三、《国语罗马字歌》,自作词。

其中的《劳动歌》,原词是:

你种田,我织布,他盖房子给人住,哼哼呵呵,哼哼呵呵,做工几点钟,休息几点钟,教育几点钟,大家要求生活才劳动。

认识字,好读书,工人不是本来粗。读书识字,识字读书,教育几点钟,休息几点钟,做工几点钟,大家要求教育才劳动。

槐树绿,石榴红,薄薄衣衫软软风。嘻嘻哈哈,嘻嘻哈哈,休息几点钟,教育几点钟,做工几点钟,大家要求休息才劳动。

在思想意识上只提出劳动是要求生活、教育和休息的,还没有能明确认识"劳动创造世界"、"劳动是生活第一需要"的基本观念。不过,就这首歌的词句以及音乐所表现的情绪来说,在当时知识分子的圈子里已经算是够前进的了。

赵元任在语言学一方面的成就虽然大,可是人民知道他是音乐家的比知道他是语言学家的多得多。由此咱们更可以认清学术为人民服务的重要性,语言研究也得在深入浅出的原则下逐渐走向普及的大路了。

白涤洲小传

白涤洲名镇瀛，以字行，北平人，其先出自蒙古白济特氏。1915年，年十六，入北京师范学校，坚苦自励，每试辄列前茅。毕业后，历任前京师公立第十七及第七小学校长，兴革得宜，训育有方，前京师学务局局长张仲苏(谨)极器重之。1920年，入国语讲习所研究国语国音，以头脑之精敏，国语之流利，故成绩斐然，为侪辈冠；黎劭西[黎锦熙]先生因引为青年同志，约其共同戮力国语运动。此后十五年间，关于国语国音之讲习、讨论、宣传、视察、编辑，君几无役不与。1926年国语统一筹备会着手增修之《国音字典》，1932年教育部公布之《国音常用字汇》，初稿均出自君手：其在国语运动史上之伟绩，殆可与陆词之于《切韵》、周德清之于《中原音韵》相比拟也。

1924年，君有志深造，毅然辞校长职，考入北京大学预科乙部。以其余暇佐顾孟余先生办理前北京教育会会务，略得微酬，借助膏火，兼供仰事俯畜之资，俭约自给，未尝求助于人，友朋援济，皆善谢之。1926年入本科英文系，1928年转国文系，从钱玄同、马幼渔、刘半农诸先生治中国声韵学及语音学，并能启发其天才，获得切实之工具。于时君已兼任教育部国语统一筹备委员会常务委员及中国大辞典编纂处整理部主任，毕业北大(1930)更任北平市立师范学校教务主任；事务丛脞，而能不废所学，且参加本所第二组之语音训练班，从赵元任先生实习听写方言。其所著《北音入声演变考》、《集韵声类考》、《广韵声纽韵部之统计》、《广韵通检》、《广韵入声今读表》等，均于此期间陆续完成，以勤敏犀利之精神，为实事求是之工作，努力猛进，迥异寻常。君所为文多归纳，少推想，长于排比统计，而不为非常可喜之论，时流或有讥其庸者，然数年之内，百忙之中，已佼佼若此，其庸亦殊不可及也！

1932年岁杪，君长子蓝及原配胜鉴溪女士，于一周之内相继殇逝，次年(1933)1月，复丁父忧；创巨痛深，悲苦异常。适傅孟真先生读君所作《北音入声演变考》，喜其创通规律，足以正讹明变，拟请君调查豫、晋、秦、陇之入声变读情况以证实其结论。君遂于是年3月应本所聘赴陕西调查方言，努力工作以排遣烦闷，六月之间，凡调查音系42县，并搜集民间歌谣多种。8月半返平，月终即到上海向本所报告调查经过，并为中华书局灌制《标准国语国音留声机片》。10月底复应刘半农先生召北来，任北大研究院文史部语音乐律实验室助教，得暇辄整理陕西调查材料。11月半与武进徐溶女士结婚，蜜月之中，不辍所业，其所作《关中入声之变化》及《关中四声实验录》内之声调曲线即于是时画成，一时传为佳话，媲美于吕祖谦之《东莱博议》：其敬事负责，有如此者。

1934年6月半，君随刘半农先生赴归绥调查方言，盛暑工作，历时三周。归来，即值半农先生之丧。于劳顿悲痛之余，复受国语统一筹备委员会命，赴长安讲演国音，8月折往武进，伴其夫人归宁，返平未及一月，又于9月23日赴郑州出席国语罗马字全国代表大会，三月之间，仆仆数千里，未尝一日宁息，体敝神疲，伤寒菌遂乘虚侵袭，归平病乃转剧，竟于10月12日上午4时殁于北平林葆骆医院，得年仅三十有五，英年溘逝，闻者无不惋惜！盖君赋性诚笃，见义勇为，舍己从人，劳怨自任：其堪供人悼伤者，固不止学术上之损失已也！

半农、涤洲逝世后，陶燠民亦以病死瑞士闻。燠民福建闽侯人，清华大学文学院哲学系毕业，曾任本所第二组助理员，著有《闽音研究》载《集刊》第一本第四分。以国内治语言学者之希而一年之内共弱三人，其在国外则劳佛（Berthold Laufer）亦于9月13日在芝加哥坠楼殒命，厄运同遭，殊可慨已！

1934年11月11日，罗常培述于北平北海静心斋。

（原刊中央研究院历史语言研究所《集刊》4本4分）

白涤洲君著述提要

甲　整理

一、《北音入声演变考》(1931 年 4 月刊入女师大《学术季刊》第二卷第二期)

自元周德清《中原音韵》以入声派入平、上、去三声，北音入声演化之迹已著。历明清两代，如熊士伯、李汝珍等皆曾有志整理，但均未得其条贯；君融贯各家之说，证以北平今读，归纳成“全清全浊变阳平，次清次浊变去声”之规律。

二、《集韵声类考》(1931 年 12 月刊入《中央研究院历史语言研究所集刊》三本二分)

《集韵》一书大系依据《广韵》，但其中反切用字及声纽韵类有无异同，尚未经人探讨，且传世版本讹舛颇多，中外学者皆无从致力。君先取诸本详加校勘，次用番禺陈兰甫氏《切韵考》方法系联《集韵》反切上字，成《集韵声类考》一篇，结果定为 39 类：泥娘不分，床禅不分，均与《广韵》不同。

三、《广韵声纽韵部之统计》(1931 年 4 月刊入女师大《学术季刊》第二卷第一期)

此文统计《广韵》反切上下字，订声纽 47 类，韵部 290 类。

乙 纂辑

四、《国音常用字汇》

1931 年由教育部公布之《国音常用字汇》初稿为君所主编，完成新定国音标准。

五、《广韵通检》（1931 年油印本）

《广韵》一书，分韵苛细，据音求字，颇难检寻。君据字典部首，遂韵改排，并附注“纽”、“呼”、“调”、“韵”及其国韵今读。

六、《广韵入声今读表》（1930 年）

君既考见北音入声演变之规律，因取《广韵》入声韵字，逐一注明今读。

七、《国音字典》稿本

国音标准既经决定采用北平音，遂于 1925 年秋着手增修《国音字典》，是年初次议决之稿本，撰写改削亦出自君手。

八、《注音符号无师自通》

此书初稿为君所编，出版在 1930 年教育部编《注音符号传习小册》之前。

九、《平民字典》稿本

此书系 1925 年为平民教育促进会所编。

丙 实验

十、《关中入声之变化》（1933 年稿）

1933 年 3 月中央研究院历史语言研究所派君往陕西调查旧关中道所属方言，历时半载，所得材料甚多。返平后先整理其中关于入声部分,以成斯篇,已刊入《庆祝蔡元培先生六十五岁论文集》。

十一、《关中四声实验录》(1934 年稿)

此文亦关中方言调查材料之一部分,实为刘半农先生《四声实验录》之惟一嗣响,已刊入《中央研究院历史语言研究所集刊》第四本第四分。

十二、《关中音系》稿

全稿包括陕西旧关中道所属 42 县方音系统,参用应用语音学及实验语音学之方法,谨严细密,惟尚待整理。

十三、《标准国音国语留声机片》

1933 年 8 月,君应中华书局之聘赴沪灌制《标准国语国音留声机片》12 张。

十四、《北平声调之研究》

此系君在北大语音乐律实验室任职时经刘半农先生指导所作之专题研究,对于赵元任先生"赏半"之说略有修正。

十五、《河北方言纪录》

稿藏北大语音乐律实验室。

十六、《黟县同音字注音》

此文将在《国学季刊》发表。

十七、《归绥方音调查》

1934 年 6 月 15 日,君随刘半农先生赴归绥调查方言。此部分材料,现存北大语音乐律实验室。

(原刊中央研究院历史语言研究所《集刊》4 本 4 分)

欢迎毗罗博士致词

一、毗罗博士(Dr. Raghu Vira)是印度当代著名的语言学家。在他主持领导下的印度国际文化研究所,各种科学技术辞典的工作和编纂"百藏"(Satapitaka)的计划都是很有成绩、很有前途的。他这次来华使中印友谊和中印文化的交流都增进了一步。我们谨以诚恳的热忱表示欢迎。

二、据可靠的记载,中印两国从第一世纪就发生文化上的接触。自此以后双方的文化使节很多。师觉月博士(P. C. Bagchi)所著的《中印千年史》(*India and China——A Thousand Years of Sino-Indian Culture Contact*)仅只是一个简略的记载。其中印度来华工作的印度学者就有102个,详检大藏中的《高僧传》、《续高僧传》恐怕还不止于此。中国学者到印度的也很多,最著名的法显、玄奘、义净是世界周知的。

三、印度对中国文化的影响

甲、翻经　从148A.D.起到1287A.D.共有译经人194人,翻了1440部、5586卷经。到了1738年清重刊《三藏圣教目录》又增加到1672部、7247卷。有许多印度失传的佛经,幸赖汉译保存。

乙、语言学

1. 悉昙章(Siddhirastu)对于汉语声母系统(initial system)和"等韵"(rime-tables)的影响。

2. 梵文(Sanskrit)对音(transliteration)对于构拟汉语古音的帮助。

a. 钢和泰(Alexander von Staël-Holstein)《音译梵书与中国古音》(*Transliterated Sanskrit and the Ancient Pronunciation of Chinese Characters*),1922。

b. 汪荣宝《歌戈鱼虞模古读考》(*On the Ancient Pronunciation of Rimes* 歌戈鱼虞模),1922。

——详见《中印研究》一卷三号(*Sino-Indian Studies* vol. I, part 3, March), 1945。

玄应《一切经音义》(约 649A.D.)(*A Dictionary of the Whole Canon*)。

义净《梵语千字文》(689 ~ 695)(*One Thousand Characters in Sanskrit*)。

礼言《梵语杂名》(755 ~ 789)(*A Sanskrit Dictionary*)。

慧琳《一切经音义》(788 ~ 810)。

法云《翻译名义集》(1151A.D.)(*Mahāryutpatti - A Glossary of Sanskrit Terms Translated into Chinese*)。

义译举例:

我执 Ātma-grāha(holding of the idea of the ego)

法性 Dharmākara

有情 Sattva(Creature, a living being)

空 Śūnya(absolute non-existente)

如来 Tathāgata

解脱 Vimokṣa(mokṣa, mukti(emancipation)(Liberation)

真如 Bhūta-tathātā

c. 汉语中的梵文借字

子 保存全部音节的:

△Bodhi 菩提　　yoga 瑜伽

Amitā 阿弥陀　　Dhāmanī 陀罗尼

丑　省去两个音或两个音节的：

△Bodhisattva　菩提萨埵 > 菩萨

Yamarāja　阎摩罗社 > 阎罗

△Saṅghārāma　僧伽蓝摩 > 伽蓝

寅　省去一个音或一个音节的：

△Arhat　阿罗汉 > 罗汉

Samādhi　三昧地 > 三昧

卯　在汉语中单音化的：

△Buddha　佛陀 > 佛

Dhyāna　禅那 > 禅

Kappa(巴利)　劫波 > 劫

辰　缩减梵音另加汉语类名的：

△Udumbara　优昙婆罗 > 昙花

Pattra　贝多罗 > 贝叶

巳　用梵音一部或全部另造谐声字(Phonetic Compound)的：

Stūpa　窣堵婆 > 塔婆 > 塔

Dakṣiṇa(右手)达嚫 > 嚫

Kaṣāya　袈裟

四、结束语

周恩来总理和尼赫鲁总理关于中印和平共处的五项原则的公告，不单可以加强中印友谊，保卫亚洲和平，而且可以保卫世界和平。

在这个基础上，又加现代交通如此方便，今后中印文化的交流一定可以超越古代。

毗罗博士的来华不过是这种交流的第一者，我们再一次用诚恳

热烈的心情表示欢迎，并祝

中印语言学在已往的基础上发扬光大！

中印友好万岁！

研究工作的性质

——国立北京大学文科研究所第八次公开讲演

一　前言

起头儿就得声明两件事,第一,这里所谓研究工作,仅指着我们研究所现在所注重的历史和语言文字两个部门来说,虽然有几个基本观点,未尝不可以应用到其他的社会科学上去,可是我决不敢牵涉到自然科学的范围,尤其是不能包括数学和逻辑。第二,我们研究所设有文学史和哲学史两个部门,文学和哲学的本身固然和史学不同,可是,研究文学史或哲学史还得适用一般研究史学的方法。1929 年罗膺中先生曾给中山大学的学生讲过一次《治学方法及其态度》,其中有一段论到文学、哲学和史学的不同说:“文学是基于情感的创造品,文学的创造以感受作出发点。研究文学的最高造诣就在养成感受力和创造力。终极所得到的仅仅是‘只可自怡悦,不堪持赠君’的‘独喻之情’。研究哲学、文学有所得的人,他的理解力、感受力越来越深,批评力越来越密,发表力越来越巧;他只是超越过浅浮的东西向那最高去处,弃其芜秽,撷其精英。老子说:‘为道日损’,陆士衡说:‘虽纷蔼于此世,嗟不盈于余掬’,都可以表现出研究哲学或文学的最高造诣。至于史学就不然了。史学以过去不可复睹的事实作对象,以现存可作证据的记载或遗物作材料。它的责任是把过去人类活动的事实,交相映射的人事,求出一个因果关系,说明它们演变的真相。贵在从一种蒙昧的事物状态之下,求出它分析的、清楚的客观事实。它只是推陈出新,一天一天开发那草昧的路;问题越来越新,分析越来越密,前修未密,后出转精,新得的条理、答案都是前古所无——这便是发明。"(据叶作仁记录的油印本节录)他这一段话,在我看是非常精要的。治文学史或哲学史的人,固然先得对于文学或哲学的本身有深澈的了解,可是一谈到"史",就离不开历史的方法。所以本讲的范围不牵涉到纯文学和纯哲学的本身。

前提既定,底下就好说话了。

二 研究释义

把本讲的范围交代清楚,咱们再咬文嚼字地谈一谈"研究"。《说文》"研,礦也",段玉裁注云:"以石礦物曰研。"从这个意思引申,便有精思审虑的意义。《易·系辞》"能研诸侯之虑",郑玄注:"研,喻思虑也",疏,"精也";《文选·东京赋》"研核是非",薛综注:"研,审也"。又《说文》"究,穷也",段玉裁注云:"《释言》同。《小雅·常棣》传曰:'究,深也';《释诂》及《大雅·皇矣》传曰:'究,谋也;皆穷义之引伸也'。"合起来讲,可以说是"切磋琢磨,穷思竭虑"的意思。在中国古书上把"研究"两个字连用的也不少,例如谢庄《改定刑狱疏》:

> 督邮贱吏非能异于官长,有案验之名,而无研究之实,愚谓此制宜革。

傅绰《明道论》:

> 依贤圣之言,检行藏之理,始终研究,表里综核,使浮辞无所用,诈道自然消。

《元史·铁木儿塔识传》:

天性忠亮，学术正大，伊、洛诸儒之书，深所研究。

又《萧䞖传》：

博极群书，天文地理，律历算数，靡不研究。

这些例子里的意义，虽然不完全一样，大致却和我们现在所讲的相差不远。再要一追究 research 这个字的语源，咱们可以说，它是从古法文 recercier 来的，往远一点讲，就可以把 cercier 推溯到近代拉丁文的 circare。它的意义是 To go round in a circle, to explore。说的详细一点，就是 That act of searching into a matter closely and carefully, inquiry directed to the discovery of truth, and in particular the trained scientific investigation of the principles and facts of any subject, based on *original* and *first hand* study of authorities or experiment。所以凡是合乎下面所说的才配叫做研究工作：

Investigations of every kind which have been based on original sources of knowledge may be styled 'Research'.

它必须有在一定范围内去探讨的精神(to go round in a circle, to explore)，必须有精切(closely)谨慎(carefully)的态度，必须有本来的(original)不转手的(first hand)材料。从前有一个学生质问我说："照先生所说的本来的材料，难道只有地下发掘出来的，或从敦煌石窟新发现的才能算数吗？"其实，这是他误会了！我所谓本来的材料并不限于别人没看见过的，只是不要转手的。比方说，你要研究文学史，不要根据谢无量的《中国大文学史》，郑振铎的《插图本文学史》，朱谦之的《音乐文学史》……；你要研究哲学史，不要根据胡适之的《中国哲学史大纲》，冯友兰的《中国哲学史》……；你要研究历史，不要根据夏曾佑的《中国古代史》，章嵚的《中国通史》，邓之诚的《中华二千年史》，吕思勉的《白话本国史》，顾颉刚的《古史辨》，钱穆的《国史大纲》……我并不是说这些书不好，其中有许多直到现在还是我很佩服的好书，我只是说你要作研究只能拿它们作参考，不应该拿它们作根据——因为它们不是原料。研究历史的人注重探讨史源，注重第一次发现(first appearance)，其实，无论研究什么都应该这样。凡是作研究的人都应该直探本源去找原料，不应该从“关于书的书”(book of books)里去展转抄袭！“大纲”、“概论”、“通史”、“述评”之类的玩艺儿，假如著者没有大错，它可以指示你门径，引起你的兴趣，可是，你要研究，即使这些书的本身是第一流的作品，你也不能拿它作根据。凡是没经自己亲眼审核过的材料是不可轻易信赖的！

三　研究工作必经的步骤

一个有系统的研究，至少得要经过下列的四个步骤：

第一得要有问题——问题的发生或者从观察精确引起，或者从“读书得问”引起。现在所讲的还是偏重读书一方面。读书得要会发疑问，随眼忽略过去，不会有问题，也就没有进益。从前张载说：

> 读书先要会疑，于不疑处有疑，方是进矣。
>
> 在可疑而不疑者，不曾学！学则须疑！
>
> 学贵心悟，守旧无功。[①]

因为会发疑问然后才想钻研，才能深入，一切研究工作都由这一念而起。凡是浮光掠影、含胡颟顸的读书人，一辈子也走不上研究的路！所提出的问题越具体越好，范围越窄越好，必须由自己体验出来的，然后才不至于隔靴搔痒，捉摸不定。

第二得要有见解——有了问题就该着手搜集材料。具体数量的事实和材料，是一切研究或实验的张本，不过材料的积聚和剖析需要

① 参《张横渠集·经学理窟》。

功力,材料的组织和融贯,需要理解。从前章实斋说:

> 学与功力实相似而不同。学不可以骤几,人当致攻乎功力则可耳。指功力以为学,是犹指秫黍以为酒也。(《文史通义·博约篇》)

单靠功力而没有理解,决不能发生意见,那便不能叫做"学"!

自然,有许多问题现在只能用归纳法去研究,一个研究者不能坚持自己的意见;但是,科学的精诣,就在研究者要有一点有价值的意见。设若事实和这意见冲突,他就立刻改变或抛弃那个意见。单是不断地统计测量决不会产生理论、原理或意见的。所以在观察若干事例或搜集相当的材料以后,就得提出一个或几个可能的假设(Hypothesis)来;根据这个假设再去搜求,便走上了研究的另一个阶段。

第三得要有证据——假设能否变成通则,就看证据充分不充分。一个严正的研究者得要抱着"有几分证据说几分话"的态度。没有证据的假设那只是"无征不信"的幻想。若是把不足作证据的硬要拉来作证据,尤其牵强附会,不足为训!比如,一个文学史的作者,因为有人在天台山国清寺见到了很古的梵文写本,又经人断定是梵曲Sukantala,他就借着这个"惊人的消息"来证明中国戏剧和梵曲的关系,并且又从体裁和组织上"细观之",提出五点引证和说明:

(1)印度戏曲是以歌曲、说白和科段三个元素组成的,中国也是这样。

(2)印度的Nayaka等于生,Nayika等于旦,Vidusaka等于丑或净,下等侍从等于家僮或从人,女主角的侍从或女友等于梅香或宫女。

(3)印度戏有前文等于中国的开场。

(4)印度戏于每戏后必有尾诗等于中国的下场诗。

(5)印度戏用两种语言:一、典雅语Sanskrit,二、土白语Prakrit,等于明嘉靖陆采的《南西厢记》和万历间沈璟的《四异记》丑净全用苏人乡语。

假如因为中国的庙里藏着一个梵曲写本,再比附上五点偶合,就想证明中国的南戏出于印度,那无异因为中国人和印度人都有一个鼻子两个眼睛,就想证明他们是同种!这种不科学的臆断就犯了把不是证据当做证据的毛病!

第四得要有结论——单有材料而没有意见,就会流于破碎,单有意见而没有证据,就会流于空疏,从材料提出假设,拿证据证成通则,自然而然地就得出顺理成章的结论来。一个研究工作若是没有果断确切的结论,那就像画龙没有点睛、做衣服没装领子一样!许多旧式的学者读书很多,材料顶丰富,可是他写出东西来永远是平摆着许多别人的说法,案而不断的没有结论!从前有两个老前辈,一个叫"活《周礼》",一个叫"活《二十四史》",一辈子也写了不少的东西,博则博矣,可是始终稗贩成说,决没有独得的创见或结论!这固然许是天分所限,却也不能不怪他们没得到研究的方法。一个真正科学的研究或实验,能有惊天动地的假设固好,但是主要的特征,还是根据特意搜集的材料,求得归纳的结论。能够提出果断确切的结论来,一个研究工作才算完成。

以上这四个步骤,在研究的过程中是缺一不可的。杜威(John Dewey)在他的《思惟术》(*How we think*)里把系统的思想分成五步:(一)疑难的境地。(二)找出疑难的所在。(三)提出假设。(四)找出每个假设的涵义。(五)证实。这便是实验主义(Pragmatism)的方法论。起头儿因为观察事例引起疑难,把疑难确定后立刻提出假设,有了假设再去继续观察,搜求证据,赶到证据充分,假设自然证实,所发生的疑难问题也自然解决了。在提出假设以前是归纳的功夫,有了假设以后是演绎的工夫,最后一步还是归纳:这种归纳演绎互用的方法对于一般的研究工作都是可以适用的。

四 举几个简单的例

为把上面所说的步骤弄得更清楚一点儿起见，我想就着前人或近人关于文史方面的研究举几个简单的例来说明它：

例一，顾炎武关于《柏梁台诗》的考证（《日知录》卷二十一）。

（一）问题："汉武《柏梁台诗》本出《三秦记》，云是元封三年（纪元前 108）作，而考之于史则多不符。"

（二）见解：（甲）年代不符，（乙）官制不符。

（三）证据：

（甲）从年代上考证：

《史记》及《汉书·孝景纪》中六年（纪元前 144）夏四月，梁王薨。《诸侯王表》梁孝王武立三十五年薨。孝景后元年（纪元前 143）共王买嗣，七年薨。建元五年（纪元前 136）平王襄嗣，四十年薨。《文三王传》同。

又按，《孝武纪》元鼎二年（纪元前 115）起柏梁台，是为梁平王之二十二年，而孝王之薨至此已 29 年，又七年，始为元封三年。

又按，平王襄元朔中以与大母争樽，公卿请废为庶人。……乃削梁八城。

又按，平襄王之十年为元朔二年（纪元前 127）来朝，其三十六年为太初四年（纪元前 101）来朝，皆不当元封时。

（乙）从官制上考证：

又按《百官公卿表》，郎中令武帝太初元年（纪元前 104）更加光禄勋；典客景帝中六年（纪元前 144）更名大行令，武帝太初元年更名大鸿胪；治粟内史景帝后元年（纪元前 143）更名大农令，武帝太初元年更名大司农；中尉武帝太初元年更名执金吾；内史景帝二年（纪元前155)分置左右内史,右内史武帝太初元年更名京兆尹,左内史更名左冯翊;主爵中尉景帝中六年更名都尉,武帝太初元年更名右扶风:凡此六官皆太初以后之名,不应预书于元封之时。

又按《孝武纪》太初元年冬十一月乙酉柏梁台灾,夏五月正历,以正月为岁首,定官名。则是柏梁既灾之后,又半岁而始改官名。而大司马、大将军青则薨于元封之五年,距此已二年矣。

(四)结论:“反复考证无一合者,盖是后人拟作,剽取武帝以来官名,及梁孝王世家乘舆驷马之事以合之,而不悟时代之乖舛也!”

据日人铃木虎雄说,宋敏求《长安志》所引《三秦记》无元封三年,也没有梁孝王的名字,但称“梁王”。这只是所据材料的出入,顾氏的考证方法并没有错误。

例二,王引之《经义述闻·尚书·立政》“义民”及《吕刑》“鸱义”条(卷四)。

(一)问题:“传于义字皆训为仁义之义,其不可通者有三:用丕训德,则乃宅人,则善人在位矣,何乃三宅反无善民邪?其不可通者一也。三宅,即上文之宅乃事,宅乃牧 ,宅乃准。传解为五流有宅,五宅三居,以为无义之民大罪宥之四裔,次九州之外,次中国之外,以及下文三有宅,三宅宅心,皆谓居恶人。此不特与上文宅乃事云云不合,且与下文则克宅之句相反矣。其不可通者二也。鸱义奸宄,解鸱枭之义,夫鸱枭恶鸟,何义之可言?其不可通者三也。郑注训义为良善,而曰盗贼状如鸱枭,钞掠良善。亦不得其解而为之辞。经但言义,不言钞掠也。”

(二)意见:“家大人曰:《说文》曰:俄,行顷也。(顷与倾同。《说文》有曰:义从我,我顷顿也。我义俄古并同声。)《小雅·宾之初筵》篇,侧弁之俄,郑笺曰:俄,顷貌。《广雅》曰:俄衺也。古者俄义同声,故俄或通作义。《立政》曰:谋面用丕训德,则乃宅人,兹乃三宅无义民。义与俄同,衺也。言夏先王谋勉用大顺之德,召然居贤人于官而任之,则三宅皆无倾衺之民也。《吕刑》曰:鸱义奸宄,夺攘矫虔。义字亦是倾衺之义。马融注曰:鸱,轻也。鸱者冒没轻儳,义者倾衺反侧也。"

(三)证据:(甲)"《大戴礼·千乘》篇说司寇治民烦乱之事曰:作于财贿,六畜五谷,曰盗;诱居室,家有君子,曰义;子女专,曰媄;饬五兵及木石,曰贼;以中情出,小曰间,大曰谍;利辞以乱属,曰谗;以财投长,曰贷。盗义媄贼间谍谗贷皆是寇贼奸宄之事,义即鸱义奸宄之意也。"(乙)"《管子·明法解》篇曰:奸邪之人用国事,则奸人为之视听者多矣,虽有大义,主无从知之。故明法曰:佼众誉多,外内朋党,虽有大奸,其蔽主多矣。是大义即大奸也。"

(四)结论:"古者俄义同声,故俄或通作义。"(已经证实的假设。)

例三,王引之《经义述闻·毛诗·终南》篇"有纪有堂"条(卷五)。

(一)问题:"《毛诗·终南》篇:终南何有?有纪有堂。毛传曰:纪,基也;堂,毕道平如堂也。引之谨案:终南何有?设问山所有之物耳。山基与毕道仍是山,非山之所有也。"(疑点一)

(二)意见:"今以全《诗》之例考之,如山有榛,山有扶苏,山有枢,山有苞栎,山有嘉卉,侯栗侯梅,山有蕨薇,南山有台,北山有莱,凡云山有某物者,皆指山中之草木而言。"(意见一)

"又如,丘中有麻,丘中有麦,丘中有李;山有扶苏,隰有荷华;山有乔松,隰有游龙;园有桃,园有棘;山有枢,隰有榆;山有栲,隰有杻;山有漆,隰有栗;阪有漆,隰有栗;阪有桑,隰有杨;山有苞栎,隰有六驳(钱大昕答问曰,《释木》云:驳,赤李,谓李之子赤者也,其即诗之六驳乎?);山有苞棣,隰有树檖;墓门有棘,墓门有梅;南山有台,北山有莱;南山有桑,北山有杨;南山有杞,北山有李;南山有栲,北山有杻;南山有枸,北山有楰:凡首章言草木者,二章、三章、四章、五章亦皆言

草木,此不易之例也。”(意见二)

“今首章言木,而二章乃言山,则既与首章不合,又与全《诗》之例不符矣。”(疑点二)

“今案纪读为杞,堂读为棠,条梅杞棠皆木名也。纪堂假借字耳。”(提出假设)

(三)证据:

(甲)“《左氏春秋》桓二年,杞侯来朝。《公羊》《谷梁》并作纪侯;三年,公曾杞侯于郕,《公羊》作纪侯。”

(乙)“《广韵》堂字注引《风俗通》曰:堂,楚邑,大夫伍尚为之,其后氏焉。即昭二十年棠君尚也。棠字注曰:吴王阖闾弟夫溉奔楚,为棠溪氏。定四年《左传》作堂溪。”

(丙)“《楚辞·九叹·怨思》执棠溪以剸蓬兮,王注曰:棠溪,利剑也,《广雅》作堂溪。”

(丁)“《史记·齐世家》《索隐》引《管子》棠巫,今《管子·小称篇》作堂巫。”“是杞纪堂棠古字并通也。”(第一次证实)

(戊)“考《白帖》终南山类引《诗》正作有杞有棠。唐时齐、鲁诗皆亡,惟韩诗尚存,则所引盖韩诗也。”(第二次证实)

(己)“柳宗元《南山祠堂碑》曰:其物产之厚,器用之出,则璆琳琊玕,夏书载焉;纪堂条梅,《秦风》咏焉。宗元以纪堂为终南之物产,则是读纪为杞,读堂为棠,盖亦本韩诗也。”

(四)结论:“且首章言有条有梅,二章言有纪有堂;首章言锦衣狐裘,二章言黻衣绣裳;条梅纪堂之皆为木,亦犹锦衣黻衣之皆为衣也。自毛公误释纪堂为山,而崔灵恩本纪遂作屺,此真所谓说误于前,文变于后者矣。”

例四,陈寅恪李太白氏族之疑问(《清华学报》十卷一期)。

(一)问题:李太白是中国人还是西域人?

李阳冰《草堂集序》:"中叶非罪,谪居条支,易姓与名。然自穷蝉至舜,累世不大曜,亦可叹焉。神龙之始,逃归于蜀,复指李树而生伯阳。"

范传正《唐左拾遗翰林学士李公新墓碑》:"……凉武昭王九代孙也。隋末多难,一房被窜于碎叶。流离散落,隐易姓名。故自国朝以来,漏于属籍。神龙初,潜还广汉,因侨为郡人。父客,以逋其邑,遂客为名。……公之生也,先府君指天枝以复姓。"

照《李序》和《范碑》所说,好像太白的先世本来是中国人,隋末被窜到西域,隐姓瞒名,唐朝神龙初年才逃回蜀的广汉。太白是返蜀以后生的,他生下来才复姓李。但是陈先生的意见却不以为然。

(二)意见:他据《新唐书·地理志》认为"碎叶条支在唐太宗贞观十八年(644)平焉耆,高宗显庆二年(657)平贺鲁,隶属中国政治势力范围之后,始可成为窜谪罪人之地。若太白先人于杨隋末世即窜谪如斯之远地,断非当日情势所能有之事实"。

(三)证据:"又考《太白集》卷二六《为宋中丞自荐表》云:'臣伏见前翰林供奉李白年五十七。'太白为宋若思作此表时,为唐肃宗至德二年(757),据以上推其诞生之岁应为武后大足元年(701)。此年下距中宗神龙元年(705)尚有四年之隔。然则太白由西域迁居蜀广汉之时其年至少已五岁矣。"

(四)结论:"是太白生于西域,不生于中国也。又考《李序》'神龙之始,逃归于蜀,复指李树而生伯阳',及《范碑》'公之生也,先府君指天枝以复姓'之语,则是太白至中国后方姓李也。"

他得到这个结论后,认为《新唐书》一九〇下《文苑传·李白传》既载不可征信之"父为任城尉,因家焉"之语,又称白为"山东人",未免进退失据。因为山东非唐代州县名,以郡望应称赵郡人,以居住地为籍贯亦应称"兖州或鲁郡任城人"。

例五,胡适《红楼梦》的著者是谁?(节录《胡适文存》卷三《红楼梦考证》,第 822 ~ 854 页)

(一)问题:《红楼梦》的著者究竟是谁?他的事迹、家世和著书的年代如何?

(二)意见:这部书第一回所说原稿是空空道人从一块石头上抄写下来的,那是依托的话;真正的著者就是那“于悼红轩中披阅十载,增删五次,纂成目录,分出章回”的曹雪芹。

提出这个假设以后,胡先生又根据袁枚《随园诗话》卷二里记载曹楝亭的一条,知道:(1)乾隆时的文人承认《红楼梦》是曹雪芹作的;(2)曹雪芹是曹楝亭的儿子;(3)大观园就是后来的随园。

从这个线索,他再用剥茧抽丝的方法去探讨,于是又根据吴修的《昭代名人尺牍小传》卷十二、《扬州画舫录》卷二、韩菼《有怀堂文稿》里的《楝亭记》、章学诚的《丙辰札记》、宋和的《陈鹏年传》、《江南通志》、《四库全书提要》谱录食谱之属存目里的《居常饮馔录》条和别集类存目里的《楝亭诗钞》条、《八旗氏族通谱》、铁保所辑《熙朝雅颂集》、《楝亭书目》等书,关于曹寅的事迹考得四条结论:

(1)曹寅是八旗的世家,几代都在江南做官。他的父亲曹玺做了 21 年的江宁织造;曹寅自己做了四年的苏州织造,做了 21 年的江宁织造,同时又兼做了四次两淮巡盐御史。他死后,他的儿子曹颙接着做了三年的江宁织造,他的儿子曹頫接下去做了 13 年的江宁织造。他家祖孙三代四个人总共做了 58 年的江宁织造,这个织造真成了他家的“世职”了。

(2)当康熙帝南巡时,他家曾办过四次以上的接驾的差。

(3)曹寅会写字,会做诗词,有诗词集行世;他在扬州曾管领《全唐诗》的刻印,扬州的诗局归他管理甚久;他自己又刻有二十几种精刻的书。他家中藏书极多,精本有 3287 种之多,可见他的家庭富有文学美术的环境。

(4)他生于顺治十五年,死于康熙五十一年(1658~1712)。

曹寅的略传和他的家世既然考清楚了,那么,曹寅究竟是曹雪芹的什么人呢?胡先生又根据杨钟羲《雪桥诗话续编》卷六所记曹雪芹事,《熙朝雅颂集》里所收清宗室敦敏、敦诚兄弟关于曹雪芹的诗,《八旗文经》里所收敦诚的几篇有年月可考的文字,考出下面几件事:

(1)曹雪芹名霑,不是曹寅的儿子,是曹寅的孙子。

(2)曹雪芹后来很贫穷,穷得很不像样子。

(3)他是一个会做诗又会绘画的人。

(4)他在那贫穷的境遇里,纵酒狂歌,自己排遣那牢骚的心境。

(5)从曹雪芹和他的朋友敦诚弟兄的关系上看来,又说:"我们可以断定曹雪芹死于乾隆三十年左右(约1765)。"又说:"我们可以猜想雪芹大约生于康熙末叶(约1715~1720);当他死时约五十岁左右。"

《考证》改定后大约半年,1922年4月19日,胡先生得到敦诚的《四松堂集》又补充了四点:

(1)曹雪芹死在乾隆二十九年甲申(1764)。

(2)曹雪芹死时只有"四十年华"。这自然是个整数,不限定整40岁。但我们可以断定他的年纪不能在45岁以上。假定他死时年45岁,他的生时当康熙五十八年(1719)。

(3)曹雪芹的儿子先死了,雪芹感伤成病,不久也死了。据此雪芹死后似乎没有后人。

(4)曹雪芹死后,还有一个"飘零"的"新妇"。这是薛宝钗呢?还是史湘云呢?那就不容易猜了。(《胡适文存》二集卷四《跋红楼梦考证》,第169~176页)

1928年胡先生得到脂砚斋重评《石头记》残本,又作了一篇《考

证红楼梦的新材料》,再把以前所考修订了两点:

(1)乾隆甲戌(1754)曹雪芹死之前九年,《红楼梦》至少已有一部分写定成书,有人“抄阅重评”了。

(2)曹雪芹死在乾隆壬午除夕(1763 年 2 月 13 日)。(《胡适文存》三集卷五,第 567、570、601 页)

他根据这些关于曹雪芹个人和他家世的材料,更提出一个进一步的假设说:

《红楼梦》这部书是曹雪芹的自叙传。(《文存》卷三,第 840 页)

(三)证据:胡先生怎样应用这些材料来证实他的假设呢?他举出了五条重要的证据:

第一,这部书的开端已经清清楚楚地说明《红楼梦》是一部“将真事隐去”的自叙的书。若作者是曹雪芹,那么曹雪芹即是《红楼梦》开端时那个深自忏悔的“我”!即是书里的甄贾(真假)两个宝玉的底本。

第二,第一回里那块石头已经明白清楚地说,“这书是我自己的事体情理”,“是我这半世亲见亲闻的”。

第三,第十六回有谈论南巡接驾的一大段,可以作曹家曾经接驾四次的映照。曹雪芹不知不觉地——或是有意地把他家这桩最阔的大典说了出来。足征这里所说的甄家、贾家都是曹家。

第四,拿第二回所叙荣国府的世次和《八旗氏族通谱》卷七十四所记曹家世系比较,可以认贾政即是曹頫,贾宝玉即是曹雪芹。

第五,《红楼梦》所写贾宝玉的历史和他的家庭环境多与曹雪芹相合。又曹寅是刻《居常饮馔录》的人,我们读《红楼梦》时看贾母对于吃食的讲究,看贾家上下对于吃食的讲究,便知道《居常饮馔录》的遗风未泯。此外,像雍正《朱批谕旨》第四十八册载有雍正元年苏州织造胡凤翚奏陈他的前任曹寅的亲家李煦亏款事,第十三册载有两淮巡盐御史奏请追还李煦所亏两淮盐款事，都可以映衬曹家衰落的情形，大概这两亲家的下场相差不远。况且"袁枚的《随园记》(《小仓山房文集》十二)说，随园本名隋园，主人为康熙时织造隋公。此隋公即是隋赫德，即是接曹頫任的人。(袁枚误记为康熙时，实为雍正六年。)袁枚作记在乾隆十四年己巳(1749)，去曹頫下任时甚近，他应该知道这园的历史。我们从此可推想曹頫当雍正六年去职时，必是因亏空被追赔，故这园子就到了他的继任人的手里。从此以后，曹家在江南的家产都完了，故不能不搬北京居住。这大概是曹雪芹所以流落在北京的原因。"我们看了李煦、曹頫两家败落的大概情形，再回头来看《红楼梦》第五十三回和第七十二回所写贾家中落的情形，就更容易明白了。"《红楼梦》只是老老实实地描写这一个'坐吃山空''树倒猢狲散'的自然趋势。"(《胡适文存》卷三，第804、853页)

后来胡先生得到脂砚斋重评《石头记》的残本后，根据它的朱批又把第十六回凤姐所说"南巡接驾"一大段，就是康熙南巡，曹寅四次接驾，和用《八旗氏族通谱》的曹家世系跟第二回冷子兴所说的贾家世系来比较，认为贾政即是曹頫那两个假设，加了一层有力的证实。于是他很果决地说：

> 故《红楼梦》是写曹家的事，这一点现在得了许多新证据，更是颠扑不破的了。(参看《胡适文存》三集，第574、575页)

(四)结论：总结上文关于《红楼梦》著者的材料，凡得六条结论：

(1)《红楼梦》的著者是曹雪芹。

(2)曹雪芹是汉军正白旗人，曹寅的孙子，曹頫的儿子，生于极富贵之家，身经极繁华绮丽的生活，又带有文学与美术的遗传与环境。他曾做诗也能画，与一般八旗名士往来。但他的生活非常贫苦，他因为不得志故流为一种纵酒放浪的生活。

(3)曹寅死于康熙五十一年。曹雪芹大约生于康熙五十六年，死在乾隆二十七年壬午除夕。

(4)曹家极盛时,曾办过四次以上的接驾的阔差,但后来家渐衰败,大概因亏空得罪被抄没。

(5)《红楼梦》一书是曹雪芹破产倾家之后,在贫困之中做的。做书的年代大概当乾隆初年到十八九年之间,书未完而曹雪芹死了。

(6)《红楼梦》是一部隐去真事的自叙:里面的甄、贾两宝玉即是曹雪芹自己的化身;甄、贾两府即是当日曹家的影子。(故贾府在长安,而甄府始终在江南。)(《胡适文存》卷三,第853、854页;(3)、(5)两条,参看《文存》三集,第569和570页重订)

以上所举的五个例,虽然长短不一,四项步骤有的完备,有的稍欠完备,可是大体上都可以算是研究工作。研究工作的价值不在乎篇幅长短,两三页的一个研究结果,可以有惊天动地的发明;几百页的大书也许是尘羹土饭的废话!自然我不敢就拿上面所举的几个例当做研究工作的代表,我不过想借他们说明研究工作的步骤罢了。在这五个例当中,我觉得王引之考"有纪有堂"和胡先生考《红楼梦》的著者两条方法最精密,证据最充分,态度最严谨。我在清代许多学者里面顶佩服王氏父子,因为他们每考一个问题,总是弄得怡然理顺,涣然冰释,让你心服口服,毫无间言!胡先生参合清代考证家和实验主义(Pragmatism)的方法比前人更进了一步。读过杜威 *How we think* 和 *Essays in Experimental Logic* 的人再看他的考证文字,自然会觉出他有一个始终一贯的方法,这里因为篇幅所限,把他的原文删节太多,读者必须参看原文,才不至于淹没他的好处。

五　什么不是研究工作

咱们在上文既然把研究的意义、研究的步骤和研究的实例都交代过了,底下还得要问,什么不是研究工作?照我的意见说:收集材料——虽然准确——不算研究;累积叙述的材料不算研究;未分析与不可分析的材料,无论如何精巧地堆积在一块,不能算研究;报告不是研究,调查不是研究。述作、习作或者是研究,但是重复人家一个原始的问题,特别避免调查研究报告,有意或无意容纳读书暗示来重行证实人家的结果,不能算是第一等研究或实验。自己暗地七摸八摸,东凑西凑,随意得到一点见解,别人无法查考,无法照样重复证实,不能算得严格的研究或实验。

拿这个标准去衡量,那么咱们可以指出来:

(1)“长编”或“资料”之类不算研究;

(2)“讲义”或“教科书”之类不算研究;

(3)“索引”或“引得”之类不算研究;

(4)标点古书不算研究;

(5)“集解”或“校注”之类,只是众说杂陈,案而不断,或拘泥版本,墨守类书,不能融贯文字的形音义,使古书的疑滞怡然理顺、涣然冰释的,不能算是研究;

(6)“调查”或“报告”之类,只是把材料有闻必录地写下来,而不能从所得的材料里找出问题、分析综合来构成系统、求得结论的,不能算是研究;

(7)没有证据的臆断,纵然有“非常异义可喜之论”,只能算是瞎猜,不能算是研究;

(8)剽窃陈言,没有本来的精神或创见,甚至于还掩蔽出处、自欺欺人的,不能算是研究。

关于这几类的具体的例证,咱们不便列举,也无须列举。只要你对于上文第二、三、四节里所说的积极的意义能够认清,你自然会辨别出什么是研究工作来了。

说到研究,当真也不是一件容易事!大概在刚一发生问题的时候,你只觉得茫无头绪,不晓得从什么地方下手;于是东翻西检,左思右想,弄得人疲精敝神,废寝忘食,没有一时一刻不想解决这个疑难;赶到左右逢源,头头是道,实证和假设符合,一旦豁然贯通,那个时候的快乐,不是身历其境的简直体会不出来。所谓研究,就是这么一个苦中寻乐的玩艺儿!王国维在《人间词话》里说:古今成大学问者必须经过三种境地:

第一期是:"昨夜西风凋碧树,独上高楼,望尽天涯路。"

第二期是:"衣带渐宽终不悔,为伊消得人憔悴。"

第三期是:"众里寻他千百度,蓦然回首,那人却在,灯火阑珊处。"

这确是亲身经历过的甘苦之谈,值得咱们大家体味!

最后,我还想把蔡孑民先师送给历史语言研究所同人的一副对联写出来,为的是让咱们大家时常互相警惕,互相勖勉,那就是:

多闻阙疑,慎言其余;遭人而问,少有宁日。

1942年1月7日写竟于昆明青云街靛花巷北京大学文科研究所。

《道藏源流考》序

道经纂集，凡历三期：自《汉书，艺文志》始见著录，厥后葛洪、陆修静、孟法师、陶弘景、阮孝绪、王延、尹文操等，递有增订，著其卷帙。顾目录虽备，而丛藏未成。此一期也。洎唐开元中编排纂辑，始以藏名，目曰《三洞琼纲》，都凡3744卷。中更唐末五季之乱，劫馀焚烬，统纪荡然。宋太宗、真宗之际，徐铉、王钦若等先后奉敕校雠，撰目以献。然纲领漶漫，部分参差，岁月坐迁，科条未究。逮张君房参斠诸本，品详异同，历时数年，诠次为4565卷。依《千字文》叙列函目，始天终宫，题曰《大宋天宫宝藏》。而撮其精要，以成《云笈七签》。及徽宗崇宁中，又诏搜访道家遗书，就书艺局令道士校定，大藏增至五千馀卷。此二期也。道藏经板之可考者，以宋徽宗时所刊《政和万寿道藏》为最古。政和中，诏搜访道门逸书，令道士校定，雕板流传，都540函。迨金章宗时，经板尚存，但颇阙佚。乃命中都十方大天长观提点孙明道搜访遗经，据以补缀，增至6455卷，刊为《大金玄都宝藏》。镂椠之事，始于明昌元年，历二年而始毕。元宋德方复遵其师丘处机遗意，旁求缺佚，增刊为7800馀卷。雕椠校雠，历时八载，仍以《玄都宝藏》称。会宪宗、世祖两朝，因释道争辩《化胡经》真伪，颁旨焚毁道经，浩劫重罹，颇有散佚。及明正统十年重辑全藏，仍以《千字文》为函次，先成天字至英字。万历三十五年，续成杜字至缨字。都512函，5485册，镂板行世，今尚流传。别有天启丙寅新刊袖珍本，则人间秘笈,见者盖寡。此三期也。

综兹三期,历时绵邈。徒以记载缺略,卷帙浩繁,儒者畏难,羽士不学。虽或撷其古本诸子,据以校勘;而于道经科条,道教宗派,鲜能挈其纲维,穷源竟委。至于摭拾日人馀绪,迻译成书,疏舛百出,尤难凭依。然则考镜道藏源流之作,讵可已乎?

1942年春,余以暇日,潜修于昆明龙泉镇北京大学文科研究所。偶于图书室邂逅西南联合大学化工系教授陈国符先生,值其翻检道藏,撮录为劳。初意其方从事于中国炼丹术之探索也;及经倾谈,始悉君病道书纪载缺略,源流不彰,于留学德国时,即假佛兰克府大学中国学院藏书,捃集史料,汇辑长编。返国任教,复以馀晷,续加补苴,草创《道藏源流考》三卷。及1946年秋,转南京资源委员会任职。更于公馀借阅国学图书馆、金陵大学图书馆、泽存书库藏书。于道经全藏外,旁及道教名山志、宫观志、佛藏传记、正史、类书、各省方志与夫唐宋以降重要文集,凡与道藏有关者均搜罗务尽。又漫游茅山、当涂、武进、吴县、上海、北京及江西贵溪龙虎山,凡载籍记其庋有道藏者,咸亲往访问。稿经数易,始克写定。于三洞四辅之渊源,历代道书目录,唐宋金元明道藏之纂修、镂版及各处道藏之异同,均能究源探本,括举无遗。其功力之勤,蒐讨之富,实前此所未睹也。培以末学,辱承下问,钦仰之馀,间有摧扬。君虚怀若谷,咸经采纳。顷全书付梓,复嘱以数言弁首。聊抒所感,序如上文。

1949年2月6日,北京

(原载陈国符《道藏源流考》,中华书局,1949年初版。北京中华书局,1963年新版)

罗常培年表

1899 年(清光绪二十五年已亥)

8 月 9 日(农历七月初四)出生于北京西直门内曹公观后西井胡同一个满族家庭,满姓为萨克达氏,隶属正黄旗。父亲名恩禄。

名常培,字莘田,又署心恬,号恬庵,笔名贾尹耕,斋名未济斋。

1904 年(5 岁)

开始识字。

1907 年(8 岁)

就学于希怡泉、崇乐峰主持的怡乐书斋。怡乐书斋后遵督学局令改为西城第四学区私立第二小学堂,校址在西直门内大街崇寿寺。除诵读启蒙读本外,兼习局定之小学课程:算术、修身、史地、格致、体操等。

1908 年(9 岁)

希怡泉、崇乐峰改就公立小学教职。重就读于北魏胡同远戚伍世舜及后公用库荣静之的私塾,读四书,进度颇速。

1909 年(10 岁)

继续读私塾,收获颇丰。《恬庵五十岁自订年谱》中写道:"闰二月开始读《诗经集注》,七月二十一日读竟。八月三日开始读蔡沈《尚书集传》、《古文释义》等。试学作文二三百字,喜套袭成调。"

1910 年(11 岁)

年初仍读私塾,后投考京师公立第二两等小学堂,小学堂设于西直门内大街高井胡同路南。校长为景佑臣。因读过四书二经、算术等课程,也能作文,因此被编入高小二年级,和老舍(舒庆春)同学。老舍说:"我从私塾转入学堂,即与莘田同班。我们的学校是西直门路南的两等小学堂。在同学中,他给我的印象最深,他品学兼优,而且长长的发辫垂在肩前;别人的辫子都垂在背后。"(老舍《悼念罗常培先生》,载《中国语文》1959 年 1 月号)《恬庵五十岁自订年谱》中写道："余以读竟四书二经，略能作文，粗通算术，遂编入高小二年级。教员中有李笃斋、李丹六、裴叔平诸人。笃斋讲《诗经》甚清晰，丹六教国文、算术，颇鼓励余之作文。入学第二次课艺竟以《论蝇虎》一篇冠全班。同学中能自总订交，四十年如一日者惟舒舍予(庆春)一人而已。"

1911 年(12 岁)

继续就读于京师公立第二两等小学堂，各科成绩优秀。《恬庵五十岁自订年谱》中写道："继续就读于京师公立第二两等小学堂，精勤攻读，各科并进，每试辄冠全班。"

1912 年(13 岁)

民国建立，督学局改组为京师学务局，京师公立第二两等小学堂改为女校。先生投考祖家街市立第二小学校。昆明夏筱琅(瑞庚)任校长。不久就原校址改立"京师公立第三中学校"，校长仍为夏筱琅。小学学生则并入报子胡同第四小学。是年先生毕业于第四小学，毕业考试结果，在两班 44 名学生中名列第一。《恬庵五十岁自订年谱》中写道："小学学生则并入报子胡同第四小学，校长初为金湘浦(声)，继改赵绍庭(继增)。时以第三年级人数过多分甲、乙两班。甲班教员为赵松龄(鹤汀，国文，算术)、夏恒福(寿延，甲乙班地理)、杨书升(伦秀，甲乙班音乐，乙班算术)、同布(荫田，英文)、桂清(馨山，修身，历史)、赵宗茂(得福，图画)、定林(逸安，甲乙班理科，甲班农业)、石学万(月樵，甲乙班体操)；乙班教员为胡荣桂(湘府，国文，农业)、续森(世臣，英文)、贵荫(养桥，修身，历史)、增禄(代耕，图画)。在当时均为上选，故余此一年内所得之基本训练尚不坏。至十二月二日至六日(夏历壬子十月二十四日至二十八日)举行毕业考试，成绩核定结果：

国文 95　英文 100　算术 100　理科 100　修身 99.5

历史 99.7 地理 100 农业 95 乐歌 100 图画 99

手工 99.5 体操 90

综计 1175.5 平均 97.96 临时考试 95.52 总平均 96.74

于两班四十四名学生中名列第一。”

1913年(14岁)

考入北京市立第三中学。名列第三。《恬庵五十岁自订年谱》中写道:“三中校长为夏瑞庚师筱琅,国文教员世虞臣(兴)……筱琅师貌颇严峻而性甚仁慈,对于贫苦学生尤体恤鼓励。世虞臣师笃守桐城义法,讲解清晰,改笔恰当。余生平识为文之径,实自此奠基。”老舍说:“到入中学的时候,我们俩都考入了祖家街的第三中学,他比我小一岁,而级次高一班。他常常跃级,因为他既聪明,又肯用功。他的每门功课都很好,不像我那样对喜爱的就多用点心,不喜爱的就不大注意。”(老舍《悼念罗常培先生》)

是年母亲因病去世,先生在家补习国文、英文、算术,兼学蒙语。

1914年(15岁)

继续在三中读书。在一些学友启发下,先生取得不少进步。《恬庵五十岁自订年谱》中写道:“自入中学后识张德言(锡伦),颇受其熏染,喜宋明理学语。董鲁安(璠)亦时以曾涤生之律身法相砥砺,因之除温习《论》、《孟》外,时披览《曾文正公家书》及梁启超《饮冰室文集》、康有为《不忍》杂志等。且自署日记为《自醒录》,并分养心、修身、接人、执事、读书、时务、附记数项。”

1915年(16岁)

中学三年修业,于学校规定课程之外,读《通鉴》、《史论》、《历代名臣言行录》之类,在日记中常有论史的言论。秋天北京学务局举办中学四年级学生会考,先生考取甲等第三名。《恬庵五十岁自订年谱》中写道:“日记中常有论史的粗浅的言论。又时涉猎理学、摘记格言,有‘闲德’之愿,而不能克制私欲。一月二十三日自定敦品条例七项:(一)己所不欲,勿施于人;行有不得,反求诸己。(二)惩忿窒欲,迁善改过。(一)洁长补短,互问互得。(四)戒盈戒满,勿矜勿伐。(五)常思己过,莫论人非。(六)慎于雌黄,谨于容止。(七)言而有信,心宜存忠。”

遵父命,在读中学的同时,又投考龙溪蔡璋的速记传习所夜班学速记。先生刻苦努力,勤奋学习,6个月就学会了并娴熟地掌握了22个声母、32个韵母的速记法,一分钟能记140个字,名冠全班。《恬庵五十岁自订年谱》中写道:“是年除在中学读书外,有三件事可以记录:(一)学习速记:二月一日(甲寅十二月十八日)父命我顶‘汪之瀛’名到西斜街速记传习所学习。因系夜班,故可不废校课。……自二月一日至十一日学完二十二声,三十二韵。二月十八日起学习拼音、简单符号、特别法庭符号并练习听写,五月四日学期考试,十日发榜名列第一,得97.5。……第二学期自六月七日起开始实地练习,由教员与学生轮流演说,当场用速记记录,归家再译成汉文。……两学期共交练习一千六百七十六面,每分钟可记一百四十字。……父亲命我学此技术,本为藉此谋得职位,补助家用;我则打算学会速记可以帮助记笔记。当时在中学所记之法书经济笔记、西洋史笔记,以及入大学后所记《左盦文论》、《东西文化及其哲学》皆由后一目的出发也。然自严亲见背后,生计日蹙,本赖此技术簪笔佣书,得以养家糊口,娶妻生子,并得工读的机会报考大学,为后此转入学术界之阶梯。尤其能多辨方言,无形中为审辨语音预加训练,对于我终身的事业皆有帮助。故学习速记的过程,实在是我一生的转捩点。……(二)投考经界局:各省地亩未升科纳税的很多,俗称‘黑地’。当时的政府想办一‘经界局’去勘察,委蔡锷作局长,兴武做帮办。九月一日闻讯,被好奇心和求知欲鼓励遂准备报考,预备国文、代数、几何、数学四科。十九日赴竹竿巷该局应试……二十六日复试。二十九日发榜列第二十六名,须当天领保证书,十月一日入学。……因为同时京师学务局举行中学观摩会考,传说取前列的有留学希望所以没有入学……(三)京师各中学观摩会考。”

1916 年(17 岁)

父亲得“血蛇瘟”急症,患病九天就去世了,那时先生还不满 17 岁。

中学毕业后,家庭经济困难,到众议院秘书厅速记科任二等技士(速记员),月薪收入 80 元现大洋,不但可以维持生活、贴补家用,还可以偿还父亲的丧葬费。这时三中夏校长劝先生应在工作余暇多念些书,积蓄一些学费,准备考文科大学,这样可以半工半读。本年秋天,报考北京大学文科中国文学门,考中第四名,从此便走进了半工半读的大学生活,每星期至少有三个半天到众议院作速记,其余时间在北京大学上课学习。入学后,对钱玄同的“文字学音篇”、刘师培的“中古文学”和“中古文学史”较感兴趣,每次上课均用速记作笔记,回家后再翻译成文言收藏起来,后来编成《左盦文论》。

1917 年(18 岁)

蔡元培到北京大学任校长。蔡先生崇尚学术自由和思想自由,主张新旧思想兼容并包,聘请了许多思想先进的教授讲授新知识。先生受到启发,一直拿蔡元培“博大而坚贞的精神”做自己追求的理想人格,赞成蔡先生的“兼容并包”的态度,崇拜他的“临大节而不可夺”的气节,服膺他那“富贵不能淫,贫贱不能移,威武不能屈”的精神。先生在自传中说:“在他(蔡先生)逝世第二天作了《博大和坚贞》一文来哀悼他,就是发挥这种思想。三十年来我所以能做到‘大德不逾闲’的地步,完全靠这种‘北大精神’的帮助!”当时的同学有伍一比

(叔倪)、孟寿椿、俞平伯、陈宝锷(剑修)、许德珩(楚荪)、傅斯年(孟真)、杨振声(今甫)等人。

1918年(19岁)

和黄婉如女士结婚。

1919年(20岁)

北京大学中文系毕业。受五四运动的影响,感觉自己学的是旧文学,而又有对新知识的要求,迫切要求学习新知识。当时北京大学哲学系如日中天,教授有胡适、梁漱溟、陶孟和、蒋梦麟、陈大齐、傅侗(佩青)等,杜威、罗素先后被请来讲学。为接受西方的学术思想和治学方法,决定在北京大学中国文学系毕业后,转入北大哲学系继续学习两年。

1921年(22岁)

此年夏,山东教育厅约请杜威、黄炎培、梁漱溟等到济南去讲学。受梁先生之约,为他的演讲做记录(速记)。后来由陈政整理出版了《东西文化及其哲学》。北京大学毕业,应聘到天津南开中学任国文教员。

1922年(23岁)

应邀到京师第一中学任国文教师兼总务长,不久又代理校长。先生接任后实行了财政公开;聘请好教员,但绝不任用私人;聘请教育界名流演讲;把校长的全部薪水捐购新图书。

1923年(24岁)

应聘到西安国立西北大学任教授兼国学专修科主任,讲授"中国文字学"和"中国音韵学"等课程。

1924年(25岁)

因军阀混战,交通梗阻,不但书报不通,就连平安家书也难送到。夏天,先生只好辞职返京,同时辞谢了河南中州大学聘请做中国文学系教授兼主任之邀。先生在5个机关约请下继续做速记员,同时兼任私立四存中学国文教员。

论文:

《清代校雠学家的方法》,1924年12月27日在西北大学的讲演。

1926年(27岁)

段祺瑞"执政府"镇压爱国学生运动,发生"三一八"惨案。北京形势险恶,许多学者心情忧忿,纷纷离京。此时厦门大学托林语堂邀请北京许多学者到厦大讲学,于是,先生同鲁迅、沈兼士等人南下到福建厦门大学任教,讲授"经学通论""中国音韵学沿革"等课程,并开始调查研究厦门方言。

1927年(28岁)

离开厦大后,应马叙伦之约到浙江省政府工作了不到3个月,又应聘到广州中山大学任中国语言文学系教授,开"声韵学"、"等韵研究"、"声韵学史"等课程,结合教学发表论文《怎样整理声韵学史》,刊中山大学《语言历史学研究所周刊》1集6期。

1928年(29岁)

任中山大学语言文学系主任。

为了研究《广韵》,每月出30元港币学广州话。

这一年赵元任到广州调查两广方言。向赵元任请教解疑,并切磋其他有关语言学的问题,两人讨论了一个多星期。事后先生常说:"赵先生在三天之内把我三年的疑问都解决了,赵和我的关系是介于师友之间的。"赵元任也讲过:"我跟莘田共事多年,关于语言文字方面,我们的思想跟意见好些都很难分得出谁的是谁的了。大致说来,关于经典方面他比我阅历的多,关于语言学的理论方面,我跟欧美的学者接触的多点,所以我出的主意比较占大部分。此外就很难分彼此了。"(《罗常培纪念文集》,商务印书馆,1989)

同年,与傅斯年、赵元任、李方桂一起参加创办中央研究院历史语言研究所的筹备工作。

论文:

《〈广韵〉声纽的讨论》(与刘文锦合署名),刊中山大学《语言历史学研究所周刊》2 集 14 期。

《〈切韵·序〉校释》,刊中山大学《语言历史学研究所周刊》3 集 25、26、27 期合刊。

《〈切韵〉探赜》,刊中山大学《语言历史学研究所周刊》3 集 25、26、27 期合刊。

《双声叠韵说》,刊中山大学《语言历史学研究所周刊》4 集 41 期。

1929 年(30 岁)

辞去中山大学教职,到中央研究院历史语言研究所任专职研究员,致力于音韵学和现代汉语方言的研究,下决心要把这门学问提高到新的科学水平。是年元旦,加入人寿保险 20 年,决心:"我要玩命,非干出名堂不可!"

在史语所,从 1929 年到 1935 年 7 年间,共完成了 4 部专著、14 篇论文,又调查了 6 县 46 个点的方言,编完《汉魏六朝韵谱》和《经典释文》的反切长篇。

论文:

《校印莫友芝〈韵学源流〉跋》,《韵学源流》1929 年由中山大学出版。同年又载《中山大学图书馆周刊》6 卷 5、6 期合刊。

1930 年(31 岁)

专著:

《厦门音系》,中央研究院历史语言研究所出版。

论文:

《耶稣会士在音韵学上的贡献》,刊中央研究院历史语言研究所《集刊》1 本 3 分。

《〈声韵同然集〉残稿跋》,刊中央研究院历史语言研究所《集刊》1 本 3 分。

1931 年(32 岁)

论文:

《〈切韵〉鱼虞的音值及其所据方音考》(高本汉《切韵》音读商榷之一),刊中央研究院历史语言研究所《集刊》2 本 3 分。

《知彻澄娘音值考》(高本汉《切韵》音读商榷之二),刊中央研究院历史语言研究所《集刊》3 本 1 分。

《梵文腭音五母的藏汉对音研究》,刊中央研究院历史语言研究所《集刊》3 本 2 分。

《敦煌写本守温韵学残卷跋》,刊中央研究院历史语言研究所《集刊》3 本 2 分。

《厦门音系序》,刊《清华中国文学会月刊》1 卷 2 期。

1932 年(33 岁)

从本年开始与赵元任、李方桂合译瑞典高本汉(Bernhard Karlgren)的《中国音韵学研究》。中研院打破不译书的成例而独译此书,把高本汉应用印欧比较语言学的一套方法介绍到中国来,使中国音韵学在传统的分类分部外,又在构拟古音方面有了有效的办法和工具。

论文:

《〈中原音韵〉声类考》,刊中央研究院历史语言研究所《集刊》2 本 4 分。

《释重轻》(副题“等韵发疑二,释词之三”),刊中央研究院历史语言研究所《集刊》2 本 4 分。

《戴东原〈续方言〉稿序》，刊中央研究院历史语言研究所《集刊》2本4分。

《刘继庄的音韵学》，刊（北平）《世界日报·国语周刊》32、33、34期，1932年4～5月。

《官话字母与合声简字》，刊《世界日报·国语周刊》39、40期，1932年6月。

《关于广州话入声的讨论》，刊《世界日报·国语周刊》41期，1932年7月。

1933年（34岁）

专著：

《唐五代西北方音》，中央研究院历史语言研究所出版。

这是我国学者用现代语音学和比较语言学的方法，利用多种汉藏译音资料结合现代方言材料探讨古代汉语方言音系的第一部专著。它利用五种汉藏对音材料同《切韵》比较，去推溯唐五代西北方音的渊源，考证它们的语音系统，然后再同六种现代西北方音进行比较，来探讨它们的流变。书中披露了唐五代西北方音中有不少前人没有谈到的特点。先生说："研究现代方音唯一有效的出发点就是古音。""必须考证出古代方音来，才能窥见周秦古音的真相。"

论文：

《释内外转》（副题"等韵发疑二，释词之二"），刊中央研究院历史语言研究所《集刊》4本2分。

《泰兴何石闾〈韵史〉稿本跋》，刊中央研究院历史语言研究所《集刊》4本2分。

《刘继庄的生平及其学术概要》，刊《齐大季刊》2期。

《〈切韵〉闭口九韵之古读及其演变》，刊在中央研究院历史语言研究所《集刊·外编》（《庆祝蔡元培先生六十五岁论文集》上册）。

《明清学者对于方音研究的贡献》,刊《世界日报·国语周刊》69、70、71期,1933年1~2月。

《西洋人研究中国方音的成绩及其缺点》,刊《世界日报·国语周刊》72期,1933年2月。

《方音研究之最近的进展》,刊《世界日报·国语周刊》73期,1933年2月。

《国音字母以前的音标运动》,刊《世界日报·国语周刊》111期,1933年11月。

《唐五代西北方音自序》,刊《世界日报·国语周刊》113期,1933年11月。

1934年(35岁)

由中央研究院借聘到北京大学任中文系教授。此时刘复(半农)病逝,中文系主任是胡适兼任,到系后,日常事务实际上由先生代理。

专著:

《国音字母演进史》,1934年上海商务印书馆出版。1959年文字改革出版社新版改名为《汉语拼音字母演进史》。

论文:

《〈古音系研究〉序》,刊《世界日报·国语周刊》142期,1934年6月16日。

《徽州方言的几个要点》,刊《世界日报·国语周刊》152期,1934年8月25日。

《白涤州小传、著述提要》,刊中央研究院历史语言研究所《集刊》4本4分。

《黟县方音调查录》(与白涤州、魏建功合作),刊《国学季刊》4卷7期。

《汉语方音研究小史》,刊《东方杂志》31卷7期。

《音韵学研究法》,刊上海商务印书馆《出版周刊》新80、81号。

1935年(36岁)

受聘兼任北京大学中国文学系主任。先生到北大后开设了语言学、语音学和音韵学某些专题课,还有一门"域外音韵论著述评",评介外国人研究汉语音韵的著作,能做而且肯做这些工作的,当时还极为少见。先生讲课条理清楚,引人入胜。语言学中某些内容,尤其涉及音韵学问题的,每每叫初学者感到艰涩,先生却能深入浅出,举重若轻,间或举某些特异的语言现象,以加深学生的理解和兴趣。先生利用刘复建立的国内最早的"语音乐律实验室"教语音学,结合方言调查的训练,教学生亲自操作,把许多音韵学史上含混不清、淆乱已久的问题搞明白了。

论文:

《关于国音的几个问题》,刊《世界日报·国语周刊》172期,1935年1月12日。

《高本汉的中国音韵论著提要》,刊(天津)《益世报·读书周刊》6期,1935年7月。

《中国音韵学的外来影响》,刊《东方杂志》32卷14期。

《中州韵和十三辙》《张洵如〈北京音系十三辙〉序》,刊《益世报·读书周刊》16期,1935年9月19日。

《〈中国音韵学〉序》,刊(天津)《大公报·图书副刊》101期,1935年10月。

《〈十韵汇编〉凡例》,刊《益世报·读书周刊》21期,1935年10月24日。

《〈通志·七音略〉研究》(景印元至治本《通志·七音略》序),刊中央研究院历史语言研究所《集刊》5本4分。

《〈十韵汇编〉叙例》,刊《国学季刊》5卷2期。

《音韵学与戏剧》,刊(北平)《华北日报》1935年9月8日。

1936年(37岁)

继续兼任北京大学中国文学系主任。

编著:

《十韵汇编》(与刘复、魏建功合编),北京大学出版部出版。

这本书是《切韵》系统韵书材料的总结,汇辑了唐写本《切韵》残本五种,《刊谬补缺切韵》残本一种及《大宋重修广韵》一种,排比对照,以利研究阅览。

论文:

《读牟应震〈毛诗古韵考〉》,刊《益世报·读书周刊》42期,1936年4月2日。

《旧剧中的几个音韵问题》,刊《东方杂志》33卷1期。

《〈榕村韵书〉正名》,刊《益世报·读书周刊》51期,1936年6月4日。

《韵文体语中所见之古今音变示例》,刊《益世报·读书周刊》74期,1936年11月12日。

《释清浊》,刊(南京)《中央日报·文史》6期,1936年12月13日。

1937年(38岁)

专任北京大学教职,中央研究院改聘先生为通讯研究员。

"七七事变"后,除了同以郑天挺(毅生)为首的一些教授维持北大残局外,加紧进行自己的研究工作,赶写《临川音系》,以工作来排解忧烦。先生说:"故都沦陷之后,是否还应该每天关在屋里埋头伏案地去做这种纯学术研究?这件事的事非功罪颇不容易回答。可是当时我在想,我既不能立刻投笔从戎,效命疆场;也没机会杀身成仁,以死报国,那么,与其成天的楚囚对泣,一筹莫展,何如努力从事自己未完成的工作,藉以镇压激昂慷慨的悲怀?假如能在危城中奋勉写成几本书……自觉对得起自己,对得起学校,对得起国家!”这段话表露了一个爱国知识分子的悲愤和执著的敬业精神。10月中旬与郑天挺、魏建功等结伴南下,乘汽车离开北平,从海路到香港,绕道梧州转赴长沙临时大学(北大、清华、南开三校组成),12月中旬到达设在南岳的文学院,任国立长沙临时大学中国文学系教授,立即开课。

译著:

《中国音韵学研究》(瑞典高本汉著,与赵元任、李方桂合译)脱稿。译本1940年初版,1948年再版,1994年缩印第一版。

这是我国语言学界一件大事,因为“三位先生全是这门学问里极精彩的工作者”(高本汉语,见该书作者赠序),他们被称为中国现代语言学的奠基人。三位先生商定的译法:一要译得忠实能读,二要改其错误,三要加入新材料,四要改用国际音标注音,五是一部分重编。这实际上是译中有审、校、改、著,没有深厚的功力显然是不能同时做到的。当时中央研究院历史语言研究所所长傅斯年称赞这部译著:“此固近年我国译学上未有之巨业,瞻望明代译天算诸贤,可无愧焉。”

论文:

《音标的派别和国际音标的来源》,刊《东方杂志》34卷1期。

《武尔披齐利的中国音韵学述评》,刊《中央日报·文史》25、26期,1937年5月。

《绩溪方音述略》,北京大学出版部排印本。

1938年(39岁)

随着抗日战争的发展,长沙临时大学迁往云南。先生随校入滇,1月下旬从长沙坐火车到广州,再从香港搭船到越南海防,转滇越铁路,2月26日到达昆明。

长沙临时大学到昆明后,4月改称“国立西南联合大学”。因为校舍不够,文、法两学院在4月至8月一度搬到蒙自上课。8月23日,西南联大蒙自分校课程结束,文、法学院师生返回昆明。

5月4日,蒙自分校开始上课。是日,蒙自分校学生集会纪念“五四”,先生应邀出席演讲。同时演讲的还有朱自清、张佛泉、钱穆。

6月28日,受西南联大1938~1939年度招考委员会聘为委员。

10月6日,西南联大校委会决定成立编制校歌、校训委员会,先生和冯友兰、朱自清、罗庸、闻一多同聘为委员。11月30日决定以“刚毅坚卓”为校训。

11月26日,西南联大校常委会决议,设立文、理、法、商、工四学院一年级生课业生活指导委员会,先生受聘为委员。

11月27日,教授会推选出席1938~1939年度校务会议之教授、副教授代表。朱自清等11人为代表,先生等6人为候补代表。后来,自1939年至1943年,先生连续被教授会推选为出席第二至六届校务委员会议的代表。

1939年(40岁)

1月9日,西南联大校常委会决定由师范学院国文系教职员筹办《国文月刊》,先生为编委。

6月,北大、清华、南开三校恢复原有的研究院、所、部。任北大文科研究所语学部导师,仍兼北大中国文学系主任。

11月,校常委会决议请先生暂代西南联大文学系和师范学院国文系两系主任。

12月5日,校常委会决议成立毕业生成绩审查委员会,聘请先生等5人为委员,先生为召集人。

老舍说:“莘田的责任心极重,他的学生都会作证。学生们大概有点怕他,因为他对他们的要求,在治学上和为人上,都很严格。学生们也都敬爱他,因为他对自己的要求也严格。他不但要求自己把

学生教明白，而且要求把他们教通了，能够去独当一面，独立思考。（老舍《悼念罗常培先生》）

论文：

《〈经典释文〉和原本〈玉篇〉反切中的匣于两纽》，刊中央研究院历史语言研究所《集刊》8本1分。

《〈八思巴字和元代官话〉自序》，刊《图书季刊》新1卷1期。

《段玉裁校本〈经典释文〉跋》，刊《图书季刊》新1卷2期。

《〈蒙古字韵〉跋》，刊《图书季刊》新1卷3期。

《从"四声"说到"九声"》，刊《东方杂志》36卷8期。

1940年（41岁）

6月16日，《国文月刊》创刊（至1946年共出40期）。

6月26日，校常委会决议，聘请先生为西南联大中文系及师院国文系主任。

专著：

《临川音系》，商务印书馆出版。

这部书首先应用史传、族谱和地方志的记载，找出客家几次迁徙的路线跟江西的关系，再从语音特点比较临川话和客家话的共同性与个别性，两方面互相参证，把"客赣"方言的亲属关系联系起来，在方言研究的著作中可算是一个典型。它虽然是一部研究方言音系的书，但已注意到收集研究方言的特殊词汇，并附加好些语源学的解释，对研究这种方言或别种方言的现代语言学、历史音韵学和方言与普通话的对应关系，都起了示范作用。

论文：

《误读字的分析》，刊《东方杂志》37卷18期，又载《国文月刊》1卷4期。

《〈古逸丛书〉影宋大字本〈尚书释音〉跋》，刊《图书季刊》新2卷

1期。

1941年(42岁)

5月,因公赴叙永分校,离校期间,校常委会决议由闻一多暂代中文系及师院国文系主任。8月回校后恶性疟疾发作,连病两个多月。

9月10日,因病未能到任,请辞中文系及师院国文系主任。闻一多请辞此两系代理主任。校常委会决议请杨振声继任。

12月18日,杨振声请辞两系主任,校常委会仍请先生担任。

论文:

《现代方言中的古音遗迹》,刊(重庆)《文史杂志》1卷2期。

《昆明话和国语的异同》,刊《东方杂志》38卷3期。

《查尔默的汉语入声尾说》,刊《东方杂志》38卷22期。

《介绍高本汉的中国音韵学研究》,刊(重庆)《图书月刊》1卷7、8期合刊。

《四声、五声、六声、八声皆为周氏所发现》(副题"恬庵说音之一"),刊《国文月刊》1卷6期。

《唐写本〈经典释文〉残卷四种跋》,刊《清华学报》13卷2期。

1942年(43岁)

2月,第一次到大理调查少数民族语言,在大理师范住了三个星期,在喜洲五台中学住了两个星期,在边疆中学生中找到发言人,先后记录了莲山摆彝(傣)语、福贡傈僳语、贡山俅(独龙)语、怒语和茶山、浪速、山头三种景颇语,以及9县11个点的民家(白)语方言。回昆明途中,在楚雄附近不幸遇车祸,被汽车撞伤,幸而治愈未留后遗症。

自1938年到1944年在联大教课和主持系务工作之外,积极对云南这个民族语言众多的"宝库"开展了大量的调查研究工作。先生自己做,也指导别人或配合别人做。先生在《语言学与云南》一文中,把1938年到1944年在云南进行的民族语言和汉语方言调查详细列出,归结为"五纲四十一目"。在民族语言方面,先生亲自往滇西调查的有十几种,积累了许多材料。单是民家语就调查过多次。后来发表了《贡山俅语初探》、《莲山摆彝语文初探》两种专著和几篇论文。先生还调查了昆明方言,1941年发表了《昆明话和国语的异同》。大多数材料先生生前都没有来得及整理,甚为可惜。先生还指导北大本科生和文科研究所研究生调查了云南的几支彝语,后来都整理出版了。先生这些学生日后都成为著名的民族语言研究的佼佼者和专家,如傅懋勣、马学良、陈士林、邢公畹、高华年等。云南话和北方话相近,音系简单,引不起方言研究者的兴趣。先生从方言研究全局出发,建议中央研究院抓紧时间调查,于是中研院组织人力调查了云南省98个县的方言(《云南方言调查》1969年在台湾出版)。先生自己也调查了昆明方言,1941年发表的《昆明话和国语的异同》起了示范作用。

这一年在北大文科研究所作了题为"研究工作的性质"的讲演,指出:"教书要深入浅出,科研要小题大做。""'大纲'、'概论'、'通史'、'述评',只能指示门径,研究则不能以此作为根据。先生说:"一个有系统的研究……第一要有问题,问题的产生或由观察精确引起,或从读书而来……第二得有见解,有了问题就该搜集材料,相当数量的事实和材料是一切研究的基础。材料的聚积和剖析需要功力,材料的组织和融会贯通,需要理解。而科学的精诣,就在于研究者要有一点有价值的意见……第三得有证据,假说能否变成通则,就看证据充分不充分。一个严正的研究者得要有'有几分证据说几分话'的态度。第四得有结论,单有材料而没有意见就会流于破碎;单有意见而无证据就会流于空疏;从材料提出假设,拿证据证成通则,自然而然就得出顺理成章的结论来。一个研究工作者没有果断确切的结论，那就像画龙没点睛，做衣服没装领子一样。”这样对研究工作的性质、步骤和方法，就了如指掌了。

专著：

《贡山俅语初探》，北京大学文科研究所油印论文之三，1942，昆明；又发表于《国学季刊》7卷3期。1952年，北京再版。

《北平俗曲百种摘韵》，1942年由重庆国民图书出版社出版。1950年北京来薰阁书店新版，改题为《北京俗曲百种摘韵》。

论文：

《从语言上论云南民族的分类》，刊（重庆）《边政公论》1卷7、8期合刊。

《评费兹哲拉尔德的〈五华楼〉》，刊《旅行杂志》16卷10期。

《答汪洋君问》，刊《国文月刊》12期。

《中国人与中国文》，刊《国文月刊》12期。收入《中国人与中国文》，这是1941年4月24日在昆明广播电台的讲话稿。

《中国文学的新陈代谢》，1942年7月1日在昆明广播电台演讲。

《什么叫“双声”“叠韵”?》（副题“恬庵说音之四”），刊《国文月刊》13期。

《汉字的声音是古今一样吗?》（副题“恬庵说音之三”），刊《国文月刊》14期。

《语音学的功用》，刊（重庆）《读书通讯》36期。

《临川音系跋》，刊《图书月刊》2卷2期。

《老舍在云南》，刊昆明《文聚》3期。

《法伟堂校本〈经典释文〉跋》，刊《图书月刊》2卷4期。

《从客家迁徙的踪迹论客赣方言的关系》，刊《中国青年》7卷1期。

1943 年(44 岁)

3 月,第二次到大理调查少数民族语言,收获颇丰,得到了茶山、浪速、山头三种景颇语的语言材料。

先生向来在从事高深研究的同时,不忘生活中的语言问题,尤其关心"国语运动"和语言教育,早期写过许多国语运动的文章,并穷源竟委地研究我国拼音文字的历史,1934 年写成《国音字母演进史》。到云南后,先生几次在广播电台演讲,或应邀为报刊写文章,谈论语文教学问题。先生主张充分利用注音符号和"国语罗马字"帮助认字,抨击官定国文教本专选文言排斥白话的复古逆流,提出中学国文教员应该讲究教学法,自己要说国语。这些意见都很可取,切中时弊。先生还在刊物上发表了一系列关于语言文字,尤其是音韵学的通俗性文章,如《误读字的分析》、《什么叫"双声""叠韵"?》、《语音学的功用》、《反切的方法及其应用》、《音韵学研究法》等,浅显易懂,启人心智。1942 年在重庆出版了《北平俗曲百种摘韵》一书,重庆《新华日报》的记者郑林曦读后在该报上写书评《给诗人们介绍一本韵书》,称:"就内容说,称得上是一本通俗的科学著作;而所附的词曲,又可以实际帮助诗人们用来合辙压韵。"这本书本来印数不多,转眼就售尽。1950 年,经作者校定,此书在北京再版,1986 年又由天津一家出版社重排出版,改称《北京俗曲百种摘韵》。可见这本通俗著作受到社会重视的程度。

论文:

《王兰生与〈音韵阐微〉》,刊(重庆)《学术季刊》1 卷 3 期。

《恬庵语文论著甲集自序》,刊《读书通讯》58 期。

《我的中学国文教学经验》,刊《国文月刊》20 期。

《语言学在云南》,刊《边政公论》2 卷 9、10 期合刊。

《昙花未现》,刊(昆明)《自由论坛》5、6 期合刊。

《从昆曲到皮黄》，刊(昆明)《正义报》副刊，1943 年 11 月 14 日。

《周秦古音之新问题及近人之贡献》，昆明西南联合大学油印出版。

《贡山俅语初探叙论》，刊《边政公论》3 卷 12 期。

老舍说："莘田虽是博读古籍的学者，却不轻视民间文学。他喜爱戏曲与曲艺，常和艺人们来往，互相学习。他会唱许多折昆曲。"(老舍《悼念罗常培先生》)

1944 年(45 岁)

1940 年在《临川音系序论》中论到赣方言和客家方言的关系，并论述了客家迁徙的过程。这是先生把语言研究延伸到文化领域的开端。入滇以后，先生把那篇叙论单独抽出，修改为《从客家迁徙的踪迹论客赣方言的关系》发表在一家期刊上。文章认为："如果有人把客家问题彻底地研究清楚，那么关于一部分中国民族迁徙的途径和语言演变的历程就可以认识一半多。"随后，先生尽量搜集藏缅族的父子连名制的语言材料和有关文献，片纸支字都不放过，逐步深入研究，在 1944 年 3 次发表文章，最后总合成一篇《论藏缅族的父子连名制》的长文，详细论证了以大理一带为中心的"古诏国"(约 8 ~ 10 世纪)的建国者是有父子连名制的藏缅族，即现在有父子连名制特征的彝族和仍存有这一特征遗迹的白族的祖先，而不是没有这一文化特征的非藏缅族的称为"白彝"或"摆彝"的傣族。这个结论得到公认，非但解决了民族史上的疑难，而且有地缘政治的现实意义。1943 年夏，在西南联大主办的文史演讲会上，先生用"文化与语言"为题演讲，建立了日后《语言与文化》一书的框架。20 世纪 80 年代后期，"社会语言学"在我国升起一股势头，自然想起在 20 世纪 40 年代先生即开创了从语言研究扩展到语言与文化、语言与民族社会历史关系的研究。

5月4日《文艺》壁报社在联大校区10号教室举办五四文艺晚会。先生应邀出席。由于参加者多,会场容纳不下,临时改换地点引起纠纷,晚会改期举行。

5月8日重开五四文艺晚会,改由国文学会主办,先生和闻一多主持,地点在新校舍图书馆前草坪。参加者有校内外2000多人。先生当时的回忆录后来发表为《第一个五四文艺晚会的回忆并怀一多、佩弦》一文。

7月26日先生和郑天挺等应邀赴大理参加撰修《大理方言志》工作。先生十分注意搜集地方方言文献和少数民族历史文化资料和民情、民俗等。当年所写的日记、随笔、散文等,艺术风格朴实自然而有风趣,显示一位博学幽默而有文采的学者风度。后来一部分著为学术论文,一部分收入散文集《蜀道难》和《苍洱之间》内。

9月教育部确定先生于1944~1945年度出国休假讲学。先生因事赴渝,二系主任由校常委会决议请罗庸暂代。

1944年美国加州朴茂纳大学邀请先生去美讲学,担任人文科学访问教授。请辞二系主任,校常委会决议请罗庸继任。朴茂纳大学在南加州的“客来而忙”(Claremont),是一所文科大学,曾授予京剧大师梅兰芳名誉博士学位。校长伊·威尔逊·莱因是一位国际知名的学者。

按照国民党政府规定,凡出国人员要先去重庆中央训练团受训,并加入国民党,才发给官员出国护照,便于买较高的舱位,并有其他方便。先生宁可领取普通护照坐三等舱,但要保持学者本色。

10月,从昆明乘火车、轮船、飞机,经加尔各答、孟买去美国。11月23日,应泰戈尔翁创建的国际大学邀请,先生作了短期学术访问,并作演说“印度对于汉语音韵学研究的影响”演说稿。后发表在《中印研究》1卷3期,1945年3月。两个月后先生到达美国。

游记散文集:

《蜀道难》由重庆独立出版社出版,1946年上海再版,1996年收入辽宁教育出版社《书趣文丛》之《苍洱之间》一书中。

论文:

《国语运动的新方向》,刊(昆明)《中央日报·星期论文》1月2日,又收入《中国人与中国文》。

《我与老舍》(为老舍创作二十周年),刊(昆明)《扫荡报》副刊,4月19日。

《从文艺晚会说起》,刊《云南日报·星期论文》,5月21日。

《论藏缅族的父子连名制》,刊(南开大学)《边疆人文》1卷3、4期合刊。

《再论藏缅族父子连名制》,刊《边政公论》3卷9期。

《三论藏缅族父子连名制》,刊《边疆人文》2卷1、2期合刊。

《推行语政与宗族融合》,刊《边政公论》3卷1期。

《贡山怒语初探叙论》,刊《边政公论》3卷12期。

《茶山歌》,刊《边疆人文》1卷5、6期合刊。

《反切的方法及其应用》(副题"恬庵说音之六"),刊《国文月刊》27期。

《音韵学不是绝学》,刊《读书通讯》83期。

《汉语里的借字》,刊(昆明)《中央日报·周中专论》7月6日。

《〈史通增释〉序》,刊《图书季刊》5卷4期。

1945年(46岁)

从1945年1月到1946年6月,在美国朴茂纳大学讲授"汉语引论"等课程。美国朴茂纳大学校长莱因对先生"在美国朴茂纳大学杰出的工作"表示感谢,赞扬先生"对学生和学校十分关切",称先生"在朴茂纳赢得了永久的地位，我们全体同人对能有这样一位学者做了这样出色的工作引为幸事”。

专著：

《中国人与中国文》由开明书店出版。

《汉魏六朝专家文研究》（整理刘申叔遗说），由重庆独立出版社出版。

论文：

《〈金元戏曲方言考〉序》，刊《图书季刊》新6卷1、2期合刊。

《师范学院国文学系所应注意的几件事》，刊《当代评论》4卷2期，又收入《中国人与中国文》。

1946年（47岁）

6～7月在美国加利福尼亚大学图书馆博览群书，进一步了解国际上语言学研究的新进展。

8月移教大西洋岸边的耶鲁大学，每周担任4小时的研究讨论班，指导研究生作博士论文。耶鲁大学校长也在先生讲学工作结束之际，对先生“在耶鲁汉学研究项目上所做的贡献，表示感谢”，并且决定聘任为终身教授，负责将家属接到美国。美国《洛杉矶日报》发行人罗伯特·伊·沃克写道：“在美国，罗教授受人怀念，自然是因为他讲课的质量高，对所教的学科十分通晓，并能有效地传授给别人。但他特别令人怀念的是，作为一个大师把他伟大的祖国，中国社会的成就和特点教给世界上另一大国的青年学生。特别是以他自己的楷模，说明一个人可以在一生中充分发挥自己的个性和才智，并以这样的榜样教育其他人更友爱、更谦虚、更有造诣、更有道德、更诚实、更宽厚、更平易近人，即使他的学生意识到他们永远不能达到他们的老师和朋友的高度。”（罗伯特·伊·沃克《罗常培在美国》，《罗常培纪念文集》398页）。

1947 年(48 岁)

暑期,在美国密西根大学举办的语言研究所的语言学会星期讲座上,会见了来自美国各地的语言学家,还选修了三种课程,对美国语言学界的情况有了进一步的了解。

游记散文集:

《苍洱之间》独立出版社出版,南京;1996 年收入辽宁教育出版社《书趣文丛》之《苍洱之间》一书中。

论文:

《王兰生年谱》,刊(南京)《现代学报》1 卷 2、3 期合刊。

《评商克的〈古代汉语发音学〉》,刊《岭南学报》7 卷 1 期。

1948 年(49 岁)

7 月 3 日,离美回国。

8 月 19 日回到北平,仍在北京大学中国文学系任教,并兼任北京大学文科研究所所长,恢复了刘复创建的语音乐律实验室。

先生很快静下心来,谢绝各方面的活动,躲进东斋斗室和北大文科研究所的小办公室,开始整理文稿和存书。秋天北大开学,先生所开的课程中有门语言学。先生在联大时开过"训诂学",试着用语言学的观点给这门传统的学问以新内容,在美国几年也留意摘录这方面的材料,这次回北大讲语言学,在某些方面就结合训诂学里的问题来讲。比如讲到意义和声音的关系,就联系清儒"训诂之声,故有声同字异,声近意同"的学说,加以语言学论点的阐发。先生曾有开拓一门"新训诂学"的设想,但紧接着是炮声隆隆,这事则无暇考虑了。

解放前夕,加紧完成《语言与文化》一书,并协助布置北大 50 周年校庆展览。南京国民党政府派飞机到北平接各大学名教授到台湾。先生留在北平。

论文:

《七七事变后的北大残局》，1948 年 12 月刊《北京大学 50 周年纪念特刊》。

1949 年（50 岁）

北平和平解放。参加筹备北京大学工会和北京市教育工作者工会的工作，又参加了北京市各界代表会议和中国人民政治协商会议第一届全体会议，以及亚洲、澳洲工会代表会议。

10 月，中国文字改革协会成立，吴玉章被选为主任，先生被选为常务理事。

专著：

《汉语音韵学导论》一册，北京大学出版部出版。

论文：

《〈道藏源流考〉序》由中华书局出版印行。

1950 年（51 岁）

《语言与文化》出版。这本书经过多年积累，用大量语言事实，包括中国的、外国的、古代的、现代的，论证语言与现代文化多方面的关系；从语词的语源和演变看过去文化的遗迹；从造词心理看民族的文化程度；从借字看文化接触；从地名看民族迁徙的踪迹；从姓名和别号看民族来源和宗教信仰；从亲属称谓看婚姻制度等等。全书只十余万字（包括附录数篇），却内容厚实，引证详细，读起来又使人情趣盎然。这本书最能体现先生一贯倡导的“有几分证据说几分话”的严谨学风，又最能见到先生深入浅出的笔底功力。先生“自信这本小书对于中国语言学新路把路基初步地铺起来了”。1950 年北大出版，只印了几千册，除送人外，很快卖完了。20 世纪 80 年代后期“社会语言学”在我国升起一股势头，自然想起曾被评为“我国第一部文化语言学或社会语言学开创性著作”的《语言与文化》，于是 1989 年由语文出版社重新排印出版。

6月中国科学院语言研究所成立,被任命为语言研究所所长。

7月起,先后派遣青年干部参加中央民族访问团到各民族地区了解情况,搜集资料,接受语言锻炼,准备调查少数民族语言。

12月9日,在语言研究所关于《马克思主义与语言学问题》(李立三、曹葆华译)的讨论会上,先生作了题为《斯大林论语言学问题与中国语言学研究的联系》的报告,提出把语言学各学科的研究和国家的实际需要结合起来,逐步开展语法、音韵、方言、语言规范化和语音实验等方面的工作。语言研究所还建立了少数民族语言研究组,帮助各少数民族创建和改革文字。

专著:

《语言与文化》由北京大学出版部出版,1989年语文出版社再版,2004年北京出版社"大家小书"第三辑收印《语言与文化》,1月至9月三次印刷。

《莲山摆彝语文初探》由北京大学出版部出版。

论文:

《中国语言学的新方向》,刊《新建设》1卷12期,1950年。

《语言研究和文艺创作》,刊《新建设》2卷9期。

《研究西南少数民族语言的重要性》,刊(天津)《进步日报》1月26日。

《第一个五四文艺晚会的回忆并怀一多、佩弦》,刊《光明日报》5月7日。

《对于大学中国语文系课程改革的意见》,刊《光明日报》6月3日。

《一年来高等教育的发展和教学研究的联系》,刊(北京)《新民报》10月5日。

《相声的来源和今后努力的方向》,刊《人民日报》12月10日。

《一年来语言学的普及倾向》，刊《进步日报》10 月 1 日。

《关于〈吴王寿梦之戈〉音理上的一点补充》，刊《光明日报》6 月 21 日。

《〈北平俗曲百种摘韵〉再版自序》，刊《光明日报》10 月 8 日。

《扬雄〈方言〉在中国语言学史上的地位——周祖谟〈方言校笺〉序》，刊《光明日报》10 月 22 日。

1951 年(52 岁)

任中央民族事务委员会委员，负责领导少数民族语言调查研究和文字规划工作。

6 月，在中央民族事务委员会作“关于少数民族语言文字问题”的报告。

7 月 31 日语言研究所举办“语文干部训练班”。

10 月派语言所研究人员与中央民族学院语言系有关民族语言教师合编语言教材，共编写了 8 个民族的 12 种教材。

10 月 6 日主持召开“西南、中南少数民族语文座谈会”。

10 月 12 日政务院文化教育委员会成立少数民族语言文字研究指导委员会。被任命为该指导委员会的秘书长。

11 月 20 日，语言研究所和中国文字改革协会联合召开“关于少数民族文字汇通方案及汉字注音问题座谈会”。

12 月，少数民族语言文字研究指导委员会召集少数民族代表及语言学、民族学专家座谈如何协助各少数民族创立或充实改进文字问题。

同月，语言研究所派出工作组去川康调查彝语。

论文：

《研究国内少数民族语文的迫切需要》，刊《光明日报》3 月 28 日，又收入《国内少数民族语言文字的概况》(中国语文丛书之一)，

1954年,北京中华书局出版。

《国内少数民族语言的系属和文字情况》,刊《科学通报》2卷5期,又载《人民日报》3月31日。

《语言研究的重点》,刊《新建设》3卷4期。

《耶稣会士在音韵学上的贡献补》,刊《国学季刊》7卷2期。

《唐写本〈经典释文〉残卷五种跋》,刊《国学季刊》7卷2期。

1952年(53岁)

2月,语言研究所派以傅懋勣为首的云南省民族语言工作队赴云南调查民族语言。

2月5日,中国文字改革研究委员会在北京召开成立大会,先生被任命为委员,分工在拼音方案组。

3月初,语言研究所派出以北大袁家骅为首的壮语工作组赴广西调查壮语方言。

5月,语言研究所派出由喻世长、王辅世组成的贵州工作队赴贵州调查苗语和布依语。

7月,《中国语文》在北京创刊,先生担任总编辑,从编辑方向、稿件内容到编辑部每个人的工作情况,都亲自过问,并亲自撰写论文。

9月,倡议并筹划在北京大学开办"语言专修科",专门培养语言调查研究人员,语言专修科开设语音学、音韵学、语言学概论、方言调查、文字学等专业课程。先生亲自授课。很多当年的毕业学生,后来成为语言研究的骨干。

先生培养人才的积极精神人多称道。北京大学袁家骅曾经说过:"莘田对于培养青年,那是百分之百的坦率亲切,肯呕心沥血地加以指点的。"除了讲课、指导研究这些身为人师的职责外,先生对学生的爱护、关照是非常突出的。先生对学生一视同仁,对学生在学问上有一得之见,先生不惜在课堂上表扬或在文章中提及;对于学生行为上的过失,先生当面批评;对于学生生活上的困难,先生设法帮助。对学生“温而严”的风范为大家所了解。在云南五年内,先生推荐去一些大学或研究所任副教授或讲师的,单中文系出身的就是10人。至于中文系历届毕业生甚至旁系的,由先生介绍去中学或别的行当任职的,更是难以计数。先生主张为人师者“要把金针度与人”。先生教导学生:“教书要深入浅出,研究要小题大做”,是出自肺腑的经验之谈。1941年先生在联大分校讲“读书八式”:“涵咏自得,采花酿蜜,剥茧抽丝,磁石引针,披沙拣金郢书燕说,过眼云烟,挦撦饾饤”。1942年在昆明北大文科研究所演讲“研究工作的性质”都是以金针度与人,正所谓“善歌者使人继其声,善教者使人继其志”。先生在云南七年,单在语言学方面口传心授,亲自带领学生操作,培养了一批又一批语言工作人才、专家、知名学者,为后来国家急需的语言工作者作了储备。

12月,语言研究所召开“相声语言座谈会”,先生亲临讲话,说:“有人以为语言学高深莫测,玄而又玄,可望而不可及。可是,活的语言来自民间,相声的语言就十分丰富多彩。侯宝林就是杰出的语言学家。”先生还说:“相声曲艺演员应该有语言学常识。欢迎大家来进修。”

论文:

《语言研究应联系实际并照顾全面》,刊《中国语文》创刊号。

《1950年苏联语言学界的辩论》,刊《中国语文》创刊号。

《从斯大林的语言学说谈中国语言学上的几个问题》,刊《科学通报》3卷7期。

《语言学的对象和任务》,刊《中国语文》1952年2期。

《从历史上看中国文字改革的条件》,刊《中国语文》1952年2期。

《为语言在文艺上的精切运用而奋斗》，刊(北京)《新民报》5月23日。

《关于少数民族语文工作的报告》，刊《科学通报》3卷7期。

《加强研究少数民族语文，为提高各族文化而努力！》，刊《中国语文》1952年6期(12月号)，又收入《国内少数民族语言文字的概况》。

《怎样学习大众的语言》，刊《语文学习》1952年9期。

《贡山俅语初探》，刊《国学季刊》7卷3期。

1953年(54岁)

积极参加和领导当时正在进行的推广普通话、文字改革、汉语规范化和研究少数民族语言文字等工作。

9月14～26日，语言研究所举行少数民族语文研究工作扩大会议，会上着重讨论了有关帮助少数民族创造和改革文字的问题，先生亲自主持。先生在发言中强调了为兄弟民族人民大众服务，必须既重视学术上的科学性，又重视工作中的政策性；必须把少数民族人民大众的利益放在首位，为提高各民族的文化而努力。先生说："过去我也写了多种专著和论文，调查了十余种少数民族语言，但只停留在个人的、孤立的工作上，没有也不可能为社会服务，只有现在由于国家的重视，语文研究工作者才有了'用武之地'。"

论文：

《中国的语言学》，刊《科学通报》1953年4期，又载《新建设》1953年6期。

1954年(55岁)

当选为全国人民代表大会代表，工作繁忙，积劳成疾，长期患高血压症，但仍坚持参加各种会议、撰写论文，为汉语规范化、文字改革和少数民族语言文字的建设，抱病工作。

代表民族语言文字研究指导委员会和中央民族事务委员会向政

务院提出《关于帮助尚无文字的民族创立文字的报告》。

论文：

《国内少数民族语言文字的概况》（与傅懋勣合写），刊《中国语文》1954 年 3 期。

《为帮助兄弟民族创立文字而努力》，刊《中国语文》1954 年 6 期。

《台词和语音学的关系》，刊《戏剧报》1954 年 4 期。

《遵照政务会议的指示，开展帮助尚无文字各民族创立文字的工作》，刊《科学通报》1954 年 7 期。

《语音学知识》（与王均合作，署名田恭），《中国语文》连载，1954 年 1 期至 1955 年 5 期。

1955 年（56 岁）

10 月，中国科学院成立哲学社会科学部，任哲学社会科学部学部委员。

4 月，先生召开“词典编纂法座谈会”，5 月又召开“汉语规范化座谈会”，为推广普通话，促进文字改革进行准备。

10 月 15 日至 23 日，出席教育部和文字改革委员会联合召开的全国文字改革会议；25 日至 31 日，先生又出席中国科学院召开的汉语规范问题学术会议；12 月 6 日至 13 日，先生出席中国科学院语言研究所和中央民族学院联合召开的民族语文科学讨论会。这三个会议都是全国性的，会上先生都被推选为领导小组成员。在现代汉语规范化问题学术会议上作了主题报告“现代汉语规范化问题”（与吕叔湘合作）。报告精辟分析和回答了为什么要在这个时候提出现代汉语规范化，关于现代汉语规范化有什么原则性的问题需要解决，以及怎样进行规范化工作等问题。它对研究汉民族共同语、促进汉语规范化都具有重要价值。

论文：

《略论汉语规范化》，刊《中国语文》1955年10期。

《现代汉语规范问题（提纲）》（与吕叔湘合作），刊《中国语文》1955年12期。

1956年（57岁）

国家成立中央推广普通话工作委员会，被任命为委员。

中国科学院语言研究所创办内部刊物《语言研究通讯》，任常务编辑。

中国科学院语言研究所聘请所内外专家成立“普通话审音委员会”，被推选为召集人。

在先生倡导下中国科学院语言研究所和教育部合作开办“普通话语音研究班”，组织各地高等学校进行全国汉语方言的初步普查（从1956年至1959年10月）。以县为单位在全国共调查约两千个点，写出方言调查报告1195种，使方言调查与推广普通话紧密地结合起来。

中国科学院语言研究所和中央民族学院联合派出少数民族语文工作队700多人，对全国少数民族语言文字进行普查，足迹遍及祖国边疆，成绩卓著。3月桂西壮文学校在广西武鸣开办。

6月，在北京召开“关于滇、黔、桂、康兄弟民族文字创立改革工作座谈会”。

10月，在贵阳市讨论通过了《民族文字字母形式问题》和《苗族文字方案（草案）》。

11月，在贵阳市布依族语言文字问题科学讨论会上，通过了《布依族文字方案（草案）》。

12月，在成都市彝族语言文字科学讨论会上通过了《凉山彝族拼音文字方案（草案）》。

此外,还主持编辑出版《语言学论文集》(自1956年4月至1958年12月共出版8辑),介绍国外语言学研究动态及成果。

论文:

《现代汉语规范问题》(与吕叔湘合作),刊《语言研究》1956年1期。

《从汉字造字和标音的历史看〈汉语拼音方案〉的进步性》,刊《人民日报》3月16日。

1957年(58岁)

2月22日,中国文字改革委员会召开第五次全体会议,决定扩大汉语拼音方案委员会。

5月6日,中国文字改革委员会第42次常委扩大会议决定,推选先生为拼音方案委员会委员(委员会由11人组成)。

专著:

《普通语音学纲要》(与王均合著),科学出版社出版,该书被列为高等学校中文系主要参考书。

论文:

《〈汉语拼音方案〉的历史渊源》,刊《人民日报》12月18日,又收入《当前文字改革的任务和汉语拼音方案》,1958年文字改革出版社出版。

1958年(59岁)

1月,全国政协派出6个宣传组,宣传《汉语拼音方案》,先生和吕叔湘为京津组负责人。

专著:

《汉魏晋南北朝韵部演变研究》(第一分册,与周祖谟合著),科学出版社出版。

论文:

《大家都来做文字改革的促进派》（与叶圣陶、胡愈之、韦悫合写），刊《人民日报》2月7日。

《〈汉语拼音方案〉与民族团结的关系》，刊《民族团结》1958年2期。

《校补本〈十韵汇编〉序》，刊《中国语文》1958年6期。

这一年冬天，先生因高血压再一次住院治疗。生病住院期间，先生仍念念不忘语言学的研究和语言科学的发展。

12月13日上午，先生医治无效，与世长辞，终年59岁。

（杨力立编）

《罗常培文集》总目

说明：

《罗常培文集总目》分为三类，一是著作，二是文章，三是外文论著。每类之下先列著作、文章等的名称，属于合著的一一署明，大都注明了出版、发表或讲演的年代，之后用罗马数字和阿拉伯数字分别标明其在《罗常培文集》中的卷次、起始页数，供读者翻检。

一、专　著

二、文 章

2.《切韵·序》校释(1928)(Ⅶ/37)

3.《切韵》鱼虞的音值及其所据方音考(1931)(Ⅶ/63)

4. 知彻澄娘音值考(1931)(Ⅶ/108)

5. 梵文腭音五母的藏汉对音研究(1932)(Ⅶ/155)

6.《切韵》闭口九韵之古读及其演变(1933)(Ⅶ/184)

7.《中原音韵》声类考(1932)(Ⅶ/260)

8. 刘继庄学述(1932)(Ⅶ/281)

9. 京剧中的几个音韵问题(1935)(Ⅶ/300)

10. 怎样整理声韵学史(1927)(Ⅶ/330)

11. 双声叠韵说(1928)(Ⅶ/336)

12.《广韵》声纽的讨论(与刘文锦合著)(1928)(Ⅶ/349)

13. 释重轻(等韵发疑二,释词之三)(1932)(Ⅶ/357)

14. 释内外转(等韵发疑二,释词之二)(1933)(Ⅶ/367)

15. 音韵学研究法(1934)(Ⅶ/391)

16. 释清浊(1936)(Ⅶ/399)

17. 释等呼(等韵发疑二,释词之一)(Ⅶ/402)

18.《韵镜》源流考(等韵发疑一,源流之四)(Ⅶ/408)

19. 拟答郭晋稀《读〈切韵指掌图〉》(1943)(Ⅶ/412)

20.《经典释文》音汇凡例(Ⅶ/420)

21.《经典释文》之版本(Ⅶ/422)

22.《经典释文》和原本《玉篇》反切中的匣于两组(1939)(Ⅶ/423)

23. 关于《经典释文》中同字异切为同音或异音的几个判断标准(Ⅶ/431)

24.《经典释文》中的齿头音(Ⅶ/435)

25.《经典释文》中的徐邈音(Ⅶ/449)

三、外文论著

1. Indian Influence on the Study of Chinese Phonology(1945)(Ⅹ/3)

2. A Preliminary Study on the Trung Language of Kung-shan(1945)(Ⅹ/19)

3. The Genealogical Patronymic Linkage System of the Tibeto-Burman Speaking Tribes(1945)(Ⅹ/27)

4. The Traits of the Chinese Language(1945)(Ⅹ/48)

5. Languages and Dialects in China(1946)(Ⅹ/59)

6. Phonetic Substitutions in Chinese Loanwords from Indic(1947)(Ⅹ/75)

7. Review to C. P. Fitzgerald *The Tower of Five Glories: A Study of the Min-chia of Tali, Yunnan*(Ⅹ/81)

8. Review to Yuen Ren Chao and Lien Sheng Yang' *Concise Dictionary of Spoken Chinese*(1947)(Ⅹ/89)

9. Nouvelles Remarques sur le Lien généalogique du Patronyme chez les Tribus de Langue tibéto-birmane(Ⅹ/95)

10. Correction de *j-* en *rj-* dans le Système du Chinois ancien de B. Karlgren(1948)(Ⅹ/106)

后　记

《罗常培文集》十卷终于出版了！

从中华书局通过郑仁甲先生提出意向，聘请尉迟治平先生参加整理、设计，并得到了严学宭先生的支持，酝酿编辑出版《罗常培文集》，到中国社会科学院胡绳院长特批了一笔经费，重新启动《罗常培文集》的整理工作，山东教育出版社承担《罗常培文集》的出版工作，中间经过了一波三折。1996年底，《罗常培文集》编辑委员会成立，由以下诸位先生组成：蔡美彪、高更生、李钊祥、罗慎仪、罗圣仪、邵荣芬、隋千存、孙宏开、孙永大、王均、杨耐思、尉迟治平、周定一。编辑委员会推举王均先生担任主编，周定一、高更生、孙宏开、尉迟治平四位先生担任副主编，邀请吕叔湘、吴宗济、马学良、邢公畹、张清常、高华年等先生担任顾问。周耀文、陈治文和杨力立等先生也为《罗常培文集》分担了具体工作。2007年初，在许嘉璐先生的关心下，《罗常培文集》得到了中国社会科学院语言研究所的支持，聘请郑张尚芳和麦耘两位先生参加《罗常培文集》后期的编校工作，增补任继愈先生为顾问。十余年来，各位顾问认真参与，各卷编委分工合作，参加编辑工作的隋千存、昝亮、2004年调入编辑组的白汉坤，以及2006年秋接手参加的王韶松、孙光兴、周红心等先生认真编校，到2008年10月终于完成最后的校样，真可以说是“十年磨一剑”了。

我们感谢所有为《罗常培文集》出了力的人，没有他们，《罗常培文集》是不可能最终问世的。

这里要说明的是,《罗常培文集》中的著作、文章撰写、出版或发表于不同时期,写法自然不一,在《罗常培文集》的整理、编辑加工中,由于历时较长,参与同一卷编校的编委、编辑大都有几个人,因此整理、编辑加工体例不尽完美、统一,有些情况下,是遵循原著还是按照目前通用的出版规范,是一个难以兼美的困难选择,因此不可避免地遗留了一些问题,这是以后修订再版时需要注意妥善处理的。

罗慎仪

图书在版编目(CIP)数据

罗常培文集　第10卷/《罗常培文集》编委会编．-济南：山东教育出版社，2000
ISBN 978-7-5328-3102-9

Ⅰ.罗…　Ⅱ.罗…　Ⅲ.罗常培-文集　Ⅳ.C53

中国版本图书馆CIP数据核字(2000)第45712号

罗常培文集　第十卷
LUO CHANGPEI WENJI　Di-shi Juan

主　　管：山东出版集团
出 版 者：山东教育出版社
（济南市纬一路321号　邮编：250001）
电　　话：(0531)82092663　传真：(0531)82092661
网　　址：http://www.sjs.com.cn
发 行 者：山东教育出版社
印　　刷：山东新华印刷厂
版　　次：2008年11月第1版
2008年11月第1次印刷
规　　格：880mm×1230mm　32开本
印　　张：13.875印张
插　　页：7插页
字　　数：328千字
书　　号：ISBN 978-7-5328-3102-9
定　　价：63.00元